VIOLENCE AND CULTURE IN THE ANTEBELLUM SOUTH

Violence and Culture in the Antebellum South

by Dickson D. Bruce, Jr.

University of Texas Press, Austin

The publication of this book was assisted by a
grant from the Andrew W. Mellon Foundation.

Library of Congress Cataloging in Publication Data
Bruce, Dickson D   1946–
    Violence and culture in the antebellum South.
    Bibliography: p.
    Includes index.
     1. Violence—Southern States—History.
2. Southern States—Social conditions. 3. Southern
States—Race relations—History. I. Title.
HN79.A133V52   301.6'33'0975   79–4571
ISBN 978-0-292-73992-5

FOR EMILY

Contents

Acknowledgments ix

Introduction 3

1. The Southern Duel 21

2. Preparation for Violence: Child-Rearing and the Southern World View 44

3. Feeling and Form: The Problem of Violence in Society 67

4. Violence in Plain-Folk Society 89

5. Slavery and Violence: The Masters' View 114

6. Slavery and Violence: The Slaves' View 137

7. Militarism and Violence 161

8. Violence and Southern Oratory 178

9. Hunting, Violence, and Culture 196

10. Violence in Southern Fiction: Simms and the Southwestern Humorists 212

Conclusion: Edgar Allan Poe and the Southern World View 233

Notes 241

Bibliography 284

Index 311

Acknowledgments

AS IS TRUE of any author, I have run up a share of debts to others in writing this book. First, I am grateful to staff members at several libraries and archives for their patience and assistance. These institutions include the Henry E. Huntington Library; the Southern Historical Collection at the University of North Carolina, Chapel Hill; the William R. Perkins Library at Duke University; the University Archives of Western Carolina University; the Alabama Department of Archives and History; the Virginia State Library; the Virginia Historical Society; the Library Company of Philadelphia; the South Carolina Historical Society; the Charleston Library Society; the Houston Public Library; and, too, the Harris County District Clerk's Office. In addition, I appreciate the help the librarians at the University of California, Irvine, gave me in my research. Irvine's interlibrary loan librarians, in particular, performed what often seemed amazing feats in finding and obtaining important items.

Several of my colleagues read and commented on the manuscript. Pete Clecak and Raul Fernandez read it all and offered valuable criticisms. Among those upon whom I imposed the task of reading a chapter or two were Francesca Cancian, Jim Flink, Mike Johnson, Joe Jorgensen, Karen Leonard, and Dickran Tashjian. All were generous and helpful, and I am grateful to them. I should also express my appreciation to the two anonymous readers for the University of Texas Press. Both not only said encouraging things about the study, but also offered valuable suggestions for its improvement.

Chapter nine of this book, on hunting, initially appeared in a different form as "Hunting: Dimensions of Antebellum Southern Culture," in the *Mississippi Quarterly* 30 (1977): 259–281. I am grateful to the *Quarterly* for permission to incorporate a revised version of that article here.

Finally, I thank my wife Mary for tolerating my spending so much time working on this book. My daughter Emily was born at about the same time I first began thinking about this study. She, too, has had to show great patience, and I hope she's pleased that this book is for her.

VIOLENCE AND CULTURE IN THE ANTEBELLUM SOUTH

Be careful, my dear Johnston, how you prepare
yourself for this voyage thro the tempestuous ocean
of life. Let reason the most expanded and compre-
hensive keep the helm, and never even for moment,
let the direction of your ship be under the manage-
ment of your passion, that most erring of all pilots.
Many bright Argosies have spread their flowing
sails to the gentle breese, entirely unprepared for
rougher weather: and when the storms of life
came on would gladly have returned to fit them
with stronger tackle. But that is a voyage in which
we can never return but always go on, and en-
counter the dangers difficulties and rocks that
encompass our path.

Advice of Charles Pettigrew to his younger brother
James Johnston Pettigrew, September 21, 1843.

Introduction

"HOWEVER CAREFUL they might be to walk softly, such men as these of the South were bound to come into conflict. And being what they were—simple, direct, and immensely personal—their world being what it was—conflict with them could only mean immediate physical clashing, could only mean fisticuffs, the gouging ring, and knife and gun play." W. J. Cash's deeply felt critique of Southern society has come in for strong and justified criticism in recent years, but there can be little doubt that he captured the image of the Old South, if not its reality, when he talked about the violent individuals who peopled its plantations and frontiers. From fairly early in America's history, and certainly by the end of the first third of the nineteenth century, the South had acquired such a reputation for violence that few people acquainted with the region failed to comment on it. The English traveler J. S. Buckingham, writing in 1842, declared that "five times as large a proportion of these [violent] crimes to population as is witnessed in the North, and ten times as large a proportion as is seen in any of the free countries of Europe" occurred in the South. His statistics may be open to question, but his impressions were widely shared. The society of the Old South was inextricably associated with violence in the minds of many people.[1]

Articulate Southerners were ambivalent about the association. Some accepted—indeed, even asserted—their propensity for violence as a positive characteristic. If they could not approve some forms of violence—the "shirking ways" of the North and Europe or the "wild practices" of the American West—not a few Southerners argued that violence itself was natural to society and, if properly employed, actually improved social health. Southern intellectuals from George Tucker to George Fitzhugh asserted an appreciation of this "fact" of life and contrasted their "realistic" assessment of the nature of society with the "baby ethics," as one writer put it, of Northern intellectuals.[2]

Not all Southerners, however, shared in a high assessment of violence. One Charlestonian, early in the nineteenth century, objected strenuously to the violence in his society, especially to that of dueling which, he wrote, "has made dreadful havoc in the morals of America, and most particularly those of the Southern States." Still others, while acknowledging their region's reputation for violence, felt it to be more a matter of fantasy than fact. Convinced that their reputation was mainly a product of misrepresentation, they were equally sure that the North was a far more violent place than the South. The South was free from the excesses of mobs and criminals, or so they liked to claim, and Southerners were unfairly tagged with a reputation created by an irresponsible and malicious Northern press.[3]

Despite the disagreement among Southerners themselves, statistics from the period tend to support the region's reputation for violence. Even if some Southerners, including Augustus Baldwin Longstreet and J. D. B. De Bow, tried to show that selected cities in the North were more violent than selected cities in the South, available statistics confirm that the South was the more violent place. Murder rates were significantly higher in the South in 1850, and although Northern rates increased between 1850 and 1860, the South maintained its rather dubious edge on the North in that latter year. While the newer Western states and territories—notably California and New Mexico—were far more violent than any Southern state, except Texas, before the Civil War, it remains the case that the South, even in its most settled regions, had proportionately more murders and homicides than did the North or the Old Northwest.[4]

The South appeared, then, to be a violent place to live in antebellum times, regardless of one's race or class. More significantly, perhaps, for the region's reputation, certain forms of violence were exclusive, or virtually so, to the South. The hot-blooded aristocrat is an old and entirely too simple stereotype in American tradition, but the fact was that Southern gentlemen were noted for turning to violence in defense of themselves or what they considered their "honor." The duel, and the notorious "code of honor" were fairly identified in the United States with the Southern region, although

Californians in the 1850s seem to have transplanted the practice to the West Coast. The identity was a strong one, and Southerners cited the practice as evidence of their refinement while Northerners added it to their own catalogue of Southern perversities. In addition to the duel, the nineteenth-century militarism of the Southern gentry was often understood to be a symptom of a violent people, as were such social rituals as the ring tournament. Finally, it need hardly be added that Southern planters had a reputation for violence growing out of the system of slavery, where physical force, or the threat of it, provided the practical foundation.[5]

But planters were not the only members of Southern society who knew violence as a part of life. Those Southern whites who were not in the plantation-owning elite also had an apparently well-founded reputation for violence, and one that took several forms. Fighting on the Southern frontier has long been a popular topic for observers of all kinds, from tourists to satirists to historians. Whether in rural areas or in frontier towns, middle- and lower-class whites were said to have made the most brutal sort of fighting a regular social event, and according to reputation, even ostensibly friendly gatherings were usually enlivened with a community brawl. The Southern frontiersman had a reputation for barbarism exceeding that of anyone else, and it grew out of some very real and very brutal practices in his community.[6]

Slaves and free blacks were also acquainted with frequent violence, both on and off the plantation. The presence of violent whites was as much a factor in the development of the culture of antebellum black Southerners as the fear of violent slaves was in that of Southern whites. But slaves were not mere passive recipients of white aggression. They frequently resisted the brutality of slaveowners and and other whites, and occasionally made violent rebellion against the system itself. At the same time, the plantation and the free black communities of the South had their share of bullies and toughs, and Southern blacks, like the whites, looked on such men of violence with mixed emotions.[7]

Southerners probably deserved some parts of their reputation for violence—although the reputation was by no means accurate in every respect—and it is clear that some kinds of antebellum violence were distinctly Southern. Southerners, black and white, thus had special reasons for needing to come to terms with violence. Their reputation alone probably forced them to talk about violence to an extent other Americans could avoid, and the existence of what were, by the second or third decades of the nineteenth century, their own varieties of violence—and very public violence at that— would not have allowed them to remain silent.

In fact, people in the Old South talked a great deal about violence. Southerners rarely exhibited the thoughtless readiness to fight that the region's reputation would lead one to expect. Because people in the South tended to be highly moralistic,[8] they saw violence as a particularly difficult moral problem, and when they had to come to terms with it, most tried to do so—to justify it or to condemn it—in a way that was compatible with their most strongly held values. However violent their actions, that is to say, they did not undertake those actions without thought for the moral implications and consequences, so that to look at antebellum violence is to find a window to some of the most powerful elements of Southern culture. Violence was not itself a "central theme" in Southern history, but it evoked some deep and often discordant themes in the culture to greater effect than even race or slavery could do.

Southerners showed little disagreement about what violence was, and most would have defined it as the use of considerable physical force against another person. Most would have agreed, as well, that there were times when such force was necessary. But such psychological or ethological notions as frustration-aggression or innate-aggressiveness often raised in connection with violence— theories, by the way, which many antebellum Southerners advanced in their own language—have only slight relevance to violence as it occurred in the Old South. Far more striking, historically at least, was the overwhelming acceptance of violence by almost everyone in the society. Any moral problems violence posed in the Old South had nothing to do with violence in itself but focused instead on the kinds of situations for which violence was appropriate. Southerners' resignation to the fact of violence may have been little more than a matter of inheritance. Europeans, Africans, and Native Americans all knew violent conflict long before they ran into each other in the New World. It pervaded their histories, their mythologies, and their lores, and given the South's place in history, one would find it surprising had the region produced an unusual number of pacifists. But what made for a "violent tenor" of Southern life—what made the South seem uniquely violent—was not only that violence seemed to occur often, but also that people there saw violence as unavoidable, as an essential fact of human life somehow built in, profoundly, to human relationships. The world was, in its essence, a violent place, and if humans should direct their energies toward controlling and confining violence, they could never make it disappear.[9]

This study explores that Southern notion of the essential quality of violence, focusing on its meaning and its implications, and also on its sources. This is not, of course, the first such effort, and there have been many explanations for Southern ideas about violence. The oldest, going back to the eighteenth century, has attributed violence to the existence of slavery. The slave system was based on force, and, according to this explanation, the habits of violent command developed in the slaveholder were carried by him into his dealings with the world outside the plantation. Complementing the vision of the violent slaveholder was that of the rebellious slave, and, it has been suggested, the general fear of slave insurrection was a major factor in Southern life, leading to an increasing appreciation of force and violence among the whites. The very existence of slavery with its inherent tensions was, according to many observers, enough to make the South a violent society.[10]

Slavery is rarely left out of any account of Southern violence, but other factors have been mentioned by people trying to explain the region's violent ways. In his influential study of Southern life, journalist W. J. Cash emphasized the frontier character of much of the South prior to 1865, suggesting that violence was a natural product of the rugged individualism encouraged by frontier conditions. Others have taken Cash's suggestion, going beyond it to claim that the very proximity of the frontier in time and space created the sort of atmosphere in which violence could flourish among all classes of Southerners. Still other investigators have mentioned other factors, including demography and ideology, and have stressed, in this, the extent to which so much about the Old South could have contributed to its violence.[11]

And yet, sources for Southern violence and for the meanings people gave it appear to have gone far deeper than the kinds of immediate factors usually cited in most accounts. To be sure, such things as regional paranoia, frontier conditions, slavery, or demography had some influence, and antebellum Southerners themselves cited many of those factors in attempting to account for their society's violence. But the significance of such factors was not so much causative as interactive. The bases for Southern attitudes toward violence lay in pervasive patterns of culture that extended well back into Southern history. To understand those patterns, one must understand, as well, something of the relationship between Southern culture and major themes in Western thought and culture during the eighteenth and early nineteenth centuries. Chiefly, one must focus on the concern many Southerners expressed about the problem of human passion.

The concept of "passion" was of basic importance to Western thought during the eighteenth and early nineteenth centuries. Referring essentially to irrational, selfish motivations, the idea of "passion" informed thinking about everything from private morals to political economy and was a constant in theories about human nature. At the close of the eighteenth century, it was generally accepted that people were by nature passionate, given to the pursuit of their own selfish ends rather than to the upholding of rational public or social good. In the realm of politics, where the view had great influence, this led to a focusing of theoretical and practical effort on coming to grips with the problem of passion. By the time of the American Revolution, Western political theorists and economists had long since accepted a "realistic" view of man which precluded transcendence of his passionate nature and precluded, as well, any argument for its complete suppression. Theorists focused their efforts on devising the sorts of systems which would restrain passion, or on those promising to put passion to some good use.[12]

The key problem was that those in the West who gave the matter much thought tended to be of two minds about the role of passion in society. Viewing it as the most powerful motivating force in any individual, they also saw that its power could drive men toward either good or evil. On the one hand, they often spoke of passion's destructive potential. To say, for example, that men allowed selfish passions for wealth and status to guide their actions did much to explain significant tensions in society. Or, at another level, most thinkers declared that the passion for power was such that, once indulged, its possessor would strive for more. If he were not checked, the result would be the emergence of a tyrant. Passion for private gain or glory was, in other words, seen as a major threat to a stable political economy, and, indeed, as the single force most likely to produce disorder in world affairs.

Yet most thinkers also acknowledged that passion was the wellspring of human action; in its absence there was little men could achieve. If lust for fame or wealth was potentially corrupting, when pursued moderately such desires led men to their grandest achievements. The desire for esteem, for instance, was necessary to spur men to perform essential social and political duties. The moderate pursuit of wealth and material comfort led to an industriousness that contributed to the general prosperity. Passions could be destructive, to be sure, but their moderate indulgence was also necessary to social survival. Passion could never be excluded from political and economic life, given human nature, nor would it be desirable to make such an effort, since there could be no life without passion, harnessed and properly directed. The point was, again, to guide passion and to put it to good use.[13]

People in the American South were hardly out of touch with Western thinking on the question of passion during this period. Like other leaders of America's Revolutionary generation, for example, Southerners had spoken often of the unbridled passion of the British monarch and, hence, had justified their move for independence from the crown. When debating the forms of federal and state governments, Southerners along with other Americans frequently referred to the necessity of devising a system that would restrain and divert powerful men's passions away from destructive excess. They were not unusual in the concerns they expressed, nor can it be said, in fact, that their ways of expressing those concerns differed from what other Americans had to say.

Throughout the West after about 1800, however, significant changes began to occur in notions of passion and its role in human affairs. These were apparent, too, in political and economic thought. On the one hand, the terms in which discussion took place began to change radically, especially after Adam Smith, with questions of private virtue and passion occupying an increasingly irrelevant place in political and economic thought. At the same time, following Rousseau and the growing romantic movement, the character of passion itself was coming to be reevaluated, coming to be seen as something not so much to be restrained and guided, but as itself a guide and as a part of the human being which should be fulfilled rather than repressed.[14] Southerners, by and large, did not share in these changes.

In politics, Southerners held to classical concerns about passion and to a view which put passion at the center of the political process throughout the antebellum period. They could, to be sure, recognize the material importance of the issues they had to face, but they would rarely fail to tie the material to the moral and to human nature. Moreover, they could never reject that vision of the political system as a structure of harnessed passions which had so stirred their ancestors in Revolutionary time and before. Hence, one may understand George Fitzhugh's comment in the mid-1850s: "Science is every day discovering that the most fatal poisons when properly employed become the most efficacious medicines. So, what appear to be the evil passions and properties of men, and of societies, under proper regulation, may be made to minister to the wisest and best of purposes."[15] Fitzhugh's words have a quaintness about them which betrays their ties to older political conceptions. That society could only be a structure of directed passion was not, by Fitzhugh's time, a very original idea.

It is important to emphasize, however, that concern about passion was not limited to the realms of economic and political philosophy. "Passion," understood in much the same way that the philosophers used it, was also a central focus in the morality of everyday life. The difference was, mainly, that the notion was not so clearly limited in popular morality to lusts for wealth or power—although it might be used in that way. Here, "passion" was more generalized and referred to any expression of strong spontaneous feelings in one's relations with others.[16] Indulging such expressions was popularly conceived as analogous, though on a smaller scale, to allowing lusts for gain or power to make one a tyrant. In either case, individual self-indulgence posed a threat to the order and stability of human relationships.

Passion was a moral danger which many Southerners feared, and minimizing its role in daily life was a moral task to which they set themselves. A Mississippi planter, Everard Green Baker, summed up the matter when, in his diary, he privately hoped "that God will give me grace to put down anything like passion—that my unclouded reason may always be triumphant, for I never give away to a burst of passion towards any one that I do not regret afterwards."[17] Other Southerners were like Baker in contrasting passion with reason and in seeing passion as a force which was not only difficult to control but as one which could drive people to act in ways they would later regret.

Both aspects of passion were important in Southern thinking. People worried to a surprising degree about the effects of passion on personality and on social relations in a way that was fairly constant from colonial times to the eve of the Civil War. The Virginia gentleman Landon Carter, for example, worried much about his being a "passionate man," one given to bursts of temper, from his days as a young man in the 1730s to his death in 1778.[18] He did so in a way that seems little different from the fears expressed by Everard Baker at the opening of the Civil War. All were convinced that passion was dangerous to anyone, man or woman, leading to selfishness, quarrelsomeness, and a loss of purpose.

One need not catalogue all the Southern uses of the word passion to make the point. Passion could refer to a great many things, including the sort of strong affection for another that by its power drove out all other interests, as well as the kind of self-appreciation which made one calculate his own worth as inestimable. Within bounds, neither sort of passion was bad. Strong affection, for instance, was essential to ties of family and friendship; pride was a "passion of the mind," as one schoolboy wrote, by which "we are often aroused from a state of inaction and idleness, to one of industry and honor."[19] The problem came when such passions became excessive, when love blinded one to responsibility or when pride became vanity and arrogance. Then such passions would cause more harm than good.

This problem of excess was made more pressing by the sense that passion was difficult, if not ultimately impossible, to control. Since man was naturally passionate, most people believed that the only thing which would hold it in check was the thin wall of restraint provided by civilization and manners. Such a barrier was weak and artificial, and there was always the chance that nature would break through the civilized veneer and that passion would exceed its proper bounds. Not a few Southerners were like Carter or Baker in looking back over a day's events or a past episode in their lives mortified at having been so weak in the face of primitive nature; and more than a few looked forward, as well, to future occasions when excessive passion would lead them, or those they encountered, to unreasonable, selfish, and disruptive acts. People are by nature passionate, Southerners often said, and whatever good their passions might create, the danger of excess was always there. The major effect of this point of view was to make Southerners remarkably pessimistic about the possibilities for a good life in this world.

It has become almost a truism to note than antebellum Southerners craved order and a stable, secure, community life. Coupled with that desire, however, was an equally strong belief in human frailty due to a passionate nature and, hence, a sense that the social order was quite fragile, needing constant guarding and care. The belief in passion and the desire for order contributed to a pessimism about human relationships which came awfully close to, and often lapsed into, misanthropy. Mistrusting themselves, Southerners were even less sure of others' abilities to stay under control. As a result, they were prepared to see a threat to social order at almost every turn. Their security, they felt, rested on a very insecure base, and they were not sanguine about its strength and endurance.

The tradition of moral concern about passion was at the root of Southern pessimism, but other factors contributed to it and reinforced it, as well. Dominant among them was religion. From colonial times to the Civil War, elite Southerners were hardly known for their religious fervor. Still, and not surprising for a conservative community, there were but few freethinkers—whatever their fame—in the South. Southerners' language shows them to have been touched by religion in ways that would have reinforced their pessimism about human nature and society. Protestants, by and large, they were inheritors of the Reformation tradition which strongly emphasized human depravity and the inability of people to escape corruption so long as they lived in the world. Their religious background, then, tended to support their rather bleak view of human nature. At the same time, their religion was mainly Arminian rather than Calvinist in that, while stressing human depravity, it also put human choice and effort rather than the arbitrary grace of God at the center of the process of salvation. Among moderate Episcopalians, this led chiefly to a religion of social morality with an acceptance of human imperfection.[20] But even among Southern evangelicals, the Methodists and Baptists, there was stress upon the human role in choosing to receive or ignore the offers of grace from God. In both cases the effect was to deemphasize the possibility of God's direct intervention into the affairs of the world. However they differed on other points, Southerners of all religious groups agreed that human beings, weak and corruptible, were also pretty much alone as they faced the trials and temptations the world had to offer.

This is not to say that Southern religion was wholly divorced from the cares of the world or that it counted people wholly incapable of moral improvement. That religion in the South attempted to come to grips with the very problem of passion and to influence individuals to lead moral, orderly lives has long been noted. The moral topics chosen by Anglican preachers in colonial times and after were directed mainly at guiding their parishioners away from the sort of selfish behavior—excessive drinking, or gambling, or swearing, or, for that matter, violence—that led to social problems. Among evangelicals, of whatever social class, piety and discipline went closely together as believers tried to create orderly communities of the saints on earth.[21] In both cases, religion identified the problems posed by human nature and worked to make man into a social being at peace with himself and with others.

But there was no utopian streak to Southern religion; few believers were convinced that such a peaceful community could be achieved in this world, however much they might be exhorted to work toward it. The distinction which evangelicals, in particular, liked to make between living in the world as opposed to living the life of the world was not, as they recognized, an easy one to maintain. Conversion and redemption, to be sure, were central to evangelical thought, but too many converts had backslid for believers to be very comfortable about any visible community of saints. Even for the faithful, as they often said, life in the world could never be too tranquil. The Christian's life, whether one were a moderate Episcopalian or a Methodist evangelical, was a perpetual struggle against sinners and temptations, worth making only because it would lead to membership in the heavenly communion above.[22] They might have been optimistic about eternal life; they had reason for little but pessimism about life here below.

Such a sense of worldly life was expressed most clearly in Southern attitudes toward death. Accounts of the dying of friends and relatives were frequently circulated among literate Southerners, and they filled the popular religious magazines—ranging from Kentucky's evangelical *Christian Register* to the *Charleston Gospel Messenger and Protestant Episcopal Register*. Class as well as denominational lines were transcended by the search for what was termed a "happy death." Always and everywhere, the focus was the same: death was not a fearsome prospect but was a step toward one's genuine fulfillment. The dying saint, by all accounts, approached his end calmly and hopefully, for it meant freedom from the burdens of the world and membership in the eternal heavenly band.[23] One would not want to suggest that all Southerners welcomed death, even when, in despair, they claimed to have had enough of worldly woes. It is sufficient to say that religion in the South treated death in a way consistent with pessimism about the nature of life in the world, and, hence, kept a steady focus on the trials of the world and the failings, moral and spiritual, of human beings. Southerners' pessimism about life in the world was strongly reinforced by their religious heritage, and reflected in the main themes of religion as it was practiced in the South before the Civil War.

Secular traditions of thought complemented those of religion to reinforce pessimism in Southern thinking. Southerners generally held to organic conceptions of society. This could mean, and often did, that they viewed society as a system, like the body, of interdependent parts. It could also mean, as it did for a long time, that bodily metaphors controlled thinking about historical processes. It was not at all uncommon, especially during the early national period, for Southerners to describe the history of nations in terms of the Renaissance figure of a progress from youth through maturity to what Virginian John Taylor of Caroline called "the decrepitude of old age."[24] The process was unavoidable, and the best any nation could hope for was an avoidance of a "misspent youth" and the prolonging of a prosperous maturity. Eternal life was not for this world.

The bodily metaphors of the early national period began to drop out of use after about 1800, to be replaced by those of violence which we shall examine in this study. Southerners spoke very rarely of society's inevitable decay, but they did speak as though their society were in the midst of a maturity from which it could all too easily decline. Organic notions implied fragility since, as Southerners seem to have understood, to change any part of a functioning system was to risk unintended consequences in the system itself; society, faced with the unusual or unexpected act, could very quickly get out of control and speed toward the chaos which had destroyed great nations throughout history. This implication of organicism remained important, even if the specific metaphors of disease and decline came to be used infrequently during the antebellum period. Organicism provided an intellectual heritage for a sense of history that maintained Southern pessimism about human action and human relationships. Not that Southerners never spoke favorably of progress in political, social, or economic life. The fact was simply that change looked dangerous and hard to control from a Southern point of view, as likely to lead to decline as to progress—indeed, perhaps more likely to lead to decline since any change would also involve at least a temporary break in a structure of harnessed passions. The secular tradition of historical pessimism, however subdued, was hardly dead by 1860; it clearly had some influence on the generations of Southerners who came to maturity during the antebellum period, reinforcing a general lack of optimism about life in the world.

Pessimism was finally encouraged by the very character of social life, by the fact, that is, that people were different. One's predictions about how others would behave could never achieve unfailing accuracy and, where society seemed so fragile, this simple fact had great significance. One cannot read the letters and diaries of many antebellum Southerners without noticing their great ability to assign universal moral significance to the most trivial events. The unexpected frustration in social life was frequently taken as a sign of perverse humanity and used as a touchstone for further thinking about the difficulties of living in a world of people. This fact of difference had various meanings according to context—whether it were in the family, or among recognized social equals, or across class lines—but given Southerners' notions of human nature, it contributed to their almost inevitable disappointment in the behavior of themselves and of others.

Southern pessimism was deeply rooted in the region, and was

part of a long tradition in Western moral thought. This pessimism, surviving in the South at a time when the North and Europe were adopting new points of view on human nature and society, was strongly reinforced by the region's own history in the nineteenth century. These experiences were such that pessimism seemed to be a very accurate approach for describing the events of the world.

The importance of organic political notions, and the fear of disruption, were undoubtedly enhanced by the state of sectional relations in the United States which were tense during the early national period, becoming increasingly so after about 1820. The Southern point of view was fairly simple and evolved fairly quickly. Southern leaders were deeply fearful that their region, with its "peculiar institution" should become a minority part of the Union, subject to possibly hostile policies advanced by the majority.[25] They saw themselves, in other words, in danger of becoming an oppressed minority within the nation, and events beyond their control made that possibility seem ever more likely. In a sense, Southerners were involved in a self-fulfilling prophecy in which basic political notions were reinforced by events which, in turn, reinforced pessimistic ideas about political stability. Here was, indeed, a fatal circle which would have worked against changes in Southern thinking.

At the same time, those visible evidences of progress and success which meant so much to Northerners were not really present on the Southern scene. Economically and socially, the South was a static region compared to the North, and this tended to work against the growth of the optimistic and democratic ideologies that would come to dominate Northern thinking during the antebellum period. To be sure, there were conservatives in the North who agreed with much of the Southern point of view, just as the South was not without its vibrant American nationalists. Nevertheless, the forces that pushed conservatism into the background in Northern social and political life were not so strong in the South that pessimism and a concern for human fallibility could not remain dominant in the ideas of the region's leaders.[26]

Finally, there was slavery, an institution which operated in such profound ways on the Southern mind. On the one hand, slavery emphasized the South's minority status in America and, indeed, the Western world, and hence the need to guard with special care the balance of political relations with other parts of the Union. Beyond that, however, the presence of a black population increased Southerners' devotion to order and stability within their region, as even they acknowledged. Predictability in social behavior was doubly important when social relations took place among such "unlike" people as Southern blacks and whites believed each other to be, so that the institution could only have reinforced Southern fears for the frailty of human relations.

Other experiences, too, may have contributed to Southern pessimism and to Southerners' retention of a primarily fearful understanding of human passions, and some will be suggested in the study which follows, but the point to be made is that much of what Southerners did during the antebellum period grew out of their pessimism and concerns. For one thing, as we shall see, Southerners devoted a good deal of effort to self-discipline and to the cultivation of well-regulated human relationships. In both cases, the main focus was to prevent the sorts of spontaneous, passionate acts which one would inevitably come to regret. There was a great deal of emphasis placed on discipline and correct deportment in every area of life. Southerners attempted to insure that human relationships would be tightly ordered. Within their own society, they held to ideals of organicism and hierarchy, putting individuals into carefully ranked social groups and trying to keep those groups as discrete as possible. Where relationships were set, well-ordered, and understood, Southerners believed, then social life itself would be regular and predictable. They would achieve a stable society. In relationships with the outside world, and particularly with the North, Southerners also emphasized the importance of predictability, and placed great value on the observance of regular, mutually understood rules and procedures for maintaining an orderly, predictable system. Careful regulation, they felt, at any level would decrease the probability of the system's being destroyed by excessive passion.

At the same time, Southerners maintained their pessimism, and it was this which, more than any other aspect of culture, had to do with their attitudes toward violence, because violence confirmed, in a very visible manner, their worst fears for human society. Southerners did not, for the most part, take violence to be a good thing, but their understanding of human nature convinced them that violence was a necessary, unavoidable part of human relations. Desiring stable, secure community life, most Southerners learned to believe that other people were likely to follow their passions, putting personal desires above the well-being of society as a whole—and, indeed, many expressed grave doubts about themselves. People in the South inevitably associated violence with this conflict between ideals and reality, and because such a conflict could never be resolved, they assumed, violence itself could never be eliminated.

That, in simplest terms, was what Southerners thought violence was about, and it is striking how they were able to apply their beliefs to a wide range of violent situations, from streetfighting to war. But those are, it must be stressed, the simplest terms. Different people interpreted matters in different ways. The roots for such a problematic world view were also complex; they were traditional, material, even theological. Still, the view itself was logically prior to such phenomena of Southern life as slavery, the frontier, or sectionalism. This uncomfortable combination of idealism and pessimism provided the cultural background for much of Southern history from at least the mid-eighteenth century to the coming of the Civil War, and its effects on Southern responses to historical and social events were profound.

To understand Southern violence, then, one must focus on the ways in which people in the region maintained their views of society and human nature. To a great extent, the most important attitudes about life were developed in childhood, when young Southerners learned what the world was like and what to expect from it. Only some Southern children were actually encouraged to be violent, but all were taught those conflicting assessments of social possibilities that supported the vision of a violent world.

They learned their lessons well. It is not difficult to trace the ways in which approaches to problems learned in childhood survived in the ways adult Southerners tried to handle almost every kind of difficulty, from the smallest spat to sectional political disputes. Those who raised Southern children gave them a model for approaching life in the world, and much of their adult life and thought would be devoted to elaborating that model, to exploring its complexities, and to extending it to cover new problems. The model itself went unquestioned, displaying remarkable tenacity even when, as in the case of slavery for instance, it did not quite seem to fit.

Hence, Southerners' sense of the possible remained remarkably stable throughout the antebellum period. It seemed adequate to most Southerners for characterizing many, if not all situations, and they saw little in life that made them feel compelled to change their views of the nature of things. They were able to bring most situations into harmony with their beliefs and because their sense of possibilities appeared to work so well for ordering and understanding social and political events, situations themselves fed back to ideas to reinforce and to further entrench them. There was not a great deal of change in the general outlook of the generations of Southerners who lived from, say, the 1770s to the 1860s, only such an evolution in ideas as was compelled by internal logic and by the interplay of assumptions and events. Attitudes toward violence, it must be said, were quite firm.

This study is, ultimately, an analysis of Southern "folk" moralities, of popularly held principles for action and evaluation. Its aim is to show the sources of the assumptions on which moral principles relating to violence were based and the ways in which assumptions and principles were learned and communicated in different social settings. Much of the study focuses on the Southern elite, for whom the moral problem of violence appears to have been the most troubling and about whom the best data may be gathered. Their main concerns about violence were summarized and dramatized with remarkable clarity in that most spectacular form of public violence, the duel. Indeed, it almost appears they were acting out what violence meant when they met on the field of honor. Accordingly, an analysis of the duel begins the book, and many of the subsequent chapters will show how other types of violence elaborated on what was acted out there. In addition to discussing violence among the elite, the study will also examine relationships between violence and culture in two other Southern communities, those of the frontier and of the slaves, in order to see how they compared to the ideals professed by articulate spokesmen for the region.

But the study makes an attempt to go beyond attitudes toward violence as such. Because violence had such potent meaning in the South—indeed, because it was the visible manifestation of the deepest of Southern moral concerns—the evocation of violence in a variety of situations could itself have tremendous emotional and intellectual impact on people in the region. After, then, a look at violence in different social settings and at Southern efforts to explain violent acts in society, on the plantation or frontier, or in war, this study turns to an examination of the role of the language of violence in Southern thought and feeling. Here the focus will be on political rhetoric, on the popular literature of the hunting narrative, and on Southern writers of fiction. Through all this, we will see how Southern concerns about passion and the Southern pessimistic outlook contributed to a distinctive understanding of events and of the place of violence in human affairs.

1. *The Southern Duel*

ON MONDAY, January 13, 1845, two men met near Beltsville, Maryland, outside Washington, D.C., to fight a duel. Congressman William Lowndes Yancey of Alabama and Thomas Lanier Clingman of North Carolina had had words on the floor of the House of Representatives and had, after some conversation, mutually agreed that the only way to resolve their difficulties was with pistols. Their decision was not an unusual one for two eminent Southerners to make during the antebellum period. Indeed, given the immediate circumstances and the tenor of their subsequent communication, the situation all but demanded that the two should face each other on the field of honor.

The duel between Yancey and Clingman, in its typical features, shows how the practice served as a ritualized expression of the role of violence in the culture of the antebellum Southern elite. On the one hand, the events of the duel demonstrated in vivid terms how violence could be used and under what circumstances. On the other hand, in the duel violent activity was itself raised to an expression of Southerners' conceptions of themselves, their society, and their world.

The dispute between Yancey and Clingman grew out of the House debate on the admission of Texas to the Union as a slave state, the major issue before the Congress that year. James K. Polk, running for the presidency on a proannexation platform, had just defeated Henry Clay of the antiannexation Whig party, giving the Democrats a mandate they felt would pave the way for Texas to enter the Union. In making their case to the House of Representatives, they called upon Southerners of both parties to follow the will of the people and to stand united in support of the South through the necessary expansion of its way of life.

Many Southern Whigs, however, were not convinced that the

annexation of Texas would be in the best interests of the South or the nation. They had not supported the initial treaty for annexation in 1844, and were not about to be pushed into precipitate support for a treaty now by calls for Southern unity. Clingman, one of those Whigs, was especially forceful in stating his party's position. He began his remarks to the House by mocking Southern Democrats who called for a united, nonpartisan regional coalition, but saved his greatest scorn for those who claimed that Polk had defeated Clay because of the Whigs' stance on annexation. Clay had not, the North Carolinian insisted, been defeated in a fair and open election. Instead, according to Clingman, Polk had won because of massive election fraud, chiefly "double voting," in several states. There was no mandate for Polk or the Democrats because the election had been stolen, and, what was worse, Southern Democrats had countenanced the theft.

> A stranger would perhaps be surprised to learn that many of these individuals, in the relations of private life, are esteemed honest and honorable men. Nothing could show more conclusively their devotion to party, than that they should thus be able to overcome their natural aversion to crime, and thus endeavor to countenance and protect the criminal, because that crime had been committed for the benefit of the party. Sir, it gives me no pleasure to refer to this occurrence. We formerly flattered ourselves that however mischievous locofocoism might become in other sections, there was in North Carolina and other parts of the South a regard for public opinion, and a feeling of personal honor among its leading members, which would keep it somewhat in the bounds of decency. But it is a tree which bears the same fruit in every climate.

It had not been, he sadly concluded, a "manly contest."[1]

Reaction to Clingman's speech was mixed. The *Charleston Courier* merely sniffed that Clingman had "made a humorous speech against annexation, in which he did not touch the subject of annexation at all, further than to show that it was not one of the issues before the people at the late election."[2] House Democrats were not so restrained in their reaction, however, and chose the young freshman member from Alabama to respond to what they felt had been a scurrilous attack on their characters. Accordingly, the next day, January 7, William Lowndes Yancey arose to deliver his maiden speech in Congress, speaking in favor of the annexation of Texas—and attacking Thomas Lanier Clingman.

Dismissing Clingman's charge of election fraud as a partisan and trivial response to a question "addressing itself so directly to the honor and to the interest of the entire Republic," Yancey could not suppress his own doubts about the character and intelligence of a representative who "was every where viewed as a betrayer of his country." Clingman, he proclaimed, was not only a traitor to the South, but one who, in opposing annexation, had "turned and flaunted the colors of [the] enemy in the face of his own friends." Clingman was like Noah's youngest son in ridiculing the people of the state which had given him so much, and Yancey's only concern was that he himself "should be pardoned if, in taking these views of the subject which the Representative from North Carolina had discussed, or rather had avoided, and of the character which he had attempted to a debate otherwise eminently dignified and worthy of that Hall, he [Yancey] should not follow him into the dark purlieus of party with which that gentleman seemed so disgracefully familiar."[3] Yancey then continued with the problem of annexation.

It was a remarkable speech. *The Mobile Register and Journal* reported that Yancey "was most eloquent and forcible from the commencement to the end of his speech. He has made a most profound and favorable impression, and taken at once a proud rank amongst the most talented and eloquent men of the House." *The New Orleans Bee*, on the other hand, found Yancey "very abusive and inflammatory in his remarks." It was not the sort of address to be ignored in the agitation over the question of Texas.[4]

Clingman himself did not choose to ignore Yancey's remarks and, from his seat in the House, sent the young Alabama congressman a note: "SIR: In the course of your remarks to-day, you declared that you wished to have nothing to say with one possessed of the head and heart of the gentleman from North Carolina, alluding, as I understand, to me, personally. I desire to know of you, whether, by the use of that expression, you intended towards me, personally, any disrespect, or to be understood that I was deficient in integrity, honor, or in any other quality requisite to the character of a gentleman." Yancey's reply was simply that he did not recognize the purported language, and he sent Clingman a copy of the relevant parts of his speech. He added, "Of the language I did use, or of my motives, I have no explanations to make."[5]

As John Hope Franklin has pointed out, "Whenever a difficulty arose in which there was a *possibility* that honor was involved, it was usually decided, just to be on the safe side—that it *was* involved."[6] Yancey would have been in no position to send a note to Clingman, since the Whig had named no names. But Yancey had attacked Clingman personally. For a Southerner of the North Carolinian's position, Yancey's assault on his character was most definitely a question of honor, one which, if it could not be peacefully resolved, must be settled with blood in the manner usual among gentlemen: he would have to challenge Yancey to a duel. Hence, when Yancey's response did not satisfy the demand for an explanation, Clingman let it be known through his friends that he had left the city for Baltimore—it being illegal to issue a challenge in Washington, should matters come to that—where he would discuss things further. Yancey, with his friend, also departed for Baltimore, arriving at eight o'clock on the evening of January 9.

The two parties continued their "interchange of views" for some time thereafter, handled, according to custom, by their friends, the seconds. The North Carolinian persisted in his demand for a "satisfactory explanation" of Yancey's remarks: had Yancey intended any disrespect? Yancey himself was no less adamant. He would stand by what he had said, and any further explanation would be "superfluous." By eleven o'clock at night on January 10, Yancey's second, John M. Huger, and Clingman's friend, Charles Lee Jones, decided to close the correspondence between their principals in the hope of arriving at an acceptable settlement. The correspondence, they felt, had exacerbated the conflict. In addition, the seconds suspended delivery of a final, intransigent note from Yancey to Clingman until the following morning, at which time the two seconds could meet to draft a substitute correspondence upon which the matter could rest. At that time, chances for a peaceful settlement seemed very good, so good, in fact, that Baltimore authorities ignored a warrant issued for the arrest of both principals.[7] The duel, it appeared, would be properly prevented by the negotiations of the seconds.

Still, when Huger and Jones attempted to draft the substitute notes, the main points remained at issue. Clingman's demand for an explanation and Yancey's refusal to provide one could not be compromised, and Yancey's previously withheld note was tendered by Huger to Jones, after all. Then, as Yancey's second reported, a challenge from Clingman followed "as a matter of course." The challenge was immediately accepted, and Huger and Jones met later that Saturday to draw up articles for procedure—eleven in all—outlining the time and place, the weapons to be used, and the number of seconds, companions, and surgeons who could accompany each principal to the field. The word to be given was, *"Gentlemen, are you ready: Fire—one—two—three—halt,"* at one-second intervals. The two men would meet at three o'clock on Monday; Sunday was, after all, no day to fight a duel.[8]

Having to evade the police, who were now prepared to arrest the principals in the dispute, the Yancey party met that of Representative Clingman at the appointed place. The parties were posted and the word was given: both men fired. Clingman's ball passed over Yancey's head and Yancey's struck the ground a few feet beyond Clingman. Neither man was hurt. Friends of the two immediately entered into consultation and the affair was settled. "Upon a suggestion of Hon. Mr. Rayner, of North Carolina, that Mr. Yancey might now retract his personally offensive remarks applicable to Mr. Clingman, Mr. Huger suggested that this difficulty existed: that Mr. Yancey considered Mr. Clingman's speech as casting personal and offensive imputations upon the Southern Democrats. Upon which Mr. Jones, as Mr. Clingman's friend, *at once disclaimed such construction*, and declared that the speech was purely political, and that Mr. C. *intended no personal imputation upon any member* of the House of Representatives. Whereupon Mr. Yancey *made the suggested retraction*."[9] Huger and Jones "accepted for their respective friends" and the affair of honor between William L. Yancey and Thomas L. Clingman was finished.

Reaction to the duel from all classes of Southerners was swift, with Yancey receiving much of the public condemnation. William G. Brownlow, in his *Jonesborough Whig*, spoke for many pious plain-folk in his scathing indictment of Yancey, and characteristically for him, of Democrats in general. Dredging up an unfortunate event from Yancey's past, Brownlow reported that the young congressman "had once killed a man in a street fight, in Alabama, and was selected by his party to put Mr. Clingman out of the way."[10] The editors of the *Houston Telegraph and Texas Register*, for all they might have appreciated Yancey's support of Texas statehood, hardly approved of the affair, declaring the principals' failure to hit each other to be "just as well as if both balls had passed through block heads."[11] But it was the censure of a journal from his home state, the *Alabama Baptist*, to which Yancey himself felt constrained to reply. The *Alabama Baptist*'s concern was moral, not political, its editors having advanced what Yancey considered to be a cruelly severe stricture that "all duelling is *murder*. . . . It is no justification in the sight of Heaven," they continued, "if this determination fails to be carried into effect."[12]

Conceding the "christian spirit" in which the editor's remarks had been written, Yancey desired nothing more than to place "the facts" before the public, and his constituents. His speech to the House—"ardent, indignant, severe if you please"—could only be owed to the character of Clingman's attack on Southern Democrats. Yancey could not have retracted, since he had not acted for self alone, and his reply shows the extent to which the question of whose honor had been assailed became submerged once an affair had begun. "I was a Southern representative," he wrote, "who in defending southern rights, and the honor of the whole Southern delegation was called to account." The "stern and inflexible laws of society" demanded that Yancey answer the call, and, unfortunately, he did not possess the "high devoted, christian character" which would have allowed him to reject the challenge. "Blame me not, then, for *accepting* this challenge," he concluded, "for not in that consists my offence, but for a far greater evil of not being a christian." In support of his actions, Yancey cited an eyewitness account of the duel: "Mr. Yancey acquitted himself in the whole transaction, with the most scrupulous propriety. He was, indeed, *unwilling to shoot at Mr. Clingman, at all; but when his friends told him that they would not accompany him upon the field, if he persisted in thus exposing his life, without firing at his adversary, he consented with the determination to shoot only at his legs.* This high and chivalrous conduct should go far to exculpate him even from the blame of those who will not justify duelling in any extremity." What it ultimately came to, in Yancey's view, was "more a matter of feeling than of reason," and if he would not defend dueling in abstract terms, he could at least make his participation understandable by reference to the specifics of the case.[13]

It was not astonishing, during the antebellum period, that two

Southerners of such standing as Yancey and Clingman should participate in an affair of honor, because dueling was taken by many to be a distinctive part of Southern life. Southerners and their Northern critics alike identified the practice with the region beginning fairly early in the nation's history. The Southern press frequently reported accounts of duels and often contained editorials on the subject, whereas many Northern journalists considered the duel an excellent example of the pernicious effects of the South's peculiar institution upon a slaveholding people.

And yet Southern opinion was anything but unanimous on the propriety of dueling. Most Southerners, regardless of whether they had ever fought, were like Yancey in their reluctance to leap to a defense of dueling in abstract terms, apart from the particulars of a unique event. Many newspapers stood editorially against dueling, even if newspaper editors were among those who most frequently occupied the field of honor.[14] Southern periodicals, ranging from small religious publications to *De Bow's Review*, also took a negative view of dueling. Ministers of the gospel were not loath to add their voices to the cry against dueling, and antidueling societies arose in many communities.

All of the Southern states and the District of Columbia had laws against dueling and most agreed in disqualifying the participants, whether principals or seconds, from holding political office. Such a law was on the books in Mississippi from the time of the organization of the territory in 1799, and many other states passed statutes during the same period. In Tennessee, where it was discovered that about 90 percent of duels were fought by lawyers, one was required to swear never to be a participant in an affair of honor before admission to the bar; North Carolina proposed to institute capital punishment in the event of a principal's death, and without benefit of clergy.[15]

Although it is hard to say whether laws were effective in curbing the practice—since it is hard to say how many duels were fought—anyone who wanted to fight a duel could find a way of doing so without much trouble. It was easy enough to evade the law simply by moving to another state, as Yancey and Clingman had done, and there are few reports of participants' having been arrested for their roles in a duel. On the contrary, it was not unusual for state legislatures to pardon those who had taken part in duels, restoring supposedly lost privileges to them: the North Carolina legislature did this in 1833, and the Mississippi legislature offered a wholesale amnesty to "fifteen leading citizens" in 1858.[16]

In a very real sense, however, law had little relevance to dueling. As Yancey had argued, disputes between gentlemen over honor had mainly to do with the opinion of society. Another Southerner, Francis Ruffin, certainly felt this was so, and confided in his diary on the anniversary of his having fought, that "All defenses of the Practice are derived from sophistry, whilst most of the arguments against it are pure reason and common sense. Yet so strong is the force of imperious *opinion*, that I may again be *compelled* to fight, and I do not know of any consideration which under certain circumstances would prevent my sending or accepting a challenge, though, if ever man had reason to refuse I have."[17] Others who had taken part in duels agreed with Ruffin's assessment. Mississippian Henry S. Foote recalled that no one, "not in close connection with some Christian denomination," could refuse a challenge "without being consigned to permanent discredit and coldly shut out from all intercourse with gentlemen."[18] He was certainly exaggerating the case, but he had no doubts, nor did Yancey, that the sanction for the duel lay not in law or morality, but in public opinion. Anyone who failed to meet his opponent on the field had to worry, rightly or wrongly, that he faced a much sterner test in maintaining his social standing in the face of public scorn. Only a known Christian, appealing to religious scruples, could refuse a challenge from another gentleman with public approval, a point both Foote and Yancey made.

Historians of the South have long noted the gentlemanly concern for public honor and esteem. Such a concern, as Foote, Yancey, and others said, was what ultimately forced men to the field— as it was called—of honor. Society's good opinion, and the fear that it should be lost, was powerful in leading men to duel. One sees this clearly in the positive defenses many Southerners formulated for the practice. George Anderson Mercer, a Georgian, reflected, "Its necessity sometimes is to be deeply lamented, but it at least tends to preserve gentlemanly deportment, and a healthy social tone" adding, "Avowed non-combatants make the most rancorous and abusive politicians."[19] When Louisianians considered an antidueling provision for the state constitution, one member of the convention declared his own fear that "ambitious persons" would more readily insult public men, secure from being called to account.[20] The duel was necessary simply because, given human nature, something beyond the law was needed to enforce good behavior in social and political relations.

Dueling, it was argued, made men careful. It forced them to watch their words, as William H. Haigh had to admit, "making them more thoughtful & respectful—bridling the tongues of the impudent coxcombs, & acting as a check upon the whole body of society." Legislative enactment would never do away with the duel; only a thorough reformation of human nature and social order could create the sorts of conditions in which the extralegal practice of dueling would be superfluous. Governor John Lyde Wilson of South Carolina, whose *Code of Honor* was published in 1838 as a procedural textbook for affairs of honor, put the case with his usual perception, writing, "I would teach immutable integrity and uniform urbanity of manners. Scrupulously to guard individual honor, by a high personal self-respect, and the practice of every commendable virtue. Once let such a system of education be universal, and we should seldom hear, if ever, of any more duelling." But Wilson was a Southerner, and his argument was rhetorical. He was not optimistic that such a system could ever exist.[21]

As the words of dueling's defenders indicate, honor was very much a public matter, involving not only one's opinion of himself, but also his sense of what others should expect him to be. Pessimistic Southerners understood that venal, selfish men—present in any community—could destroy a gentleman's reputation by their invective or their insinuations, and the duel was protection against this. Its threat was preventive, and, given the low expectations most Southerners had of their fellow men, the practice provided a recourse that many felt society could ill afford to lose. The message of dueling grew out of both considerations.

Duels occurred in the South for various reasons. Some grew out of personal differences, as when two South Carolinians almost fought in 1858 after one had joined the other on an afternoon's ride with a young lady: the challenger viewed the act as a "violation of courtesy."[22] Duels resulting from personal difficulties were not nearly so numerous, however, as those growing out of political life, and more particularly out of the ways in which differences were publicly expressed, as in the Yancey-Clingman affair.

Indeed, as the meeting between Yancey and Clingman shows,

political debate often became quite personal during the antebellum period. That Yancey's attacks on Clingman were highly personal is beyond doubt, and, in fact, when several years later the North Carolinian saw a debate with Edward Stanly taking the same course, he recalled his earlier meeting with Yancey. He promised Stanly, however, that any affair between them would not end as happily as the previous one with Yancey. Politics that became personal could also become violent. When Judge A. G. Magrath of Charleston was nominated for a seat in Congress, the *Charleston Mercury* blistered the judge for Unionist leanings, accusing him of putting his own "blighted ambition" above the needs of the state. The judge's brother, Edward, called the paper's editor out for those remarks, and the latter, William R. Taber, was killed. Magrath withdrew his name from nomination.[23]

The events usually leading up to most affairs of honor in the Old South indicate that political or personal differences were only tangentially involved in a point of honor, however much such differences were ostensibly at issue. When a writer for *Harper's* sarcastically suggested that in a duel, "the process of ratiocination was exceedingly luminous, and so simple as to be adapted to the commonest capacity. It was based on the theory of some supposed connection between saltpetre and a change of opinion,"[24] he displayed only a vague understanding of the causes of dueling. It is clear that no one went to the field with any thought of changing anyone else's mind. Yancey and Clingman were on opposite sides of many political issues, but neither would have claimed that a desire to convert his opponent on the annexation question had led him to Beltsville. Every Southern Whig representative had voted against the annexation treaty of 1844, but Yancey did not become embroiled with them all. Similarly, in the later difficulty between Clingman and Stanly, Clingman expressed no opposition to the latter's attacking his position on the issue then before the House, and only feared that Stanly should make the attack personal.

Still, that political differences of the sort described here did lead to questions of honor shows how, at the simplest level, duels related to culture. The kinds of attacks in political life that would take two men to the field of honor generally involved accusations of a man's allowing selfish dispositions to triumph over his duty to contribute to the public good, as when Clingman was accused of mere partisanship at a time of grave national crisis. Others, like Magrath, were similarly charged with putting personal fame over public good. Here, in its clearest form, was that conflict between social ideals and notions of a passionate human nature which led Southerners to view violence as inevitable in life. Individuals in public life had a special responsibility to uphold the public good, and the sort of accusation that generally led to the field was one that the individual had abrogated his responsibility in favor of selfish and expedient goals. Put another way, it was an accusation that a man could not control his passionate nature.

And, again, it was passion that ultimately set the duel off. Hostile critics made much of the role of passion, owing everything about the practice to passion run amok, or, as the Reverend John Blair put it (in an antidueling sermon entitled, tellingly, "On the Impetuosity and Bad Effects of Passion"), "the madness of a quick and inflammable temper." Another critic, writing under the name "Honestus," tied dueling to class and then to the lack of restraint that led to all sorts of vicious habits of self-indulgence: duelists were the same men who "drank free, gambled, and blasphemed," and all, he added, had likely "seduced and disgraced some unfortunate girl." Most defenders of the practice, of course, would have vehemently denied Honestus's view, but few would have disagreed with William Yancey's contention that engaging in a duel was "more a matter of feeling than of reason." In fact, most did assert that passion, in its noblest form, was the major force leading men to resent aspersions on their characters, as well it should. Virginia scholar George Tucker and Governor Wilson both went so far as to defend dueling on the ground that it preserved a manliness and courage otherwise found only in less civilized states of society.[25] The problem, again, was neither to suppress nor to transcend passion, impossible and undesirable tasks in any event. The problem was, as always, to keep passion moderate and within bounds once it had been provoked by insult or resentment, and this the duel was supposed to do. The duel, ultimately, was a drama in which two contending moral forces, passion and restraint, occupied center stage. The specific form dueling took in the Old South, the structure of events and characters in every duel, grew out of the ways in which Southerners sought to come to grips with their basic moral task.

The duel may be seen as both a method and a proof for the possibility of restraining passion. On the one hand, various aspects of dueling procedure were designed to channel volatile passions into controllable, though clearly not harmless, forms. On the other hand, as a duel progressed, the participants demonstrated that they could make such an effort successfully. A duel began, not with the issuing of a challenge, but with the exchange of notes by principals and their seconds. The exchange of notes had to be full enough to establish that there was, indeed, a point of honor under dispute, and what took place between Clingman and Yancey was not unusual in either its volume or its form. Clingman, in his initial note, showed the kind of judgment demanded of a potential principal. Not rushing to resent Yancey's remarks—though they had been abusive and aimed at him—Clingman framed his note as an attempt to establish whether the Alabamian "intended towards me, personally, any disrespect," and so on. The tone was both inquisitive and respectful, and that, according to Governor Wilson's textbook *Code of Honor*, was as it should have been.

What Marquis James called "the code in its purest ray," "a word and a challenge,"[26] was not the *Code* at all. Governor Wilson's *Code of Honor* was meant to insure a "civilized" practice of dueling by setting forth stringent rules—codifying, in fact, many existing procedures—to govern the conduct of principals and seconds and, thereby, to regulate and limit the actions each could take in a trying situation. Put briefly, once a possible insult had been offered, the *Code* attempted to reduce the level of spontaneity and, thus, any chance of further outbursts of unrestrained passion in subsequent conversations between the two disputants. Clingman's response to Yancey's letter, regardless of whether he had read the *Code*, followed Wilson to the letter. "Let your note," Wilson had advised, "be in the language of a gentleman, and let the subject-matter of complaint be truly and fairly set forth, cautiously avoiding attributing to the adverse party any improper motive."[27] The point was to insure that nothing occurring once negotiations had begun would give further grounds for resentment while putting the anger of the principals into an apparently controlled form. The language of communication, mannered and mannerly, would prevent passion's too free expression.

Another device for containing passion was the use of seconds for all communication between the principals. According to Wilson's *Code*, "When you believe yourself aggrieved, be silent on the subject, speak to no one about the matter, and see your friend, who is to act for you, as soon as possible." Principals and seconds were not to be in consultation once the exchange had begun, and, as Wilson said, the second was to have complete custody of his principal's honor, using only his own judgment for every decision. The principals were irritated, while the seconds were "cool and collected." The degree of responsibility taken on by the seconds for even the occurrence of a meeting on the field cannot be overstated. Wilson himself estimated that "nine duels out of ten, if not ninety-nine out of a hundred, originate in the want of experience in the seconds."[28]

As the *Code* made clear, a second, or "friend," did more than deliver notes between the two principals. Instead, the seconds were responsible for all negotiations taking place between the parties from the delivery of the first insult to the acceptance of a challenge. One did not take the duties of a second lightly. When Clingman sent a note to Yancey, for instance, the first person he called upon as friend would not even bear the communication without permission to tell Yancey he had approved of the Alabamian's words.[29] Most of the notes in a correspondence were composed by the principals, but each man's second communicated primarily if not exclusively with the second of the other party, and they were within their rights mutually to agree to withhold a principal's note if they felt that by doing so they could prevent the affair from ever reaching the field. In addition, throughout the affair the seconds determined what could be retracted and accepted, often, as Wilson's *Code* required, in the absence of any consultation with the principals. In the Yancey-Clingman affair, Yancey's friend Huger elaborated on Yancey's adamant refusal to explain—trying several versions—and Clingman's friend Charles Lee Jones was the one who continually maintained that none of the elaborations was adequate for his principal's satisfaction.

If the seconds performed their duties capably, they could prevent hostilities. By withholding several crucial notes, the seconds did much to head off a meeting between Roger Pryor and John Potter, so much that Pryor ultimately tried to address a note directly to Potter—and it too was intercepted and withheld.[30] When the seconds were inexperienced, the results could be tragic. The correspondence in an affair between Daniel Dugger and Virginia congressman George C. Dromgoole shows that Dugger, at least, had no desire to fight with his challenger, an old friend, and that he even wished to apologize in an acceptable manner. He went so far as to tell Dromgoole's second, Hiram Haines, at one point, "that if there was an act of his life which he sincerely regretted" it was the one that broke up his friendship with Dromgoole. Haines then, without his principal's knowledge, offered Dugger a "memorandum" proposing "that if Mr. Dugger feels regret at the hastiness of his course, that he shall so express himself and in such terms as gentlemen ought to use and be satisfied with when made." Dugger's response to Haines was an attempt to apologize while, at the same time saving face.

> I agree with you that the personal difficulty between Gen. Dromgoole and myself ought to be settled without resort to a hostile course. In furtherance of that object therefore I have had to say that I ought under the circumstances to have [asked] an explanation of Gen. Dromgoole at the time he used the exceptional language to me [Dugger, feeling insulted, had simply hit the General instead]. While I would not seek the adjustment of this difficulty by a resort to hostile measures, yet I would not shun or decline the responsibility which such difficulty might devolve on me. But being convinced as I now am that Gen. Dromgoole was unconscious of having used insulting language to me, I cannot hesitate to express my regret for having acted hastily towards him. Having thus expressed regret for the precipitancy of my course in resenting the insult as I thought intended by Gen. Dromgoole, I cannot doubt that it will be received by him in the same spirit in which it is offered and be considered by him as honorable reparation for the indignity of which he complains.

This, to Haines, was not "in accordance with the memorandum" and hence the challenge was tendered. Haines had improperly required too much of the challenged party, and when the two old friends met, Dugger received a wound from which he died several weeks later.[31]

The Dugger-Dromgoole affair was, in fact, a good example of how a duel should not be conducted. Dromgoole had drunkenly insulted Dugger who, without asking explanation, struck him. The difficulty had, however, been resolved on the spot, and should have been dropped. The time between the alleged wrong and the beginning of negotiations was to be as short as possible, as Wilson advised, and this was usually the practice. But Dromgoole waited almost twenty days before calling Dugger to account. In any case, it is less than certain that Dromgoole, having tendered an insult and received a blow, had any right to demand satisfaction of Dugger, but the rules on this point were highly confusing. The duel did no one credit, given the existence of a code of honor, and it is small wonder that Haines, as well as Dugger's friend Thomas Goode Tucker, went to a Richmond newspaper independently, to defend their actions to the public, or that Haines also felt constrained to write to Dromgoole's brother Edward in defense of himself. Not surprisingly, though a duel was no barrier to political advancement, Dromgoole's political advisors feared that this sort of sloppy affair could hurt the Congressman immeasurably.[32]

Critics of dueling, like its defenders, recognized the crucial role played by seconds. A writer for a Boston publication exaggerated only slightly when he claimed that "the principals in such affairs should be passive instruments, with no other function than to pull triggers at word of command," and he found this a compelling argument against the practice. "What a scandal to an age of civilization, that A and B should shoot each other because C and D did not know what they were about, and had not the sense necessary to the adjustment of an affair of honor!"[33] Daniel Dugger, for one, might have agreed.

The formalities of the duel, then, because they were intended to keep the passions in check, manifested Southern concepts of human nature, illuminating their implications. In using stiff, even stereotyped language in their notes, and in relying so heavily on seconds, principals were not attempting to evade taking action themselves, as the Boston critic implied—they would, after all, have to face the bullets themselves. Instead, these practices reveal a larger sense of unpredictability and distrust with regard to human action. Southerners worried about the passionate side of human nature because, though indispensable, it was liable to break loose, uncontrollably, in fits. Social decorum and stability were fragile, and all too vulnerable to the strains accompanying any affair of honor.

The point of much that followed in a duel was to prove that

one could withstand its strains and still remain cool. Once negotiations had broken off, events took place relatively quickly. First, having failed to secure a satisfactory agreement, the offended principal's second would issue a challenge which, more often than not, would be accepted. It was considered bad form to refuse if one had agreed to enter into negotiations at all. Then, the seconds would meet to draw up rules for the affair. These rules were intended to establish equality between the principals and, as in the case of the Yancey-Clingman affair, they were usually quite explicit, identifying weapons, and once the parties had reached the field, the position each man would occupy and whose second would give the command to fire. Finally, principals and seconds would make preparations for the fight—which could range from a crash course on how to use a dueling pistol to drawing up a will in case one were shot. A day or two later, the meeting would occur.

On the field, once the men were in position, the duel began with the command to fire. A duel could be stopped after the first fire, regardless of whether one of the principals were hit, and Yancey was not unusual in his private determination merely to fire without hurting his opponent. Daniel Dugger proposed to do the same, but was dissuaded by his second's refusal to serve in such an instance. In any case, it was the seconds' duty to meet after a fire to see if honor were satisfied, and sometimes it was satisfied by a meeting and an ineffectual exchange of shots. So frequent did bloodless duels seem to some observers that, after reporting one such encounter, the *Columbus* (Georgia) *Enquirer* wryly editorialized, "We are tired of these bloodless fights and now give due notice that if somebody don't get killed pretty shortly we will quit noticing such contemptible freaks of martial honor. If men will fight we want them to do the thing a little less like they were taken with a shaking. Some uncharitable people have already surmised that of late there are no *bullets* used by these *braggers*. We venture no opinion on the subject ourselves."[34] An opponent of dueling apparently concurred, declaring that there would be no need for formal opposition should there be "a public sentiment created which would stigmatize a duel in which both parties come off with their lives."[35]

Matters were not always so easily concluded, however, and a duel could last over several fires until either party was shot. One duel in New Orleans, for instance, lasted for three fires before one of the principals was killed; the fight between western Virginia leader Sherrard Clemens and O. Jennings Wise just before the Civil War actually went through four, at which point Clemens was shot and the affair settled. After a fire in which either party was hit, the duel had to stop, and it was the duty of the injured principal to declare that he had been wounded. The challenger could clearly demand no more, and, if his opponent were shot, had to claim satisfaction; if he himself were hit, he could only withdraw from the contest and grant his opponent permission to leave the field.[36]

The seconds in one New Orleans affray met with difficulty in just this regard. After the first fire, neither party had fallen. The challenger asked for an apology which his opponent refused to give, and at the second fire, the challenger was killed. Afterward, it was learned that the victor had been wounded on the first exchange of shots; the fight should never have reached its fatal conclusion since both seconds and the wounded man should have seen to it that the affair was halted. The wounded man had been unwilling to see his opponent satisfied, however, and had concealed his injury in order to continue. The seconds of both parties were, it was said, "in a very embarrassing position."[37]

The point was that in all these cases, the principals went through with the duel, even if it meant standing and shooting—and being a target—over several fires. The New Orleans deception was unusual and out of line, for in most duels what stands out is the willingness of men to abide by the rules as they risked their lives on the field. And it is this, of course, that made the deliberately "bloodless" duel so significant, because such duels originated not by prior mutual agreement, but by each principal's decision to put his own life on the line while not placing that of his opponent in jeopardy. The drama of the duel was contained in the risk each participant had to take as he sought to defend his honor on the ground.

Some Southerners went to great lengths to emphasize that their participation in a duel had more to do with risk than with combat. According to an anonymous account (perhaps apocryphal) of a meeting between Joseph Cheves and William Trapier, the demonstration could take a spectacular form. "This was the duel where Cheves drank champagne before every shot, toasting his opponent, William Trapier. . . . Cheves had not wanted to fight, and had had a basket of Champagne brought along, and before every shot called for it and drank to Mr. Trapier, then fired in the air." Other Southerners had a less festive attitude. Francis Ruffin, aware of the power of passion, worried that it might force him to shoot a man in a duel, and hoped it would never happen. At least one man, a New Orleanian, was led to suicide by, among other things, having killed a friend in a duel. There was, some duelists recognized, a big difference between obtaining satisfaction and killing another man.[38]

Satisfaction was the end of any duel. Its importance was obvious, but its meaning was anything but clear. In some duels, as in that between Yancey and Clingman, satisfaction involved a negotiated resolution of differences, made possible after each man had undergone a fire. In others, there seems to have been no resolution at all, simply an agreement, for the future, to disregard the difficulties that had brought the principals to the field. One thing certain is that demonstrating one's skill at shooting by injuring an opponent was secondary, and even revenge was to have had no place in motivating the principals.[39] Here, too, the process and its risks were most important. Satisfaction came as one proved his ability to behave as a principal should; and as he made his opponent take the same risk.

Whatever the historical origins of the duel, and however much combat may have been its traditional focus, as the practice developed in the antebellum South, it tended to look less toward combat and more toward the individual principal himself. Only a few men went to the field seeking a satisfaction that came from killing an opponent; most found satisfaction though little or no damage was done. The practical meaning of the duel lay in its opportunities for risking one's life in proof of honor and reputation.

The dramatic meaning of the duel, however, was more important. Responding to aspersions on his character or, in a sense, claiming to defend a code of duty and decorum, the duelist was also acting out the moral conflict that occupied so many Southerners, that between the natural, passionate man and the social man of discipline and restraint. As each principal went through the procedures of a duel, he proved by his actions that the two key forces in human action—natural passion and civilized restraint—could achieve some kind of equilibrium. On the one hand, the duel provided formal channels for controlling passion while defending oneself, by directing anger into conventional courtesies between principals as, through their seconds, they communicated with each other. On the other, by demanding that a gentleman confront the powerful fears and emotions evoked in the face of possible death, and still display coolness, the duel allowed each principal to experience vividly the forces of nature that challenged civilization. In a duel, natural instinct was brought head on with the social injunction to maintain a discreet and agreeable deportment in the most trying situations, so that, given the stakes, the character of each of those forces was unmistakable. Any risk short of one's life would have been insufficient, because self-preservation meant proving oneself inviolate under *any* possible circumstances, and no other circumstance could ever equal the challenge posed on the ground. The duel, then, did not involve a denial of passion under provocation but embodied, in a particularly intense way, the heroic struggle on the part of every man to face up to both the civilized and "primitive" parts of his nature, denying to neither an essential role in the human condition.

The duel dramatized, quite spectacularly, two main Southern ideas about violence and, indeed, about social relations in general. As it progressed, the duel showed the extent to which Southerners associated passion with violence, as well as the pessimism which made them feel the necessity for a method of violent response. It also revealed their understanding that the only effective way to control passion was through tightly constricted formal procedures. So long as procedures were observed, and individual spontaneous action was restrained by rules, then violence itself could be controlled and kept in bounds. A man might have to defend himself violently, but he need not lose his self-possession in order to do so.

The striking connection of dueling with the antebellum South, then, grew out of the South's focus on passion and the problem of restraint. To see the strength of this connection, one must emphasize the extent to which dueling continued to occur in the American South at a time when it appeared to be dying out everywhere else. Moreover, one must also stress that nineteenth-century dueling in the South was something more than a carry-over from colonial times. There had been little dueling anywhere in colonial America, and, despite a few flare-ups in the early national period, the "sudden and fantastic acceptance" of dueling in the lower states after 1800 was unmistakable.[40] Richard Buel has suggested that one reason for the growing acceptance of dueling in the South lay in the fact that the practice, with its close ties to social status in the South, provided a way for members of the gentry to distinguish themselves from the common man. As Buel argues, in the South during the early national period, there was less a question of whether an elite would rule than of who should be fit for the elite; among New England Federalists, who shared much of the Southern conservative world view, there was a genuine question of whether they should continue "to wield the authority they believed themselves entitled to" in an increasingly democratic society. Hence, they had less use than Southerners, concerned about individual rather than corporate status, for such a practice as dueling to indicate a man's standing.[41]

Buel is, in large measure, right. Certainly, dueling reflected Southern ideals of social hierarchy, since there was a strict convention that duels were to involve only gentlemen, and that one should never fight with a social inferior. For Governor Wilson this precept was so important that his *Code* advised anyone receiving a note from a stranger to "ascertain his standing in society" before making a reply, and there are innumerable stories of challenges rejected, with no loss of face, because of the social inferiority of the would-be challenger. If there were an unwritten law to cover some kinds of social transactions in the Old South, as has often been suggested, not every Southerner was fit to be guided by it; the activities of the duel were not such that just anyone could participate in them.[42]

But, clearly, there was more to the duel than the simple assertion of one's own social status. Southerners never talked about why they began dueling in the nineteenth century, so that one can only read between the lines of what they said about the practice once it had become established. To some extent, the aristocratic past of dueling provided its appeal in a society which wanted to maintain a hierarchical order. But hierarchy itself had more profound connections with the deeper Southern concern for passion. That is to say, Southerners closely related high social status to an ability, carefully cultivated, to control one's own passions. Hence, even the somewhat impetuous John Randolph—himself a proponent of dueling—gave some not unusual advice to a young relative in 1807, urging the young man against "any indulgence of *sudden* suggestions of your feelings," adding, "I am deeply interested in seeing you turn out a respectable man, in every point of view."[43] The thrust of Randolph's advice was simple: being a gentleman required an ability to act with restraint; the man who could not was unfit to demand the respect due to someone of stature. For Randolph (and his was the common view), the markings of social hierarchy were closely bound up with a conception of human nature and society in which the restraint of passion was an individual's primary moral task, since being a gentleman and succeeding at the task were one and the same thing. Thus, again, only gentlemen could fight duels, because only gentlemen could act with restraint.

By 1800, such ideals of hierarchy and self-restraint were becoming outmoded outside the South. The sorts of fears that led men to view life as a contest between passion and virtue were coming to be replaced by more material views of social process and a reevaluation of human nature. At the same time, hierarchy was being challenged by more democratic points of view that made the individual, whose rights were in his person and not in his property or status, the essential element in social organization. Southern leaders were aware of these changes and even had to confront them in political life, but unlike even the New England Federalists, who were at least willing to modify their rhetoric to keep up with the changing times, elite Southerners stuck to more traditional views which kept both hierarchy and passion at the center of social and political processes.[44] Dueling, one may suggest, asserted both distinctiveness and tradition in a striking way, because the duel did not merely verify that hierarchy existed. More, it was a way of dramatizing those concepts of human nature and motivation, focusing on the problem of passion, which Southerners believed lay at the bottom of gradations in a hierarchical social order. In other words, dueling was not only a symbol of Southerners' devotion to a hierarchical social order, but also a dramatization of their reasons for that devotion.

Again, the point is that the South seems to have changed less than the North during the early national period, so that interest in the duel was a measure of the tenacity with which Southerners clung to classical ideas about human nature and society and of their desire, as well, to express their tenacity in an increasingly individualistic, egalitarian world. One indication, perhaps, of the extent to which the North had moved away from older conceptions may be seen in the most famous duel to occur in that region in the nineteenth century. Whereas a Southern man faced more vilification for refusing a duel than for fighting, Northerner Aaron Burr found his reputation virtually destroyed after he killed Alexander Hamilton on the field of honor. But an equally important indication of how things had changed in the North lies in Hamilton's belief, prior to the fight, that should he refuse the challenge, he would so lose public credibility as to find his political influence seriously eroded.[45] It was not simply a matter of the New Yorker Hamilton's having somehow adopted a Southern sensibility. Rather, both he and Burr retained that classical view of human nature and society that had dominated in colonial and Revolutionary America, one that stressed the problem of passion and the necessity of hierarchy, at a time when Northern sensibilities were changing, as Burr lived to regret. This suggests that the duel had been available to gentlemen throughout colonial America, and it would continue to appear available as a course of action in the early years of the United States. Its meaning had probably been everywhere what it would continue to be in the South up to the time of the Civil War. After 1800, however, the ideas which gave dueling its meaning were increasingly confined to the South, and, as Southerners became aware of this, they saw in the duel an expression of their distinctive character and of the views which, they felt, made them distinct. Southern conservatism and Southern distinctiveness were, that is, symbolized in the practice of dueling, and this would account for its growing acceptance after 1800.

Dueling was a survival of older ways in the South. Its aristocratic European past may have contributed to its antebellum popularity in the region, but what actually made the duel important, symbolically, at least, was its continuing compatibility with what most Southerners thought about human nature and society. After the Civil War, the hierarchical, carefully ordered world of the Old South lost its strength, and the basic concerns upon which that world had been based no longer had much power to organize life in the region. Despite sporadic attempts to revive dueling, the practice itself died, for all intents and purposes, as antebellum concerns came to seem increasingly irrelevant.[46] For antebellum Southerners, nevertheless, dueling, stylized and ritualized as it was, had much to say about themselves and about the nature of violence in society.

2. Preparation for Violence
Child-Rearing and the Southern World View

THE DUEL dramatized Southern perceptions of the individual and his relations to other people. In the form and substance of their actions, duelists vividly expressed a profound mistrust of self and society, focusing with clarity on problems of motive and behavior, thought and action, in social life. In proposing to control a passionate humanity by observing outward form and in emphasizing the necessity for human violence, duelists portrayed, dramatically, the crucial themes in Southern attitudes toward physical conflict. Southerners learned both these themes early, and well, when they were growing up.

It would be convenient for a study of violence if Southern children had, in fact, been brought up to be self-assertive, impetuous, and violent. On the frontier, this was often the case.[1] But in child-rearing practices, there were genuine class distinctions in the Old South. Those Southerners who felt they belonged in the planter elite tried to raise their children to be members of that hallowed group, and this desire led to distinctive practices on their part. The distinction is apparent in regard to violence. The sons and daughters of Southern planters were not raised to be aggressive individualists. In fact, every effort of Southern child-rearing was directed toward the opposite goal, toward the repression of impetuosity and the channeling of self-assertion. At the same time, however, the ideas which children were taught to have about themselves and society reinforced the sense of social insecurity that contributed to most Southern notions about violence.

This chapter, one should note, focuses mainly on Southern boys, for it was among males that violence was most common. The reason men were more given to violence than were women is not hard to find, nor is it particularly profound. These were people who were part of a long cultural tradition which associated violence with the male role, so that—with some significant exceptions, which we shall see—violence was a response to situations which was available to men but not to women. At the same time, women were taught the same lessons of childhood that will be outlined here. They were discouraged from acting with unrestrained passion and inculcated with a strong sense of social insecurity. The fact that they did not often turn to violence, at least not against each other, had more to do with traditional sex roles than with other differences in what they were taught to believe about human nature and society.

It is hard to know how different the elite Southern family was from that of the Northern United States or of other parts of the Western world. In its broadest forms, especially in its nuclear focus, the orientation of husbands and wives, parents and children toward each other, and the presence of servants, the elite white Southern family differed very little from the sort of well-to-do family which has dominated in the West for at least the last two or three centuries.[2] These features were as important in the raising of Southern planters' children and in the character of family life as they were anywhere, so that if there were anything unique about Southern child-rearing, the differences resulted mainly from variations on the basic form caused by the peculiar characteristics of Southern society.

There is much evidence on which to base an understanding of Southern ideas about child-rearing. Southerners—children and adults—wrote frequently in letters and diaries about the problems and joys of family life, and they seem to have agreed with each other, at least tacitly, as to what the main concerns in growing up were. Moreover, their ideas about child-rearing tended to be remarkably coherent and systematic as they considered the various aspects of life which parents and children had to face. One sees this coherence most strikingly, however, not by pointing to a large number of families, picking and choosing the evidence to fit some system, but by examining the efforts of a single family—not an atypical one—to mold the children into good, proper adults.

The Pettigrew family of North Carolina embodied many of the virtues most Southern plantation families approved. Conservative, influential, pious, and prosperous, the Pettigrews were a close-knit family—though not unusually so—and one in which the concern for discipline, order, and, above all, high moral standards occupied first place in the mind of every member. As one commented to an old friend of the family, James C. Johnston, in 1846, "The position that our family occupies in the public eye is highly flattering. But let it not be forgotten, that the higher our rank, the more circumspect it is necessary that we should be. For any blunder of ours would afford pleasure to the envious who never allow an opportunity to escape for putting the worst construction on the errors of those who are above them."[3] No one in the family would have been likely to disagree with the sentiment.

Pettigrews were not always in the upper ranks of Southern society, but by combining hard work and good connections, they had risen fairly high by the opening of the nineteenth century. The first Pettigrews moved from Scotland to Pennsylvania in 1740, and the immigrant James Pettigrew's family, including thirteen children, settled in North Carolina in 1760. One son, Charles, went on to make his home in Warrenton where he was engaged as a tutor, remaining there when his father and the family moved on to South Carolina in 1768. Appointed schoolmaster in Edenton in 1773, young Charles at last found his place, and he eventually became rector of the Episcopal parish. He also acquired land, and, by 1782, he had begun to develop his first plantation, Bonarva, in an association with several of his parishioners. His holdings in land and slaves never stopped growing, and at the time of his death in 1807, his will included not only the original plantation of Bonarva but also a second, Belgrade, where he lived out his life, and lands as far away as Tennessee. The plantation "regime" he founded was destined to endure for three-quarters of a century.[4]

Charles Pettigrew—minister, tutor, and planter—was the founder of the Pettigrew family of North Carolina. In 1778, he married Mary Blount, and she bore five children, of whom only two, John and Ebenezer, lived for more than five years. John was born in 1779, attended the fledgling University of North Carolina and undertook the study of medicine, but died suddenly in 1799. Ebenezer, born in 1783, did reach maturity, and he inherited and built upon the family holdings. Moreover, he had a large and rather successful family of his own, including two daughters and seven sons. Both daughters and three of the sons reached maturity and expanded the influence of the family in Southern society and politics.

These two generations of Pettigrews met every Southern criterion for what a family was supposed to be like.

Ten years before his death, the founder of the Pettigrew family, concerned about what course the lives of his two sons might take, published a moralistic little pamphlet entitled, *Last Advice of the Rev. Charles Pettigrew to His Sons, 1797.* In its evocation of death, its advice, and, it might be said, in the fact that it should have been printed at all, the pamphlet epitomized the Pettigrew approach to child-rearing. Thirty-four years later, Ebenezer would send copies to his own sons, away at school, with the admonition to "read them with attention." And, indeed, the Reverend Pettigrew's concerns, hopes, and fears were those of many dedicated Southern fathers even up to the time of the Civil War.[5]

Charles Pettigrew's ideas about child-rearing grew out of that vision of the world which most Southerners shared, a vision which emphasized the difficulties and temptations posed by life. He was, as a result, convinced that every youngster required substantial guidance in order to live well. "Could I stay but long enough to guard you from the rocks and shoals which are so numerous, and so dangerous to youth, as just launching out into the troubled ocean of this life," he wrote, ". . . the bed of death would be rendered comparatively soft, easy and comfortable."[6] The problem was, of course, that at some point the boys would have to make it on their own, and it was this that gave their father the most trouble, for he was sure that his sons, like all people, were too weak to navigate a proper course without constant careful vigilance. The Reverend Pettigrew's perspective on child-rearing is easily summarized as uncertainty magnified by a not unusual pessimism about human nature and the future.

Because of what Pettigrew thought about the nature of life in the world, he was most interested in training his sons to approach that world with both a proper respect and a pessimism of their own. Like most Southern fathers, he encouraged his sons to work hard—to follow his example in accumulating property—but he also warned that wealth brought problems of its own, problems arising from the very simple fact that "the world is envious and ill-natured," particularly toward those who were successful and possessed of property.[7]

The perversity of the world posed a major challenge to a

good life and Charles Pettigrew knew it took great discipline to meet that challenge. But he did not encourage his children to meet it aggressively. Certainly he expected his sons to maintain what he called "firmness," and, in the tradition of the South, to be men of "honor," but Charles Pettigrew's conception of honor could not have been further from that sense of personal sovereignty so often associated with the word. Instead, the father encouraged his sons to "cultivate the softer tempers, in the exercise of resolution and firmness," and, indeed, to avoid having too much self-confidence, "for such is the imperfection of human nature, that men are often deceived in themselves, while exposed to the eye of the world, in a very different light from that in which they are accustomed to view themselves."[8]

Charles Pettigrew taught his sons honor and resolution, but he most certainly did not teach the kind of hyperindividualism so often associated with the South in the early years of American independence. In fact, it might be said that he taught them to strive for the opposite character, as he urged them to shun an overt self-assertion and to be cognizant of the opinions of the world. One could not, after all, be too independent in a world of envy and malice, a world in which others were waiting to take advantage of any misstep on one's part, and Charles Pettigrew was convinced that in such a world, the best prescription for life was to "act always on your guard."[9]

Reverend Pettigrew felt confident he could give his sons the discipline they needed to remain "on their guard" so long as they stayed under his guidance, but he was worried about what would happen to them once outside his control and especially in the event they should come into contact—as they inevitably would—with the wrong sort of companions. At about the time of the publication of his pamphlet he withdrew the boys from the University of North Carolina because of the "pernicious habits" of most of the students. He was convinced that his sons would adopt bad habits themselves should they stay longer, and he had the evidence of a large tavern bill to reinforce his fears. The younger son, Ebenezer, was not pleased by his withdrawal from the school—although, at the ripe age of twenty, he too would worry that a young friend, on his way to Chapel Hill, might have his "principles depraved." The point was, however, that no matter how well one raised his own children, self-will could not be prevented in the children of others.

It was not that the Reverend Pettigrew wanted his sons to avoid all company; it was simply that company had to be of the right sort, and such company was not, in his view, easy to find.[10]

The fears the elder Pettigrew expressed for his sons were not unusual in Southern families; the problem of bad company worried many people, and it remained an important theme in Southern child-rearing up to the time of the Civil War. As late as 1860, Southern thinker George Fitzhugh warned parents to guide their children strictly and carefully. As for those who urged greater freedom, such a position was nonsense; the real issue was clear, and the alternatives only two: "The child turned out into the streets, amid temptations to crime and the teachings of evil associations, is no more free than the child in the nursery, learning lessons of religion and virtue from its parents."[11] If Charles Pettigrew lacked Fitzhugh's gift for vivid contrast, he would probably have been pleased that, sixty-three years after he had written his pamphlet, his views were still alive.

The main point to emerge from Pettigrew's views of family and society was his belief that his family was qualitatively different from the world of a larger society. For one thing, Pettigrew never seemed to have seen his sons as anything but potential victims of corruption, and he certainly never expressed any fear that they should corrupt others. Everyone else's children were what Fitzhugh would call "evil associations"; one's own were only likely to suffer. The home, by contrast with the world outside, was a seat of safety and virtue, where children were well-protected from the dangers of bad company. Charles Pettigrew felt that there were two worlds to live in, that of the home and that outside, and the two could not have been in greater opposition.

John Pettigrew, the elder son, died before he could have a family of his own, but the younger, Ebenezer, married and fathered several children. He never rejected his father's precepts, although, since he had thoroughly imbibed that rejection of self-confidence his father had taught, he never tired of expressing his regret that he "did not follow [the pamphlet's] precepts in the fullest sense of the word."[12] Beyond his desire to follow his father's guidance at every step in his own life, moreover, that same avoidance of self-will and of bad company that had so preoccupied Charles Pettigrew was a major focus in Ebenezer's own efforts to raise his family.

Ebenezer Pettigrew and his children were great letter writers.

His wife of fifteen years died with the birth of their eighth child in 1830, and Ebenezer was left the unenviable task of managing his affairs and raising his family. He handled it by sending the children for much of the time to others, but, a concerned father, he wrote to them frequently. Never chary with advice, Pettigrew tried to exert as much influence on his children's development as he could, so that his letters to them, and theirs back to him, were tantamount to conducting a family life in writing. Ranging from the most prosaic to the most significant matters in the children's affairs, the correspondence between Ebenezer Pettigrew and his children shows clearly what much Southern child-rearing was about.

Like his father, Ebenezer Pettigrew encouraged his children to work hard and to exercise strong discipline and self-restraint. Also like his father, Ebenezer Pettigrew felt that the world posed great dangers for growing children, and he was convinced that they required strong parental guidance if they were to become good men and women. His children, for their part, never openly rebelled against their father's teachings.

One reason the main themes of Pettigrew child-rearing survived for at least the next two generations is that Ebenezer Pettigrew and his children continued to accept that view of the world which had so dominated the thought of the Reverend Charles Pettigrew. If anything, the pessimism deepened with the passage of time and the events of life. Even at the relatively youthful age of twenty-two, Ebenezer would describe an incident, the loss of a girlfriend, in terms of what it told him of universal significance: "I have long been of the opinion," he wrote to a friend, "that this is a wourld of crosses, losses & disappointments, & am prepaired to bear every thing with firmness, hoping there is a better in store." Even the slightest-seeming misfortune inevitably led Pettigrew to universal reflections, and in a world that he came to describe as "the hell of them all," his reflections were seldom pleasant.[13]

Family relations and, it must be added, those rare close friendships the Pettigrews allowed themselves, continued to stand in stark contrast to the sense of society that followed from Pettigrew pessimism. One could expect little but friction and corruption in social relations, but family relations were not supposed to be so troublesome. One of Ebenezer's sons, Charles, acknowledged this distinction when he commented to his brother James Johnston Pettigrew that, "the intercourse of friends and relations should not be regulated by those circumscribed and oftentimes contracted views that may, perhaps, with great propriety, influence our connection with the mass of acquaintances. You cannot be aware of the pleasure that an unrestricted intercourse with those we love, is able to afford every right minded person."[14] It was, in fact, a removal of constraints and a continual expression of affection that held the family together, contrasting that world with the world that lay outside.

The family was, then, sharply distinguished from the rest of society as an arena for action. Other Southerners agreed with this view. South Carolina author William Gilmore Simms, for example, emphasized this distinction when he wrote approvingly of his son, "He will resent the smallest indignity of another boy, but a single sharp word from his mother, or myself, will flood his eyes with tears." Simms, no blind advocate of violence and fighting, assumed that there were some people a man should stand up to, but they should not include members of one's own family. A few who saw the tendency toward social dichotomy in Southern life also saw its dangers. When members of the Charles Colcock Jones family were led to go their separate ways after a fire destroyed their home, Mary Jones wrote to her sons that she saw the hand of Providence. Their ties had become too binding, she suggested, and God had used the fire "to invade the circle which our blind affection might have contracted into selfishness." Still, few were so perceptive as Mrs. Jones, and the tendency she feared was clearly but an exaggeration of a social outlook most Southerners felt made perfect sense.[15]

The contrast between family and world was maintained, most people believed, by the love family members were to feel for each other. In the words of one writer for a women's magazine, "The foundation of all domestic happiness between husband and wife is the consciousness that each entertains of enjoying the undivided affections of the other,"[16] and such a family man as Ebenezer Pettigrew went to great pains to cultivate that consciousness not only in his marriage, but throughout the family. However much he attempted to be restrained and on guard when dealing with most people, he let his attachments appear quite emotional when it came to his wife and children. He expected the same from them, and, it seems, they did not try to disappoint him. Indeed, the giving and receiving of affection occupied first place in everyone's mind.

One need not doubt that, at least among the Pettigrews, this affection was genuine. One need only note Ebenezer's grief at the loss of his wife to indicate the depth of his affection. It has been said that after her death "he became a social bore by his habit of showing her miniature to one and all, while with tears streaming down his cheeks, he recited her virtues." In like manner, Ebenezer's son William actually had visions of his father after the latter's death. And, whatever the depth of affection in fact, it was the paramount motif in family correspondence.[17]

The Pettigrews were not unusual in the depth of feeling they displayed. Southern men often had to travel, and being away from their families could be emotionally trying for them. Gazing, like the pious and reserved Charles Colcock Jones, for instance, at a miniature of his wife, the traveling man displayed a sense of being cast adrift when he had to leave his home. Ninian Edmonston's comments to his wife were not unusual; he wrote, "words cannot express my anxiety to see you and my little children but circumstances has separated us and providence withe time can only bring us to gither again which will be sweet union with me." The usually good-humored Charles Minor, in fact, almost turned back to Virginia before completing an important trip to New Orleans, so great was his sense of absence from his home and wife.[18] The wives usually expressed a similar sense of loss when their husbands were away.

What one sees in Southern planter families is, in fact, quite consistent with a much longer process, occurring mainly in the eighteenth century, in which the nuclear family in the West began distinguishing itself from the society at large, identifying a private life quite separate from the social one and emphasizing that separation. Moreover, in assigning to affection the chief power for holding the family together, in seeing affection at the bottom of proper family relationships, Southern planters were also joining in trends that seem to have been developing throughout the West. The old-style, authoritarian patriarchal family form was being eroded throughout much of Europe and America in favor of a style of family life which emphasized mutual duties based on ties of affection, and this was no less true for the South than it was elsewhere.[19]

At the same time, however, Southerners did not go as far with this trend as others seem to have done. Strong believers in the dangers of passion, they could, like Mrs. Charles Colcock Jones, grow quite concerned about a potentially blinding affection. Beyond that, many of the changes occurring in the family outside the South were based on that reevaluation of passion which Southerners, by and large, refused to accept. Describing the process in England, Lawrence Stone has discussed the development in the late seventeenth and eighteenth centuries of the "Man of Sentiment," one who "was easily moved to outbursts of indignation by cruelty and to tears of sympathy by benevolence." This ideal, he suggests, had great influence on English family life during the period. There is little evidence for such a type in colonial America, but it is clear that a similar sentimentalization of family relations became significant in the North, particularly after 1800. Southerners, however much on the surface they appear to have shared in this trend, inevitably stopped short of approving sentimentalism. William Hooper Haigh, as sensitive as anyone, spoke for many Southerners when, responding to a popular poem, he wrote that "sentiment in a woman is bad enough heaven knows—in a man 'tis intolerable & disgusting . . . [sentimentalists] create an unhealthy & sickening atmosphere, filling the brains of the young & credulous with false theories of life and making them the poor, blind dupes of a bewildered fancy." Haigh was, to be sure, talking about poetry, but, in true Southern fashion, he recognized that the moral implications went far beyond literature. Affection was one thing, but sentiment, "ill-regulated & disordered fancy," was not a good tie to hold human beings together.[20]

The implications of such a view were apparent whenever the issue of affection in family relations was brought to the fore. Despite such claims as that of Charles Pettigrew that one could speak freely among family and friends, no one really belived that to be entirely true. One had to control emotion as carefully in the family as elsewhere, as may be seen in Ebenezer's approach to family relations. He enjoyed evocations of love, as he showed clearly in a letter to his wife, after about a year of marriage. Proclaiming his love for her, Ebenezer was overcome and wrote, "I have writen untill I cannot forbare droping a tear, I will therefore turn on to something else. I hope you will favor me with some things of a similar nature in your next. I mean similar in Language."[21] On the surface an outburst of emotion and affection, Ebenezer's letter was also a description of what affection was supposed to mean in his family. The language of affection was what he sought from his wife, and it was to be a language similar to his own. He demanded analogous signs of affection from his children. On one particularly striking occasion when his son William had failed to provide the appropriate complimentary close to a letter—"your son"—Ebenezer was distraught. "I suppose," he complained in a return letter, "I must submit to be forgotten, but I hope my God will not forget *me*."[22] Children, and all family members, were expected to observe the outward signs of affection, the "similar Language" that held things together.

The frequency of correspondence in the Pettigrews' lives may have led Ebenezer to emphasize language, but the fact remains that he spent a great deal of time and energy advising or chastising his children on their use of language. And Pettigrew was not alone in his concern. Even the usually fiery William Lowndes Yancey felt only slight hypocrisy in advising a young friend, about to be married, to avoid hastily expressing anger toward his bride. Yancey was moved to give his advice, he explained, because once, in Yancey's presence, "in a little irritation, too suddenly indulged in, you swore hard. A perfectly bred man," Yancey admonished, "should never swear." The point was, for Yancey, that the young man appeared to have a weakness of self-control which could destroy his marriage, a weakness revealed by a single use of intemperate language. A marriage, or a good relationship between parent and child, depended on a consciousness of affection, but that consciousness itself depended upon the proper expression of feelings between individuals. How one used language was, therefore, a major index of a more general ability to maintain proper human relationships; when people could not convey their feelings acceptably, or when they were careless about how they talked to each other, then they struck at the foundation of close family ties.[23]

The emphasis on proper, careful language was paralleled by other features in child-rearing practices. For one, it conformed to the rigidity with which children were described as separate from adults in all areas of life, and particularly in the moral sphere. Such a sharp discontinuity between childhood and adulthood as the Pet-

tigrews saw is not characteristic of every society, but the Pettigrews took it as unquestioned that children were not simply small
adults. Children could not make their own decisions in life but had
to be passive recipients of adult guidance, and particularly family
guidance—or that of their teachers—until they reached maturity.
"To let a boy hack his own way," Ebenezer once wrote his youngest son, James Johnston, "is to ruin him forever." Children's roles
were well-defined and wholly subordinate to the advice and direction of adults.[24]

Children were taught to develop a strong sense of their own
position within the family, and discipline was frequently justified
by reference to that position rather than by appeals to reason or to
principle. It was clear to Ebenezer Pettigrew that he need brook
no explanations or justifications from his children when they disagreed with him or with other adults in positions of authority, and
it was equally clear that he was not required to justify his own actions to his children. The fact that he was their father was justification enough for any action, and reason enough for their obedience.
Significantly, his children, at least as they grew older, did not disagree with this point of view. Obedience was, in fact, a function of
affection. As twenty-five–year–old William Pettigrew once commented, true affection would "induce the young party to listen to
the experience of the older and prize his good opinion." William
James Bingham, the boys' teacher, was of the same opinion. After
James Johnston had been through a rebellious period in school, his
teacher wrote to Ebenezer that although the offenses were "unimportant"—the chief one had been drumming softly on a bench—they
were nevertheless offenses and, hence, inexcusable. But the worst
thing, according to Bingham, was that young Johnston had put on
a "mannish air." A much happier Bingham would write of Johnston, a couple of years later, that he "submits very readily to lawful
authority. A more submissive & docile pupil no teacher could desire." Age and position brought their own authority, and the child
had to recognize, even to appreciate, his subjection to it.[25]

Thus the fear of bad company that so troubled Reverend
Charles Pettigrew and his son Ebenezer drew support not only
from a generally pessimistic social outlook, but also from the strong
sense of structure and form that dominated Pettigrew ideals of
proper family life. All associations with one's peers were potential-

ly corrupting because they were associations with one's peers. Whenever a child took his cues from people his own age instead of adults, he was taking advice that was bad by definition. Stepping outside that pattern of ascribed roles that, for most Southerners, was the foundation of social order, such a child was merely looking for trouble. Hence one may appreciate John Randolph's concern about changes he saw taking place in the society around him. Writing to a young relative in 1807, Randolph declared, "A petulant arrogance . . . marks the character of too many of our young men. They early assume airs of manhood; and these premature men remain children for the rest of their lives. Upon the credit of a smattering of Latin, drinking grog, and chewing tobacco, these striplings set up for legislators and statesmen; and seem to deem it derogatory from their manhood to treat age and experience with any degree of deference." They may be at home in the tavern, Randolph went on to insist, "but placed in the society of *real* gentlemen, and men of letters, they are awkward and uneasy: in all situations, they are contemptible."[26]

Because Southern children were expected to fit into a narrowly defined system of roles rather than to "hack" their own ways, the main focus of disciplinary practice was the eradication of self-will in children. As a result, the moral virtues which such a family as the Pettigrews prized most highly had as a common denominator the development of the strictest sense of discipline. Certainly no Pettigrew was ever to conform to the stereotype of the high-living Southern aristocrat, any more than was John Randolph's young relative, and the children were expected to eradicate self-will through the cultivation of industry, self-restraint, and obedience to those in positions of authority. They were urged to be diligent in their schoolwork—they should "waste as little time as possible," their mother had advised before her death—and to direct their efforts only in the proper direction. James Johnston Pettigrew, for instance, did exactly the wrong thing when, as his teacher complained to Ebenezer, "he began to rely too much on his scholarship & his quickness, read other books, or amused himself with other things, so as not to leave himself time to get his lessons thoroughly." Learning to do what was expected of one was a crucial part of growing up, whether it involved learning properly to express affection or learning that kind of disciplined diligence in school work that would fit one for carrying on the responsibilities of life when one reached maturity. The expectations of others rather than personal fulfillment were to guide Pettigrew actions, and the discipline to learn and to appreciate those expectations was a focus in child-rearing efforts.[27]

There was much in Southern family life that corresponds to what Richard Sennett has described as the response of families in mid-nineteenth century London and Paris to "the turmoil of public life." As Sennett has tried to show, the earlier sense of the family as a refuge from the larger world, united by ties of affection, had to face a severe test in the nineteenth century, as psychological theory tended to discount older ideas of "natural sentiment" in favor of cultivated feeling as the basis of family relations. Everyone had to display, in a way others would recognize, that he, or she, had learned to be part of the family.[28] In the South, whatever impact such ideas may have had was strengthened by the more general sense of social insecurity which Southerners possessed. Living in a slave society, and being greatly concerned about the fragility of social relations, Southerners sought through the inculcation of careful family behavior to create at least one area in which there might be peace and stability. Beyond that, their emphasis on outward form was the clearest way of addressing the old problem of the evil tendencies of man—given his passionate nature and his sinfulness—by ensuring that his natural feelings and desires were carefully contained in strictly observed conventions of behavior. When people behaved conventionally, they also behaved predictably.

This emphasis on outward form suggests that even the supposedly peaceful family circle was feared to rest on a fairly weak base. There was a feeling that family life should, and perhaps could be different from life in society, but, at the same time, there seems also to have been a belief that feeling still had to be carefully channeled if the ideal closeness of the family were not to be disrupted. Family members were no less prepared for misbehavior from each other than they were to find corruption in the world at large, and Ebenezer Pettigrew was not the only adult to read ingratitude or a lack of proper affection into a child's failure to toe the mark with utter precision. Susanna Clay, in a letter to her son, the Alabama senator, expressed the deeper concerns of the situation when she told him, "your memory must recall my affectionate care of your youth, my self abnegation for your future," concluding her thoughts by exclaiming, "Human nature is always depraved!" Mistrust and the dangers posed by human nature were no less important in family life than they were in Southern views of society at large.[29]

This sense of insecurity about family life in the South was probably enhanced, moreover, by the presence in the household of people other than kinsmen. Also on hand and playing a major role in bringing up the children were house slaves, whose place in the family must have sent some kind of message to planter children. That Southern planters sought to claim some kind of "family" status for their slaves, constructing the whole plantation on a family model, is well enough known. And the use of the word "family" was more than an ideological word-play. There is no reason to suspect, for instance, that sheer propaganda had much to do with the planters' frequent references, in letters or diaries, to the "family," black as well as white. There was, nevertheless, something very unusual about the place occupied by slaves in the planter family. At the very least, given the well-documented Southern fear of slave violence, the already problematic vision of the family as stable—an island of peace in an unpredictable, dangerous world—would have been further weakened for Southern planters and their children. Slavery, and especially the presence of house slaves in the family, must have posed a significant challenge to the familial atmosphere Southern parents wanted to cultivate.

Evidence concerning the effects of slavery on Southern white families is, to say the least, scanty, and one can only speculate on how the presence of slaves in the household influenced relations between white parents and their children. Philip Greven, in his valuable study of family life in early America, has suggested for the colonial aristocracy a "genteel" family type, which, like those of the antebellum period, put affection and family intimacy at the center of life but which, unlike antebellum families, tended to indulge the child's will, with less concern being given to the question of discipline than to the cultivation of "love and reverence." It is Greven's view that, in large part, such relationships were possible among the elite since having slaves (or servants in the North) meant that parents' "feelings were unqualified by the daily confrontations of so many parents with children." Whatever may have been the case among the gentry of colonial times, the antebellum elite showed few characteristics of Greven's genteel type, coming much closer to the "moderate" colonial type which, like the antebellum elite, valued hierarchy and taught self-control and "temperate self-denial" as the most appropriate behavior in children and adults.[30]

The point here is not, of course, to argue with Greven's useful categories, nor even to try to fit the families of antebellum planters into them. It is, rather, to emphasize something of what gave those families their form. Above all, it may have been the presence of slaves in the household that had the greatest influence on the Southern view of family relations. Although it is certain that slaves did much of the drudgery of child-rearing in the Old South, it is not at all clear that Southern children thought of such slaves as surrogates nor that parents felt that the presence of slaves relieved them from the main task of disciplining their children. Indeed, as the Pettigrew case shows, even the sending of a child to boarding school, as was done with the Pettigrew children, did not make either Ebenezer or his wife feel that they had put the work of discipline into someone else's hands. Teaching discipline was the main task of parenting from the Southern point of view, and one did not forego that task simply because there were slaves around nor even because the children lived outside the household. Slaves, for all their work in nursing and child care, did not divide authority in the planter home. Indeed, racial views were too strongly held in the South for such a division to have occurred, and there is little if any actual evidence to suggest that it did.

The central effect of the presence of slaves, then, was most likely to have kept Southerners from feeling too sanguine about the possibility of peace in the family circle. Blacks and whites were so different, from their point of view, that it must have been as though there were always outsiders present, and outsiders about whom white Southerners were never entirely comfortable. Affection and a measure of trust were often present, to be sure; but security was an altogether different matter. Couple this with the sorts of external pressures on the region which made Southerners uncomfortable about human relations in general, and about slavery in particular, especially after about 1800, and the importance of discipline and control to a household becomes clear. And, in contrast to Greven's early American "moderates," the devotion to discipline and order was based not so much on the belief that humans could be easily trained to be temperate and virtuous but rather, on the Southern belief in the danger of human relations where control was not clearly, firmly, and visibly exercised.[31]

The connection between child-rearing and violence was subtle. Again, Southern children were not raised to be aggressive individuals; nor, for that matter, was violence a part of child-rearing. Indeed, just as parents sought to inculcate discipline in their children, they also tried to avoid passion in their own actions. Everard G. Baker confided in his diary, "I have one fault & a serious one in my discipline of my children I allow myself to get too much in a passion sometimes & speak too harshly." He went on to say, "I never give away to a burst of passion towards any one that I do not regret it afterwards, & especially towards my dear little children." Under most circumstances, a fit of passion in an adult said more about the governor than the governed, as one twelve-year-old Virginian acknowledged when he commented that his teacher simply did not "know how to govern as well as he might that is he ought to govern more by principal [*sic*] than by punishment."[32]

Given this perspective, corporal punishment was not highly valued by most Southerners. Good values, they felt, were best taught to children by precept and example, not through violence. One raised children well by winning their affection and love—those crucial ties in the Pettigrew family—and by giving them a living example of what benevolence and unselfishness could contribute to life. Southern romanticizers of earlier, less decadent ages, whether they wrote in the 1820s, the 1840s, or on the eve of the Civil War, often saw the success of this mode as a distinguishing feature of the "families of the former age." According to one writer, in a rather typical paean to Southern motherhood, "She ruled, not with an iron rod, but firmly, gently, and the child loved her none the less because she taught it the word obedience." The point was, as he said, "we do not ask you to *force* the young child to obedience, but win it by the power of persuasion, and by constantly setting before it the picture in its most attractive lights."[33]

Southerners were not unanimous on this. A few defended corporal punishment as the only way in which children could be made obedient. A writer who signed himself "C. C." felt that physical punishment was necessary for children simply because of their immaturity, because they could not be dealt with like adults: "Now children as they are less capable than adults of being governed by reason, must be the more governed by bodily punishment. When the child becomes a youth, perhaps confinement and reproof will answer, and when the youth comes to manhood, you may rely on argument alone."[34] As this writer's comments show, the task of reconciling structure with feeling was not the easiest thing a person could do.

In any case, corporal punishment never received unmixed approval in the South, and the weight of opinion seems to have been against it. As a sign of parental passion, it could undermine the efficacy of parental example and, thus, the sense of pattern that defined correct family relationships. Moreover, to the extent that the family was held together by external signs of love among the members, a display of anger, and especially of violence, could work to the detriment of family strength. Finally, one must note, the introduction of violence into the family circle could only have undermined that feeling of the family as separate from—indeed a refuge from—the world that was so important to many Southerners.

Although the evidence is hardly conclusive, Southern parents appear to have acted consistently with their attitudes so far as spanking their children was concerned. Charles Minor was probably being typically facetious when he recorded in his autobiography that he was "flogged once every day—for the first *seven* years of my life making in all *2555* whippings I got in those first 7 years."[35] In most families, spanking seems not to have been such a matter of course; even Minor remembered that being forced to breakfast on milk and bread was the more common punishment for misbehavior in his childhood. It is to the point, for instance, that when William Bingham, young James Johnston Pettigrew's teacher, gave the boy a few disciplinary whacks, he felt constrained to send a long explanation to Ebenezer.[36] Most importantly, the evidence does not indicate that spanking was the usual method of keeping planter children in line: Southern children would not have learned that violence should be a regular method for solving problems from their direct dealings with their parents or teachers.

Still, Southern children were not ignorant of violence; it was not something from which they were sheltered all their lives. Indeed, violence must have impinged upon their lives at a fairly young age. A young Virginian, Launcelot Minor Blackford, whose childhood diary provides a superb glimpse into the lives and activities of Southern children, reported numerous outbreaks of violence in play with friends and schoolmates, though much of it was not serious. Frequently, for example, children would "form into armies" and charge into each other for wrestling, or sod-throwing, or, in winter, a snowball fight. Such activities were thought of mainly as play, and the children were careful to avoid letting things get out of hand, to the point at which roughhousing "would if continued produce numerous fights (real)."[37]

More seriously, some children's violence does sound remarkably like that of adults, and it grew out of situations all too similar to those leading up to duels. The fifteen year old "Lanty" Blackford, for example, founded a debating society with his friends, and reported on one evening that the debate "grew very warm occasionally and threatened once or twice and that pretty plainly an out-break of fisticuffs" which, he was happy to say, was avoided.[38] Other youthful debates did not have such fortunate conclusions. Even James Johnston Pettigrew, for instance, once had a fight as a result of a college debate. And politics often entered into juvenile violence in other ways: William W. Stringfield, a young Tennesseean whose father was a schoolmaster, was once set upon by a companion for having "in a jovial way talked some" about Democrats.[39]

Outside the home, at school for instance, unfocused violence was a part of growing up. College life, in particular, was distinguished by "rowdyism" and bad company of the sort that troubled three generations of Pettigrews, and students engaged in all sorts of pranks—many violent, all disruptive, and most encouraged by heavy drinking. A readiness to fight, in school and out, over questions of words, was often a fast route to status, or so it seemed to many students who, it must be noted, claimed to prefer other paths for themselves.[40]

Rioting was, in fact, a serious campus problem, both inside and outside the South. Some of it was simply a matter of rowdyism. Students would get drunk and get into fights among themselves or with people in the town. Occasionally the causes were more clearly defined. A riot occurred at Columbia College, South Carolina, in 1822 when members of the junior class refused to attend prayers and recitations. Another riot with similar causes occurred at the same school in 1850. The consequences of such student rioting could be quite tragic: J. A. G. Davis, an eminent Virginia legal scholar, was shot to death by a student when he interfered with a riot at the University of Virginia. Since students were often armed, other riots had similar results.[41]

Campus rioting was inconsistent with the kinds of values Southern parents tried to give their children. Indeed, at least one Southerner, William Grayson, saw it as a symptom of social failure. Children left the home and family too soon: "The end of education is to improve the manners, morals, and mind of the Student. Our system operated lamely for these purposes. To refine the boy's manners he is taken from the guidance and restraints of home and placed in rude barracks, with other boys his own age, removed from the checks imposed by female society and by older persons of his own sex and left entirely to their boyish devices."[42] For Grayson, it was a matter of bad company, which a boy's peers were by definition.

Looked at another way, however, college rioting may be evidence of the force, if not the efficacy of Southern family ideals. As Grayson's words make clear, and as is shown by so much that Southerners wrote about child-rearing, the separateness of the family was a major factor in the moral education of young people, an effective restraint on their tendency to act immaturely and passionately. College rioting may have been one response, and not a surprising one, to leaving such an isolated world. Believing, as they did, in strongly differentiated sex roles, and identifying violence with the male, young boys embarking on the world showed by rioting the kind of defensive assertion of masculinity that ultimately exaggerated the manly behavior associated with, for example, dueling.[43] College rioting was, most simply understood, a way of blowing off steam. It was also, however, an important way of moving from the closed world of childhood into the world of being an adult, in a distinctively male way.

It does not detract from this explanation for rioting that here was one form of violence upon which the South could not claim a monopoly. Indeed, most major American colleges experienced similar outbreaks during the antebellum period. The reason for this sharing probably lies in the fact that the Southern family, with its great stress on insecurity, was still but a variation on a more general

American pattern that also emphasized affection and the role of the family as a refuge from the trials and temptations of the world, as we have seen. Hence, the need to break out was not exclusively Southern, but was shared by youths throughout the country. For boys, at least, the college riot was a way in which this need could be met.

And, it must be emphasized, rioting did not conform to major Southern values. Such mindless violence caricatured adult masculinity but did not portray it. The acts of college rioters were aberrations without long-range influence or significance for understanding violence in the Old South. At least a few Southerners who looked back on their own rioting did so without pride or pleasure.[44] The defensive masculinity of the college prankster or bully, though some men never outgrew it, was commonly a passing thing. The important relationships between child-rearing and violence in the Old South were far more subtle and complex, founded more on deep-seated values than on any hyper-masculinity.

One sees the tie to deeper values in the fact that, while Southern parents did not encourage their children to be violent, they themselves neither preached nor practiced pacifism. On occasion, one did have to stand firm against the malice of others. Even Ebenezer Pettigrew, whose resignation to the world was profound, could still be backed to the wall, once noting during a political dispute, "I have long thought I had some of the character of the Rattlesnake. It never acts but defensively it never strikes without giving fair warning & when it does strike, it is fatal." Indeed, he did not eschew violence as an appropriate response to the attacks of others. When his friend Edward Stanly was involved in an altercation with Henry Wise in which Wise had struck Stanly, events almost led to a duel. The matter was settled short of the field, but even Ebenezer would comment to his friend that he himself would have hated to take the blow "without killing or at least trying to kill him."[45] There was evil in the world, and when others did act with malice, no man had to submit tamely. Indeed, this was the point of view generally held in the Pettigrew family. When young James Johnston got into his fight at school, his brother William was not reluctant to advise, "as far as it can be done, we should live peaceably with our associates; but, as we cannot always do so, it is necessary occasionally, to resist. And when our honor demands resistance, it should be done with courage." Ebenezer, it must be added, offered no criticism at all of his son's action. One may recall, as well, Simms' approval of a son who would "resent the smallest indignity of another boy." Self-respect was important to Southerners, and if their sense of it did not correspond to the cocksure impetuosity of the stereotypical Southern dandy, few, not even Pettigrews, felt that one should not be prepared to defend himself physically. Striking back was never to be done in any way other than defensively and reluctantly, but this did not mean it was never to be done at all. There were times when violence was considered quite appropriate.

Not encouraged to be violent, then, Southern children were not prevented from believing that violence might be necessary in some situations. They learned, that is, not to be surprised by its occurrence nor by the occurrence of the sorts of social difficulties that made it necessary. Ironically, such a resignation to violence was inculcated by the emphasis on form and procedure that Southern parents laid on their children, especially by their encouragement of the use of restricted modes for expressing feelings and desires. When one cannot express his emotions in words, then the ability to use language is itself inhibited in such a way that new and difficult feelings or situations are hard to describe and, thus, hard to come to terms with.[46] Where, as in the Old South, such a situation holds, it tends to limit the range beyond which situations become unpredictable and unfamiliar. Southern children were brought up to accept only a few highly formalized techniques for approaching other human beings, and when those techniques were ineffective, as they would often appear to be, people raised that way were likely to despair of using normal means for solving problems. They learned to turn to violence only when no other course of action seemed available, only when they were backed to the wall. The problem was, of course, that they could become backed to the wall rather quickly.

Indeed, Southern children probably had one example right from home to persuade them of how appropriate violence could be, and this was the example of the slaves. Again, Southern planters liked to speak of their slaves as, somehow, family, but they also had to claim that slaves, unlike other family members, were ultimately governable only by physical force. That is, the doubts about corporal punishment which applied in regard to their own children definitely did not apply when planters dealt with slaves, even those of the household.[47] It is hard to know for certain how the children were affected when they saw such violence, but one may speculate on what its message was. Perhaps, to an extent, the message was a racial one: simply that—as everyone seemed to believe anyway—corporal punishment was the only discipline that blacks could understand, however sad the "fact" might have been. In this regard, as we shall see, the "family" metaphor served the double duty of justifying an oppressive relationship while putting the best face on slaveholder violence. But if the message were more than racial, it would have been a difficult one for planter children. On the one hand, the family could not have been a refuge while black slaves were there. Undermining security, as we have suggested, slavery also brought violence into the planter home, as the children must have known. On the other, the violence of slavery, as an example, proved that white Southerners, men and women, did recognize a place for violence in dealings with other people.

It is important to note, as subsequent chapters will show, that Southern child-rearing encompassed a substantial gap between ideals and expectations. Taught to value discipline, order, and harmony, Southern children also learned that other people—and, it was implied, even people in the family—were likely to act in ways that disrupted all. To the extent that aggression and frustration are closely connected, Southern parents encouraged a resignation to violence by virtually building frustration into their children's view of the world.[48]

The meaning of violence in the Old South grew out of a perspective on human nature and society that Southern children learned in a variety of ways. The connection between child-rearing and violence was, thus, not a simple one, and it can only be seen in detail by examining how Southern adults usually talked about the causes of violence and their beliefs about how physical conflict could be kept in proper bounds.

3. Feeling and Form
The Problem of Violence in Society

WHITE SOUTHERNERS, at least those who thought themselves part of the plantation elite, were expected to have learned to
be moderate, amiable and temperate, to act excitedly and violently
only when there appeared to be no alternative. Most adults tried to
live up to those expectations and attempted, as well, to instill such
behavior in their children. And yet many Southerners were given
to violence, whether ritualized in the duel or in the less formal
street fight. There were conflicts between prominent men in all
the major Southern cities, from old and sophisticated Charleston on
the Atlantic to raw and unsettled Houston in the West. Frequently, minor quarrels led to death for one of the parties as tempers
flared or grudges festered. Southerners were taught not to value
impetuosity and malice, but impetuous outbursts and malicious
feelings were often the order of the day in community affairs.
Nevertheless, when people in the Old South had to account for the
violence in their communities, they did so in ways that were
consistent with the view of the world they learned as children.

Violence among well-to-do-Southerners was, above all, a measure of the character of social relations. Southerners, as is well
enough known, led active social lives, and they liked to talk about
the ways in which their understanding of social graces and social
ties made them better than people from other parts of the country.
The problem was, however, that they approached social life in
terms of that view of the world they had learned as children. Society, they felt, could be wonderful. They also had to consider that
society was composed of people, and people, as any child knew,
were not to be trusted.

Southern social life, particularly that of the planters, was noted
by travelers (and even more by Southerners) for its charm and
hospitality. The diaries and letters of affluent men and women

were filled with accounts of balls, parties, and an endless round of visiting—often for an afternoon, frequently overnight. Even the unexpected guest could count on being well entertained in the home of a friend or acquaintance, and entertaining itself was almost certainly the main form of recreation in the antebellum South.

There was, however, something artificial in what C. Vann Woodward has called the Southern "propensity for living it up." One Charleston woman captured that artificiality when she wrote to a friend that she was spending her time "paying off visits," an offhand remark that nonetheless reflected a sense that visiting, sociability, and the trappings of hospitality were all part of that network of obligatory appearances that comprised Southern social life. One not only had to entertain, one also had to be entertained. There was an obligation to participate in social affairs, and it was that sense of obligation that made social life work.[1]

Southern society, like family life, rested on a fragile base composed mainly of outward signs. Southerners felt snubs readily, and just as easily gave them, often unawares. Social life was filled with misunderstandings or, on occasion, outright incivility; friendship, as one writer suggested, was distinguished only by its "instability." More importantly, Southerners felt social gaffes quite keenly. One woman, having felt obliged to make a visit, was not offered the hand of her hostess—and remarked that "the repulse was so great that we found it difficult to rally again." John Berkley Grimball, visiting in the home of Pierce Butler in Philadelphia, recorded in his diary that his host "never puts himself out of the way for the purpose of entertaining any one," adding as a note, "To remember this when our positions are reversed"—a reminder he later struck from the page.[2]

Southerners handled social tensions in the same way they managed family life, through the careful observance of those formalities by which anyone could depersonalize and ritualize dealings with others. It was the assertion of self and of feeling that Southerners were raised to dread, and the social formalities they relied on as adults provided them with excellent protection. Never raising one's voice, "even when angry," observing the proper amenities in conversations and correspondence, and the proper decorum on social occasions, all preserved harmony and tone in community life, and were carefully cultivated by most affluent Southerners. The same John Berkley Grimball who had been so miffed in Philadelphia even went so far as to diagram stable settings at formal dinners he attended so that, when giving one himself, he could do it in the manner of "men of acknowledged taste." The so-called gentry style of the antebellum South was a rigidly controlled and carefully cultivated one that covered up a great deal of insecurity in social relations.[3]

Although it is never safe to equate two different and historically separate societies, there is much in Southern social life reminiscent of Huizinga's characterization of a medieval Europe in which life was "regulated like a noble game." The metaphor is apt, insofar as Southerners appear to have viewed social life as an activity composed of well-defined, objective roles governed by clear, impersonal rules. Although Southerners would never have put their own perceptions in quite that form, their approach to social life and social events betrayed a point of view in which the individual became so submerged in a setting of acts and styles that personal fulfillment was supposed to be subordinate to turning in a good performance.[4]

The metaphor of a "game" is also useful because it emphasizes the organic view of society which most Southerners shared. The metaphor does not trivialize Southern life, but it does point to its superficial character; that is, to its quality as a masque or tableau of impersonal but well-regulated and, thus, integrated parts. Southerners conceived of social life as having an integrity of its own, separate from their personal lives. It consisted of nothing but the modes of action dictated by its rules; and rules, among antebellum Southerners, were not made to be broken nor to be manipulated for personal advantage. They were made to govern behavior, protecting people from others and from themselves.

This Southern sense of social life was directly related to their more general attitudes toward matters of form. Great value was placed on rules and appearances, and one would expect this from Southern child-rearing practices. Indeed, such an emphasis was an adult extension of the restricted behavior and strong discipline people learned as children. Matters became complicated, though, because most people also learned as children to expect the worst in others and, particularly, to expect that others were even less capable of discipline and self-control than themselves. Only a fine line separated the social pessimist from the misanthrope, the man who, in Francis Ruffin's words, "came at last to imagine, that, like Cain, his hand was against every man and every man's hand was against him."[5] This social pessimism contributed to the Southern love of formality, inasmuch as the observation of outward forms kept the inner man at bay, but, clearly, it also made the social organism seem a very fragile structure.

Hans Toch has suggested in a psychological study of violence that where people see human relations as power-centered and one-way, they tend to view violence as an acceptable form of social conduct. This is so whether they see others as tools to serve their own purposes or feel vulnerable to manipulation by others.[6] Presumably, such people would direct their violence toward those whom they either used or feared: individual, group, or, vaguely, institutions. Something like Toch's notion helps to illuminate the understanding of violence most often expressed by antebellum Southerners. Southerners feared other individuals. They believed, because they had been raised to do so, that people were selfish and impulsive, all too willing to put personal desires above social order. They feared social anarchy more than power, but, to draw on Toch's notion, they also knew that their own security depended on stable, reciprocal social relations—and selfishness could destroy stability. They were vulnerable to being hurt and left out, to put it very simply, and a survey of the usual causes of their violence shows that physical aggression was a response to that sense of vulnerability.

Southern violence was, first, largely personal. Such writers as D. R. Hundley made much of this, saying that if violence had to occur, at least the violent Southerner "seldom murders in cold blood," asserting that, in this regard, the South "even has an advantage over the North."[7] The advantage may seem a dubious one, but, nevertheless, violence in the South did conform to the sort of pattern Hundley implied. Physical conflict in the region was almost always personally motivated; indeed, Southerners took it for granted that people did not act violently without some sort of personal motives, at least among the upper class. Social crises leading to violence were supposed to grow out of personal relations.

The Southerner was, A. B. Longstreet wrote, "quick of temper, sensitive to insult, and too quick to revenge it." Longstreet was even willing to admit that on this score, Southerners were almost as violent as the people of the North. Insults, intended or not, genuinely were "fighting words" in the South, even among gentlemen, because insults could not be ignored. Insults generally, including those that led to duels, were aimed at a person's integrity and honesty and, thus, at his fitness to be a part of a community of well-bred men. Such words were probably the major single cause of violence in polite society.[8]

Attacks on the individual led to much violence, but unwarranted intrusions into the family circle caused a good deal of difficulty, too. The crime of passion was not unknown in the South, and many of the more spectacular murders in the region were committed by wronged husbands. It is doubtful that adultery was common in the region, and when it occurred, especially among the elite, the consequences could be tragic. In one prominent family, the father of the adulterous wife rushed to town to put her paramour to death—but her husband had beaten him to it. Arrested and indicted for murder, the man attracted both sympathy and attention because of his social standing. Less spectacularly, Southern men frequently fought over women before marriage, as one suitor would attack another out of jealousy. No wonder the usually acute Charlestonian, Jacob Schirmer, could only sigh, after mentioning a fight between two prominent local citizens, "Oh! tis Woman."[9]

Family ties being close and important in the South, family members often leaped to the defense of each other. When one's father was assaulted, or brother, sister, or any relative, many Southerners felt it to be a virtual duty to avenge the attack—whether it had been verbal or physical—by violence. William Lowndes Yancey's son assaulted a local editor in Montgomery on his father's account, and the famous caning of Charles Sumner by Preston Brooks was defended as an act of family loyalty.[10]

The causes of violence were, in general, consistent with Southern perceptions and social tensions. Violence itself was exacerbated by the practical steps some Southern men took as a result of their perceptions. Ever ready to see a threat at the hands of others, a Southern man might be prepared, as well, to punish any attacker who should appear. It was for this reason that so many Southern men, even of the highest station, went about armed. As Judge Peter Randolph, wounded in an affray, told the court in Richmond, he "went prepared at all times to repel an attack." Even the upright Charles Colcock Jones, Jr. once gave his mother cause to worry on account of his carrying a pistol at he went about. It was remarkable, and worrisome, how many gentlemen were prepared at all times to turn a minor altercation into a killing, and such preparedness could only have occurred in a community where social pessimism could so easily turn into social fear.[11]

It is important to note that Southerners never saw violence as anything other than a response. They suffered intrusions, but they never intruded on others, just as most young men were led astray but did no leading. Although observers might disagree, there was never a violent man who looked upon his actions as other than a response to a presumed wrong—although, in retrospect, he might regret responding with force. Few if any Southerners, however, ever saw themselves in the role of insult giver, interpreting their own actions in defensive, reactionary terms.

One can only speculate as to why this was so, since insults and attacks were given often enough; but, again, one may refer to the game-like quality of social life, as well as to the pessimism that informed the social perspective. Many people were simply disposed to see disruptive potential in even the most innocent sorts of acts. If social life was as structured and as fragile as it so often seems to have been, then one could always find something at which to take offence—the joke, the thoughtless gesture, the careless remark. And not a few tragedies proceeded from trivial causes.

Sheldon Hackney, in a study of the more recent South, has suggested that the region's violence grows more out of homogeneity than diversity,[12] a notion that may be applicable to elite society in antebellum times. Southerners certainly sought homogeneity in their society, and they aimed to achieve it through the emphasis on outward forms of behavior and control of these forms. The depersonalization and ritualization of society implied that individuals were expected to behave in roughly similar ways, and it also implied that nonconformity would not only be fairly obvious but would also be seen as contrary to the well-being of the community. This perhaps gave an edge to those "intrusions" that so often led to violence among the elite.

Certainly, most Southerners did not turn to violence, or did so only rarely. When they felt the pain of a social snub they reserved their anger for a diary page, or confided in a close friend. For one to become violent, something else had to be there, and that something was, as usual, "passion." Thus Southerners displayed a remarkably ambivalent attitude toward violent men. Given their social views, acts of violence were often understandable, if not justifiable. Given their morality, however, the man who gave vent to passion hardly met the community ideal.

There is much that links the violence of a fight to dueling, and many Southerners did view the duel as part of a general tendency toward violence and licentiousness; but, in intent and in practice, dueling was very different from fighting or murder. The duelist fought for his honor. Facing death on the field proved his mettle and brought its satisfaction to him. The world of the fight was a wholly different one. The fighter sought to give rein to those "revengeful passions" which in general Southerners deprecated. Thus, when D. J. McCord, a prominent Charleston attorney, was invited to the field of honor by a local physician, he refused the challenge—as was his custom—but went to the doctor's home, dragged him out, and the two fought to exhaustion. When the doctor tried to call the fight to a halt, McCord answered, "D'n you, I have enough energy left to whip you" and began to fight again. In a fight, unlike a duel, the object was, purely, to defeat the opponent, or even to kill him.[13]

Nor was satisfaction the object of a fight to the extent that revenge was. When William Lowndes Yancey shot and killed Dr. Robert Earle in a South Carolina fight, he wrote to his brother that "the blood of the only man who ever called me 'a d——d liar' is now, unwashed, upon your stock, & there let it remain, a legacy to my son, & a warning to others who feel like browbeating a Yancey."[14] It was the shedding of blood and not the facing of death that motivated a man physically to attack another, and the man who launched an attack was looked upon by society quite differently from the duelist. If most duelists escaped prosecution, those guilty of assault or worse crimes often did not. Yancey, for one, was convicted of manslaughter and had to leave town.

The duel, unlike the street fight, was one outgrowth of the carefully cultivated style of the Southern gentry. A fit of passion may have led to the problem but duelists quickly assumed the kind of behavior of which society approved, and instituted procedures to maintain order. Thus dueling was a more nearly acceptable, though violent, mode of handling social problems, one from which the revengeful passions were conscientiously excluded. The street fight not only admitted the passions, but brought to the fore impatience, revenge, and a rejection of order. The results may have been the same whether one fought for revenge or dueled for honor, but the procedures and the symbolism were very different.[15]

There were times when any man, no matter how strong his self-discipline, could allow his passions and personal feelings to have the upper hand. Still, most people felt that an exceptionally violent man was, simply, an exceptionally passionate man—that it was a matter of innate temperament. Miles Taylor, in his defense of Preston Brooks after the caning of Sumner, put the notion succinctly: "Well, sir, it is well known that where there is a temperament which is easily excited to acts of kindness, and which is impulsive in the discharge of the courtesies, it necessarily, also, is one keenly sensitive to injury; and that it is just as impulsive in resenting what seems to be a wrong, as it is doing a kindness."[16] Where feelings were stronger than discipline, regardless of the good actions that might result, the potential for violence was as great as that for kindness. Some people were simply more sensitive than others.

Temperament aside, other Southerners had other ways to account for the passionate man. For many, not surprisingly, it all boiled down to a matter of discipline. Good discipline came mainly from a proper upbringing and constant effort; but, clearly, discipline was the major factor separating the violent man from others around him. Thus it was, of course, that young men, hacking their own ways, were particularly given to acts of violence. Adults, as one lawyer claimed, may grow "grave and prudent as adults should be," but youth often gave vent to those passions which prudence and experience would have taught them to hold in check.[17]

The one thing that, more than temperament or age, led to passionate outbursts was drinking. Drinking among the gentry was common and often heavy. Every party had its punch, and every formal dinner its great variety of wines. As a result, not a few Southerners worried about the effects of drinking on themselves and their society. The conscientious Everard Baker went further than most in giving up all alcoholic beverages, even wine, in the belief that only abstinence would lead to happiness and prosperity, but many Southerners, looking around, saw a close connection between drinking and disorder, including violence, in their society.[18]

It was, after all, a connection that would have been hard to miss. Many a crime was, as Jacob Schirmer said, an "awful instance of the effects of Liquor." The reason was that a man "in his cups" was not at all the same man as when he was sober. A gentle, harmless individual, normally the picture of responsibility could, when addicted to drink, undergo a noticeable change of personality—he could, like one Virginia merchant, exhibit "those evidences of impatience and ill temper which belong to Drunkenness, but which were altogether alien from his sober heart." The sober man, no matter how violent, could refer to cause for his affrays. The drunkard, so many Southerners believed, was often violent simply because his passions were out of control. And the passions were almost inevitably violent. In fact, the only major form of mindless violence in the Old South, the college riot, grew out of drinking.[19]

Not surprisingly, given the effects of intemperance, many Southerners hoped to bring an end to the use of alcoholic beverages in the region, basing much of their case on the relationship between liquor and crime. One citizens' group, petitioning the Virginia legislature to prohibit the sale of liquor in the state, suggested that four-fifths of all crime resulted from drinking, while another group claimed, more conservatively, that three-fourths was a likely figure.[20] Whatever the number, many citizens in the South were convinced of the evils of drink and that drinking and violence were necessarily connected. Not a few felt that total prohibition was the only way to bring an end to the link.

The violent man was the passionate man, the man who, for whatever reason, tended to let his passions go out of control. He was also, it must be added, a man. Most Southerners tended to believe that although women were certainly subject to passion, their passions were of a different order. George Fitzhugh, rarely at a loss on any subject, remarked that "when danger is inevitable, women display more fortitude than men. They possess passive, not active courage."[21] Fitzhugh's was the accepted wisdom of the day. Few Southerners thought about violence among women, and, indeed, there are few accounts of any occurring. Words, not blows, were supposed to be the weapons in female society.

Still, women were often said to drive men to violence. Andrew Pickens Butler made much of this in defense of his nephew, Preston Brooks. Brooks had felt compelled to attack Charles Sumner, Butler declared in the Senate. "I would trust to the instinct of woman on subjects of this kind. He could not go into a parlor, or drawing-room, or to a dinner party, where he did not find an implied reproach that there was an unmanly submission to an insult to his State and his countrymen. Sir, it was hard for any man, much less for a man of his temperament, to bear this."[22] There is no better statement of that "gyneolatry" W. J. Cash wrote about than this.[23] Woman was not simply reduced to an object in the notions of male Southerners, but was made a symbol, a cause, in that area about which men felt such ambiguity, the area of violence. Where passion and discipline came into conflict, it was woman who took the blame.

It is, incidentally, hard to find women who fiercely pushed their men into acts of violence. Brought up to share the social values of their culture, most women, like most men, if they talked about violence at all, did so with sorrow or with scorn. Few, if any, found the impetuous, violent man to their liking.[24]

To Southerners, anyone could, for one reason or another, lose control of his passions and become violent, but the problem was a matter of class as well. The formalities of social life were, at best, thin protection against an outbreak of feeling, but they were better than no protection at all. Thus, many people believed that, for all their problems, those in the elite, the "aristocracy," with their manners and their training, were far less likely to commit acts of violence than were people who lacked the requisite breeding. Those outside the elite, whatever their financial achievements, lacked even the thin veneer of easy formality that prevented passionate outbursts in polite society, or so many Southerners felt. Class was, after all, more a matter of behavior than of money,[25] and the propensity for violence was a major way, according to the gentry, that those outside their group behaved.

Violence was used as a discriminator to great effect in the work of Daniel R. Hundley, whose *Social Relations in Our Southern States* remains valuable for its analysis of social stratification in the antebellum South—from the planter point of view. Like many Southerners, Hundley recognized that class involved not only economics but also differences in life-style and values among distinct categories of persons. Although he identified numerous criteria for class difference, predominant among them was that of manner, for the difference between the "Southern Gentlemen," Hundley's ideal type, and the "Cotton Snob" was clearly that between the man for whom good manners were "easy and natural" and the one whose affectations rendered him "both ridiculous and contemptible." It was a matter of knowing how to behave and being able to do so consistently and easily.[26]

But for Hundley there was a distinct class within the South, distinguished for the violence of its members, which he called the "Southern Bully": "a swearing, tobacco-chewing, brandy drinking Bully, whose chief delight is to hang about the doors of village groggeries and tavern taprooms, to fight chicken cocks, to play Old Sledge, or pitch-and-toss, chuck-a-luck, and the like, as well as to encourage dog-fights, and occasionally to get up a little raw-head-and-bloody-bones affair on his own account."[27] In part, according to Hundley, the matter was one of money. Hardly industrious, the Southern Bully was usually out of work and, "as a general thing he is poor."[28]

Not all bullies were, however, poor; for class, again, involved more than economics. There were also the sons of "Southern Yankees"—men who, wherever they were born, behaved like stereotypical Northerners in their dedication to self and money over honor and community—and these young men matched their fathers' self-indulgent greed with a self-indulgence of their own vices. Such youths, whatever their wealth, were as improperly prepared to live as gentlemen as was any Southern Bully. Hence, Hundley could string together a list of adjectives that summarized the selfish character of such a young man, emphasizing a selfishness that gave passion a free rein. He was, according to Hundley, "an ignorant, purse-proud, self-conceited, guzzling, fox-hunting, blaspheming, slave whipping, uproarious, vulgar fellow! who is at all times as willing and ready to pink a fellow-being as to wing a pheasant, or to shoot a hare."[29] Violence and licentiousness were closely associated in one who, with his improper upbringing, was really little better than a Bully with more extensive resources.

The reason such a set of discriminators as breeding, background, and wealth went together for Hundley is not hard to see, nor is it hard to understand why the character of the Bully, the violent man, should have represented the absence of that concatenation of features which made for the Gentleman. Southern children were, again, brought up to understand the importance of well-defined, highly structured roles, as well as the extent to which depersonalized, ritual behavior dominated, and had to dominate, social relations. Society could hold together only so long as people played their roles skillfully. When people were incapable of playing, passion and its concomitant violence were just below the surface, ready to break through. In the case of those outside the elite, who had not learned to play the social game consistently, the propensity for violence was greatest.

Other Southerners made the same connections between violence and class as Hundley did. One writer, bemoaning the rise of new wealth, looked back on an older society, centered in Charleston, that was infinitely more refined, and characterized it in a way that juxtaposed, strikingly, violence and manner: "There was no violence, no bullying, no brutality, then, and there; but the deportment of old and young was such as it would have been in a ball room."[30] All of life was a social occasion, a time to put on one's best manners. And so long as people knew how to behave that way, there would be no violence. A defense attorney, arguing on behalf of a lower class client who had murdered his wife, made the point with even greater clarity:

> I know not if it is not at this day to be received, that a husband might lawfully correct his wife in moderation, *modica castigatione, verberibus et flagellis.* Let me not be mistaken. This is indeed an inadmissable principle in all classes of any refinement or delicacy of sentiment and manners, where a single word or look in anger or disdain, would be far more poignant than blows, and which instead of bruising the body, would break and burst the heart. But in the class of these unfortunate persons, nothing is more common than such chastisement, on both sides of a pair, who might more often be thought by the passerby, to be "twenty in a house than one." It would certainly be a strained and forced presumption of malice, to kill.[31]

When a member of the "refined classes" resorted to blows, it was an indication of social crisis of the most severe sort. For the lower classes, unable to regulate their feelings, a resort to violence was common and not nearly so loaded with a sense of crisis. The meaning of violence was, from the point of view of the elite, much better understood by themselves than by anyone else.

Separating insiders from outsiders, an emphasis found in Southern child-rearing, applies very well to the subject of class and violence. Elite Southerners drew sharp distinctions between themselves and others, and one of the ways they could talk about those distinctions was in terms of the extent to which one could expect self-control from someone else. The further one moved from the self, and especially as one moved across class or racial frontiers, the less self-control one felt other people were likely to exert.

Indeed, members of the gentry even had a hierarchy of forms of violence to be used among themselves and with those outside the group. For "Southern Gentlemen," there were really two choices when one desired revenge: fighting or caning. The choice depended upon whether one wanted to hurt or to disgrace his opponent. One would not fight a social inferior as an equal, and the instrument of castigation had to be different: a horsewhip, perhaps, or one might decide, as one gentleman did, not to fight at all but merely to shoot a potential attacker down and be done with it.[32]

"There seems to be," according to *De Bow's Review*, "an almost complete wall of separation between this class [criminals] and what I may call the comfortable classes of society—the people of education, of middling property, and the wealthy. To associate with ignorance and vice is no pleasure to the educated and refined."[33] "Southern Gentlemen" certainly liked to see things that way, and one of the ways they characterized that wall between themselves and the less "comfortable" classes was in terms of violence.

Every element of upper-class Southern life was supposed to work against violence. Children were taught to be careful in their actions and amiable in their dispositions. Social life itself was constructed in a way that was meant to minimize conflict by rendering encounters impersonal. There were even some writers who claimed that it was the social isolation of plantation life that prevented the violence found in, say, Northern cities by enhancing the discipline of youth: after all, everything, including drinking, was "done at home under parental and feminine observation, and therefore excess can never go so far."[34] Southern social philosophy emphasized harmony—though it taught one never to expect it—and discouraged rather than encouraged violent acts.

To the extent that Southerners themselves made any correlations between the strength of community and the presence or absence of violence, they generally felt that the presence of large numbers of people created an atmosphere in which violence was most likely to occur. As one writer put it, "the pleasure of social intercourse, up to a certain undefined and undefinable point, is eminently promotive of virtue; beyond that point it becomes the fruitful parent of dissipation, vice, and crime. It has truly been said, a crowd of philosophers is but a mob. Men collected together in large numbers, unless rigorously supervised and governed, become mad and drunk with excitement, lose their reason and self-control, and zealously aid in perpetrating deeds of violence and crime, which, as individuals, they shudder at the mere mention of."[35] It was a primitive version of crowd psychology, but one which captured quite well the pessimistic foundation of Southern values. One was safest, and most secure, when one had the least contact with other people, and then such contacts had to be tightly controlled. If many people came together, the possibility of violence greatly increased.

The violent man was, ultimately, a deviant in polite society. If not explainable by class, then he could only be explained by reference to a peculiar temperament or a poor upbringing. The seed of passion may have been present in everyone, but it was the man careless of the discipline which was necessary to social life who was most likely to become violent. Violence went against the grain of Southern values and attitudes, but those same attitudes made violence seem an unavoidable part of human life.

The best way to control violence was for everyone to behave himself, but given the inevitable shortcomings of human nature and society, many people recognized that this was hardly a satisfactory approach to the problem of violence. Physical conflict meant a breakdown of social rules, but not surprisingly, due to the Southern faith in proceduralism, not a few people felt that when one set of rules broke down, the best solution was to look for another set to replace it. They turned to the law. That Southerners had mixed feelings about the law is well-known, but there was little about the culture to make one think, as stereotypes suggest, that their feelings toward the law were entirely negative. Given the well-documented rage for order, and for a depersonalized order at that, one would more likely expect that Southerners, in society as in politics, would approve the rule of law as a counter to arbitrariness and disorder in their lives. And many did.[36]

There was, as William Lowndes Yancey once intoned, "in the South, an habitual reverence for law and order,"[37] and many Southerners supported Yancey's contention. In the rhapsodic words of a New Orleans minister, "Amid all the busy scenes of life, the eagerness of competition, and the violence of conflicting passions, LAW lifts up her majestic front, calm, unmoved, and unaffected by the various changes which agitate us, like some lofty mountain towering far above the surrounding plain, unshaken by storms, and ever irradiated by heaven's own light."[38] Most Southern writers took a similar, if less poetical view of the nature of the law, describing it less in terms of its negative role in providing sanctions against crime, and more in terms of its conservative functions of providing "security" and regulating human "engagements."[39] The law provided an objective and impersonal set of rules for guiding social life.

And the law, many Southerners felt, was all that stood between civilization and anarchy. As one prosecutor informed the jury in a Virginia murder trial: "The wicked and unruly passions of men, if let loose, unbridled and unrestrained upon society, would delight in scenes of blood and death. Hence the tender regard which society—law—extends to life and liberty, is not confined to those accused of crime, but the value of every man's life is recognized."[40] The law, like all social forms, stood in contrast to passion and disorder, and because of this it was treated with reverence.

Indeed, in its objectivity and impersonality, the law must have represented society in its most perfect state. Passionless, procedural, and impersonal, the law reduced the resolution of social conflicts to a matter of applying the correct rules in any situation. Removing feeling from social affairs, the law was, so far as those who upheld it were concerned, what every aspect of social life should be like.

A similar sentiment informed Southern views with regard to punishment. Revenge was never desirable in human society, and it was no better, so many felt, as a principle of punishment in law. J. A. G. Davis, the Virginia legal scholar, murdered when he interfered with a student riot, wrote that punishments were devised to prevent crime through a fear of the consequences. "They are inflicted," he added, "because other wise it would be useless to denounce them." Prevention and regulation comprised the goal of punishment, and not a few Southerners congratulated themselves that the law had progressed far beyond the days when vengeance and brutality were standard practices in the punishment of crime. In fact, a surprising number of Southerners—neither eccentrics nor "Transcendentalists"—spoke out against capital punishment, chiefly on the ground that the practice admitted, as the law should not, the principle of revenge.[41]

The problem was, of course, that the law was not simply an abstract set of principles, nor was it on any pinnacle, "unmoved and unaffected by the various changes which agitate us." It was, instead, an all-too-human institution, existing only in its practice. That very fact, according to some writers, made for its inadequacy. Much of the problem, some authorities felt, was with the legal profession. The lawyer had to have some sense of morality, some devotion "to distinguish a bad from a good cause," and many lawyers lacked either the desire or the ability—or both—to make such a distinction. Too often lawyers put the client above everything else so that, as one attorney wrote: "The safety of society is totally disregarded, and the preservation of the guilty Cain, though covered by the blood of the righteous Abel, is regarded as a first duty, both by Bar and Jury." The lawyer, far from upholding truth and justice, might well become the "agent and supporter" of "bad passions" and, thus, by his devotion to his client, pervert the very law he was supposed to uphold.[42]

Hence, one of the problems which worried many in the South was the ability of a good lawyer to obtain acquittals for known criminals. The acquittal obtained by skillful arguments and packed or ignorant juries was not unknown in the Old South. In such cases, moreover, the people often felt a need to take the law into their own hands, lynching the presumed guilty party. Antebellum lynching was primarily a frontier phenomenon and just as often involved whipping or tarring-and-feathering as it did hanging. But, as an extralegal method of law enforcement, lynching was quite controversial in the Old South.[43]

Actually, lynch law had few defenders among articulate Southerners. Those who did defend the practice, or who found it at least understandable, referred mainly to the fact that the spirit of the law often was sacrificed to its letter in the acquittal of known criminals, but, as Southerners, their approval of lynching was usually qualified. Like a writer who signed himself "P.P.," they saw lynching not only as a product of frontier conditions in which law was not yet established, but also as a matter of class, pointing out that small farmers—desirous of order but not bred to it—were most given to the practice. Even defenders of lynching, however, expressed the view that the practice should never become common. They merely put the burden on the legal system to stamp out the kinds of conditions which made less formal modes of justice necessary.[44]

Those who defended lynching did so, then, in a manner that accorded well with Southern culture—proposing extralegal violence only when normal procedures failed, and then proclaiming that the "best people" never engaged in the practice anyway. The record would not bear their defense out. "Southern Gentlemen" often joined their less affluent fellow citizens in attacks on local wrongdoers, and, like the small farmers, frequently felt the need to organize vigilante or "regulator" bands in an effort to bring order to their communities.[45] Conservative in intent, such efforts represented a real sense of social crisis in community affairs.

Mob violence was not, however, any more a Southern than a Northern or Western phenomenon, as Southerners were fond of pointing out to their critics.[46] Moreover, it posed grave social dangers. Lynchers, as one writer put it, "tear down the most sacred barriers of a common protection,"[47] by challenging those dispassionate, impersonal standards upon which society had to be based. The New Orleans minister put it even more tellingly: "Let the mob rule, and let lynching be tolerated, and who *can* be safe? Who can then even *conjecture*, what course may ensure him safety? In such a state of things, there is no law to guide him, no tribunal to which he can appeal, but the power of the multitude, swayed by their own lawless, uncurbed, and ever varying passions!"[48] The law, like society, could survive only as long as form triumphed over feeling.

The greatest debate over law among Southerners came, in fact, from the very problem of feeling and form. To some Southerners, the inadequacy of the law lay not in its inability to convict all the guilty, but in the fact that, rigidly enforced, it could lead to the punishment of men whose acts of violence were committed in defense of self or of family. On the one hand, many Southerners agreed, in the case of such private wrongs as insults, one had to act on his own because the law provided inadequate redress or none at all for the wronged individual. On the other, given the volatile nature of the passions, a man might well act violently in a fit of anger and under extreme provocation when normally he could maintain that veneer of sociability which kept society together.

Southern law certaintly recognized the right of self-defense. It was, according to J. A. G. Davis, "founded on the law of nature, which confers on every individual the right to defend and maintain the possession of that which belongs to him, by those means which are necessary to attain this object."[49] The problem, so many believed, was to figure out the kinds of situations in which that right of self-defense was applicable. Did it, for example, apply to those "private wrongs" which so often led to violence—to insults or to social gaffes—or did self-defense relate only to threats to life or property. The problem of self-defense was vastly complicated by a perception of society in which every individual was already on the defensive against violations of peace and order in relationships with other people. The difficulty of dealing with the problem of self-defense was one of the thorniest Southern law had to face in the antebellum period.

This difficulty was shown with particular clarity in a Charleston trial held in 1805, that of Richard Dennis for the murder of James Shaw. Dennis's father had been abused by Shaw, and the son took it upon himself to avenge the wrong done to his father. The defense made much of both the family feeling displayed by the defendant and of Shaw's own actions following the young man's notice that he could not let the matter rest. Dennis's lawyer summarized the events, and the case, this way:

> The prisoner at the bar, bearing no malice or antipathy, having no animosity, entertaining not even the slightest personal dislike to Mr. Shaw, was unexpectedly betrayed into a contention with him by a violent assault and outrage which was committed upon his father by the deceased, and which under the impulse, he interfered in and opposed. . . . I will prove to you by indubitable testimony, that the deceased, instead of treating this conduct of the prisoner as he ought to have done . . . instead of admiring the generous spirit, and applauding the filial piety of the youth, did conceive, and treasure up in his bosom the most implacable hatred and re-

venge—declared at the moment that he would inflict personal chastisement upon him, and would kick him; and that true to his rash and vindictive menace he did actually kick him in the public market place, making him, thereby, an object of scorn and derision to the scoffing multitude.[50]

As if that were not enough, Shaw not only refused a challenge from the young man, but threatened him with a whipping—the kind of violence reserved for inferiors and slaves. Ultimately, young Dennis, lying in wait, shot his would-be assailant down.

The problems in the case were great, but they were not unusual, and they captured major conflicts between social values and the law and, thus, conflicts within Southern culture. The problem of provocation and that of the readiness to perceive a threat to oneself and to one's family both figured prominently in the Dennis case, as they did in many others.[51] Moreover, notions of social class and hierarchy entered into the affray in a manner that virtually summarized Southern ideas on the subject.

But the central issue in the Dennis case, as in others, was that of the passions, their nature and effects. Dennis had killed Shaw, the defense argued, in a quite understandable fit of passion, which Shaw had inflamed, and the defendant could not therefore be guilty of malicious, premeditated murder. It was an argument defense attorneys would make throughout the antebellum period. If being in a state of passion would not excuse an act of violence—Dennis's lawyers were trying to get the charge reduced to manslaughter—it should mitigate the crime, and the law had to recognize that the passions were too volatile, unpredictable, and powerful to be controlled in the event of extreme provocation.

A defense based on passion as in the Dennis case emphasized what Southerners thought the nature of the passions to be. Such a defense proposed, in J. A. G. Davis's words, "the want or defect of *will*" in extenuation of a criminal act,[52] an indication of the extent to which Southerners opposed passion to control, and an indication, as well, of how desperate a situation would have to be for a Southerner to turn justifiably to violence. That one would act violently implied a provocation so extreme that the individual himself could no longer exercise control over his actions—and it was only such a loss of control that made violence understandable.

And the law, ultimately, had difficulty in coming to terms

with this problem of passion, at least in the opinion of many defense lawyers. Since the law was more concerned with regulation
than revenge, or so it was said, it offered little to one who was insulted or whose home had been invaded. All too often, particularly
in the case of a private wrong, the best one could get from the law
was prosecution for misdemeanor, a fine, and a "gentle admonition
to behave better for the future."[53] Giving no vengeance, the law
offered nothing to quiet the passions once they were excited.

More than that, however, there was a real problem in submit-
ting an act committed in passion to a judgment rendered in terms
of a rigid, impersonal set of rules. It was not that Southerners believed it could not have been done; it was simply that two contrary elements of social life and values came into conflict in such a
situation, and the proper resolution of that conflict was never clear.
Quite a few Southerners, recognizing the importance of passion in
human life, tended to feel that, where the provocation was serious
enough, passion and revenge had to be expected and condoned.
Thus it was that the judge in the trial of Colonel John A. Winston
of Alabama for the killing of a physician who had "debauched" the
Colonel's wife could "rejoice that the law which I was sworn to
execute, allowed me to discharge him."[54] Crimes of passion, coming into conflict with the principle of law, were frequently ex-
cused, given the nature of man.

But not all Southerners felt that the conflict should be resolved
in favor of the passions. After all, the man who acted passionately,
no matter how provoked, was still acting without discipline, and
Southerners prized discipline. They might not prosecute duelists,
but those who avenged wrongs with passion and without regard to
rules frequently went to court and often felt the full force of the
law. Young Dennis, for one, was not helped by the efforts of his
lawyers, and according to accounts of his conversations with the
Reverend Richard Furman, "The violence of his passions, he at
first, rather urged as an excuse for unjustifiable actions; but afterwards acknowledged it was the effect of sinful indulgence, which
he then lamented."[55] Perhaps that was the thought he took with
him to the gallows.

Such convictions were important to those whose job it was to
uphold the law. The prosecutors in the Dennis case had not argued
that the young offender did not act as many would have in his

place, but, in the words of the attorney general, "After evincing his spirit, would it have been unmanly in him, Gentlemen, to have Mr. Shaw bound over? That was the course he ought to have taken. But he chose to take the law into his own hands, and therefore stands he now at the bar for judgement." The judge in the case agreed with the attorney general. In charging the jury, he declared that there was too much vengeance in society, and added, "If juries do not give their aid in stemming this torrent, there will be no personal safety or security in society." The law was not always upheld, as it was in the Dennis case, but its success was important to many Southerners for whom order was a necessary and important protection from the violence of human nature.[56]

Violence, when it occurred, occupied a peculiar place in Southern life, and Southerners were never quite sure what to do about it. Looking sometimes with pride at their own unwillingness to tolerate personal abuse or insults and considering their readiness to resent and take action as a mark of nobility, many Southerners, if they themselves did not fight, were loath to condemn those who did. And, indeed, if the violence did not graduate beyond a fistfight or a caning, and there were no serious injury, most altercations were never taken before the law. Fights were noted but rarely dwelled upon. Still, there was that nagging sense in the minds of many people that fighting could get out of hand all too easily and that, above all, the habitual fighter was a man who had not learned his culture very well. Even fighters were known to share this sentiment.

Violence was both a logical outcome of Southern social thought and a contradiction to it. Taught fear and mistrust, many Southern men were ready to see threats everywhere and, frequently, were prepared to respond should an attack occur. At the same time, stepping outside a law that offered no revenge for personal wrongs, they undermined that very order which, alone, could prevent abuse in a hostile world. Violence, in other words, posed a real cultural dilemma for antebellum Southerners.

What all this suggests is that, ultimately, when an affluent Southerner turned to violence, it was a signal of his belief that the social order was in irredeemable trouble. That is, given the conservatism of "Gentlemen" and "Snobs" alike, it is probably less accurate to talk about a propensity for violence among members of the gentry than it is to talk about violence as a response to any perception that the social game was not proceeding according to rules, and that things had come to such a pass that rules could not easily be reestablished.

The problem was, of course, that their social pessimism, bordering on the misanthropic, predisposed them to see a crisis in the making at every turn. Guarded against their neighbors and fellow citizens—and not too sure of their families nor even of themselves—Southerners went forth into society convinced only of its instability. When their convictions appeared true, many were ready to throw caution to the winds and strike back at the danger.

4. *Violence in Plain-Folk Society*

PROPENSITIES FOR violence, many Southerners thought, were closely related to social and economic class and to the environment in which people lived. Accordingly, when Southerners talked about their most violent citizens, they tended to focus their attention on those who lived outside the plantation elite, and on the environment which such people created and maintained. They focused, that is, on frontier and town life.

At first glance, the juxtaposition of frontier and town appears to be a strange one, but within the framework of Southern culture, the two were conceived of in remarkably similar terms. For one thing, there was a factual basis for such a connection. Outside the plantation system economically and socially, many Southern whites found an opportunity for livelihood in town just as others saw a hope for advancement in following the frontier. Indeed, frontier settlement and town-building were virtually simultaneous acts in most parts of the Old South.[1] To the extent that frontier areas retained much of their original character up to the time of the Civil War, the connection was an obvious one to make.

But there was a conceptual link between frontier and town that was even more powerful in the minds of many Southerners. One may recall a writer's comment that a mob of philosophers is no less a mob. What was crucial, so far as many people were concerned, was the size or diversity of a population. Where a population was large, or where it was composed of diverse elements, then one could never expect the kind of carefulness of manner that preserved decorum and prevented violence. Given the upper-class Southerner's model for the social world, frontier areas and towns both almost had to be violent, for they were both conceptually contrary to the ideal of plantation society, and in the worst possible ways.

It was because of this model that Southern frontier communities, in particular, acquired a reputation for excessive violence that has come down to the present. The reputation was built, to some extent, on fact, but was encouraged by such factors as tradition, literature, and, of course, humor—particularly the widely enjoyed works of the Southwestern humorists.[2] Whatever its sources, however, there can be little doubt that the frontier's reputation for violence, and that of the town, were powerful influences on Southern culture.

That European or Northern travelers to the South should have been taken with the apparent violence of such communities is, perhaps, not surprising. But even Southerners from the elite could rarely venture to town without reporting a few "Southern Bullies," or, as Caroline North wrote in her diary from Charlottesville, "rough looking men" and "queer and hard visaged people." The same was true of the frontier. Charles Minor, passing through Kentucky on a trip from Virginia to New Orleans, described the only way of fitting into the environment in his diary: "Walked over Louisburg. Having purchased a gun and bowie knife, I walked on my head a little higher than usual . . . Set all Kentucky at defiance & bloods! let a rascally Texan say *Turkey* to *me*!!" If Minor could take it all in great good humor, others had more trouble. When Jacob Young, a Methodist itinerant, was sent on his first frontier circuit, he could only remember, "I felt like a stranger in a strange land."[3]

It is difficult to separate fantasy from fact in looking at frontier or town violence. So strong was the reputation, and so biased is much of the evidence, that it is even more difficult to know what white Southerners who were neither articulate nor affluent thought about violence. There is some suggestion, made even at that early day, that frontier folk, in particular, indulged a "sly chuckle over their somewhat dubious reputation," encouraging their detractors with stories if not with behavior. Gullible editors, even on the frontier, were occasionally taken in by hoaxes of a sort that added to their neighbors' violent reputation. This reputation for violence had a life of its own, and one which necessarily interferes with any picture of how the people themselves thought and acted.[4]

Those Southerners, then, who have come to be called the "plain-folk" were supposed to be a people far more given to violence than the plantation elite. Fighting and brawling among themselves, these sturdy yeomen—and towndwellers—were also said to be the Southerners most likely to engage, misguidedly or understandably, in vigilantism, lynching, and urban mob violence. The question of the extent to which these plain-folk actually did have distinctive attitudes toward violence is a murky one, and one to which their reputation only suggests an answer.[5]

The most obvious difference between plain-folk attitudes and those professed by the elite was that violence was never given the connotations of desperation most planters assigned to it. The Reverend James Finley, raised on the Southern frontier, recalled that "if such a disastrous thing as a quarrel should break out, the only way to settle the difficulty was by a strong dose of fisticuffs," and he acknowledged that quarreling and fighting often occurred between the "best of friends," under the influence of "the brown jug."[6] A few plain-folk would assert violence as a good thing, but many accepted physical conflict as a normal means of settling disputes.

Indeed, to a greater extent than planters ever could, plain-folk saw violence as simply a part of social life. In the words of Mississippian Reuben Davis, "Their creed was generally simple. A man ought to fear God, and mind his business. He should be respectful and courteous to all women; he should love his friends and hate his enemies. He should eat when he was hungry, drink when he was thirsty, dance when he was merry, vote for the candidate he liked best, and knock down any man who questioned his right to these privileges."[7] Those who, like Davis, looked back fondly on plain-folk life, gave violence a place, and saw it as an element of the directness and openness of the people of the Southern frontier.

The violent planter was a deviant. The violent yeoman was not. However common fighting may have been among plain-folk, it remained the case, as Jeremiah Jeter recalled, that "combat brought no disgrace on the pugilists."[8] The comments of plain-folk—although as deeply tinged with romanticizing as those of outsiders were with disdain—make it clear that the man among them who turned quickly to his fists needed no special explanations. Nor was he likely to look upon his actions with any degree of remorse. Violence had a normal quality about it which members of the plantation elite could never have approved.

For all this, it must be emphasized, the plain-folk shared certain crucial aspects of the planters' world view, particularly its social pessimism and mistrust of others. Those who were religious would have agreed with pious planters that the world offered few rewards, that it was a place to be endured but not enjoyed. They accepted, as well, a rather bleak view of human nature.[9] Unlike the elite, however, plain-folk did not turn to formalism in order to construct adequate social relations out of undesirable materials. Indeed, if the reputed diversity of frontier communities be at all accurate, such a course would have been impossible, anyway. Instead, they took the opposite course and proposed blunt honesty and assertion as the best protection against harm from the selfish disposition of their fellow men. One had to fight fire with fire.

Where planters sought to maintain a language and bearing that prevented spontaneous expression of thought and feeling, plain-folk seem to have sought just the opposite for their communities. W. H. Sparks, looking back on a frontier upbringing, summarized the difference at the same time that he made a case for plain-folk virtue: "I doubt, however, if the habit of open and unrestrained expression of the feelings of our nature is not a more enduring basis of strong character and vigorous thought and action, than the cold polish of refined society."[10] And he linked this virtue to both frontier primitivism and national survival, citing Nathaniel Macon as his authority for the claim that "bad roads and fist-fights made the best militia on earth; and these may have been, in some degree, the means of moulding into fearless honesty the character of these people."[11]

David Hines, a self-styled picaresque hero, made the contrast all the more clear when he described his meeting with the notorious Southern outlaw, John Murrel. Hines, trying to cultivate the image of the refined rogue, found his more celebrated frontier counterpart wanting in "manliness" and "self-reliance," and the problem was one of manner. "To one, like myself, who was something of an aristocrat in bearing, feeling and language, his familiarity and mode of speech were sometimes inexpressibly offensive."[12] This question of manner was hardy trivial to many articulate Southerners, although Hines had some fun with it, and the distinction between plain-folk and planter was most apparent in precisely this regard.

Honesty, free-speaking, and violence were all supposed to have characterized plain-folk society. The planters sought to minimize the potential for conflict and violence through the observation of impersonal, restricted forms of expression. The plain-folk, by contrast, made much of their approval of speaking one's mind, and claimed to accept violence willingly as a natural concomitant of that freedom. Their assumptions about human nature and society were quite similar to those held by the Southern elite, but their methods for dealing with a human world were different and, as a result, their attitudes toward violence took a very different form. They could readily appreciate the existence of "fighting words," for the honest, straightforward insult very clearly had a place in the social setting of plain-folk life.[13]

The question here, as in the case of the planters, was one of self-consciousness. The plain-folks' reputation for violence grew out of a belief in the diversity of their communities, a belief which they, too, tended to accept. It is doubtful that plain-folk neighborhoods, with a few exceptions, really were more diversely composed than those of the plantation elite, and it was certainly not the case that plain-folk were more tolerant of differences than were members of the elite. The important point is that plain-folk saw their communities as made up of people who were likely to disagree, but in ways that could not be smoothed over or ignored. Society itself was a conglomerate of people, bound not by any sort of contract, but only by the fact of being in the same place at the same time. Conflict was, in such an instance, inevitable.

The sense of diversity in their society was exacerbated for the plain-folk by the simple fact of geographic mobility. Plain-folk moved around more than any other white Southerners, and most black ones, for that matter.[14] Seeking better lands and opportunities—and usually finding neither—plain-folk moved with great frequency throughout the South, and into the Northern border states, as well. This great mobility could only have affected their perceptions of others. Society looked diverse because its personnel changed so often.

Frontier and town communities looked different from those of the plantation elite. At the same time, plain-folk, like their more pretentious fellow Southerners, sought social stability. For those outside the "aristocracy," and especially for people on the frontier, the need for stability was enhanced by practical concerns. Frontier folk depended on each other to a startling degree.[15] For putting up houses, clearing fields, getting in the harvest, starting up a household, even for moving about, plain-folk required the assistance of people around them. The problem may be simply put. Plain-folk needed social stability. They needed an ongoing set of social relationships in which disagreements did not completely disrupt cooperation and survival. Unable, however, to accept the planters' approach to stability through the cultivation of artificial manners, they readily turned to more direct methods of handling difficulties, chiefly knocking down the opposition. Geographic mobility and the need for practical stability did not make for a violent society. But mobility (which made society appear unstable) in combination with social pessimism and with a lack of faith in manners, did.

Now, if elite Southerners learned the value of formality when they were children, plain-folk learned the virtue of direct action at the same time. Plain-folk child-rearing practices were informed by the same combination of social pessimism and concern about diversity that so influenced adult attitudes toward violence. Richard Bartlett has described the first of these factors well by pointing out that, on the frontier, the child was "looked upon as a little rascal rather than as an angel or cherub."[16] Plain-folk parents, unlike, say, an Ebenezer Pettigrew, did not assume the innocence of their children, and approached disciplinary problems with a sense of the corruption of the child. Misbehavior was to be stopped or punished, but the tendency to misbehave could never be blunted.

This point of view was reinforced by the practical character of the plain-folk family. It was, above all, a functional unit, the primary economic unit to which most people belonged, and its functional character tended to outweigh its expressive role in an individual's life. Everyone in these nonaffluent families had some kind of task to perform, and children as well as adults had to contribute to the economic survival of the group. They had to work, and their work had to be done independently and well.[17]

Larger economic forces, too, contributed to a functional focus in plain-folk families. To the extent that many plain-folk sought to improve their standing in society, members of the family had to be prepared to seize opportunities as they arose, and often to the detriment of family ties. Bartlett has suggested that much of the coldness observers ascribed to the American family, particularly on the frontier, in the nineteenth century had little to do with an absence of affection and everything to do with the cultivation of the kind of family bonds that would be easy to sever.[18]

Plain-folk children had to grow up quickly and they had to know when it was time to leave the household. As a result, plain-folk family life tended to take a different form from that of the planter elite. The focus of planter-family enculturation was, as we have seen, on the development of formalized expressions of senti-ment which gave evidence of strong family ties—reassurances that the emotional core of the family was intact. Plain-folk families, given their functional emphasis, focused more on individual and practical concerns. It may have been, in part, a matter of time: the plain-folk family had to inculcate independence, with little thought given to ways of channeling feeling into formalized, non-instrumental directions.

The difference here was manifested clearly in plain-folk atti-tudes toward corporal punishment. There is, as Bartlett reminds us, a stereotype of the sadistic, tyrannical frontier father, and though that stereotype may be more symbol than fact, it seems to have been the case that plain-folk parents thought more highly of physi-cal punishment than did those in the elite. Many autobiographers were like David Crockett in remembering fathers who believed that a good branch of hickory was a first rather than a last resort for the correction of a willful child. One did not channel or control potential problems, one simply stopped them, and violence was the most efficient means.[19]

The use of corporal punishment carried over into the country schools. One cannot imagine a local schoolteacher's feeling obliged to explain his use of the rod to a plain-folk parent, as Bingham did to Pettigrew, and, in fact, most people who grew up in plain-folk communities remember a very different situation. According to Jeremiah Jeter, a good supply of rods was just a part of the furnish-ings in most schoolhouses, and teachers were not reluctant to use them:

> The virtues of the hickory were well understood by all the discipli-narians of the school-room, and its penal application was held in extreme horror by all the unruly urchins of the region. It was em-ployed with more or less freedom and severity, according to the

temper and views of the pedagogue. Some irascible teachers used it, occasionally, at least, with unquestionable cruelty; while others employed it to terrify rather than punish. Castigation was inflicted usually by retail; but in some cases by wholesale. One teacher frequently flogged his pupils by the bench. Ten or a dozen were called up at once, and each received his share of the whipping. The punishment was not severe. While those at the head of the line were receiving their stripes, those at the other end were sniggering, and by the time the infliction was ended all were in a glee.[20]

Such an account as Jeter's shows the readiness with which schoolteachers could use violence; it shows, as well, the extent to which some teachers felt it to be the best method for governing unruly charges. Its efficiency seems to have been assumed.

Plain-folk children were more frequently exposed to violence than were those of the planters, learning to accept it from those in authority as part of the governing process. Physical punishment certainly did not undermine the authority of a teacher or a parent. Indeed, the opposite seems, in some instances, to have been the case: the teacher who could not defend himself, whether in a ritual turn-out or in his efforts to discipline his pupils, could be in a great deal of trouble. Should a student fight back, and win, a teacher might expect very little success in the future.[21]

The acceptance of violence was shown as well in the treatment adults accorded violence among children. The idea that children had to be watched to keep them away from bad company was not remarkably important in plain-folk families. Children, as many recalled, were pretty much left on their own, especially when it came to having fun. "No restraints," as one woman remembered, "were laid on our sports, except the injunction to 'keep out of mischief.' "[22] And keeping out of mischief certainly did not include avoiding fights. Indeed, fighting may have been a favorite sport.

"Backwoods boys," according to the Reverend James Finley, "were brought up to the trade of 'knock down, and drag out.' "[23] They were encouraged in the trade, in many cases, by their parents. Dr. Daniel Drake, recalling his Kentucky boyhood, wrote that his strongest disagreements with his father came over the issue of fighting: "A boy by the name of Walter, from mere mischief for we had no quarrel, struck me a hard blow and cut one of my lips, which I did not resent, as most boys would have done; but quietly put up with it. When I went home at night, and was asked the cause of the assault, Father blamed and shamed me for my coward-ice."[24] Andrew Jackson's mother apparently raised violent resent-ment to a general principle. Some Southerners saw in this the roots of more serious adult violence, but many plain-folk families seemed unconcerned. A sense of the necessity and utility of vio-lence was inculcated early, and even a frontier youngster who did not like to fight—William Physick Zuber of Texas, for example—could recall a time when inflicting a severe beating on another boy was the only way to bring a halt to childish "persecution."[25]

Adolescent and even adult violence were not, however, purely functional. After all, D. R. Hundley had virtually identified the Southern Bully with plain-folk communities, and such an identifi-cation was not entirely unfair. It is clear that plain-folk did some-times fight for fun, and, although the character of the bully was not universally appreciated—most plain-folk reserving their fighting for more serious occasions—nevertheless, he was a character who could make strong impressions. Not simply content to react violently to some kind of threat, such bullies strutted haughtily at any gather-ing, provoking and encouraging others to violent response.

Even among children—or perhaps especially among children—similar provocation was not unknown, as William Zuber's having to quiet a tormentor makes clear. Jeremiah Jeter even reported a ritualized provocation, motivated perhaps by jealousy, in the form of a custom known as "school-butter." According to Jeter, a "dar-ing" boy, when passing by a school, would cry, at the top of his voice, "School-butter! school-butter!" in order to ridicule the pupils inside. When he did, the scholars would throw aside all their work in favor of chasing the offender. If they caught him, he was usually forced to run the "gauntlet," that is, to run between two lines of boys who were armed with sticks. The punishment was not, apparently, an easy one.[26]

What all of this adds up to is a distinctive idea of the nature of violence in plain-folk communities. It is not that they valued violence or saw it as a meaningful form of manly action. It was rather that violence was one of several available forms of action in society. "Even the strictest of them," as Reuben Davis wrote, "made no scruple about a social glass, or a lively dance, or a game of cards, or even an honest hand-to-hand fight under due provocation."[27] Davis was clearly exaggerating the situation. Many plain-folk were far from making "no scruple" about those things. But, in identifying social violence as simply a part of social life—no worse, at least, than a social glass—he summarized what most plain-folk themselves described the situation to be.

Plain-folk defended their violence on the rather simple ground of naturalness, and this was something of an ideal for frontier life. Jeter, whose accounts of such violence are so useful, made the point rather clearly when he commented on the unlocked doors of frontier houses and barns: "Fighting is a great evil. It indicates a low grade of civilization, but between bullies and thieves, we unhesitatingly give preference to the former. Bullies are governed by false views of life and duty, but they may have within them the elements of which heroes are made."[28] Honesty was an ideal for community life, and if fighting were a price one had to pay for it, then the price was not too much to ask.

This view of honesty shares much with the pessimistic view of the world we have seen in the planters. A peaceful society could not exist, it appears, if men were honest. Honesty brought conflict, and conflict brought violence. One would not want to call the plain-folk view misanthropy, for it is doubtful that they thought their assumptions through enough to form a coherent theory of human evil, or even human unpleasantness. But, like planters, they were armed with mistrust, with expectations of the worst in their fellow man, and this influenced their actions toward other people. What travelers and affluent Southerners took as an excessive quickness of temper and what they condemned in plain-folk, was an almost inevitable consequence of a deep-seated mistrust of others, a mistrust which the planters themselves shared. It was because of this mistrust, perhaps, that towns were centers of violence and why, in fact, even rural gatherings were marked by fighting.[29] Mistrusting others, fighters were prepared to establish their own position, physically, in any social encounter.

The difference between plain-folk and planters had primarily to do with an understanding of the efficacy of symbols, of the power of language or gesture to accomplish things. The plain-folk attitude towards symbols was summarized by what was supposed to be a maxim of Andrew Jackson's: "Take time to deliberate; but when time for action arrives, stop thinking."[30] Violence, when it occurred among plain-folk, was sudden; it was also supposed to be conclusive. It was supposed to settle any issue once and for all, with neither grudges nor disputes remaining. One could, as the Reverend Finley suggested, settle difficulties with a "strong dose of fisticuffs." This too, contrasted with what the Southern elite thought, since for them, violence and disorder were virtually synonymous. Plain-folk fought, even if for sport, to prove some kind of superiority. Violence, they believed, could settle problems, and could do so with finality. Physical conflict was itself a part of their understanding of order.

It is usual to explain plain-folk violence by reference to individualism—either frustrated or excessive—and to a brutality born of frontier hardships. However much frontier conditions may have contributed to plain-folk violence, anything like "individualism" must represent such a complex of specific traits as to be of very little use for understanding plain-folk life. Far more important was a sense of social relationships as threatening and a belief that only immediate action could stave off any danger.

This view of plain-folk society receives an interesting and enlightening confirmation in one of their forms of expressive life, balladry. The ballads, essentially sung narrative poetry, entered plain-folk community life from a variety of sources. Some originated in their own communities and told of spectacular events in local or even national history; others came from other parts of the United States. But those which are most useful for this study, because the most is known about their history, are those English and Scottish traditional ballads which have come to be known as Child ballads, after the great collector Francis James Child. Child's classic collection of these ballads was published in the late nineteenth century. Drawing on European and American sources, he attempted to classify and trace the sources of traditional balladry in English. His ballads either antedate or were contemporary with the period of Southern settlement, and, since they remained a part of plain-folk life up to the present, it is likely that the plain-folk of the nineteenth century knew them, too.[31]

It is unfortunate that most of what is known about the traditional ballads pertains to the period after the Civil War. This is when the earliest American collections were done, although a few of the ballads appeared in pre-War songsters. One would guess, however, that the lives of the ballads before the war were very little different from what one can see afterward. Certainly, if one compares the early versions in Child with those in twentieth-century Southern collections, one can say that there was continuity in the sense of social relations and human life that the ballads portrayed. Moreover, the kinds of settings for ballad singing that post-bellum observers described were those which antebellum plain-folk knew as well. At log-rollings, house-raisings, parties and dances, good singers rendered the "old-time songs." There was a continuity that allows one to use these ballads to look back on plain-folk life.[32]

The traditional ballads seem peculiarly appropriate for a study of plain-folk notions about violence. Many of the ballads—60 of Child's 305—were stories of violence. Those that were not tended to present a picture of social relations out of which violence could grow. Not that the ballads were some sort of reflection of a violent plain-folk world. Alan Lomax's comment about the Native American murder ballad "Rose Connelly," that cold-blooded violence "came naturally to people whose ancestors were Indian fighters, bear hunters, moonshiners and feudists" and that the "old Border ballad tradition, which linked love and death, fitted the code of the backwoods," is a far too simple characterization of both plain-folk life and the ballads. Balladry did, sometimes, deal in cold-blooded murder; plain-folk, by their accounts, did not, however violent they may have been otherwise. The connection was a subtle one, but it illuminates what plain-folk social ideas were about.[33]

Traditional ballads popular in the pre-War South did not tell plain-folk stories, nor were they unique to the plain-folk. Sung throughout this country, in Britain, and on the Continent, the ballads presented situations which captured the plain-folk imagination by their qualities, not because the situations themselves were familiar. One may claim with certainty that few plain-folk girls ran away with gypsies. Few plain-folk youths were stabbed by a siren of the woods. The events of many of the ballads were spectacular, even exotic, and were hardly part of everyday life. The ballads were sensational, and in that lay much of their power to move.

What made them powerful was that, however sensational the ballads were, the stories they told were not impossible. Dealing with unrequited love, with seduction, with cold-blooded murder, or, for that matter, even with humor, the ballads presented events that—if exaggerated—could happen, all things being equal. The ballads presented a picture of potentialities based on a rather con-

sistent portrayal of human nature and of the content of social relations, and it was in this that they were most closely connected to
plain-folk life.

The fact that the ballads were not uniquely plain-folk stories
does not undermine their relevance to the community, but it does
place certain conditions on how one may treat them. Plain-folk did
not learn their culture nor did they give a distinctive expression of
their world view when they sang traditional ballads. What they
did do was to give accounts of spectacular events and circumstances
in a way that, to them, was understandable, so that they felt they
had some kind of handle on the extraordinary possibilities of human
relations. If one looks at the ballads, then, one can see how those
narrative poems cohered with and even elaborated on some difficult
but significant social concerns. People enjoyed the ballads and
were moved by them because they conveyed so much that people
believed could be true.

There are many aspects of the ballads one could focus on. The
tradition is rich and varied. Questions of motivation, or the role of
accident in human affairs, even of class consciousness, enter into
ballad verse in striking ways and could be related to plain-folk society and culture. More significant, however, given the view of
plain-folk developed here is the overriding sense one gets from the
ballads of human ties as being potentially deep and dangerous. Indeed, the ballads seem to say, the deeper one allows ties to become,
the more dangerous they are. Strong attachments to others are
never likely to bring satisfaction.

In some of the ballads, the problem was simply one of uncertainty or unreliability. One could never count on others to live up
to their obligations as husbands or wives, parents or lovers. More
pronounced, however, were the themes of callousness and cruelty.
Strong attachments, according to these songs, could be blinding,
indeed, even debilitating. Ballad characters pine away when their
love is not returned; the long absence of a loved one could lead to
death from grief. More significantly, however, strong ties made one
vulnerable, because others were all too likely to hurt anyone who
was weakened by excess affections.

An individual could be sure of how he felt about someone,
but not about that other's feelings for him. Love might be returned
with callousness. Seduction might be followed by attempted murder. If some ballad heroes, "Lord Bateman" for instance, felt com-

pelled to keep their vows, others were like "Lord Thomas" who, in one of the most popular ballads, left "Fair Eleanor" in favor of the "Brown Girl's" wealth—a decision which led to tragedy for all concerned. Family loyalty could not prevent family callousness or even family brutality. Worse, ballads told tales of infanticide, fratricide, and sororicide motivated by causes ranging from nothing through trivia through jealousy. No tie of affection was sacred, so far as the ballad stories were concerned. The "Johnnie Randal" who dined with his sweetheart in the evening found himself poisoned the following day and he died. Being open and trusting of others was not safe, for they could well respond with deceit and murder.[34]

The ballads did not condone deceit and murder. Some would-be seducers were undone; some would-be murderers, killed before they could commit the deed. The wife who abandoned her hard-working carpenter husband and their child to go off with a stranger went to a watery grave and, according to the ballad, to hell. Nor, however, was there universal retribution. The point was not the climax, but the situation of mistrust and danger which was found in almost every ballad. The main point was simple. Cruelty and even physical violence could come from anywhere, even from those one trusted most—a lover or a member of the family.[35]

The "old-time songs" did not "teach" violence. They did not even teach mistrust. They were almost more important for what they left unsaid than for what they made explicit. A ballad like "Lord Randal," for instance, described the murder of a young man by his true love. It did not address her motives. Ballad characters acted with resentment or cruelty, even with violence, almost without motive. This did not make a ballad any less powerful. What everyone could understand was that people might behave cruelly, and it was this understanding that made any ballad work.

Plain-folk learned certain attitudes toward people and society when they grew up. If the events of the world did not provide enough reinforcement for those attitudes, their expressive forms—ballads for example—contributed their own kind of support. Still, the role of violence in plain-folk society may be clearest in that sort of community which brought the sources of violence to a peak, the frontier town. It was in such towns that local bullies found an arena,[36] and the frontier town became a focus for the plain-folk's violent reputation. Such a place, in spectacular terms, was Houston in the days of the Texas Republic. Outsiders and citizens alike considered violence one of the most pressing of problems, posing both physical and moral dangers to anyone there.

Houston's reputation for violence was strong and widespread. In part, the town's notoriety resulted from the independent status of the Republic of Texas and its presumed role as a haven for criminals from the United States. Texas became, in the eyes of many, "a community of unprincipled adventurers," and Houston occupied a central place as a major town in that community. Stories of Texan violence circulated throughout the United States, and even in England, adding to the Republic's poor reputation.[37]

Houstonians themselves—at least some of them—were concerned about their city's reputation, and about that of the whole Republic. If larceny were a more common crime than violence, the *Houston Telegraph and Texas Register* was probably correct in editorializing, "There is nothing that tends more to injure the credit of our country abroad, than the opinion that our streets are often the theatres of brawls, where the bowie-knife and pistol are permitted to do the work of death with impunity. The impression, however erroneous, has made Houston and Texas by-words of contempt in many parts of the United States." Comparing their own city to those in the States, Houstonians had a standard against which their own city appeared sadly lacking.[38]

According to some, moreover, the violent tenor of life they saw in Houston could have economic as well as moral and social consequences. Francis R. Lubbock, in his memoirs, recalled that Houston failed to get a carriage factory when the uncle of a local merchant arrived from New Jersey to check the prospects for such a venture. Visiting the Congress of the Republic, then in session, the uncle was astonished by a shoot-out between two senate clerks. Running from the chamber, he was almost knocked over by a wounded man, and when he crossed the street to escape that affray, another man "with his bowels protruding from an immense bowie knife wound" rushed past. Needless to say, Houston did not get the factory.[39]

It is unlikely that the visiting uncle witnessed a typical Houston day—though one can understand his reluctance to stay and find out. Houstonians fought, and there were frequent brawls, but criminality appears to have involved crimes against property about as much as it did those of violence, at least in the eyes of the law.

In fact, citizens and travelers differed greatly on the extent of violence in the city. Gustav Dresel, who visited Houston in 1838, reported frequent brawls among well-armed men and said that the police were virtually powerless to maintain peace. Other visitors did not agree. William Kennedy, an English visitor to the city a year later, found the criminal laws to be "rigorous" and assured his readers that "in none of the new States of the Union is the law so certain to be carried into effect against a real offender, through the instrumentality of a jury, as in Texas." It was taken as a measure of the relative peace of the community by at least one native that of the three men who served as city marshal during the decade of the 1840s, not one had to kill another man. The apparent frequency of dangerous violence, and its significance, depended very much upon whom one asked.[40]

Yet the problem, as many Houstonians saw it, had less to do with the frequency of violence than it did with the kind of violence that marked their community; specifically, with its quickness. As Francis Lubbock remembered the situation, "very few brutal murders or assassinations took place; generally when killings occurred they were caused from sudden difficulties and in hot blood."[41] However well this spoke for a people who did not bear grudges, it posed peculiar sorts of problems for those who would have understood and thus controlled violence in their city.

More respectable Houstonians never stopped being amazed at the triviality of quarrels that could lead to homicide. Some members of the community did seem shockingly hot-blooded:

> On the evening of Sunday last Mr. Wm. Wood, then on a visit to this city, was requested by a friend to ride his horse a short distance to try his speed, the horse a few moments previous had been left in charge of a man by the name of Jones. Wood jumped upon the horse, and while riding him, was called upon by Jones to stop; as he did not stop immediately, Jones became irritated and after calling again used insulting language, Wood in return used some harsh epithets and stopped to dismount: when Jones coming up stabbed him with a Bowie knife, in such manner that he died on the second day afterwards.[42]

The cause was ridiculous and had nothing to do with malice, the classic concomitant of murder—although Jones was to be executed for this and other crimes.[43] The problem was paradigmatic: hot-tempered, armed men, on a sudden irritation, in a confrontation that led to death.

According to many, it was just such preparedness to fight that led to the greatest trouble. Citizens of frontier Houston, a virtual "instant city" founded on the heels of a difficult war, were said to be even more given to going around armed than were the citizens of more settled places. Pistols and bowie knives, it seems from contemporary accounts, were standard adornments for male Houstonians and, in the opinion of Lubbock at least, made men "ready to resent insult and wrong without waiting for the slow process of the law."[44] One newspaper declared that firearms were "hourly discharged in the precincts of the city," and the writer added: "If all who are in the habit of shooting were skillful enough to hit a barn door, we should be under no necessity of making this complaint; but as we have recently witnessed *marksmen* who might aim at a whole barn and miss, to hit a bystander: we shall take the liberty of recommending that no description of firearms be discharged within half a mile of the city, unless required by the most urgent necessity."[45] The very presence of armed careless men contributed to a dangerous atmosphere by making any quarrel a potential homicide.

Violence in Republican Houston clearly conformed to the general patterns of plain-folk violence. It was largely personal violence, growing out of some kind of dispute between two men. More than that, however, it was almost certainly encouraged by a constant preparedness for physical conflict on the part of many people. The fact that so many men apparently went about armed was significant. Frontier Houstonians displayed in this their sense of human nature and social relations, and there was, as among more elite Southerners, a preemptive quality to their actions. Houstonians' preparedness also highlights the differences between plain-folk attitudes and those of the Southern gentry. Quarrels between perfect strangers were rare among the elite; their difficulties tended to grow out of clearly defined social or political relationships, even in the case of an inadvertent insult. Quarrels picked by frontier Houstonians needed no such background. Simple contact was a more crucial force than any well-charted but fragile relationship among actors.

One other point should also be made. There is very little evidence of fighting without pretext during the period. The shoot-'em-up and gang violence of the cattle frontier seem to have been rare in frontier Houston, as does the pure, formalized sport of the twentieth-century "fightin' and dancin' club." To be sure, liquor and gambling in themselves contributed to violence then as they have done in more recent times, but always there was the presence of a quarrel to set things off. Indeed, even "bullies" had to pick a quarrel to start a fight. A dispute, however trivial, was inevitably the first cause of a Houston fight, emphasizing, again, the extent to which violence was supposed to be a symptom of social conflict and tension—the price of honesty.[46]

Still, all this quarrelsomeness, as most Houstonians recognized, resulted from somewhat deeper causes, and they tried hard to figure out what those causes might be. Some, noting the usual qualities of a Houston summer, posited a direct connection between climate and quarrelsomeness. "We have noticed," in the words of the *Telegraph and Texas Register*, "that as the warm season sets in quarrels become frequent among loafers and dogs, who generally exhibit more scratches on their noses or ears, as the weather becomes more warm and oppressive." The *Morning Star* was in agreement: "Any man that quarrels in hot weather, should be set down as a blackguard."[47]

There was much, however, in the year-round environment that seemed to many to encourage violence. A theory was said to be current "that it is necessary to mingle a little whiskey, rum, or brandy with the water of many of our streams, to render it wholesome," and drunkenness and violence were all too common partners. Moreover, the exciting, competitive atmosphere of gambling led many Houstonians to violence. Vice and violence were as closely connected in Houston as they were elsewhere in the South.[48]

However, Houston's youth and her background were the factors most observers cited in order to explain the city's violence. Houston was founded near the end of a war, before society had settled and before many of the soldiers had found gainful employment. Armed and disorganized, many of the ex-soldiers turned to less than innocent pastimes. But it was rapid growth and the resultant diversity of population that impressed many thoughtful observers. According to one, writing on the Republic as a whole, "The new settler in mingling with his fellows, witnessing no common or uniform manners, customs, or language, sees no pattern to which he may conform, and hence each one retains his own previously formed habits, nor even thinks of adopting any model." There was, in other words, no real protection against violence in the absence of common forms of behavior.[49]

Houstonians' understanding of violence in their own community was, thus, primarily environmental. There were, to be sure, a few extraordinarily bad men. "Lem M'Guire" was a noted villain in the region, one who from childhood was given to attacking the innocent and wicked alike—including officers of the law—and every frontier had to face similar characters. In addition, Houston, like most Southern towns and cities, had its share of "rowdies." But if Houston life had its violent tenor, it was one to which a cross section of the population seemed to be subject, including the most affluent citizens. Even members of Congress had their affrays during the time that Houston was the capital of the Republic, and it is no wonder that one observer wryly suggested, "When 'Houston' was founded it became for a time the resort of all the gamblers in the country, until its citizens decided, by a large majority, to turn Congress adrift, and make them seek some other place upon which to inflict their concomitant nuisances." Violence in the setting of a frontier town, was, in great part, a result of the social milieu.[50]

There was undoubtedly some truth to the popular explanations. The diverse elements who settled early Houston probably did bring with them a diversity of manners and morals which could lead to conflict. Moreover, the fact that the Republic was independent of the United States must have attracted a fair number of fugitives from American law. But beyond that, Houston's early settlers must also have brought with them a belief that manners and morals were not much protection against violence anyway. Common models for behavior, such as the Eastern planters attempted to develop and maintain, might well have reduced Houston's violence, but such models were not given much place in an action-oriented society such as that of the Southern plain-folk. The most likely explanation for violence in Republican Houston as elsewhere, is that conditions reinforced culture in a way that made for a noticeably violent town.

Houstonians who wanted to control violence, like other Southerners, looked mainly to the law. It is, however, hard to say how well the law worked. Laws were on the books against violent crimes, and even the usually pessimistic *Telegraph and Texas Register* felt that, by 1840, the local grand jury had made headway in bringing "miscreants" to justice. The members of that body themselves had declared a year earlier that by their efforts "the moral tone of Society" had been improved and that "the property and persons of the citizen are secure in this as any other well regulated community."[51] But the situation was not all that clear. Edward Stiff, perhaps because of a bad personal experience, described the city's police as "entirely worthless," and the same *Telegraph* that commended the grand jury had less kindness for the judiciary, too many of whose members released murderers on low bail. The court records tend to support the paper's concern. Not a few of those indicted for murder were released on bail—and promptly jumped it, heading for parts unknown. A perhaps more serious short-circuiting of the law lay in the fact that few indictments for crimes of violence, including murder, appear to have resulted in a judgment of any kind.[52]

Thus it was that Judge J. W. Robinson became something of a hero when he had to handle the murder trials of David Jones, whose crime has been recounted above, and John C. C. Quick, who killed a man with whom he was gambling. Overruling all motions, Robinson sentenced both men to die and, learning of the poor conditions of the jail, ordered that it be done quickly. The editors of the *Telegraph* were delighted: "A couple of halters may ere long cause them to entertain more *elevated* notions of the morals of our fellow citizens," the paper suggested, and, following the execution, printed a letter from "A Citizen" declaring, "The result will doubtless prove of the utmost advantage to the public peace." The record suggests, however, as does the space given to Quick and Jones, that exemplary executions were rare in early Houston.[53]

It would be easy to exaggerate the violence of frontier Houston, as it would that of the frontier South as a whole. To be sure, the antebellum West was more violent than the rest of the country, and Texas especially seems to have deserved its violent reputation. It is doubtful, however, that Republican Texas at its wildest saw more violent crimes than Texas today.[54] Yet, the violence of a place like Houston was important because it betokened, in very clear terms, the most significant plain-folk attitudes toward physical conflict. Mistrust, immediacy, and a readiness to do battle were all markedly clear among the violent men of frontier Houston.

Still, spectacular as Houston's violence was, one cannot assign the bulk of the violence in plain-folk society to bullies, rowdies, and frontier ne'er-do-wells, because the evidence suggests that fighting was fairly widespread in the community, as widespread, perhaps, as the kinds of social attitudes which seem to have supported it. If, as I have suggested, violence were taken to be an acceptable form of social conduct in plain-folk communities—and not just the sensational ones like Houston—then one would expect people to have assigned to physical conflict a functional role. And this was the case.

A consequence of the plain-folk view of violence is that one can speak, in regard to that group, of such a thing as conservative violence. Its most spectacular form was vigilantism, and, if contemporary sources are to be believed, plain-folk tended to provide most of the participants in such movements. The goal of vigilantism was relatively simple: "by one single act of justice—when the law cannot be depended on—to free the country forever from the danger of becoming the den of thieves and murderers." Based, often, on an exaggerated notion of popular sovereignty, vigilantism could only have existed where a substantial number of people believed that violence could itself be a constructive force leading to social stability.[55]

There is no doubt that vigilantism could and did lead to frequent excess. Vigilante bands exacted harsh and sometimes sadistic penalties from those whose crimes they sought to stop. But their sense of power and function was shown even more clearly in the treatment they could accord to people who opposed vigilante methods:

Some Texas marauders lately crossed the line into Louisiana and took forcible possession of a citizen in the parish of Caddo. After they had carried him into the territory of Texas, it was proposed to bury him alive. With this intention, a grave was then dug—the unfortunate man being a witness to their movements. He stood helpless, counting each shovel-full of earth, as the quick termination of his life; surrounded by a gang of desperadoes, ready to crush him beneath the clod, and from whose sentence the escape was death. Overpowered with the frightful fate before him, he bounded

from his keepers and rushed into an adjacent thicket; but before
his steps had measured many paces over the earth, a heavy volley
of musketry brought him to the ground. . . . His body, after being
cut up, was hung upon the branches of the neighboring trees. . . .
The deceased man . . . had thus offended them: he had, with
others of his fellow citizens, declared himself openly to be opposed
to them. . . . The citizens of our border country have witnessed
these men, under the name of Regulators or Moderators, commit-
ting in the territory of Texas some of the most barbarous cruelties
of the 19th century.[56]

Certainly, many plain-folk were opposed to the outrages of Regulator bands, particularly since the line between Regulators and
criminals was usually difficult to draw. This was the case for instance, with the notorious Shelby County Regulators in Texas in
the 1840s. Originated to combat the high crime rate in the area,
the Regulators were themselves infiltrated by bad elements and,
ultimately, yet another group had to be formed to combat them in
a kind of vigilante war. To many in the area the ascendancy of
such a vigilante group comprised, as the *Houston Morning Star*
described it, a "reign of terror," but some of the respectable found-
ers of the group remained with it to the end. The goal of the movement was stability, at least in its inception, and stability could be
achieved by fighting criminals and other opponents alike.[57]

Plain-folk provided the rank and file for most vigilante movements, although it may have been that the leadership in some areas
was drawn from what representatives there were of the elite in the
population. If this were the case, it would certainly speak for the
power of the environment to influence action, since most articulate
Southerners tended to oppose vigilantism and lynching on grounds
that were quite consistent with other concerns. Proceduralism was
a protection against social evil in many aspects, and law was the
only barrier against mobocracy. For them, the means of justice
were, in themselves, important. The essence of vigilantism was the
ignoring of means. It is a cliché in talking about such movements,
as H. Jon Rosenbaum and Peter C. Sederberg have noted, to say
that the ends are thought to justify the means, but in the context of a
proceduralistic culture like that of the Old South, the presence of
people who acted on such a belief was quite remarkable. Many
respectable folk on the frontier seem to have opposed vigilante

movements of any sort, and went along with the editors of the *Houston Morning Star* in rejoicing when "Judge Lynche's gang" was unable to do its work. But some planters and not a few plain-folk saw the necessity for such actions in their new country.[58]

Most apologists for lynching defended the action as the only substitute for law where law had not yet been established, but the facts suggest that such apologies may be only partially correct. Certainly one would have to strain to apply that defense to anti-abolitionist lynchings in the South after the 1830s, and it was the case, as James Leyburn noted, that lynch law could persist long after institutional law arrived.[59] The more pressing problem was one of achieving stability out of diversity, a problem to be solved most adequately through violence. Combining misanthropy with a sense of the uselessness of external forms, plain-folk treated lynching in much the same way they treated other forms of violence.

For plain-folk, in fact, vigilantism often appeared to be preferable to the law. This was certainly true in the case of an 1835 vigilante uprising in Vicksburg, Mississippi, in which five gamblers were hung. According to H. S. Fulkerson, local gamblers had made themselves a public nuisance, and the people were at first not entirely sure what to do about it. "The law was resorted to, but its 'delay,' together with the money of its violators, rendered it inoperative. The question—a grave one—of the right of any whole community, organized under the legal sanctions common to all civilized countries, to its life, when in peril, and to its preservation by taking the law into its own hands, began to move the people, and was decided in the affirmative."[60] The procedures of the law did not have the sort of certainty of result plain-folk desired. Thus, it is important that when the members of a notorious Alabama vigilante band, the "Slicks," were brought to trial for their violence, several were acquitted and the rest were assessed only for damages and court costs. The findings, by a jury of their peers, were interpreted as a vindication for the Slicks' effort to purify "the moral atmosphere."[61]

Plain-folk desired homogeneity in society as much as did the planters, but felt they had to go about achieving it differently. The planters focused their efforts on achieving harmony, maintaining it through the subordination of difference to form and manner. The plain-folk, allowing for honesty, nevertheless had no patience with real diversity. Vigilantism and the active suppression of unpopular or troublesome elements, would have been more compatible with plan-folk views.[62]

Still, spectacular as vigilantism was, an even more meaningful demonstration of the plain-folks' understanding of violence came from a most unexpected source—the religious sects. For the plantation elite, religion and interpersonal violence did not mix. Indeed a religious man could even turn down a duel without losing face. For plain-folk, however, there was no inconsistency in being religious and using one's fists. In the words of Reuben Davis, "Minister as he was, my father never doubted that it was part of his Christian duty to knock down any rascal who happened to deserve such discipline. People had not begun to write about muscular Christianity in those days, but they understood and practiced it."[63] Fighting was often said to be necessary for the preservation of piety, especially on the frontier, and in a way that was consistent with more general plain-folk attitudes toward violent action.

Frontier religious people, especially the preachers, maintained a sectarian view of themselves and their role in society for much of the antebellum period. An embattled minority, as they saw themselves, contending against sinners and infidels, frontier preachers sought to bring order to disorderly communities through the power of the Word of God.[64] But many recognized that the Word's power was frequently insufficient by itself and acted on the assumption that it was impossible to fight a holy war without violence.

It sometimes seemed that one had to be as gifted with his fists as with his tongue if he were to succeed as a frontier preacher. Some, in fact, may have been more noted for their fists. Peter Cartwright—preacher, politician, and folk hero—was especially well-known as a fighter, and a story of his giving a licking to Mike Fink was widely disseminated, even though it was false.[65] But Cartwright himself recalled an evangelistic career that included its share of fighting, and he was not alone.

Frontier preachers were plagued by "rowdies," men who attended services at camp-meetings and elsewhere solely to create trouble. Some, according to Cartwright, actually came with the intention of doing the preachers physical harm, and preachers had to act violently in self-defense. Cartwright, given his reputation, was singled out as a target for special abuse, but every preacher learned early in his career that the holy war had physical as well as spiritual dimensions. William McKendree, later to become the first American-born bishop of the Methodist Episcopal Church, began his service on a circuit in Virginia in 1790. His first audience was not promising—"some drunk, some cursing and swearing, and others offering the preacher grog." They had cowed the regular preacher; he was "on his best behavior, for fear of a whipping." McKendree, with the power of God's Word, and a little help from the weather, was able to preach the crowd to submission, but, as he understood, anyone who feared for his physical safety was unlikely to be much of a preacher.[66]

Thus there was a certain amount of preventive and precipitate violence on the part of frontier religious leaders. James Finley once threatened to horsewhip a man who talked in a meeting, and Jacob Young, anticipating rowdies in a congregation, recalled that when anyone "would not obey orders, I would take hold of them and lead them out of the congregation. They soon saw that I had a great deal of muscular power. Although they threatened, no one laid violent hands on me."[67] Even the venerable Francis Asbury saw some value in violence. Aware of the presence of rowdies at a camp-meeting, he declared, "You may be in great danger from a quarter you little suspect. It is true that Methodists are not a fighting people, but they are not all sanctified—they may be provoked to retaliate, and they are very numerous on this ground. If it should come to that, you will get the worst of the battle." His words, it was reported, made for a very quiet evening.[68]

Pious plain-folk may have lost their fondness for recreational "knock down and drag outs" when they found religion, but they did not lose their belief in the efficacy and necessity of violence. Violence, for them as others, was not a last desperate resort, but rather a useful tool for achieving and maintaining order, given the aggressive sinfulness of most men. Religious men, the frontier preachers and believers nevertheless shared with other plain-folk the sense that action was more effective than symbolism in the ordering of human affairs.

5. Slavery and Violence
The Masters' View

SOUTHERN PLANTERS contrasted themselves with other whites on the basis of their understanding of the moral significance of violence. Plain-folk, for example, looked mainly at the practical side of physical conflict—if they thought about it at all—and had absolutely no appreciation for the fact that violence and passion could destroy proper human relationships. The planters themselves claimed a different point of view. They were, above all, remarkably moralistic. Indeed, one reason they saw so many crises in their lives was probably their interpretation of almost every event as a moral situation with far more than immediate ramifications. Moreover, they were not only highly moralistic, but their morals taught them such virtues as amiability, prudence, and, ultimately, a rejection of impetuosity and violence. With all this, however, these same planters were also slaveholders, maintainers and defenders of a brutal and violent system of forced labor. Much of the region's reputation for violence—indeed, probably all of it—came from the fact that slavery not only survived but even thrived in the South. And the leading men and women in the region, moralistic as they were, held other men and women in bondage.

The problem of how such a moralistic people could engage in slavery has long intrigued historians. Equally intriguing is the more limited problem of the relationship of attitudes toward violence to the plantation system. Since violence meant so much to those of the plantation elite, it is important to ask to what extent the violence of slavery, which no one denied, conformed to more general attitudes toward violence. One may also ask whether the interplay of values and attitudes toward violence with the demands of the plantation system had any effect on ways in which Southerners understood the institution of slavery. A discussion of the slaves' perceptions appears in chapter six.

Southerners were aware, and they were reminded of it often enough, that the system of slavery rested, ultimately, on violence. Corporal "punishment" was, as they were willing to admit, the one thing that made slavery, and slaves, work, and the necessity for physical force was, they acknowledged, endemic to the system itself. The free laborer, dependent upon his wages, could be made to work and to obey orders by the threat of their loss. The slave, whose livelihood was "assured" by the master, could only be made to work by the threat of violence.[1] The problem was, therefore, not whether violence should play a role in the slave system, but rather what its role should be.

Given the general tenor of Southern attitudes toward violence, the problem was not an easy one. During the early national period, when Revolutionary rhetoric was still in vogue and some Southerners worried about the conflict between rhetoric and the reality of slavery, they also worried about the role of violence in the slave system. Jefferson, the most famous of worriers, saw slavery as "a perpetual exercise of the most boisterous passions" and feared for the disposition to "tyranny" it produced in the slaveholding class. Others, whose doubts about the system were a good deal weaker, still expressed some fears. In his pamphlet advice to his sons, the Reverend Charles Pettigrew complained, "To manage *negroes* without the exercise of too much passion, is next to an impossibility, after our strongest endeavors to the contrary; I have found it so. I would therefore put you on your guard, lest their provocations should on some occasions transport you beyond the limits of decency and christian morality." There was the problem of passion in master-slave relations, as there was in any social relation, and it was on this problem that articulate Southerners concentrated much of their attention. It was, moreover, a problem that cut two ways. On the one hand, the slaveholder faced enormous difficulties in himself, as he tried to control his own passions in dealing with his slaves. On the other, as the leader of a plantation world that included himself, his slaves, and, sometimes, white employees, he had the job of controlling the general level of passion in what he felt really was a little community.[2]

These were difficult jobs, and in the handling of slaves, the problems were made worse by the simple fact of the relative positions of master and slave. As a writer for the *Southern Quarterly*

Review noted in 1854, "In taking from the negro all power of resistance, we leave the master a prey to unbridled passions that may some times betray him into excess."[3] In society at large, every man was answerable for every action—even on the field of honor, if necessary. The slave certainly was in no position to issue a challenge to his master when the latter stepped out of bounds, and this, according to many Southerners, placed added responsibility upon the slaveholder.

Here, as elsewhere, Southerners looked to order, and particularly to order expressed through outward form and behavior, to contain passion. Slavery itself came to be described as a kind of crucible in which the planter's ability to act with self-restraint received its ultimate test. It is no wonder, then, that after pointing out the difficulty of the test, one writer could contend that "The situation of a master, so far from seeming a thing to be coveted, does indeed bring with it relations of fearful responsibility."[4]

Southerners talked about the order they felt a plantation should have in the numerous essays on plantation management they wrote and published during the antebellum period. These essays all had as a purpose advising planters to establish regular systems of governing their slaves, including rules for overseers and guidelines for themselves. If such "constitutions" were often "more ideal than practical," they represented an attempt to bring order to a troublesome system.[5]

The focus in the management of any plantation was supposed to be the establishment of a proper relationship between master and slave. Southerners wrote frequently about the humanity of the Southern slave system, but on one point they would not compromise. The master's authority had to be absolute; the position of the slave, one of "unconditional submission."[6] John Stuart Skinner—hunter, planter, and editor—discussed the issue following a tour of Mississippi and did so in terms that most planters would have agreed with. Noting the lower South's reputation for the particularly harsh treatment of slaves, Skinner wrote, "The treatment of the slave there is such only as befits the relation of master and slave. Absolute, unqualified authority is asserted and exercised on the part of the master—The slave yields implicit obedience, and in return for it receives constant protection and paternal treatment. It is the only system compatible with the interests and happiness of both parties."[7] Southerners had a feeling for what social relations ought to be like. Actors in social roles had carefully and closely defined parts. The rules for interaction were well-known, and any deviation from those rules could lead to chaos. What was true in white society was no less true in the relationship of master to slave.

Social rules, stated or unstated, held personal and, thus, antisocial desires in check, for it was personal will—ambitious, selfish, and violent—that led to social problems. This was true in the relation of master to slave. For one thing, to let the slave have his way would be to undermine the whole system. Skinner made this point in his essay on Mississippi. "Whenever the authority of the master becomes qualified—whenever his dominion is relaxed, and the submission of the slave ceases to be absolute, the relation between the two loses its homogenious [*sic*] distinctness. The one is no longer master, the other no longer slave, in the sense and degree of absoluteness which produces uniformity of action and feeling between them." Where roles were well-defined and conscientiously observed, then there could be stability, and in stability lay peace. One writer even asserted that, "it greatly impairs the happiness of a negro, to be allowed to cultivate an insubordinate temper," not that he had ever asked, of course. Southern writers were assured that no one could live in a society, including that of the plantation, without a clear system of structure and order.[8]

The slave had to be kept in his subordinate place in the plantation order, and this could be done only through the use of some degree of corporal punishment, but the planter had to maintain his place in a plantation order, as well. He, too, could not give free rein to personality and passion, particularly in the inflicting of punishment on the slaves. In part the issue was a moral one, since passion should never be one's guide in any situation. It was also a practical matter: a whipping inflicted while one was in a passion could get out of control, and the slave could be seriously injured or killed. But the real issue here, as in other areas of life, was one of impression management, of putting one's best and most proper front forward in dealing with other people.

The slaveholder had to project an image of authority and responsibility, and nothing could undermine that image more than a display of passion. Southerners had a fairly clear picture of what an authoritative man was like. Self-command and command of others went hand in hand. The man who got in a passion with subordinates was the man who did not know his place, whether he were a parent, a teacher, or a slaveholder. One had to appear calm and self-possessed, in full command of himself and certain of his actions. All these notions came through in the recommendations of a committee of Alabamians for plantation procedures. Urging, in all matters, the use of reason instead of force, they also encouraged the most proper deportment on the part of the master. Thus they suggested that orders issued to slaves should always be given "in a mild tone," and recommended that the slaveowner "try to leave the impression on the mind of the negro," that any order given, "is the result of reflection."[9]

More than that, the passionate slaveholder would also appear to be the irresponsible figure of authority. Nothing could be worse, many authorities agreed, than to have a slave think "that he has been whipped not for his own benefit, but purely to gratify the . . . feelings and satisfy the rage" of the one inflicting punishment.[10] Revenge and personal gratification through violence were not looked upon favorably in any area of Southern society, not even in the management of slaves.

The plantation was supposed to be a system in which places were known and rules observed. Regularity and order were to be its main features. The slave's behavior was to be highly predictable and the master, in turn, was to be predictable in his own actions. Not surprisingly, then, Southern writers were consistent in claiming that the way to run a plantation was not through the use of severe and frequent punishment, but through the use of certain punishment. The plantation could work only as long as the slaveholder acted with "perfect uniformity" toward his slaves. This, according to most authorities, caused slaves to see that it was the "fault" that brought on their punishment, and not the caprice of the master. More than that, certain punishment was the only way in which one could ensure similar uniformity in the conduct of his slaves. Where an offence might be punished in one instance and ignored in the next, "the ill-disposed will always risk the chances of escaping punishment altogether."[11] Certainty of punishment made it unnecessary for physical punishment to be inflicted with severity; in most cases, writers assured their readers, it could prevent the need for any punishment at all. If the rules were "simple and well known" and the punishment of infractions inevitable, experience proved that "the amount of whipping done is very small, frequently months elapsing without a blow being given."[12]

Southerners answered the problems of plantation management in much the same way they answered all social problems: through an attempt to develop a fixed ideal form and image that would display the proper approach to a relationship. Most of the advice in the essays on plantation management had to do with the proper demeanor for a slaveholder to assume in the presence of slaves. "You must learn to manage yourself," R. S. Blackburn advised readers of the *American Farmer*, and the way to do it was through careful attention to manner: "a low tone of voice is recommended in speaking to negroes. This is a wise suggestion, as it must necessarily be attended with a *low tone of temper*."[13] The slaveholder, in other words, had to learn the proper manners no less than did the social aristocrat. Being a slaveholding gentleman did not come naturally.

One problem in all this was, many writers thought, the use of overseers or even black drivers in the day-to-day management of slaves. Drawn, it was generally believed, from outside the planter class, white overseers had neither the interest nor the background to prevent their being cruel to the slaves. Most of those who tried to guide slaveowners to proper management of their slaves made it clear that the overseer should have no discretionary powers of punishment. In the words of one who signed himself "Pee Dee," "Nothing is more common or more pernicious, than to invest your overseer with discretionary powers in inflicting punishment. Passion, prejudice, or ignorance often makes him abuse it. The negro does not go to his master for protection, for he will find none there, but must quietly submit to the despotic will of one but little his superior. It would be almost impossible to organize any regular system under such government."[14] Few writers were so hard on the character of the overseer as this "Pee Dee," but the belief that overseers had to be watched lest they harm the "system" of plantation order was frequently repeated by writers on the subject. Only those to the manner bred had much chance of maintaining order in this, as in all areas of human society.

Defenders of the South and its institutions, whether they wrote for public or private consumption, represented themselves in terms of that image of paternalism which recent historians have so carefully described. The slave and the slaveowner stood to each other "as protector and protected," wrote Thomas R. R. Cobb. The relationship was classically "patriarchal." The slave, like the planter, had to live in a hostile and violent world; but, unlike the planter, was unable to protect himself from that violence. It was, therefore, the duty of the slaveholder to provide protection, and such a role was the one in which slaveholders or their spokesmen most liked to describe themselves.[15]

This relationship received its most important expression in regard to the actions of lower-class whites. William Bolling of Virginia was only one of many planters who would rather lose an overseer than allow unnecessary, arbitrary whipping on his plantation, and, similarly, he was not at all unusual in prohibiting the patrol—those whites who policed an area looking for possible runaways—from coming on his land when he felt they had acted "cruelly" toward one of his slaves. Bolling was acting as many felt a slaveowner should. Planters were often advised to act protectively toward their slaves, to "give a willing ear" when the slaves had complaints about their treatment: "They will then look up to him as their great arbiter and protector in all difficulties, which will inspire both respect and confidence, and he will find them much more true in his interest than they are generally supposed to be." It was as protector, as a "father" that the slaveholder was to act in his role.[16]

The language of paternalism bore an important relationship to the use of violence on the plantation, a relationship emphasized by William Gilmore Simms' comment, in a letter to John Pendleton Kennedy, that "In fact our system is *not* slavery, but a relation between white & black not dissimilar to that of Guardian & Minor." The language of paternalism was more than just a convenience and as Michael Wallace has suggested, it represents a common language shift in American history that takes place when there is a need to legitimize violence. Violence being legitimate when parents use it to discipline children, it must also be legitimate, by extension, in the parallel relations of masters and slaves. But, given the special circumstances of Southern parents' understanding of corporal punishment, the use of such language becomes all the more important. It also signified reluctance, the notion that physical action was being undertaken only as a last resort and not in a way that would undermine the essential harmony of the master-slave relationship. Such language tied slavery in with some very deep concerns in Southern culture.[17]

The essays and advice on slavery published in agricultural journals and elsewhere in the antebellum South show a concentrated effort to make the institution conform to widely accepted ideas of an orderly social system. They were, of course, talking about slavery as it ought to be and not, perhaps, slavery as it existed, but, nevertheless, they tried to propose a way in which the institution could be made a consistent part of their culture. The regularity with which such essays appeared may be a measure, as well, of their having achieved only limited success, but these writings tell us much about the ideological requirements of white slaveowners in the Old South.

Yet if the essays on plantation management grew in part out of white ideological needs, they were also the result of the whites' inability to come to terms with the black people around them. White Southerners never "knew the Negro," protestations to the contrary notwithstanding. The issue was one of culture and economics, not experience, and it was a problem that went back to 1619, remaining unresolved by 1861 or even 1979. What Southerners did know was that anything worked best when it was carefully and observably ordered, and this was what the plantation management essays told them a plantation could be like. Thus the deeper intellectual and emotional problems of human nature could be, for the moment, set aside.

But the issues themselves would not go away, because white Southerners were never very clear as to the "nature" of Africans and Afro-Americans, and their confusions became particularly obvious when they had to face up to blacks' responses to violence and their capacity for it. Their confused confrontation with the problem of violence appeared occasionally in the essays on plantation management, but played an even more important part in the self-conscious defenses of slavery that began to appear shortly after the Revolution and that appeared more and more frequently as the antebellum period progressed.[18] Concentrating on what they saw as the redeeming or even ideal qualities of the slave system, pro-slavery writers, like the agricultural essayists, tried to bring order to a troublesome system, but the order they sought was intellectual rather than social. Their attempt forced them to discuss not only the nature of the African and Afro-American, but the nature of the slaveowner as well.

Southern writers, regardless of immediate interest, were all agreed that blacks needed discipline and that whites had to give order to every area of black life. The Negro, according to Edmund Ruffin, was "lazy, improvident, sensual, social and timid . . . always needing a guardian or a master to coerce him to exertion," and this pretty much summarized the official line on African and Afro-American character. In that fascinating mixture of environmentalism and determinism of which Southern polemicists were so fond—and which betrayed so much of their confusion—it was this conception of character that so fitted blacks for slavery.[19]

The famous, or infamous, debate over the biological, taxonomic relationship between blacks and whites is not a matter of concern here. Suffice it to say, as is well enough known, that Southerners of the nineteenth century assumed the inferiority of Afro-Americans as a given, however much they differed in their explanations for it, and derived from this assumption much of their defense of slavery. What was most important to them was that Negroes required white guidance to survive. Samuel Cartwright, a leading Southern racial theoretician, came up with the most ingenious notions along these lines when he posited a major difference between whites and blacks in terms of will or control. "The white man," he informed readers of *De Bow's Review*, "has an exaggerated will." By contrast, he declared, "The Nigritian [*sic*] has such little command over his own muscles, from the weakness of his will, as almost to starve, when a little exertion and forethought would procure him an abundance." And it was this, he concluded, that made slavery such an effective system of labor: "It is not the whip, as many suppose, which calls forth those muscular exertions, the result of which is sugar, cotton, breadstuffs, rice and tobacco. These are products of the white man's will, acting through the muscles of the prognathous race in our Southern States."[20] Cartwright's explanation was unusual, but it was merely a somewhat fanciful way of stating what many other Southerners believed: "The character of the negro is much underrated," one "H." had written twenty years earlier. "It is like the plastic clay, which, may be moulded into agreeable or disagreeable figures, according to the skill of the moulder."[21] Like the child, the slave was a creature of his environment who could be shaped in the proper way.

It was this "will-lessness" that, in fact, most clearly fitted blacks for slavery. Certainly, such a weak-willed people would be unable to govern themselves, except, as John L. Carey wrote, under "the strong rule of a single man." Southerners had, they thought, ample evidence from both Africa and the Caribbean to back up their belief—and they loved to collect negative reports from both places—so that they could claim to be dealing not in abstractions but facts about the African character. Facts taught that white government was necessary to black well-being. One cannot miss the truth of W. J. Cash's acerbic comment: "To have heard them talk, indeed, you would have thought the the sole reason some of these planters held to slavery was love and duty to the black man."[22]

The successful planter could, most writers claimed, keep order on the plantation without much resort to whipping or to outside authority. And this meant not only keeping the hands busily at work, but also keeping order within the slave community. Again, white control was necessary to black life, and plantation owners loved to write about their efforts toward fulfilling this duty. Much of the work of the planter involved, for instance, keeping the quarters in repair and keeping the slaves themselves neat and clean. Once the slaves had become accustomed to such order, one writer assured his fellows, "It is found seldom necessary to use the whip to enforce this rule," and another, in agreement, added that as conditions became neater, "from being a quarrelsome and unmanageable set, his people now assumed the harmony of a well-regulated family."[23] The language of the family described, again, the plantation ideal.

Social order, too, was important among the slaves. Most guides for the management of slaves included provisions against fighting among slaves and, to reinforce such provisions, recommendations against permitting slaves to quarrel among themselves and against allowing the use of profanity. Planters and overseers made sharp distinctions in regard to who could punish whom, all in an effort to enforce social order. They, if not the slaves, drew class lines in the slave community and urged that, for example, black drivers be "kept aloof" and superior to the other slaves as the only way of maintaining their status as representatives of the master. Other writers sought to strengthen order in the community by, for instance, punishing young slaves who insulted their elders or by making sure that a wife was never forced to strike her husband, "for fear of its unhappy influences over their future respect for and kindness to each other." There is so little that appears calculated or hypocritical in these various efforts; the main aim was simply to duplicate social ideals in the plantation community as a way of maintaining peace and stability.[24]

The difference between plantation and society was, however, that on the plantation there could be no thought of self-discipline. Discipline of any kind could be achieved only through corporal punishment. As late as the 1830s, though, many Southerners worried about the effects of whipping on the slave at least as much as they worried about its effects on themselves. According to one writer, there were many slaves "whom the whip would ruin,"[25] and many others urged methods other than the whip for enforcing discipline. Still there developed, certainly by the 1840s, an apologetics for whipping based on the assignment to blacks of further, but consistent, traits of character.

The irrepressible Dr. Cartwright summed up the argument for whipping when he wrote that slaves

> also require as a right when punished, to be punished with a switch or whip, and not with a stick or the fist. In this particular the ethnical law of their nature is different from all the other races of men. It is exactly the reverse of that of the American Indian. The Indian will murder any man who strikes him with a switch, a cowhide, or a whip, twenty years afterward, if he gets an opportunity; but readily forgets blows, however severe, inflicted on him with the fist, a cudgel, or a tomahawk. A remarkable ethnological peculiarity of the prognathous race is, that any deserved punishment, inflicted on them with a switch, cowhide, or whip, puts them into good humor with themselves and the executioner of the punishment, provided he manifest satisfaction by regarding the offence as [atoned] for.[26]

Cartwright's view was reinforced by other commentators. Chancellor Harper pointed out that while a whipping would be degrading to a freeman, it was not so to a black slave, and Alabamian Matthew Estes wrote that "the Negro feels no sense of shame or disgrace, on account of corporal punishment." Estes did add, however, that "whipping tends to degrade and ruin the Negro," an addition which reveals much about the dilemmas proslavery writers had to address.[27]

It is doubtful that Southerners convinced even themselves of the truth of their statements about corporal punishments, and Estes' contradiction shows how poorly apologetics fit with the slaveholders' own best instincts. It might be noted, as well, that few writers had anything at all to say about the fact that whippings hurt. The important thing, however, was to put their conceptions of black character into an intelligible, familiar framework, and their apologetics certainly did that. Not degraded by a cowhide, but unwilling to accept a caning, the Negro slave was the exact opposite not of the Indian but of the Southern Gentleman. White Southerners had their hierarchy of classes, and particular forms of violence were thought to be appropriate for each class. The Negro, like the middle- or lower-class white, and like the gentleman, had his place in that hierarchy.

Slaveowners tried to convince themselves that their efforts were successful. "The *paucity of crime* among the blacks, compared to the lower classes of the white population to the North, is remarkable," declared Thomas Cooper in 1835, and Southern spokesmen, both before and after, had similar remarks to make. The Florida eccentric, Zaphaniah Kingsley, went even further in claiming that, under a good system, blacks had become morally superior to most whites. Not a common position, Kingsley's nevertheless took one element of the proslavery argument to a logical conclusion.[28]

It is possible to read the proslavery delineations of a nonresistant, "Sambo" nature in the slaves as either accurate accounts of white perceptions or as wishful thinking on the part of slaveholders, and both such readings have been advanced by historians. But it is also possible to read such accounts as attempts to develop and define a category, cognitive and moral, into which black people could be placed. Constructed almost entirely out of negative attributes, the "Sambo" figure was a neat social category for slaves. Not only did it describe blacks' character in a comforting way, but it also defined white roles that cohered with role expectations in other areas of social life. Moreover, it gave the social relations of slavery an ideational base that must have been useful in a period when the institution was under attack throughout the Western world. In a status ordained by God, the Negro "is really in his highest and most favorable position as a human creature" as a slave in the American South.[29] The planters had done their duty and made a crop as well.

"They are," wrote future fire-eater John Quitman to a friend, "a happy, careless, unreflecting, good-natured race, who, left to themselves, would degenerate into drones or brutes."[30] The problem, as many Southerners saw it, was to know which result— "drones or brutes"—degeneration would bring. And if their Sambo stereotype should have led them to expect the former, their fears pointed all too clearly toward the latter conclusion.

George Fredrickson has written cogently of the dualistic black image that grew up in the white mind of the antebellum South,[31] and there is much evidence to support his characterization of Southern thought. The dualism was most apparent when Southerners tried to talk about the slaves' capacity for violence, for if the theoretically weak-willed slave existed only to be the muscular extension of his master's mind, the slave of real life often opposed and brought fear to his master, and was intractable in the face of the most drastic disciplinary efforts.

Some slaves, like some masters, simply had a "naturalistic disposition" for making trouble, and, as with whites, it was often a matter of youthful exuberance, easily handled, according to one authority by "pulling an ear, or a sound box." In their private papers, however, slaveholders frequently spoke of the slave who "rebelled" against the master's authority, and often enough the "rebellion" took the form of violence, threatened or real, against the slaveholder himself. Violence, stabbings, murders—all were recorded frequently enough to make it appear that, for many Southerners, what their discipline prevented was not their slaves' "degeneration," but their own murders.[32]

Slaveholders saw an undercurrent of violence in black life, at least in the absence of white control, and though they only occasionally faced up to that concern in their writings, it was often present in one form or another. Thus, for example, Peter Camden, after an exposition that was intended to be, according to its title, *A Common-Sense, Matter-of-Fact Examination and Discussion of*

Negro Slavery, concluded with the not-so-sober "NUT FOR ABOLITIONISTS TO CRACK/TERRIBLE MURDER OF A YOUNG GIRL BY A SLAVE," an account of a violent murder committed without the slightest provocation. It would be too much to suggest that all slaveowners lived in constant fear for their lives. The terror of a Mrs. Chesnut who, in her famous diary, revealed a steady and almost overwhelming fear of being murdered by her slaves, was hardly typical, but one can say that the "Sambo" image was less widely and less wholeheartedly accepted than apologists would have made it appear.[33]

For the most part, Southerners were able to contain their fear. Given their faith in order and procedure, they seem to have believed that they were safe. It is significant that Southerners could lucidly discuss the possibility that a slave should be able legally to act in self-defense against a master or overseer—although only a few white Southerners would actually have granted that right. Of equal significance is the extent to which some Southerners made an effort to preserve due process in the prosecution of slaves, even for crimes against their masters. So long as the system and the society were in good order, most Southerners claimed they had little to fear from the slaves.[34]

They were far more concerned about the character of blacks outside the system—whether this meant an unruly individual on the plantation, or members of the free Negro communities North and South. Matthew Estes was one of many Southerners who pointed to crime statistics to show how "our Slaves, in fact, are not guilty of one-tenth of the crimes which are committed by free Negroes at the North."[35] In the eyes of many, and with that usual confusing mixture of environmentalism and determinism, blacks in a condition of freedom were a particularly violent group, and they were, Samuel Cartwright theorized, much worse to each other when free than the whites ever could be to them: "In slavery the stripes fall upon the evil disposed, vicious buck negro fellows. But when removed from the white man's authority, the latter make them fall on helpless women and children, the weak and the infirm."[36] Crime and violence, no less than indolence, were the natural propensities of the black population, and would emerge once they were out of their masters' control.[37]

Southerners took black violence very seriously. Among free

Negroes, it was evidence of what could happen should white control ever be relaxed. Among the slaves, violence indicated a disastrous failure in the plantation order. Intellectually, moreover, any form of violent action by blacks was a stepping out of that character which whites had so carefully constructed in the interests of slavery. It was for this reason that resistance and rebellion were virtually synonymous in the white mind. Plantation order, like all order, was fragile and organic, and any deviation from the structure could only be seen as a challenge to the entire system.[38]

The brutal image of blacks came most clearly into play, however, not when Southerners talked about actual violence so much as when they worried about potential violence, particularly the possibility of slave insurrection. It is difficult to know the extent to which Southerners were possessed by a fear of insurrection; the evidence is, at best, ambiguous. But it was a problem they were aware of, and they had to address it in their writings on slavery.

The official line was to dismiss the possibility of insurrection. In part, proslavery writers assured their readers, it was a matter of the character of the slaves. There were, Edmund Ruffin claimed, certain "good qualities more prevailing in the negro race—of good disposition and kind feelings, docility, and obedience to the ruling powers, even in cases where they have been injudiciously and improperly and even unjustly treated."[39] This was why they had put up with supposed abuses in Africa, and this was why, by implication, they would never revolt against authority in the South.

In any case, the slave system itself was devised in a way that guarded against insurrection. For one thing, on a well-managed plantation there could be sufficient supervision to prevent "the concealment of all kind of roguery," including, one suspects, plotting and conspiracy. In addition, white Southerners liked to say that their own kindness prevented slaves from having even the desire to revolt. And by this they meant not so much that slaves were treated with lenity, because that, as Reverend Charles Pettigrew told his son Ebenezer back in 1802, "will not do it—it will make them worse." It was rather the giving of order and discipline to an otherwise unruly, weak-willed people that comprised good treatment, and it was that order which stood between slaves and insurrection. And, as usual, Southerners loved to contrast their own position with that of "the men of property in the North," where the lower classes were "too numerous to be controlled." Not a few claimed greater security for the South.[40]

Still, there had been episodes in Southern history that looked like slave insurrections, and there had certainly been revolutions in other parts of the New World in which slaves fought against masters. To explain such episodes, Southerners turned most frequently to that device which has served the region's ideologues up to the present time, the outside agitator. The Southern fear of outside agitation has been traced by historians with great thoroughness, and it need only be pointed out here that such an explanation was absolutely essential given the Southern need to impose intellectual as well as social order on their world.

Samuel Cartwright, making it perfectly clear why only outside agitation could ever cause slaves to revolt, repeated a common phrase when he said "There has never been an insurrection" of slaves against their masters. Referring, as usual, to "ethnical elements," particularly to weakness of the will, Cartwright wrote, "There have been neighborhood disturbances and bloodshed, caused by fanaticism, and by mischievous white man getting among them and infusing their will into them, or mesmerizing them."[41] Only outsiders, particularly abolitionists, had enough will for black freedom to bring about an insurrection, or so most writers claimed.

Abolitionists were not, however, the only ones who wanted to bring about insurrection. Some other whites had their own nefarious purposes, and the most significant insurrection scare in Mississippi was thought to involve not an abolitionist, but the infamous outlaw John A. Murrel.[42] Another and in its way more frightening source of discontent among the slaves was believed to be the presence of free Negroes in the region, and whites were convinced that few of them were respectable. At various times during the antebellum period agitation for the expulsion or enslavement of free blacks reached a high pitch among white Southerners.

Interference in the slave community would have meant a sundering of that order which Southerners liked to think existed in their society. And if little actual interference occurred on the plantations, the fact of abolitionism, of a calling into question of the social and moral order, certainly reminded Southerners of the ideal character of the system they had constructed. The proximity of abolitionism, wrote one border county slaveowner, "destroyed the tie between master and slave," for it encouraged doubt about that ideal social relationship upon which Southern notions of their own society depended.[43]

Southern spokesmen claimed that the main result of outside agitation was to increase their own policing of the slaves. William Drayton wrote: "In some of the states it has, indeed, been necessary to pass rigid police laws to protect the country from insurrections; but these laws remain a dead letter, until the interference of insidious and evil men excites and stirs up the slaves, and renders caution and severity indispensible for the safety of the master."[44] Propagandistically, of course, such words turned abolitionist efforts upside down by claiming that attempts to help the slaves, wrongly focused, actually made conditions worse for them. But there was more than propaganda involved, or, at least, the propaganda was framed in terms that any Southerner could appreciate. Order brought security, stability, and mitigated against violence. Interference and violence were inseparable.

Slaves, then, were blacks who were properly put in their place, in both an intellectual and a social sense, by slaveholders and Southern polemicists. Slaveowners claimed to expect no trouble from slaves in the absence of outside agitation, and they moved quickly when they suspected some such agitation was afoot. Abolitionists, or suspected abolitionists, were the most common targets of lynch law in settled communities, and if Southern whites like William Bolling, for instance, could see such acts only as a "disgrace" to the parties concerned, others, including many of the "best people" would join vigilance associations in an effort to preserve order in their communities.[45]

Still, nothing so challenged the Southern belief in the docility of slaves as a rebellion, actual or suspected, in their midst. The rumors that accompanied a rebellion were extreme in their portrayal of blacks, and the white response to any rebellion, rumored or real, was usually fairly extreme itself. To be sure, there was some effort following the major uprisings to preserve the semblance of due process in the treatment of those involved, but most historians seem to agree that the semblance was the main thing preserved. In the panic following such an episode as the Vesey conspiracy or the Turner rebellion, the most important thing to many Southern whites seemed to be getting the rebels convicted and out of the way before their influence could spread any further and before more trouble could occur, and many a conviction could be obtained on the most questionable sort of evidence. Beyond that, the most serious plots—whether, like Turner's, they led to violence, or, like Murrel's, they were more fantasy that reality—often led to an orgy of lynching and white violence against slaves, suspected whites, and even those whites who sought to stand for genuine due process in the affair.[46]

Whites, it appears, may have wanted to claim that their slaves were docile, but their actions attested to other feelings. It is not at all clear that they really thought of slaves as timid and weak. Indeed, personal responses to even the rumor of insurrection seem to have matched violent actions of summary "law" in their intensity. The slightest cause for alarm brought terror to many Southerners. One woman wrote that she was "almost deprived of my reason" when a plot was suspected in her neighborhood. Thus, for example, although the Nat Turner rebellion has generally been thought to have operated against abolition in Virginia in that crucial year of 1832, some Virginians argued from that insurrection in behalf of emancipation. In the words of legislator John A. Chandler, "Has slavery interfered with our means of enjoying LIFE, LIBERTY, PROPERTY, HAPPINESS and SAFETY? Look at Southampton. The Answer is written IN LETTERS OF BLOOD, upon the floors of that unhappy county." He was supported by at least one group of petitioners who looked at Southampton and declared, with a certain logic, "Tell us not of the labor & hardships we shall endure when our bond servants shall be removed from us . . . They are, in our esteem, less than the small dust in the balance compared with the burden of our fears and our dangers." And the petitioners, a group of "females of Augusta County," noted, in words much like those of the renowned Mrs. Chesnut, "we cannot know the night, nor the unguarded moment, by day or by night, which is pregnant with our destruction." The possibility of insurrection caused some Southerners to doubt the system's ultimate worth to them. It caused many more to fear for its security and, as is well known, fear of a loss of control over the slave population was a major stimulus to Southern overreaction in the sectional dispute leading up to the Civil War.[47]

If the thrust of any theory lies in the predictions it allows one to make, then the confusion of the Southern mind was shown nowhere more clearly than in the predictions Southerners made about blacks after emancipation—should the unthinkable occur. To take Quitman's dichotomy of "drones and brutes," Southern writers, regardless of what they had written before, came clearly down on the side of the brute. Forgotten were weakness of will, indolence, and all the other features of the good-natured "Sambo," because Southerners were sure that abolition could bring only race war, and they were not at all convinced that the whites would win.

Existing side by side with a Sambo incapable of assuming power was an African savage, given to acts of incredible brutality, or so many white Southerners believed. Slavery itself existed in Africa, after all, and involved "the most savage and cruel forms of slavery. The ingenuity of an enlightened intellect," wrote Thomas Cobb, "could scarcely, by effort, devise the numerous and skilful and horrid cruelties of these barbarian masters." If Africans could not assume the responsibilities of slaveownership, one could hardly conceive what they might do in war. John Fletcher wrote that Africans could kill and eat their captives "with a clear conscience," and Josiah Nott reported "on the authority of an eye witness" that Haitians did just that. "Revolutions, tumults, and disorders" were the "ordinary pastime" of freedmen, according to some experts, and they expected nothing else in their own region, should abolition occur.[48]

Thomas Jefferson had to "tremble" for his country when he acknowledged that in the desire for liberty the black man might well be the equal of the white.[49] Later writers from the South shared Jefferson's anxieties, which they voiced when contemplating emancipation. Blacks, they declared, would, if free, almost certainly claim political and social equality, and, should equality be denied, they would, to take William Drayton's scenario, "fall upon the whites, and wrest, or attempt to wrest, the political power of the Southern states from their hands, at the point of the sword. Whatever might be the final result—the immediate consequence would be a war of extermination."[50] Other Southern writers envisioned a similar sequence of events. The result of abolition must be, according to Augustus Baldwin Longstreet, "the whites must yield their territory to the blacks, and move away; or the whites must put the blacks, or the blacks must put the whites, to the sword."[51] The two groups could never live together in peace.

Nothing of the Sambo enters into these visions of the future, nor is there anything of that tie between master and slave about which Southerners had so much to say. Both the Sambo figure and that idealized tie were purely products of the slave system and of the rules that made up that system. John L. Carey said as much when he described a society after emancipation as one in which "one-half of the community is directly antagonistic to the other!"[52] Not a few Southerners, that is to say, sensed the artificiality of the system they had conceived.

The writings of proslavery Southerners were rhetorical in character, but this should not obscure one crucial factor in their presentation. Few proslavery writers addressed their efforts to the nonslaveholders of the world or believed that their writings would persuade those outside the system to a proslavery point of view. Rather, their writings were akin to preaching to the converted and were mainly concerned with exegesis, with interpreting the "facts" of slavery in a culturally acceptable way. The proslavery writers were their own audience.[53]

That they were presenting an idealized version of slavery is beyond question. Moreover, they were making the case that the ideal could become reality. "The treatment of slaves in this country, always lenient, has improved since the revolution," wrote William Drayton in 1836; and a quarter of a century later the Mississippi historian J. F. H. Claiborne made the same point when he said that as Southerners grew more secure with the institution of slavery, the condition of the slave would continue to improve. Things were getting better all the time for Southern slaves, and only abolitionist interference would arrest progress in the region.[54]

The questions are, then, why Southerners should have needed such exegetical works in defense of slavery and how the exegesis, as rhetoric, fit into the culture upon which it drew?

Robert Toombs, in one of those speeches proslavery ideologues liked to make before Northern audiences however little the hope for success, made a most revealing point. Like many proslavery polemicists, Toombs acknowledged the existence of evils in slavery:

> The condition of the slave offers great opportunities for abuse, and these opportunities are frequently used to violate humanity and justice. But the laws restrain these abuses and punish these crimes in this as well as other relations of life, and they who assume it as a

fundamental principle in the constitution of man, that abuse is the unvarying concomitant of power and crime of opportunity, subvert the foundations of all private morals and of every social system. No where do these assumptions find a nobler refutation than in the general treatment of the African race by southern slaveholders.[55]

Shades of transcendentalism on the plantation! For, indeed, Southerners were precisely the ones who assumed that "abuse is the unvarying concomitant of power" in society as in politics, and they had made that principle the foundation of both "private morals" and their "social system." Yet, when they tried to defend slavery, it was that "fundamental principle" which they had to reject.

There was, as we have seen, a certain tendency toward misanthropy in Southern social ideas that was far from the picture Toombs and other proslavery spokesmen painted of the slaveholder. The ideal of gentlemanliness through conscientious impression management which pervaded agricultural essays in Southern periodicals was far from consistent with the main themes in Southern culture than was a proslavery argument based on a human potential for good.

But more startling than a picture of innate goodness in the slaveholder was the assertion of innate docility in the slave. To achieve such a view, the proslavery writer essentially had to play off two important notions—normally complementary—against each other, and he did so with doubtful success. Usually, for Southerners, social distance and a propensity for violence were directly related. Violence was likely to be a part of any community whose members could not learn proper manners, and the farther one moved from the planter elite, the less chance there was that people could learn the easy amiability of a gentleman. It was far more likely that the natural man of passion, and violence, would assert his dominion. And yet, many apologists tried to proclaim the opposite of African slaves. Bondsmen, they argued, were more than willing to have the natural, passionate man subdued and put under the control of the slaveholder, and without a fight. The natural man was a creature of passion, but the natural African was docile, with no natural passions to be restrained or controlled. The argument was not really compatible with important Southern assumptions about human nature.

Proslavery writers tactily acknowledged this, and in their predictions rather than in their accounts of slavery, wrote in ways far more consistent with their own beliefs and far more honest with themselves. In these predictions they described scenarios that drew upon ideas and values which were frequently expressed in other areas of life. They acknowledged, certainly, the frailty of any system of order and discipline and their sense that order and discipline had to be artificial, imposed against the tendencies of human nature, and, by implication, against the desires of the slaves. Forced order was the only kind that could exist on a plantation.

Hence, the cultural problems posed by slavery were brought to a head by the issue of violence—not only the violence of the slaveholder, but also that of the slave. There was no way in which Southerners could reconcile the "brute" with the "drone," but, by the same token, there was no way in which they could reject the one image in favor of the other. The system of slavery demanded both.

The relationship between slave and master had to be a social, human relationship. Slaves had to be moral, sentient beings if they were to be capable of acting within an orderly system based on discipline and obedience. At the same time, slaves also had to be amoral, inferior beings if they were to participate in a relationship in which they were wholly subject to the will of the master. The problem was, of course, that each attribute had its drawbacks. The humanity of the slave might make slavery wrong. At the very least, it would entail those normal tendencies in human nature that troubled a few Southerners of the Revolutionary generation and that led their descendants to predict race war. On the other hand, when Southerners described the inferiority of the slave in terms of docility, they did so in a way that contradicted their most basic ideas about human nature. Amorality, weakness of will, and violence were too often connected in the Southern mind to make such a creature a comfort to have around.

In blacks, white Southerners created an image in which two exclusive categories of being came together. The enormous demands of the system of slavery served to insure that neither category would become predominant and to maintain an irreconcilable conflict in the Southern whites' image of their slaves. The literature of proslavery can be understood in terms of this serious cultural

problem. Southerners had to talk about slavery and slaves to themselves because of a need to reconcile the system with their culture.
They would never be able to do so, and they would produce more
and more polemic in the attempt. This is not to say that Southerners felt any guilt over slavery, nor even that they faced some kind
of pre–Civil War "American Dilemma."[56] It is to say that slavery
made intellectual and moral demands which, ultimately, could not
be met but which Southerners felt hard pressed to try to do something about.

It was because of their confusion about the image of the
blacks, too, that Southerners made the kinds of predictions they did
about the abolition of slavery. Lacking a clearly defined, unambigu-
ous image for blacks, they relied on a social role, that of slave,
which accomplished much the same thing that taboo does in other
areas and for other peoples—it removed Negroes from normal social contacts. Should that social role be violated, the result had
to be cataclysmic and wholly unpredictable. Even the weak-willed
could win.

Violence was, for white Southerners, more than a terrible fact
of life. It was a characteristic of social experience that, however
necessary, inevitably posed difficult moral problems. This was particularly true in slavery. Unable to trust themselves and forced to
reconcile the system with that mistrust, white Southerners were
even more worried about their slaves. They were so worried, in
fact, that they had to construct a characterization of the slave that,
some must have felt, was culturally invalid. Slavery did not determine the shape of Southern culture, but the slaveholders' attempts
to make slavery and culture compatible, particularly on the question of violence, were clearly aimed at a nearly impossible achievement.

6. Slavery and Violence
The Slaves' View

SLAVEHOLDERS tried to maintain that on a well-ordered plantation, the whip was rarely if ever used. Violence was subordinate to order, so far as they were concerned, and, according to their claims, a good master could minimize the use of physical "punishment" by imposing discipline and rules on the conduct of the plantation. Good order and good discipline made for a peaceful plantation community. Slaves themselves saw things differently.

The question of the slaves' perceptions of slavery, including the role they assigned to violence, is a difficult one to answer. Since much of the testimony on slavery was taken from ex-slaves, propagandistic intent and the passage of time clearly influenced much of the information. Still, the testimony of ex-slaves is not useless for an understanding of slave culture, and, to some extent, its usefulness is enhanced by those factors which have led many historians to suspect its validity. Ex-slaves, like all Southerners, described violence in terms of certain types of individuals and types of situations, but the lack of immediacy in their testimony gave ex-slave descriptions a formulaic quality. The conventions they relied upon to talk about violence were strict, and from them one can get a picture of that persistent set of values, ideas, and attitudes according to which they understood the violence in their lives.[1]

The various kinds of ex-slave sources—personal narratives, folktales, abolitionist autobiographies—all came together on the subject of violence. Matters of region, plantation size, even time, were irrelevant so far as basic attitudes toward plantation violence were concerned. Violence was an important influence on slave culture in the nineteenth-century South, and the basic attitudes toward violence were both consistent and widespread.

All the various ex-slave sources are agreed, moreover, that arbitrary violence was inseparable from the system itself. It was what made the institution work; it set the tone for relationships between slaves and Southern whites; and it set the tone, as well, for the quality of life led by those in bondage. Violence was one of the inescapable facts of life in slavery, regardless of the individual's attitudes toward the institution in general, and regardless of whether one actually suffered its effects. It was, in one way or another, the universal yardstick according to which the experiences of slavery were judged.

The South was, fugitive slave William Craft proclaimed in a letter to *The Liberator*, a "barbarous land of whips and chains!" and many others who experienced the institution of slavery first-hand agreed with Craft's assessment. Ex-slave Austin Grant, looking back on slavery time, remarked, "They didn' give us nothin, I tell you, but a grubbin' hoe, and axe and the whip," a connection which made the whip tantamount to hard work in the slave's life. Certainly, all slaves did not have the same bleak view of slavery that Craft and Grant expressed, but their sense of the ubiquity of the whip was common enough to form a major theme in what ex-slaves had to say about the institution.[2]

As slaveowners defended the slave system, its essence was rules. They professed to make slavery an extension of Southern society in general by creating a plantation work force governed by order and discipline. As blacks described how that system had worked, they saw mainly caprice and a lack of discipline in the actions of slaveholding whites. Some ex-slaves, to be sure, looked back to life on well-managed, relatively nonviolent plantations, but most saw such an experience as exceptional. However honest whites may have been with themselves in claiming that order was a chief characteristic of plantation life, blacks seem to have felt that impulse and passion were really in charge. This does not mean that either whites or slaves were lying. The question is not who was right, but how members of each group perceived the system.

The ex-slaves' impression of slaveowner caprice came in part from the lack of authority they felt in many areas of life. The problem of how to pace one's work, for instance, was an important element of this, and proper pace was always a matter of the master's or the overseer's judgment, not of any agreement between masters and slaves. "Slowness" was a major cause for whipping on most plantations, but the pace at which work was to take place seemed to be based on no consistent measure. Indeed, the essence of the ex-slaves' understanding of the nature of plantation life was to be found in the character of those masters who perversely disregarded the usual rules, or who seemed to behave as if operating with no consistent standards at all. Maggie Wesmoland summarized the view when she recalled of her own master, "I never did know what suit him and what wouldn't."[3] The problem many ex-slaves remembered was not that of sticking to rules; the trouble was that, whatever one did, it seemed impossible to avoid provoking the master into violence.

Ex-slaves talked about this problem in a number of ways. Some emphasized the inconsistencies in whatever rules there were. Others recalled receiving severe whippings for circumstances over which they clearly had no control. Still other ex-slaves described slaveholders like a Mr. Tabb, of Kentucky, who provided a teacher for the plantation so that his slaves could learn to "read and write and figger": he would, nevertheless, question his slaves on occasion, and, if they told him they had been learning to read, according to one, "he would near beat the daylights out of us."[4] Rules, in other words, never seemed to be fixed from the point of view of the slaves. If master or mistress wanted to use the lash, there was no protection for a slave to be found in rules.

No less than slaveholders, slaves developed a model for looking at the slave system. For the slaves, however, the use of violence had less significance for its function in keeping order than for its role in maintaining the power of the plantation owner, or the mistress, to control every aspect of slave life. Hence, most ex-slaves tended to recall the last symbolically, as it established a general authoritarian relationship rather than as a means of fixing punishment for specific "offences" against plantation discipline. That is, most ex-slaves who tried to describe the causes of violence talked less about its function than about the character of slaveholders. Such character was explanation enough for the violence of plantation life.

The main point of the ex-slaves' worst memories spoke to this concern. In every slaveholder, there was supposed to be a potential for violence, and slavery provided violent men and women with opportunities for exercising that potential. Hence, former slaves often remembered slaveowners for whom violence seemed to be its own reward. For some, it seemed, whipping was a mode of relaxation—exercise, or, if someone else actually did the work, a time to light up the pipe or to enjoy a drink. Fugitive John Warren even told of a master and overseer who gave a little of their brandy to the victim, to keep him going and to prolong their "fun."[5] Another master, John Thompson's, forced his slaves to whip each other, a practice which "seemed very amusing to himself and his children."[6]

Other ex-slaves talked about the causes of plantation violence in a way that further emphasized the arbitrary character of the violence and its roots, not in functional needs, but in the power of the master. For instance, many talked about the slaveholder who simply took out all of his—or her—problems on the slaves so that, as Louis Hughes remembered, the amount of whipping usually depended upon "the humor of the madam" rather than on the behavior of the slaves.[7] Others, of course, focused on a different sort of passion from that of anger. The association of violence with power and power with sex which has so captured the Western pornographic imagination and which loomed so large in the writings of Anglo-American abolitionists was often advanced by ex-slaves as they attempted to account for the violence of Southern whites. Most commonly, it was said that whites used the threat of violence to have their way with women, or they might offer sex as an alternative to the lash, once having found a pretext for whipping. But a very few people also recalled slaveholders who were genuine sadists, for whom the whipping of a stripped woman seemed to provide the greatest pleasure.[8]

Many of these sorts of events probably occurred, but, as remembered, they had symbolic importance as well in characterizing the master's desire for domination as the essence of the slave experience. To slaves, it seemed domination was desired by slaveholders largely for its own sake. Charlotte Foster, from South Carolina, was not unusual in replying vehemently to the question of why slaves were beaten, "Just because they wanted to beat 'em; they could do it, and they did."[9] This, in the opinion of many ex-slaves, was sufficient to account for slaveholder brutality and, moreover, it correctly summarized the position of the slave—available to be whipped, whether the beating ever occurred or not.

Much of the slaves' view of plantation violence was conveyed when they talked about its causes, but their impressions were no less clearly expressed when they talked about the act of violence as such. On the one hand, they emphasized its excessiveness. The one description which appears over and over again in ex-slave accounts and memoirs, in one version or another, was that slaves were whipped "until the blood ran," often to the floor or to the heels. Whether such whippings were common, the stories ex-slaves told usually bore out Louis Hughes's contention that "it was common for a slave to get an 'overthreshing.' "[10]

In addition, violence went hand in hand with helplessness as ex-slaves described the violent act. Just as they spoke of their subjection to pointless cruelty, they also emphasized the helplessness of their position when they described the mode of punishment on the plantation. The tying up of slaves in such a way as to render them totally helpless when under the lash was noted by most ex-slaves. They remembered vividly the ways in which slaves could be bound so as to make resistance or even relief from the blows of the lash impossible. The most common description was that the hands were bound and the victims strung up so that their toes barely touched the ground. A few even recalled an experience in which movement was rendered painful: one woman reported that her sister was held down by having her head put under a fence rail so that any movement when the whip struck her back would force the victim to choke herself.[11] W. B. Allen told of the victim who was hung by the thumbs for the usual whipping: "Then while still agonizing from the effects of the beating he had received and the torment of suspension by his thumbs, he was further tortured by having his wounds 'doctored' with salt and red pepper. Often strong men would tear their thumbs out at the roots and drop to the floor unconscious."[12]

The tying up was an important part of the punishment for ex-slaves, emphasizing as it did the extent to which they had had to submit their bodies, inevitably stripped, to the will of the master. The more grotesque postures imposed by the "buck" or "buck and gag" or the "Rolling Jim" could only have made things worse. It is no surprise, then, that J. W. Loguen once resolved to resist "punishment" solely out of a fear of being bound: "He was willing he should take him on the leg and whip as long as he pleased—giving him a chance to dodge the blows. But he firmly resolved not to be tied and whipped by a mad man, or any other man."[13]

That there were slaveholders who matched the types found in ex-slave atrocity stories is likely, although their typicality may certainly be questioned. Still, what was important about them was that they demonstrated, or at least the stories about them dramatized, the kind of violence slavery made possible, a possibility shown to even more striking effect in the accounts of ex-slaves who remembered that their own masters were not so bad. Those former slaves who wrote antebellum autobiographies in the cause of anti-slavery tended to emphasize their own victimhood or that of those they loved, but even those who were not beaten or who lived on plantations where whippings were uncommon had to face the threat. And some recalled, as well, the ways in which a nonviolent master could use a threat as effectively as the lash. Sam Kilgore, who had been held in Texas, summed it up:

> Dat place am so well manage dat whippin's am not nec'sary, Massa have he own way of keepin' de niggers in line. If dey bad he say, "I 'spect dat nigger driver comin' round tomorrow and I's gwine sell you." Now, when a nigger git in de hands of de nigger driver it am de big chance he'll git sold to de cruel massa, and dat make de niggers powerful skeert, so dey 'haves. On de next plantation we'd hear de niggers pleadin' when dey's whipped, "Massa have mercy," and sich. Our massa allus say, "Boys, you hears dat mis'ry and we don't want no sich on dis place and it am up to you." So us all 'haves ourselves.[14]

One cannot help but be impressed by the extent to which slaves on plantations with "kind" masters still knew about the brutality of the "next plantation,"[15] knew, that is, about the potential for violence in slavery even when they themselves looked back upon relatively peaceful times.

Ex-slaves, then, expressed a view of slavery which gave an important place to the violent slaveholder. He was, indeed, virtually by definition a violent man. Thus, when ex-slaves tried to evaluate masters, they did so less by whether one had used the whip than by whether the whip had been employed understandably. The good master could be many things, but he was not necessarily one who refrained from violence. He could well be like Solbert Butler's master: "He was good to 'em. An' he whip 'em good too!"[16] The ex-slaves described a model for slavery, in other words, in which violence and conflict were the core of what it meant to be a slave. It was not necessarily a model in which slaves viewed all whites as enemies, although some did feel that way, and more than a few looked back on the slaveholder with revenge in their hearts. For most, however, the nature of the conflict was more profoundly based in a perception of difference between whites and blacks, and a sense that whites were bent on demanding obedience by virtue of their ability to exert arbitrary power rather than through some rule-governed system of duties and obligations. Violence and power, not reciprocity, were the bases of slavery, as ex-slaves remembered it.[17]

Again, it would be a mistake to claim from this that either whites or blacks were set upon giving a false view of slavery. Masters and slaves need not have seen matters identically for the system to have worked. Indeed, the substantial gap, the contradictions between what slaveholders claimed slavery was like and what slaves perceived, may have operated functionally in support of the system. The slaveholders' ideal of order was clearly preserved in the vision of plantation life they propounded and, no doubt, believed. So long as they could see order in the system, they could justify it to themselves. By the same token, the slave's perception of caprice undoubtedly reinforced a belief that to be a slave was to be subject to the master's personal will rather than to a well-defined set of rules; it increased, that is, their sense of the power of the system and of the slaveholder, and made his authority seem greater. The disagreement between masters and slaves ultimately reinforced the system.[18]

In the final analysis, then, conflict and arbitrary rule dominated the memories of plantation violence expressed by former slaves. The whole thrust of such violence was, in their minds, to underline the slaveholder's authority. A perhaps apocryphal story from Georgia virtually summarized the ex-slaves' understanding: "One day a man gitting whipped was saying 'Oh pray master, Lord have mercy!' They'd say, 'Keep whipping that nigger God damn him.' He was whipped till he said, 'Oh pray Master, I gotta nuff.' Then they said, 'Let him up now, 'cause he's praying to the right man.' "[19] There was to be one source of authority in the slave's life, the master, and his "emblem," as Kenneth Stampp has rightly said, was the whip.[20]

A conflict model of master-slave relations emerges fitfully from the memories of those who were held in bondage. It appears in sharp relief in the expressive forms of slave culture, and most clearly in those which related most directly to the slave experience, stories of "John and Old Master." Although not collected until twenty to thirty years after slavery, the stories have a pattern to them that indicates a persistent tradition in structure and style. It is from this tradition that one can see something of what the slaves thought of their lives.

The wily slave "John" has often been described as a trickster figure who personified a slave belief that the weak could triumph over the strong. In fact, no such character emerges from the great number of stories about John that were told in the years after slavery. The figure who does appear in the tales admitted no sense of weakness in his dealings with whites—in fact, he asserted his equality with Old Master—and, often failing to triumph or, indeed, suffering defeat at Old Master's hands, John dramatized the continuing conflict that ex-slaves described in plantation life.

All the John and Old Master stories used conflict as the basis for their plots, but the variations on that single theme were several. John himself often initiated conflict by breaking obvious rules—stealing a pig, eating master's dinner—and sometimes used trickery to stay out of trouble. But it was not an unusual story in which John was caught by Old Master and, implicitly at least, punished for his deed.[21] Nor was it unusual for John to turn his trickery against the other slaves, as when he owed the receipt of a gift to having "cursed the master": "Thereupon two or three of the men went to the house and began cursing the master to his face, and he in turn gave each a handsome flogging. As soon as they could, they, of course, went for John to find out what he meant by telling them such a tale. His reply was, 'Yes, I did curse him, but I cursed him at the big gate.' "[22] No less significant, finally, were those stories in which Old Master himself outwitted and made a fool of John—playing "the Lord" to frighten a slave who prayed for freedom, or blacking his face in order to trap a thief.[23]

Those who told the stories did not judge them on the basis of who won and who lost. Old Master's wit was admitted, and stories of every sort seem to have been enjoyed equally. It was the situation that mattered in the stories, and the situation was one of constant conflict in which neither character could gain anything more than a temporary triumph over the other. Both John and Old Master would come back to fight another day.[24]

The stories did not question the existence of slavery. John rarely—never in the early stories—sought permanent freedom; nor was Old Master persuaded to make the offer. The situation of slavery was a given, and the stories demonstrated the playing out of conflict, between equals, within that system.

This conflict model, implicit in memoirs and explicit in such expressive forms as folktales, gave such a place to violence that many slaves simply accepted it as a price one had to pay for maintaining his own humanity. Canadian fugitive John Little was not alone in his determination that, as long as his master "could find whips, I could find back." One had to make the choice, and there are many stories of slaves who knew they faced a beating for going off the plantation, for instance, but who went anyway. One man who received such a whipping, for going to visit a woman on a neighboring plantation, recalled, "Some gal! Was worth that paddlin' to see that gal." Violence was a part of life—the ultimate fact of a social system based on conflict—and living with violence, not escaping it, had to be a goal in the slave community.[25]

This goal was usually approached, as is well enough known, by a heavy reliance on careful, even deferential behavior in the presence of whites—just as ritual deference may account for the frequent professions of devotion to "Old Master" in the interviews ex-slaves gave to Southern whites years after the fact. As W. B. Allen told an interviewer boldly, "No, sir, a Negro may be humble and refuse to talk outside his race—because he is afraid to—but you can't fool him about a white man!" The point, of course, was to play the sort of part that would minimize danger in dealing with whites. There is some evidence that children were taught the roles of slavery by their parents and by other slaves, and, it is clear, learning careful behavior for confronting whites was the most important thing many slaves felt they could do. Unpredictability in human relations, for slaves no less than Southern gentry, was answered by the careful masking of spontaneous response, and the fragility of relationships was clearly understood.[26]

Slavery, for slaves, was not simply a matter of what did happen on the plantation but, more, of their beliefs about what could happen. It was a system of potentials and the potential for violence made it work. Accordingly, the occurrence of violence did not have to be great. It only had to occur often enough to remind slaves of the kind of world they were living in. The writers of one of the classic studies of ex-slave narratives, *The Negro in Virginia*, missed the point when they claimed, "Just as front page stories of crimes in America do not prove that criminals constitute the majority of the American population, so it may not be assumed that all masters and mistresses took advantage of the opportunities for brutality that slavery threw their way." It was the presence of those opportunities that ex-slaves remembered most vividly.[27]

Herbert Gutman has rightly warned against the contention that slave belief and behavior involved little more than responses to master-sponsored stimuli. However, it seems equally clear that living with the presumptions of the slaveowner was the central problem slaves faced, and it had major impact on the development of antebellum Afro-American culture in the South. To be sure, other sources may have reinforced the slaves' view of the violence of slavery, but given the data, it is difficult to know how deeply these sources were rooted in Afro-American history and culture. The slaves' version of Protestant Christianity developed simultaneously with that of the Southern plain-folk and derived from the same sources. The view of humans as untrustworthy and potentially violent, the view according to which slaves understood their masters, would clearly have been reinforced by religious beliefs which emphasized the sinfulness and weakness of humanity—as black religion, like that of whites, appears to have done. There were major differences between antebellum black and white religions, but on this issue they seem to have agreed. Similarly, much of Afro-American folklore can be shown to have roots in slavery time, but much, too—including the John and Old Master stories—may go back farther in time, having developed in African societies and cultures. Here, too, may have been a source which gives some historical depth to the views of human nature and society implicit in ex-slaves' accounts of slavery and of the relationships of master to slave. But such sources as religion and folklore were strongly influenced by the setting of slavery. Insofar as attitudes toward violence were concerned, there is little reason to deny that the demands of the plantation were sufficient to account for the views slaves had of violence in plantation life.[28]

The power of plantation demands may be seen in the impact of the system on life within the slave community. This impact was felt, by many, as early as childhood. A large number of ex-slaves looked back on childhood with little but pleasure. They recalled having spent most of their time at play, frequently with the master's children, and many slaveowners did not allow children under fourteen to work. Their play was usually innocent, marbles and ball, although a few remembered having got into quite a bit of mischief around the plantation.

Ex-slaves juxtaposed the relative freedom of childhood with the painful realization of slavery. For some children, of course, the introduction to slavery came harshly when a parent was sold away. Samuel Boulware remembered the sight of speculators who would "cut de little nigger chillun with keen leather whips, 'cause they'd cry and run after de wagon dat was takin' their mammies away after they was sold." Few, however, had an introduction stranger— or more symbolic—than that of the ex-slave who recalled, "Me and old master's daughter used to play together all the time and one day we was out in the field playing together and old boss come out and slapped her jaws and give me a hoe and from that time on I was in the field." Nothing captured the experience of slavery more vividly than such an abrupt transition from free child to field hand.[29]

If some were impressed by a transition to slavery, others recalled an experience of slavery so total that even as children they learned what it meant to be enslaved. As Henry Bibb summed up his early life, "I was brought up in the Counties of Shelby, Henry, Oldham, and Trimble. Or, more correctly speaking, in the above counties, I may safely say, I was *flogged up*; for where I should have been receiving moral, mental, and religious instruction, I received stripes without number, the object of which was to degrade and keep me in subordination."[30] Many slaves reported a life of bondage almost from its beginning.

Some ex-slaves recalled having been put to work at an early age, and they remembered making the connection between work and violence quickly. Sally Williams was given light tasks at the age of nine and had to try hard "to escape the threatened whipping" should she get careless. Other children learned through pain to do the owner's bidding. Tom Hawkins, forced to tend a fire in his mistress's room all night, was frequently awakened by a pop on the head from her long stick when he tried to get a little sleep.[31]

Given their view of the slave system, it is not surprising that many ex-slaves also spoke of incidents in which children were made the recipients of sadistic violence on the plantation. John Thompson even reported that young children were used by his master to train the son in the ways of command. Calling the children out, the boy required them "to sweep and clear the yard from weeds &c., in order that he might oversee them. Then, whip in hand, he walked among them, and sometimes lashed the poor little creatures, who had on nothing but a shirt, and often nothing at all, until blood streamed down their backs and limbs, apparently for no reason whatever, except to gratify his own cruel fancy."[32] Whatever the generality of the event Thompson described, it put childhood in a familiar perspective, emphasizing the strength of the model for plantation life according to which many slaves lived.

If violence could enter into childhood, ex-slaves remembered the part it played in social relations within the slave community. Even some of this violence came from the planters, an extension of planter-control into the most intimate details of daily life. One ex-slave reported that people on his plantation were required to have a Saturday night bath, a requirement enforced by the whip. Even courting and marriage were governed by whipping. "If a boy went with a girl and spoke things that he shouldn't he could get a whipping for that," according to a former slave. And one slaveowner was remembered to have performed a not very touching marriage ceremony with the words, "Now, by God, if you ain't treatin' her right, by God, I'll take you up and whip you." There was little that slaves did which the master did not try to control.[33]

In this one may see, yet again, the contradictory perceptions of slavery possessed by masters and slaves. What the slaveowners tended to characterize as necessary discipline for an otherwise unruly people, slaves tended to view as unnecessary interference with their lives. In point of fact, neither understanding was entirely right, since slaves succeeded notably at constructing their own communities with their own norms. Operative here, again, was the ex-slaves' sense of what a slaveowner could do, and a belief that a master would do anything he set his mind to.

One job which slaveowners did perform that many ex-slaves remembered gratefully was that of preventing violence within the slave community. A few owners, to be sure, deliberately set their slaves to fighting, and if there were not many Thomas Sutpens among slaveholders, at least one former slave, Moses Roper, recalled how slaveowners could make their slaves engage in a free-for-all in a way that chillingly anticipated a similar scene in Ralph Ellison's *Invisible Man*.[34] On many plantations, however, there was no need for masters to bring about fights among the slaves, and the owners' efforts were directed in the opposite way.

Fights occurred in the slave community for a variety of reasons, and only a few ex-slaves agreed with the assessment, approved by Southern whites, that "slaves warn't civilized folks den—all dey knowed was to fuss and fight and kill one 'nother." In general, Eugene D. Genovese's comment that violence grew out of a "flash of passion" seems to account for most of the fighting that took place. Jealousy, a spur of the moment quarrel, or even fighting for fun were all causes of violence—and the problem of motives that so troubled elite white Southerners was not of much importance to those who talked about violence in the slave community.[35]

Quarreling and fighting were punished on most plantations. According to Northrup, the quarrelsome slave could receive some two hundred lashes—only runaways were liable for more. One ex-slave even recalled that the only cause for an automatic whipping on his plantation was fighting among the slaves. Slaveowners, everyone agreed, tried to keep down violence among their slaves, if not within themselves.[36]

Again, this sort of social control did not go unappreciated in the slave community; for many ex-slaves who looked back on the institution with some fondness, this was its main selling point. As Shang Harris told an interviewer, "Folks nuse to have fights sometimes at de frolics but dey didn't do no killin'. Hit ain't like dat now." And North Carolinian Anna Wright agreed: "Back den de bossman seed to hit dat dar wus law an' order in de town an' in de country too fer dat matter, an' dem wus de good ole days." Hence, many slaves contributed willingly to the maintenance of internal order. Slaveholders could count on parents to punish children who misbehaved and, conversely, parents appear to have occasionally taken recalcitrant children to the slaveowner for his brand of discipline.[37]

There are many questions about the slave community one would like to answer but cannot. The data are so heavily weighted toward descriptions of relations between whites and blacks that internal relationships, except in the broadest form, are difficult to pin down. Perhaps the best one can do is to propose some tentative characteristics of social perceptions on the basis of scanty information, and by analogy with what is known about Afro-American society in the South during later periods when blacks lived, to use Charles Johnson's phrase, in the "shadow of the plantation."[38] There were, to be sure, different forces at work on black communities in the postbellum South. But many patterns of later culture may be relevant.

Violence in postwar black communities, at least from about 1880 through the 1930s, conforms to descriptions of those "flashes of passion" that flared up among slaves. Disputes could start over the merest trifles, and fighting out differences when they arose was a normal, even an encouraged mode of action for children and adults alike.[39] One cannot be too sure how accurately data from years later reflect back to slavery time, but this picture from the postbellum period does indicate a view of social violence similar to that of the Southern plain-folk. Violence, where it could safely be exerted, could solve problems.

Certainly, slaves perceived such a use of violence on the part of the slaveholders. Within their own communities, however, the sources of that view lie in perceptions of others shared by all Southerners. Slaves had reason to feel the insecurity of affective ties. This does not mean that they failed to feel strongly for friends and family members. Their affections were deep. Nevertheless, such ties could not have provided the sort of refuge from a hostile world they gave to planters simply because the ties themselves were so vulnerable to external forces. Slaves could build communities, but they could not count on achieving stability in whatever they built. Frustration was inherent in community life.

Violence in the slave community may have been, in part, a deflection inward of hostility toward whites and white presumptions.[40] It may have been, as well, the product of the sort of mistrust of other people that was bred by the unpredictable conditions of plantation life, a mistrust manifested by a readiness to fight. One finds such mistrust in a fairly uncomplicated form in ex-slaves' attitudes toward whites. It is hard to see in their accounts of slave communities largely because of the focus of much of the data.

A model for conflict and mistrust in Afro-American social relations does, however, emerge from their folklore. To the extent that folklore is conservative, conveying persistent and pervasive ideas and feelings, it can tell us something at least probable about long held social views. Afro-American folklore was imbued with conflict in its presentation of all social relations. The actions of "John" against his fellow slaves in such a story as "Cursing at the Big Gate" certainly described a situation in which trust was absent, but one sees a similar theme in most Afro-American folklore, from religion to animal stories. Early blues songs, for instance, presented an image of relations between men and women marked by hostility and mistrust, and Afro-American bad-man heroes likewise portrayed a misanthropic perception of society. One must be careful about trying to understand the nineteenth century from twentieth century data. Still, the consistency of themes of conflict across genres and the fit of such themes to the scanty evidence on violence in the slave community may help us to understand something of the kind of society in which that violence occurred.[41]

Above all, the character of violence as it was usually described as having occurred in the slave community indicates that the same reliance on careful behavior with which blacks approached whites did not exist in relationships among blacks. One can see in this community setting the kind of direct approach to difficulties that marked plain-folk life. The evidence is sketchy, to be sure, but its tendency is to show a very different approach to social relations among slaves from that with which they confronted the white world. Slaves must have lived in two different settings, shifting their actions according to whose presence they found themselves in.

Violence within the slave community was based on a different behavioral code from that which governed relations with whites. Both codes were there, but some slaves probably leaned more toward one than the other, however skillfully they could switch their behavior back and forth. When switching failed, however, some slaves took direct action against the main source of difficulty in their lives, the slaveholder. There was some ambivalence toward these resisters in the slave community. Slaves who valued order remembered the resister, especially the runaway, as a peculiarly vicious type.[42] Most slaves did not, however, share such a negative view, and the opinions they did hold can be understood only in terms of their sense of the totality of the slave system.

The "insubordinate" slave was a dangerous figure to whites on any plantation, one who could inspire others to imitate his challenge to the master's authority. Because of this, ex-slaves recognized how hard masters worked to mobilize sentiment against such a figure. Christopher Nichols, who escaped into Canada, told of how, when a slave ran away, everyone else on the plantation was put on half allowance until the fugitive returned. Others recalled that slaveowners used to scare black children with the threat that a runaway would seize them if they did not behave.[43]

In spite of such efforts, many ex-slaves reacted proudly to the resisters who had been among them. Even Henry Clay Bruce, who condemned the "hard character" of many resisters, could also put into a class of "superior blooded slaves" those "fighting fellows, or those who knew when they had discharged their duty, and by virtue of knowing this fact, would not submit to any kind of corporal punishment at the hand of their master, and especially his overseer." The slaves, by Bruce's account, developed an ethic toward violent action that—like the slaveholders' own professed ethic—related violence to desperation and that also placed great value on personal independence in a world that made such independence difficult. Other ex-slaves would have agreed with Bruce's views. J. W. Loguen's mother was remembered as a woman who, whatever she had to endure from her master, fought all comers, "white or black, male or female," if they acted against her in a way that she felt was contrary "to her own estimate of rights and wrongs." Joseph Badgett of Arkansas also remembered his mother with pride because of her willingness to face the whip rather than compromise: "She was whipped because she was out without a pass. She could have a pass any time for the asking, but she was too proud to ask. She never wanted to do things by permission."[44]

Former slaves, in their reminiscences, counterposed their essential independence as human beings to a system that aimed at total control over them. If, to many, this simply meant that slaves had had to learn to live with whippings, to others it had meant the necessity of resistance, in some way, to the slaveowner. "Resistance," George Rawick has suggested, "flowed from the network of informal organization of that slave community and assumed forms that took their meanings from that community." By and large, this meant that resistance on the plantation was conservative and individualistic, confined to asserting one's own unwillingness to submit to the efforts of the slaveholder to establish total control.

At the same time, it also meant that few people described nonco-operation as anything like political resistance to the slave system.[45]

The most common form of resistance was also the simplest. Many slaves who were normally deferential, and who usually tried to do as they were told, would not let anyone whip them. Their resistance was an individual matter, frequently growing out of little more than exasperation over continued punishment. Much of this resistance was a matter of impulse, a spur-of-the-moment decision by one who simply wanted no more whippings, although a few slaves were not whipped as a matter of course on the plantation. Only occasionally would a slave plan ahead. One who did was Lucendy Hall, whose mistress had the habit of hitting slaves on the head with her fist: "One day the slave woman filled her child's hair with pins, heads down, points up; when the white woman hit the little mulatto slave girl, her fist was filled with pins."[46] Such pre-meditated, imaginative resistance was, however, rare among slaves.[47]

There was precious little in the way of collective resistance to slavery, and that, too, was frequently a matter of impulse. There were, for example, some brawls between patrollers and slaves. Occasionally, too, slaves could count on other slaves to come to their assistance in fighting with the master or overseer—although, given the sanctions, it was best not to expect too much. The most elaborate form of group resistance usually came in playing some sort of trick on the patrollers. Sam T. Stewart, of North Carolina, recalled that since the "patterollers" came to his plantation every Saturday night, the slaves had an opportunity to set a trap by stringing grape vines across the road. "Then we would run from them. They would follow, and get knocked off their horses." Such trickery, whether malicious in intent or not, obviously posed little threat to the system as a whole.[48]

The conservative character of slave resistance was consistent with the more general view of the plantation system. According to some ex-slaves, any show of independence was most likely to be counterproductive. W. B. Allen remembered that, "Sometimes a stripped Negro would say hard things to the white man with a strap in his hand, though he (the Negro) knew that he would pay dearly for it; for when a slave showed spirit that way, the master or overseer laid the lash on all the harder."[49] The most one could expect, so Allen felt, was the opportunity to vent some anger.

In any event, according to many former slaves, slaveholders

were determined to do their whipping, whatever it might take. One particularly determined master, it was said, was unable to whip a strong woman on the plantation, so he simply waited until she was confined with a pregnancy and had at her then. Other masters compelled slaves to help them, and one particularly enterprising slaveholder not only got a gang of helpers, but also tricked a vulnerable old man into getting drunk enough to be taken without a fight.[50]

Even those who did feel there was something to be gained made rather modest claims for the efficacy of resistance. Perhaps the greatest were made by J. W. Loguen who claimed, after himself resisting a beating, "Should all slaves, or any considerable portion of them manifest the same dignity and spirit, their masters would succumb to their manhood and give them freedom, or treat them justly—which, in effect, is to free them." This kind of freedom within slavery was about as much as any ex-slave ever claimed for resistance, and most thought it brought them far less. For a great many, resistance was simply the only way of getting "shut of the whip," and that only for themselves. That resistance should work at all was less than certain. As one fugitive said, "If they find a man determined and resolute not to be whipped, they will let him alone: but in other places, they will do it any rate."[51]

Resistance, given the nature of slaveholders, was uncertain, so that many slaves probably engaged in it out of a sense of having nothing to lose. John Thompson finally became so tired of whippings from the overseer that he told his master, "You alone have the right to correct me, sir. Had you been made acquainted with all the facts in the case, you would not have had me whipped so; and if the overseer strikes me again, I will kill him and be hung at once, that there may be an end of me." Many ex-slaves remembered people who would "just as leave be dead as to take the beatings," and there are stories of those who, in fact, made just such a choice.[52]

When slaves resisted punishment, then, they had to do so with a full recognition of the strength of the institution. It is a measure of that recognition that many slaves who ran away sought nothing more than to "fall into the hands of a better master." But there was, in addition, a recognition that given the discrepancy of resources between slaves and slaveholders, there was little hope for a total overthrow of the system. As Frederick Douglass wrote in describing a thwarted escape attempt, "The fact is, I never saw much use of fighting where there was no reasonable probability of whipping anybody," a statement which might be taken as a paradigm for most slaves' beliefs. The only way to get away from slavery was to get out of it altogether, and many, like Douglass, chose that as the ultimate form of resistance.[53]

Slaves may not have renounced their humanity, but most sought to adjust, in as peaceful a way as possible, to the demands of the plantation system, for that was the only way to minimize violence. A few slaves, however, did not make their peace with slavery. Some escaped to the North where they became active and eloquent spokesmen for the freedom of those left behind. Others, refusing to leave the South, actually attempted the violent overthrow of the system. The question of what made some of those in bondage look for its complete demise and feel that they could play some part in bringing about the end is not easy to answer.

Frederick Douglass was among those who sought an end to slavery. Born and brought up a slave in Maryland, under shifting circumstances, Douglass escaped as a young man to the North, where he became one of abolition's most articulate spokesmen, and an able advocate, as well, of other reform causes. Douglass's own perceptions of slavery were not, perhaps, typical of those who hoped to bring an end to the institution, but they do provide insight into what it took for an individual to come to accept the possibility that such an end could be accomplished.

Douglass once expressed, in a speech in England, his own view of the process of coming to see the need for freedom:

> When I was treated exceedingly ill; when my back was scourged daily; when I was whipped within an inch of my life—life was all I cared for. "Spare my life," was my continual prayer. When I was looking for the blow about to be inflicted on my head, I was not thinking of my liberty; it was my life. But, as soon as the blow was not to be feared, then came the longing for liberty. If a slave has a bad master, his ambition is to get a better; when he gets a better, he aspires to have the best; and when he gets the best, he aspires to be his own master.[54]

Douglass was mainly concerned here with arguing that slaveholders had to be oppressive for slavery to succeed, and this account hardly accords with his own autobiography. But he does seem to have been accurate in one important regard. Slavery, in and of itself, was not enough to make slaves try to bring about freedom; rather, the desire for freedom seemed to come more from a perspective on slavery that looked beyond the immediate difficulties of plantation life.

Literacy, in Douglass's case, had much to do with his alienation from slave life. Learning to read from an indulgent mistress, Douglass developed his skills through self-education in the *Columbian Orator*, a book which contained, among other things, a dialogue on slavery, as well as classic addresses on "the rights of man." From such a background Douglass developed what might be called a detached view of slavery, an ability to see the institution in terms of its relations to abstract principles and to human dignity. Douglass was able to generalize, to say, "It was *slavery*, not its mere *incidents* that I hated."[55]

Douglass saw, above all, the inevitability of a large gap between what he felt he could be and the life he would have to lead as a slave. As he wrote in his famous open letter to his former master, Thomas Auld, "The very first mental effort that I now remember on my part, was an attempt to solve the mystery, Why am I a slave? . . . When I saw the slave-driver whip a slave woman, cut the blood out of her neck, and heard her piteous cries, I went away into the corner of the fence, wept and pondered over the mystery."[56] All slaves experienced sadness, or rage, or bitterness when seeing or undergoing violence. What made Douglass different was his recognition that violence should not be a normal mode of behavior in human society.

Others who rebelled against the system brought similarly formed perceptions to their experiences. Nat Turner, probably the best known rebel, spoke of his own appropriately miraculous literacy in explaining his role in the revolt he led. His direct reading of the Bible—not filtered by plantation evangelism—probably informed those messianic revelations leading up to his revolt. William Wells Brown, who became an active abolitionist, reported only rudimentary learning while a slave, but he served under a great variety of employers—working for a time on a steamboat—which considerably broadened his experiences beyond the world of the plantation.[57]

Such a breadth of experience was not, perhaps, a necessary condition for desiring abolition, but it certainly widened the "prodigious chasm between what he was and what he aspired to be in this, the only life he had" that Stephen Oates has spoken of with regard to Nat Turner. It did so by increasing and making more significant one's aspirations by giving him a vision of alternatives that other slaves simply did not have. Moreover, the element of direct experience was of crucial importance. It was not enough to imbibe the notion of freedom from a slave preacher—as Turner and Denmark Vesey learned when trying to gain recruits to their cause. To experience the alternatives first hand, to see them as Brown did, or to have the direct experience of reading for oneself the message of freedom could only have made the possibility of another sort of life seem more real.[58]

People like Douglass, or Turner, or Brown, or Vesey, were unusual; they certainly thought so themselves. Douglass owed his own distinctiveness to the fact that very few slaves "were not held in awe by a white man," to the efficacy, that is, of oppression. Despite all his feelings of empathy for those still enslaved, he could not get away from the sense that, even with those who had become free, there were "marks of slavery in their tempers and dispositions" no easier to eradicate than the marks on their backs. Such a sense of superiority was shared by insurrectionaries including Vesey and Turner. Vesey, for example, had little patience with those who refused to follow him, telling some they deserved to be slaves. Turner referred to his own "uncommon intelligence." The power of the slave system was not lost on those who sought to overthrow it. They shared that perception with all who were slaves and acknowledged, too, that it would take someone exceptional to do anything about it.[59]

Insurrectionaries and abolitionists were, in the final analysis, individuals who aspired to be more than slaves, and thus felt the limits of slavery with particular poignancy. The literate man who could contrast his own condition with the worlds he explored by reading, was particularly unfit for slavery. A freedman, like Vesey, who nevertheless had to confront discrimination after achieving freedom and who even faced slavery itself since his wife and children were slaves and were often kept from him, was not less aware of the gap between hopes and reality.[60] A man whose ambitions were formed outside the slave system was likely to grow increasingly dissatisfied with the limits it placed upon his life.

Much has been made of the religion of the slave insurrectionaries, in particular, and indeed both Vesey and Turner were religious fanatics. But the main thing which religion did for those who hoped to get out of the system, or to bring it down, was to provide them with a ground for believing that they could succeed, that the fight could be won. Sharing with most slaves a sense of the totality of the system, even the most ardent revolutionaries felt a need to call on a higher power, a sense of divinely ordained destiny, to justify their belief that the revolution would succeed. In the short run, moreover, it was not unusual for insurrectionaries to claim protection from physical harm. A slave who confessed to conspiring to revolt in 1812 informed his captors that a gifted fellow slave would "conjure me clear" so that he could safely go about the work of killing his master, and the plotters who joined with Vesey included one Jack, "who could not be killed." Insurrectionaries thought the system could be destroyed, but they looked beyond that system—even to conjure or providence—for the force that would tip the balance in their favor.[61]

The revolutionaries—Prosser, Vesey, Turner—sought an immediate and violent end to slavery. Others, those who had made their way to the North and joined the abolition movement, looked for a more peaceful solution as long as they thought such an approach might work. Abolitionists like Douglass, stationed in the North, looked for emancipation to come of its own accord, "trusting," as Quarles has said, "to what they conceived as the slow but inevitable operation of religious and equalitarian principles." But people faced with an institution like slavery have been known to lose patience, and, more and more, as time passed, moral men, including Douglass, would come to conclude that a violent system had to be brought to a violent end.[62]

Frederick Douglass recognized, from the beginning, that slaveholders were not going to be persuaded, on moral grounds, to emancipate their slaves, but he also believed, for much of his early career, that moral force exerted from the outside would be sufficient to bring about the end of the system. When, for example, in the National Negro Convention of 1843, Northerner Henry Highland Garnet proposed a resolution that would have urged Southern slaves to revolt, Douglass, joined by William Wells Brown and others, opposed the resolution on the grounds that "there was too much physical force" in it. Douglass believed, as he told a British audience, that "slavery shrinks from the light," and that by exposing its realities to the outside world, sufficient force of opinion would be brought to bear to end the institution.[63]

Douglass's dawning understanding of racism, more than any other thing, led him, however reluctantly, away from his gradualist views. And what his understanding chiefly involved was the recognition that, however much he stood as living proof of the invalidity of white assertions of black inferiority, that proof was unlikely to convince any Southern slaveholder of his wrong—nor was it likely to have much effect on Northern whites, for that matter. Whites preferred to see their stereotypes fulfilled, Douglass came to realize, and those stereotypes would be fulfilled regardless of what any black man or woman might accomplish. "Properly speaking," he wrote in his newspaper, "*prejudice against color* does not exist in this country. The feeling (or whatever it is) which we call *prejudice*, is no less than a *murderous, hell-born hatred* of every virtue which may adorn the character of a *black man*."[64]

Douglass's ability to generalize had led him to see slavery and its abolition in moral terms. His long experience had brought him back to the recognition of white unity which many ex-slaves perceived, and which would inform his own autobiography. More than that, it had led him to a belief that violence, not morality, was the language of American race relations. Slaveholders, he told a Free-Soil convention, "not only forfeit their right to liberty, but to life itself," and only a decade or so after he had begun his work, he despaired of a peaceful abolition to slavery. Morality was not enough, he editorialized: "One might as well hunt bears with ethics and political economy for weapons." And a year later, he would conclude, "The only penetrable point of a tyrant is the *fear of death*. The outcry that they make, as to the danger of having their *throats cut* is because they deserve to have them *cut*." The man who, seventeen years before, could not approve of Garnet's call for slave insurrection, was to make John Brown his saint.[65]

Douglass's was a dawning awareness. It took him over a decade to achieve it. But it was built on perceptions that many slaves, if not pacifistic Garrisonians, shared. As Loguen wrote to William Lloyd Garrison, "I am with you in heart. I may not be in hands and head—for my hands will fight a slaveholder. . . . I am a fugitive slave, and you know that we have strange notions about many things."[66] One of those "strange notions"—and one which even nonfugitives with a fondness for old master agreed with—was that there was a massive potential for violence within slavery and that conflict, not moral principle, gave the system its form. Only a few felt that they could do much about it, but they knew that whatever they did had to recognize that central, pervasive quality of conflict that made slavery work.

Stephen McCray, who had been a slave in Alabama, was asked to evaluate slavery. "Every time I think of slavery and if it done the race any good, I think of the story of the coon and the dog who met. The coon said to the dog, 'Why is it you're so fat and I am so poor, and we is both animals?' The dog said: 'I lay round Master's house and let him kick me and he gives me a piece of bread right on.' Said the coon to the dog: 'Better then that I stay poor.' Them's my sentiment. I'm lak the coon, I don't believe in 'buse."[67] Violence, to McCray as to so many former slaves, was the meaning of slavery, and no amount of good treatment from a slaveowner could blunt that central fact of their experience. What rewards there were in the system were transient and tempered by the knowledge of what lay just below the surface. To be sure, not all slaves were Stephen McCrays, or Frederick Douglasses, or Nat Turners. Many no doubt constructed a satisfying life within the system. But few could ever evade that central violent tendency which, everyone knew, was slavery's core.

MOST OF THE VIOLENCE we have looked at earlier in this study has been interpersonal violence—dueling, fighting, even, to a degree, the violence of the plantation. The violence of war poses very different sorts of questions since, in general, war is thought to represent a legitimate function of the state, a form of collective physical conflict which does not offend the norms of any but political or religious pacifists. Indeed, one may distinguish between violence and force on precisely such grounds. One may ask, however, the extent to which people in the antebellum South made such a distinction and the extent to which, by contrast, their understanding of the violence of warfare cohered with their understanding of violence in general. The answer is somewhat surprising, given the reputation of the Old South—and the New—for its martial spirit.

The question of a Southern "martial spirit" has interested historians and essayists since before the Civil War. The image is well enough known. Southerners, enchanted with notions of chivalry and familiar with the novels of Sir Walter Scott, adopted this cavalier mode as their own, and like the knights of old, sought glory through military exploit. Fond of military trappings in time of peace, they found true honor in time of war when, rich or poor and regardless of cause, they answered the call to arms.[1]

Many antebellum Southern spokesmen accepted the notion that the South had a special fondness for the military, at least so far as entering the profession was concerned. "The people have a natural military character," wrote one, "and the conspicuous rank which their officers have usually taken in the several wars in which the country has been engaged, has shown that this spirit needs nothing but proper preliminary training to ensure the most permanent and wholesome efforts." Character was an adequate explanation for this 1842 writer, but other commentators had more studied reasons to account for the military spirit. D. R. Hundley, for example, harked back to a notion that had been accepted in one way or another since the time of the American Revolution when he wrote than landownership led the citizen of the agricultural South to feel "an interest in the permanence of his country's institutions," and thus a readiness to defend them.[2] For George Fitzhugh, the martial spirit was a product of the slave system and the peculiar social and "racial" position of the Southern gentry. "A master race," he assured readers of *De Bow's Review* on the eve of the Civil War, "improves upon itself, and practices as severe a drill as it subjects its inferiors to." He continued, "The gentlemen of the South are better horsemen, better marksmen, have more physical strength and activity, and can endure more fatigue than their slaves. Besides, they have the lofty sentiments and high morals of a master race, that would render them unconquerable. Their time is occupied in governing their slaves and managing their farms—they are slaves themselves to their duties, and have no taste for that prurient love of licentious liberty which has depraved and demoralized free society."[3] A social system which produced a conservative, well-disciplined elite was one which also produced a martial people, or so Fitzhugh argued.

There were, moreover, elements of social life which betokened a martial spirit in the Old South. Certainly, the apparent love of military titles among Southern men would seem to indicate a military tone to society. The number of colonels and captains in the Old South was staggering, and, once one had achieved such status, the use of the title outside of military contexts and in ordinary correspondence was expected. In addition, the symbols of chivalry caught the fancy of quite a few Southerners. They referred to themselves as "the chivalry" in their polemic, and even staged mock tournaments—jousting at rings rather than people—complete with the trappings of bygone days. More prosaically, there was a love of military attire, and of the flashiest sort, that appears to have affected even the most conservative gentlemen.[4]

The trappings of a martial spirit, and a rhetoric of chivalry, abounded in the Old South. It was, to be sure, a stylized militarism for much of the antebellum period, but there is no doubt that it was a spirit which, in capturing the imaginations of many young Southerners, led quite a few to the battlefield when the opportunity arose. Young James Lawson Kemper, possessed of dreams of glory, was one young Southerner who hurried to Washington when the war with Mexico loomed in hopes of receiving a commission. And, as an officer on his way to the action, he reported that at the first intimation of battle the air was filled with "valorous vaunts and some of the tallest talking" from the Southern troops. Of another Southerner, albeit a Northern immigrant, it was said, "The battlefield and its glory, the clangor and the charge rose up like a gorgeous pageant to dazzle his imagination," and this Mississippi fire-eater, John L. Quitman, was consistently drawn to military adventure, whether at the behest of his government or without his country's approval.[5]

Still, as John Hope Franklin has pointed out, the martial spirit was not always a part of the Southern reputation. New Englanders worried about the South's willingness to fight in the American Revolution, and, in the War of 1812, even though Southern Congressmen deserved their reputation as War Hawks—and even though New Englanders threatened to secede due to opposition to the war—Massachusetts supplied more recruits than Virginia and the two Carolinas combined. As late as the eve of the Civil War, Southerners felt called upon to respond, in one way or another, to aspersions cast on the Southern will to fight.[6]

Moreover, however much Southerners resented Northern aspersions on their military history, they too had misgivings about their society's ability to wage a war. Throughout the 1850s, writers from the region expressed the fear that, should the South be forced into war with the North, the people would be unprepared to mount a defense. As late as 1860, Virginia leader Nathaniel Francis Cabell would confide that "we must arm & discipline our people, nor must the Military Spirit ever again be allowed to become dormant as in time past," implying that the South had been something less than a martial society. If many Southerners approached the Civil War convinced of the South's military superiority, at least in terms of spirit and talent, others were not sure that the talent had been developed or that the martial spirit would be lively enough to carry the day.[7]

To the extent that there was a Southern martial spirit, it was late in developing and, even then, fraught with inconsistencies.

Most historians, noting the outsized proportion of Southerners in the Mexican War, have dated the tradition to the 1840s or 1850s, but even then one may find reason to question its existence. However true it was that Southerners dominated the army in Mexico, outnumbering troops from the free states by almost two to one, according to one contemporary account, Southern men hardly flocked to do battle. In some counties of Virginia, for example, efforts to raise companies of volunteers for the war were wholly unsuccessful and had to be abandoned.[8]

Many Southerners, moreover, were quite critical of those who linked chivalry with military life. Some, including young Charles Colcock Jones, Jr., felt that cavalier words were mere bluster. "With many," he wrote, "an extra jet of courage is apt to burst forth the farther we are removed from the scene of danger." When a fellow Princetonian left for Mississippi to join a Cuban expedition, Jones wrote of the young adventurer's resolve, "Am rather inclined to believe, however, that this was only spoken—not meant."[9] D. R. Hundley cast a sarcastic eye on the chivalric pretensions of some young Southrons:

> Place vis à vis to such a Knight of the Past, behold the dwarfish dimensions of our Cotton Knight, who ambles daintily forward on the back of a docile gelding, holding a sharpened stick under his arm, and gallantly and gloriously endeavoring to thrust the same through an iron ring, which is suspended by a rope of twine from an horizontal beam! . . . Tremble, O Cuba, and quake with much fear, O States of Nicaragua and Costa Rica, for the old lions have refreshed themselves, and the young lions are preparing against the day of battle![10]

Chivalry, he recognized, was a ridiculous show and had little to do with the realities of war.

But for some critics, the mixture of chivalry and war was more than silly. It was dangerous in its effects on military actions. "We have acted on the principle that the conferring of rank, of itself, makes the general; and rely almost exclusively for our protection against military invasion, upon the 'native courage' and 'indomitable energy' of our people," wrote one Southern critic of his title-happy society.[11] Bravery and daring were valuable, but they were not substitutes for experience and knowledge in military leadership.

However much Southerners admired the bravery of their

soldiers, they could hardly admire the results of their daring. An essayist in *De Bow's Review* wrote with disapproval of the severe losses sustained in the early days of the Mexican War, claiming that they resulted from "the rashness and impetuosity" of the troops.[12] Incompetence in leadership and rashness in the making of decisions could result in a loss of life that was unacceptable even in war.

Southerners had, then, strong doubts about the value of a "martial spirit," at least insofar as that spirit was connected with the "pomp and clash of arms" of cavalier warfare. At least one Southern polemicist, J. D. B. De Bow, even had his doubts about the regional character of what martial spirit there was in the land. Perceiving a rising military spirit in 1850, De Bow felt it was more a national than a peculiarly Southern phenomenon: it was a spirit "diffusing itself through all classes of society" in the United States, he wrote. And he was not at all sure the rising spirit was to his country's advantage.[13]

Still, the image dies hard. Marcus Cunliffe, in a superlative essay on the Southern military tradition, has indicated the lack of foundation for the stereotype while pointing out, nevertheless, that the idea had some currency even before the Civil War. But there are greater problems in dealing with the Southern "martial spirit" than that of the correspondence of the ideal to reality. For one thing, there is some question as to the currency of the idea itself and, more particularly, as to the period of time during which the idea had any widespread adherence in the region. It may be, as Cunliffe himself has suggested, that almost everything about the "Old South" is a "post-1865 invention."[14] More importantly, however, the image of the chivalrous warrior most frequently identified with the Southern martial spirit fits very poorly with conservative Southern social ideals. The man of chivalry was, after all, one who sought personal glory through violence, and both personal glory and personal violence were looked upon with ambiguity, if not disapproval, by people in the antebellum South. The character of the ideal soldier was unlikely to be distinguished by such attributes.

And, in fact, it was not. The character of the military man was ideally like that of any social being. According to Fitzhugh, "Timidity and rashness are alike to be avoided"; the virtues of the soldier were "patience, perseverance, and the love of home, with the spirit of enterprise and adventure." And the only way to achieve such virtues was "adequate experience and the full practice of discipline," as one Colonel Gardner put it. Even Quitman's admiring biographer, J. F. H. Claiborne, had to back down a bit from his earlier accounts of one for whom the battlefield was a gorgeous pageant, when summarizing the general's finer qualities: "His courage amounted to indifference to danger; he was cool and self-possessed, without a particle of bravado." And such were the qualities of any gentleman.[15]

The cavalier image would not have fit comfortably with other, more conservative themes in Southern culture, nor, for that matter, would have an intense militarism. Southerners, for all their reputation for a martial spirit, were simply not as given to the glories of militarism as stereotypes would suggest. Seeing something of the ideal man in the soldier, to be sure, it was more that they felt the military experience could create a situation in which a man's best qualities would emerge. They longed not for war, but for the kind of men who could act effectually should war occur.

The military experience of most Southerners was anything but glorious. Many took part in military activities because of the militia laws of their states. In addition, as the antebellum period progressed, all had to think about war, first during the expansionist 1840s and 1850s, and then as the threat of sectional conflict grew ever greater prior to the coming of the Civil War in 1861. In none of these cases does the South emerge as a society armed and ready to do battle.

The militia system formed, for many years, the basis of both Southern and Northern military systems. All of the states had "Militia Laws" requiring adult white males to attend regular musters and, theoretically, to be prepared in the event of a military threat. Such companies, being both part-time and impermanent, preserved the notion of a citizen soldiery and, ideologically, represented the continuing force of conservative convictions against the establishment of a "standing army"—a permanent military body owing allegiance only to itself and to those in power.

The problem was that so far as military necessity was concerned, the militia system was a dismal failure, as most people seem to have recognized. Its failure was almost certainly epitomized by the character of those musters which were designed to train a citizen army. As much a social occasion as anything else, the militia muster was nothing so much as a proof of the incompetence of those it was expected to train—and those officers who were supposed to do the training. One writer, in a general essay on the state of Georgia, summarized the disorder of a muster: "Once every year or two they have what they call a militia muster, and if there is anything on earth which is truly ludicrous, and, at the same time, disgraceful and contemptible, it is one of these '*musters*.' Get two negroes, one with a reed fife and the other with a broken-headed kettle-drum—then parade several score of men, boys and old women, helter-skelter after the music, with every alternate person bawling out: 'Shoulder-Arms!' and you will have some idea of a Georgia *muster*." The essay referred "the curious" to A. B. Longstreet's *Georgia Scenes* for "amusing and instructive details" of the practice.[16] A Northern writer, remembering a Virginia muster, wrote, "I could easily see why it required three-fourths of an hour for the Virginia troops to form a hollow square around the gallows on which old John Brown was hanged," and noted that Virginia exercises were even more ridiculous than those in less "martial" Massachusetts.[17]

The militia was not overwhelmingly popular with those expected to serve. In Virginia, apparently, a far smaller proportion of the population actually attended muster than should have been expected—at least this was so in 1850. According to the critic of the Georgia militia, in 1851, "Not one half of the offices are filled, and, as to each company's containing sixty-four privates, it is frequently the case that in one of the militia captain's districts there are not even a half-dozen privates." Muster day was, to be sure, a major social event in most Southern towns, but the militia itself had little to do with its appeal.[18]

The militia was, of course, a source of titles for Southern gentlemen. The Georgia critic's implication—that there were captains without troops—does point up the fact that the number of officers in relation to men in Southern militia was quite high when compared to the ratio in the North. Not that the attainment of a title had much to do with military ability. When J. G. Harris was appointed Lieutenant Colonel of an Alabama militia battalion, he wrote in his diary that "I am perfectly ignorant as to any military tacticks." A Virginian, offered two posts in the militia, declined them both with the remark, in his diary, "The absurdities of a militia muster." The meaning of a militia title had, in other words, very little to do with martial spirit.[19]

To be a colonel or a captain in the militia was wholly honorific and was mainly a measure of status. Such titles were usually the result of a popular election, and generally went to men of stature in the community. The officerships confirmed rather than conferred status on the holder. The one thing that seems to stand out about such militia titles is that they were titles of community service, indicating a willingness for personal sacrifice for the defense and preservation of society. Professions of such willingness were prized in Southern social and political rhetoric as representative of the ideal stance of the individual toward his community; it was the essence of what Southerners meant when they talked about "duty." The man who was elected captain or colonel, and accepted the post, was acknowledged by his fellow citizens to be a leader and was himself able to assume a title indicative of his devotion to duty at very little personal cost. Only a few men could allow such an opportunity to pass them by. The military title was a good outward sign of moral worth.

If there were a few militia companies noted for their efficiency and order—the Montgomery True Blues, for instance—most Southerners appear to have expected little. The stereotype of incompetence was both clear and pervasive. North Carolinian William H. Haigh, seeing a ticket to a "Soiree Militaire," found its appearance a little vulgar. "This may be the style military," he wrote in his diary, "but it has the semblance of a *Militia* performance." There was little in the way of military glory attaching itself to the militia, most people agreed.[20]

More seriously, such an organization as the militia could offer little of the military prowess that would be necessary in the event of war. As early as the second decade of the nineteenth century, Secretary of War John C. Calhoun proposed a rigorous defense policy that involved a reorganization of the militia to establish a more permanent military force. Similar moves were made at various times in the antebellum period. The most ambitious, perhaps, was that of Secretary of War Joel R. Poinsett in 1840. Poinsett's plan would have divided the country into military districts, providing for both active and reserve forces numbering 100,000 each. The plan would have strengthened and nationalized the military, as many Southerners recognized, and not all approved. Thomas Ritchie, for example, was an articulate spokesman for Virginia Democrats when he wrote to Poinsett, "You are charged with the design of establishing a Standing Army of two hundred thousand men; with proposing a system without precedent in our annals, tyrannical and oppressive in all its details, and without a parallel in the history of free Governments." The militia system, for all its faults, still provided for a citizen army, and thus served as an ideological safeguard against arbitrary and, in this case, national government. The South was not, in 1840, so martially enchanted as to give up other, more traditional ideals.[21]

Only a few reforms in the militia system were ever made and these involved, primarily, deemphasizing the mustering of line companies in favor of more permanent volunteer companies from whom more could be expected. In Virginia, in fact, the line companies with their annual musters were abolished altogether in 1853, only to be revived in 1858 as sectional tensions grew greater.[22] Other states, too, had their volunteer companies, and it was widely recognized that such an organization offered far more than line companies for the defense of the state, except when impending crisis made a massive mobilization of men seem necessary.

Many Southerners, like Americans everywhere, recognized the need for a professional military, or at least for professional military leadership if the country were to be adequately defended, and they felt that the only way to provide for professionalism was through the establishment of a regular system of military education. An educated group of officers would constitute, not a standing army, but "a nucleus for an effective citizen-soldiery," and its training would be a far better expenditure of state funds than was the support of a militia system.[23]

Southern attitudes toward military education paralleled notions of what made a good soldier. A writer for the *Southern Quarterly Review*, commenting on Henry Wager Halleck's important *Elements of Military Art and Science*, used his essay as an occasion to extoll the virtues of a military education. Remarking that military service could "seldom be made to advance the private interests, or answer the ends of the individual," this writer saw the military professional as one who had put the interests of the state above his own—and argued that the state should provide for military education. The important thing to the essayist was that military heroes were made rather than born. To be sure, leadership required certain significant traits of character—courage, firmness, and intelligence—but a knowledge of the theory of warfare on the basis of which to interpret information on the battlefield was the product of education and was the only guarantor of military success. And this writer, too, hoped that such an educated group would form the "nucleus" of an efficient citizen army.[24]

Other Southerners agreed. While "mere theoretical military knowledge" could not make a great leader, raw courage had its own drawbacks and often led to pointless and excessive loss of lives. Only when there was a proper combination of action and discipline, brought about through training, could the soldier behave competently and effectively. Thus, according to one writer, "Courageous conduct in battle is always a consequence of complete military education." In soldiering, as in life, it was disciplined action that was the most effectual form of behavior.[25]

Not surprisingly, Southerners rarely encouraged military education in purely martial terms, although a few, including a writer for the *Southern Quarterly Review*, acknowledged that some young men were sent to military school because of their "supposed 'martial spirit.'" Even this writer felt, however, that the military "system" of education was generally superior to other kinds, and it was this that most Southern writers focused upon when they wrote about military schools.[26]

B. J. Barbour, in an address to the literary society at the Virginia Military Institute, spoke for many when he told the students that "your institution was formed less for the chances of war than for the more solid triumphs of peace, of science, and of morality."[27] A military education, because it fused thought and action, was simply good training for manhood.[28] When thought and action had to be joined together, as was the case with the military, the main result was to temper both, preventing both rashness in action and a lack of discipline in thought. Such temperateness was admirable in every area of life. The future Civil War hero J. E. B. Stuart, just beginning his training at West Point, acknowledged this virtue of military education when he urged that a younger cousin follow him to the Academy:

I believe four years training at West Point would be the making of him. It would be the means of strengthening his constitution, establishing his health, and making him, both physically and mentally, emphatically a *man*. For one to succeed here, all that is required is an ordinary mind and application, the latter is by far the most important and desirable of the two. For men of rather obtuse intellect, by indomitable perseverance have been known to graduate with honor; while some of the greatest geniuses of the Country have been found deficient, for want of application; Edgar A. Poe for instance.[29]

Southerners loved discipline and order, and they certainly found it when they looked at the form and substance of a military education.

Military schools were popular in the South, as they were elsewhere and as they have continued to be, because of the education, scholarly and social, they gave to their students. To the extent that they did have any special appeal in the South (they probably did not, though even antebellum Southerners claimed they did)[30] that appeal lay in the way in which the emphases of military education, particularly its practicality and discipline, corresponded closely to more general Southern social values. The martial spirit was far less important than the spirit of order in the encouragement of Southern military schools.

There is no reason to think that Southern arguments for military education were offered hypocritically. A society with the chivalric symbols of the South could have claimed to be training the "knights" of the day, after all; and Southerners had no need to put on a mask of pacifism for the outside world. Certainly Southerners recognized the potential need for competent military leadership as the 1840s and 1850s progressed, bringing wars of expansion and increasing conflict with the North. But Southerners also believed that in war or peace, society needed a certain type of person and that military education could mold such men. Moreover, the training was accomplished for ends that were clearly social rather than individual, and thus schools with a military form were recommended with special strength to those who had to provide the funds. The strength of such schools was in their long-term contribution to the society Southerners idealized.

Southerners never really denied the importance of an effective military, and they would come to sense the need for strength more and more in the late antebellum period. At that point the Southern back was to the wall and regional polemicists, having proclaimed for years that the South would react violently to antislavery success, had to claim that it could do so effectively. Before 1860, however, not all Southerners were convinced that a martial spirit was good for society. In particular, during the American wars for empire in the 1840s and after, Southern opinion was sharply divided on the subject of warfare and military activity.

The last two decades before the Civil War were decades of American expansion to the West. Whipped up largely by the New York press and the doctrines of "Manifest Destiny," Americans looked far afield for new territory and new people to bring into the American sphere. Their government sent them into Mexico, and for a time they thought of bringing "All Mexico" into the Union. Other Americans looked with longing to the north, to Canada, to augment the geography and population of the United States. A few adventurers, the filibusters, made forays, or at least planned them, in an attempt to "conquer" parts of Mexico, Central America, and the Caribbean—despite the often active opposition of the American government. Many Americans of the period dreamed of empire, and some, though by no means all, attempted to act on their dreams through diplomacy or military adventure.

Southern support for expansionism was never better than mixed, and, for many years, Southerners' positions on various expansionist enterprises were determined by factors far different from any martial ideology. Party lines, racism, traditional views on "standing armies," and economic expectations all had a good deal more to do with Southern opinions about expansion than did an uncontrollable "martial spirit" infecting the population. The South, particularly the Southeast, was often the least cordial part of the country toward expansionist schemes, especially those directed toward Mexico and its dark-skinned population, and primarily on racist grounds. Even the more bellicose Southwest ranked far behind the West and the Northeast in warmth to expansion.[31]

A similar division of sympathy appeared in regard to those presumably quintessential Southern cavaliers, the filibusters. Although there was a great deal of popular enthusiasm for several of the filibuster expeditions, notably the Lopez expedition into Cuba and William Walker's ludicrous Nicaraguan enterprise, the most likely assessment of Southern sentiment places support for those adventures at no more than a bare majority. Nor was political disposition highly relevant in determining one's stand toward adventurism. Such fire-eaters as William Lowndes Yancey and John L. Quitman were exponents and defenders of filibuster imperialism, as one might expect, but Texan Louis T. Wigfall, as rash as any Southern politician, was a sharp critic of William Walker and his activities. Opinion was far from unanimous about filibustering, and far from predictable, as well.[32]

Southern responses to expansionist wars were determined by a variety of factors, but arguments for or against wars of conquest were predictably framed in terms of moral notions about war as a phenomenon. Those who opposed expansionist warfare, or who had misgivings about it, worried primarily about the problem of means by which territory could be acquired. Thus the Alabama Whig Henry Washington Hilliard, who opposed the conquest of Mexico mainly because he feared that the new territories would be closed to slavery, could attack the war as one of "aggrandizement," proclaiming that if the United States desired conquest, "we should have selected some other adversary, and not have made the point of our lance ring against the shield of our weakest neighbor." Such actions were, he declared, "indecent." Polk, the expansionist president (and a Democrat), "boasts of the advantages which he has won, by tearing from a feeble neighbor some of her finest territories, and adding them to our own possessions."[33] Hilliard spoke not only a Whig line, but one formed from a clear sense of class and class obligations put into the language of international relations.

Even some expansionists expressed a marked distaste for wars of conquest. De Bow, for one, assumed the inevitability of expansion and dearly longed for the admission of Cuba as a state in the Union, but he decried the martial spirit which would acquire Cuba by conquest. Only negotiations with Spain should be used to extend American sovereignty, he informed his readers, and added, "There are honorable means of achieving our purpose, and, if these fail, the purpose itself becomes dishonorable." An essayist in the *Southern Quarterly Review* who asserted an ultimate "natural right on the part of our race, to possess the earth," nevertheless wrote that filibusters were those "who never reflect, and obey only their impulses" or those others "who suffer selfish calculations to supersede all considerations of country." The war of conquest, whatever its end, was not a manifestation of all that was honorable in the human spirit, and some Southerners, however they felt about the goal of expansion, were not sure that the end justified the means.[34]

Others, however, were unabashed imperialists, and their views point to a major division in Southern political ideals. Some writers, including J. F. H. Claiborne, adopted a position quite similar to that of the proslavery ideologues when he asserted that "Civilized communities provide guardians for the helpless and imbecile, and defenses against the lunatic and the outlaw," and, thus, that it was the American duty to conquer and rule such a country as Mexico, "with or without her consent."[35] There were many who agreed with Claiborne's view and, like those who were not so imperialistic, they spoke in familiar terms. Those who were capable knew best how to plan the lives of those who were not, and the strong often had to impose their will through violence.

There was a basic area of disagreement between imperialists and others that crossed sectional lines, to an extent, paralleling the intellectual division of conservatives and democrats from the Jacksonian period onward. The issue here was one of order and how it could be maintained. Those who favored expansion at any price, including conquest, most frequently argued that conquest, by removing forces of disorder or by adding slave territory, was absolutely essential to the maintenance of social order in the South and political order vis à vis the North. "Conquest," declared Claiborne, "is essential to eternal repose." Their case was strengthened, more abstractly, by the widespread assumption that any relationship between parties in which the dominance of the strong was not fixed was an unstable, unbalanced relationship. Other Southerners did not agree, even those who desired additional territory. De Bow, never cool to expansionism, remained opposed to wars of conquest. Such talk involved merely the "giddy dreams of the day," he wrote; and, as for the martial spirit, no society could safely do anything that would "unduly excite it." A lust for conquest could itself be inimical to the order of society, and thus was not to be encouraged. Whereas the imperialists looked for a continual fulfillment of the ideal of order, those who opposed such adventures felt that the order existed, but was too fragile to be disrupted by unnecessary militarism.[36]

It remained only for the ideologues of the late antebellum period, such men as George Fitzhugh or George Frederick Holmes, to articulate the darkest view of the right of conquest. Agreeing with Claiborne as to the right of the strong to rule the weak, both Fitzhugh and Holmes went a step farther in their awareness of the fact that the "weak" might not submit. Fitzhugh, citing the precedent of Moses and Joshua, declared that "from their day to ours the strong have been conquering the weak—subjecting them to better rule, and improving their condition, when they were susceptible of improvement and civilization, and exterminating them when they were not." Holmes, who believed that conquest was essential to the health of society, must have agreed: "Conquest, extension, appropriation, assimilation, and even the extermination of inferior races has been and must be the course pursued in the development of civilization." Fitzhugh and Holmes were, to be sure, men given to thinking the unthinkable, and to voicing their thoughts, but their words were neither more nor less than a clear statement of what any imperialist must acknowledge, a positive assertion of the negative realities of conquest.[37]

The honest words of Fitzhugh and Holmes point, as well, to the main lines of a Southern anthropology of war, an implicit theory of why wars occurred and the nature of the effects of war on society. Chivalrous or not, Southerners generally saw war as one element of man's natural disposition toward his fellows. In the 1805 trial of Richard Dennis for the murder of James Shaw, one of Dennis's lawyers argued for his client, who had killed Shaw out of revenge: "Can you require then of a youth to feel for his country's wrongs, to wield a sword in another's cause, and to be a stoic, an apathist in his own—No—self love and social is the same."[38] Southerners did not separate war from other forms of violence conceptually, and they recognized that war, like fighting or dueling, was occasionally necessary for the maintenance of society.

War, they claimed, sprang from the same passions that led to violence generally. The difference was one of degree and direction, more than anything else; plus, of course, the fact that war was a collective enterprise. Still, the motivations were the same, and more than that, grew out of a potential for instability in relations between nations that was similar to that found between individuals. Hence Southern attitudes toward war were quite similar to their attitudes toward other forms of violence in society. "We admit that war is one of the greatest of evils," wrote one, "but it is only to be averted by constant preparation to meet and repel the attacks of unjust or ambitious neighbors. Its source is in the evil passions of our nature."[39] Another writer, who also defended the necessity of war, framed his argument in terms of that sense of social distance which appeared so often in Southern thought: "Next to my family, I naturally love, and feel most concern for my neighbors of the same community; and an extension of the same principle of our nature, tells me to defend my country against, and love her better, than the rest of the world. If as a nation, she is attacked, there is no civil magistrate to whom an appeal can be made, and I am bound to assist in her protection by force. This force I am only justified in using, so long as the wrong-doers persist in the wrong which called it forth."[40] War was necessary for the same reason violent self-defense was necessary, because one had the duty to defend himself and his friends and family against unwarranted attack. This writer was sure, moreover, that forceful defense would be necessary since, "owing to the relations which the God of nature has established between different nations, as well as between man and man, we cannot abandon all means, both of offence and defence, and rely solely for our own self-preservation on the justice and innocence of our conduct."[41] De Bow put the matter more succinctly: "Man is not the friend, where dominion and power are concerned, but the enemy of his fellows."[42] Given such a view, it is clear why many Southerners were unable to justify a war of conquest.

War was the product of human nature, but Southerners were not early day devotees of notions of innate aggressiveness. Rather, they saw war as part of human society because relationships among human beings were inherently given to conflict. This was because human beings were innately passionate, and passion was most nearly synonymous with self-indulgence, with the gratification of personal or national desires at the expense of social harmony. What Southerners acknowledged in their writing on war was, then, that such passion was a fact of life and that people could not deny that fact, but did have to come to terms with it, to order it through self-control and, in the case of the imperialists, through the imposition of control on those who were unable to subordinate desire to honor.

War was a necessity, but it was a dangerous necessity. For

some, notably Fitzhugh, the common danger it posed could strengthen ties within the community—or so he would write when the Civil War was imminent. But then Fitzhugh's fear of order imposed by force was hardly notable. Other writers, who could achieve a greater distance on the subject, felt that war had to be a temporary state of affairs. "War is not the business of life," wrote one essayist, and whereas Fitzhugh would speak approvingly of society's "admiration of distinguished warriors," this earlier thinker, writing ten years before Fitzhugh, would urge that "the people should not be excited and led away from their ordinary pursuits by the dazzling mania of war." War and threats of war, according to one expansionist, meant an end to that "calmness and deliberation" which were necessary to human affairs. War signaled a cessation of normal relationships between nations, just as personal violence meant a disruption in society. It was, thus, undesirable in itself and, as one writer claimed, the only proper goal of warfare was "the successful and honorable termination of the state of war."[43]

Bellicosity and, to use Fitzhugh's phrase, "The Love of Danger and of War," became Southern traits late in the antebellum period, were not universal, and, like mounting defenses of slave society in the 1840s and 1850s, may have represented an effort to reconcile their perception of an increasingly difficult reality with their culture. Southerners understood violence as the opposite of order. When the national order could be characterized with ever greater accuracy in terms of its fragility, Southerners were placed in the position of having to come to terms with their own beliefs. This meant, above all, that they had to confront their own sense of the necessity of violence in the event of a loss of order, and to justify that perception they had to create an apologetics for war.

Theirs was not a martial spirit. If Southerners did show a fondness for the military, they still by and large spoke of war as an evil, an attitude that was consistent with their more general views of society. Where they may have shown a disposition for military activities was in their sense, a rather simple one, of international (or intersectional) relations. Such relations, they felt, could not be secure, for nations, like individuals, could not be trusted to deal fairly and honestly with each other. It was that insecurity, and not a confident chivalry, that gave the South whatever martial spirit it may have had.

8. *Violence and Southern Oratory*

BECAUSE violent acts had such potent meaning for most antebellum Southerners, it is not surprising that violent words and symbols were important, as well. Southern writers and speakers could evoke violence in quite telling ways to make their points. Calling up their audiences' notions of what violence said about human nature and society, articulate Southerners were able to convey messages ranging from politics to metaphysics, and from ideas to the deepest sorts of emotions. The symbolic role of violence in the Old South was closely tied to more general attitudes toward physical conflict.

Words and images of violence were important in antebellum Southern politics, but their role was not simple. Southerners were less given to bellicosity than the stereotype would suggest, and most political leaders of the day would have been quick to disavow belligerence as a political tool. Certainly, they were far less pugnacious than are many twentieth-century politicians. Yet, for all that, the most militant regional spokesmen were widely known as "fire-eaters,"[1] and they had widespread reputations for political extremism. In part, such reputations must have grown out of a style and imagery in Southern oratory that depended heavily on evocations of violence for characterizing political affairs. Violent imagery was the most frequently used figurative language during the period. Its use, however, and the response such language was meant to evoke, had much more to do with very deep cultural concerns than with making reckless threats against a hostile world.

The evocation of violence in Southern politics is most clearly shown in the major form of political expression, oratory. Southerners themselves placed oratory above the written word for political communication, and educational efforts in the region tended to include turning students into good speakers as part of the curriculum. Even more, perhaps, than other forms of political action, oratory was what many Southerners thought politics was all about.

Historians have, in general, taken a mixed view of the role of oratory in Southern politics, approaching it from the "pragmatic-minded" position that rhetoric and reality were quite distinct, that eloquence was either a cover for "real interests" or that, more likely, oratory was simply a symptom of the romanticism that pervaded every aspect of antebellum Southern life.[2] While such a point of view certainly has some truth to it, it only begins to get one to an understanding of the role of oratory in the Old South, as a symbol of regional identity, and as a form of political expression through which Southerners were able to communicate their feelings about what society and culture should be like.

It would be as foolish to quarrel with the notion that Southern rhetoric and the hard realities of politics were somehow different as it would be to dispute the general inadequacy of language to capture situations of life. However, one need not take the words politicians say at face value to acknowledge that, at least in the short run, the ways in which they talk about events, including those of politics, can play a crucial part in the kinds of responses they are likely to develop to deal with those events. The classic purpose of oratory is persuasion, and, because of this, oratory has usually been closely tied to the values and assumptions of the society in which it occurs, even when the practitioners are themselves the rankest hypocrites. This is because, in trying to persuade, the orator must do nothing so much as to provide with a way of putting specific political events into an understandable context. To use Doris Graber's term, the orator creates "hypothetical patterns of reality" by his choice of analogies and causal linkages when he describes events. Taking powerful, but culturally relative imagery and stereotyped analogies and using them to urge a particular understanding of a situation, the orator makes the values of his society graphically real, and, as a casuist, shows how they should be applied to life in the world. The successful orator, in other words, defines a political reality his society can understand.[3]

Antebellum Southerners recognized the power of oratory, and they identified its art with their region. Whether they should have considered the country above the Virginia state line to be "north of the region of eloquence," as James Johnston Pettigrew once described Baltimore, is, of course, debatable.[4] Many of the country's greatest orators were Northerners and two of the South's, William Lowndes Yancey and Seargent S. Prentiss, grew up in the North. But Southerners nevertheless liked to think of oratory as a native art, and approved the tone it gave to their politics. As the Southern mythologizer John Witherspoon DuBose wrote in his biography of Yancey, "As with the slaveholding Athenians, they read not many books. Oratory and conversation supplied the wholesome friction of minds." He went on to add that, "the impartation of knowledge by the art of making truth beautiful . . . was a genuine social advancement."[5]

The reason for this positive view of oratory, where it involved more than simple regional chauvinism, had much to do with the traditional antebellum Southern understanding of human nature. If a few people during the period deeply feared the power of oratory to stir up a society that should remain calm, most recognized oratory as the means of bringing necessary passion into political affairs without, at the same time, subduing reason. In "true oratory," the traditional balance between passion and reason was struck, as Yancey, for instance, noted in a speech, and this was all to the good of society. According to the Alabamian, good oratory "addresses itself not to reason only, but to the affections, without which man would resemble more a fiend than a true man." The virtue of oratory was that "it stirs the blood in the bosom of age and arouses the energies and directs the hopes and aims of manhood."[6] The position was familiar. Reason alone could not make society work; passion had to be there to spur men to act, and this, in Yancey's opinion, was what oratory could do.

Yancey's view was generally shared by those who commented on oratory during the period. Reason, they acknowledged, had to have first place, but reasonable conviction was nothing unless it were buttressed by emotional support; thus any rhetorical performance had to bring both together. Like Yancey, other Southern orators were acknowledged to be effective speakers in part because of an ability to combine personal mildness with extreme words,[7] and orators who were unable to combine both reason and emotion in a single speech were usually said to be deficient, however admirable their arguments. Jefferson Davis, for example, was admired by one newspaper writer for his "pure, chaste, Socratic reasoning, calm as hope," and compared favorably with the more florid orators of the 1840s. But, the writer went on to say, "Could he only animate the perfect, somewhat inanimate statue of his eloquence with some of the strong outlines of passion; could he, after he had convinced the judgement by his inimitable style of passionless argument, rouse the will and the passions, enlist the feelings and captivate the imagination, he would rank among the foremost of our Mississippi orators."[8] A certain amount of emotion, carefully presented, was what made an orator good and what, some claimed, distinguished Southern speakers from their "plodding" fellow Americans.[9]

Giving a role to passion in oratory did not make political speaking strictly analogous to violence, although historians have occasionally drawn such a connection. To be sure, Southerners made little distinction between oration and debate, and adversaries were imaginatively present, if not physically so, at any political occasion. Moreover, speakers were often commended or condemned in violent terms, as when Burwell Boykin said of a performance by Clement Claiborne Clay, "You made the fur fly every pop, and every wind of the lash went to the red." Many duels were the products of oratorical conflicts or, it is fair to say, their newspaper equivalents, and, no doubt, many people conceived of public discussion as something like an oratorical "Field of the Cloth of Gold," to use Tom Watson's apt, if somewhat sarcastic, characterization.[10]

Still, Southern oratory was not meant to be somehow violent, nor was it meant merely to whip up the crowds. Given the well-documented antidemocratic focus of Southern thought, neither aim would have been acceptable to most politicians, and they distinguished clearly between the orator and the demagogue. By the same token, Southern orators expected their speeches to have some influence and most would have agreed with Seargent S. Prentiss's assessment of the situation: "The natural bent of my mind is to dry and pure ratiocination, but finding early that mankind, from a petit jury to the highest deliberative assembly are more influenced by illustration than by argument, I have cultivated my imagination in aid of my reason." Prentiss was, it has been said, almost too florid for Southern tastes, but what he attempted to do was a goal for most of the region's speakers. Putting imagination to essentially conservative purposes, Southern orators sought to fuse reason and passion. Such a complex synthesis was the central guiding force in Southern political rhetoric.[11]

One sees this to a great extent in the Southern view of debating as a part of political life. Southerners, like many Americans, were sure that proper positions and better leaders would emerge from the open contest of political debate. But whatever the adversary system was expected to contribute to the exposition of the "truth" by Southern speakers, it certainly enhanced their ability to bring together passion and reason. Because the frame for political discussion was inherently competitive for Southerners, the character of the orator, like that of the duelist, was an idealization of the kind of individual who expressed, by his actions, crucial elements in the Southern ethos. "He must be," as Hugh R. Pleasants wrote, "as cool and as calm, upon all occasions, as the pictures on the walls around him. He must never lose his self-possession for one moment, or for one moment cease to remember that he is in the presence of an adversary who is always ready to take advantage of his slightest mistake." Or, as William Gilmore Simms put it in a letter to William Porcher Miles: "Lose yourself always in your subject, and Be Bold! Bold! Bold! as was written on all the chamber doors in the Enchanted Castle of Spenser—over all but *one*, upon which was written—Be not *too* bold!" The problem was the familiar one of remaining cool in the heat of battle.[12]

Southern orators were able to meet such demands of political discussion in several ways. A presentation of personal mildness was one way. Another was the use of arguments that were exceedingly logical and legalistic. Southerners were fond of careful constitutional argument, and of framing all their speeches in terms of such cautious argumentation.[13] If this fondness derived in part from the usefulness of such arguments for the defense of Southern institutions, particularly slavery, it also derived from a more general preference for clear rules and restraints in the governing of all social relations.

In addition, Southern political language, like language in other areas of life, was tightly controlled. The same reliance on stereotyped phrases and forms that appeared, for example, in family letters, was also present in political speech, and to a surprising degree, considering the fame Southern orators achieved.[14] The use of florid imagery was rather sparse and limited in the speeches of even the most renowned of Southern orators. However radical Southern political views, they were only rarely stated in colorful language, even up to the opening of the Civil War.

Indeed, the same effort to impersonalize expression that influenced so many areas of Southern social life also marked the practices of Southern orators. They made effective use, for example, of the exordium—that opening section of any oration whereby the orators hoped, in the words of New Englander John Quincy Adams, "to prepare the minds of the hearers," and, in particular, "to interest them in favor of the speaker."[15] It was a rare orator, whatever his reputation, who did not spend at least a part of the exordium proclaiming his own inadequacy as a public speaker and his own lack of self-esteem. Whether it was a young Patrick Henry or a mature Robert Barnwell Rhett, the "confession" of one's oratorical inadequacy was well-established in Southern custom. Such modesty minimized the personal stakes of any speaker in the response of an audience to his message.

Not that one could suspect for a moment that any Southern speaker was unaware of either his power or his popularity. A matter of form, the modest exordium not only emphasized the absence of personal interest in a position—and the "utter disregard of self" was a Southern political imperative at least since the time of the Revolution[16]—but it also minimized the personal character of the emotion generated by a speech, as well. Whatever else oratory was supposed to be, it was not supposed to be either trivial or personal. It was supposed to deal in truth, and truth was emotional as well as intellectual. The Southern orator thus presented himself as the mere vehicle of a nonpartisan reality, albeit as a vehicle who deserved a hearing.

Such a modest pose coupled with a usually mild presentation meant, it need only be noted, that when any orator did become overwrought with excitement, his agitation could lend even greater significance to the event by defining it as one of great and general peril. This was so even in the case of an orator so given to excitement as Robert Barnwell Rhett, a man who, on at least one occasion, expressed public regret for his own actions in a speech.[17] Still, a comment on one of his speeches appearing in the *Charleston Mercury*, a paper favorable to Rhett, shows how an orator's agitation could be interpreted: "There were times during the speech of Mr. Rhett when the excitement rose far above what is commonly called enthusiasm at political meetings, and seemed akin to those strong workings of the heart and the convictions that characterized the period which tried men's souls."[18] The excitement at one meeting, the *Mercury*'s editor realized, could evoke that period of American history during which everyone agreed on the necessity of dramatic political action.

Stylistic strategy was an attempt, then, to synthesize reason and emotion in the organization and delivery of a speech, and in the presentation of the orator. This sylistic rhetorical pattern followed from the general sense of rhetorical purpose subscribed to by Southern orators and it contributed to the context according to which their words must be understood. Whatever Southerners had to say, and on whatever issue, they hoped to move their audiences to action through the evocation of that underlying dilemma which was such an important part of the ethos of the region.

Southerners used little imagery, and what they did use was quite limited. Analogies to nature, metaphors of pain and disease, and evocations of violence do not account for all the imagery in the repertoire of a Southern political speaker, but they account for most of it, and all three were used in strikingly similar ways. Southerners had, as has often been noted, an almost overwhelming concern about problems of order and disorder, a concern they themselves frequently acknowledged, and each of the three major kinds of imagery allowed them to portray that concern to great effect. Such was, in fact, the focus of most of their flights of rhetorical fancy. Violent imagery, however, was particularly useful for evoking Southern social and political concerns because, unlike the imagery drawing on nature or illness, violence itself could be a fact of political life. That is, while natural and bodily imagery were clearly metaphorical, metaphor and reality were powerfully combined when a Southern orator spoke of violence.[19]

The single source which provided the greatest stock of Southern orators' violent imagery was the American Revolution. Although, to be sure, they noted other violent episodes in human history and sometimes spoke of violence in the abstract, there was something overwhelming about the Revolution. It provided the basic themes on which most specific images elaborated. Now, speakers could have emphasized many aspects of the Revolution, including its ideology, leadership, or success—and, in fact, they touched on all those—but they chose to speak most frequently of its violence. It had been a Revolutionary War, above all else, and the "blood of patriots" was an important fundamental in Southern oratory. No examination of the violent imagery of Southern oratory can stray far from its grounding in Southern ideas about the American War for Independence.

For one thing, the American Revolution had been a period in which the noble passions had stood up to the violent force which would have crushed lesser feelings. The purported willingness of patriots to risk all they had was noted as exemplary by many Southern orators. In the words of unionist William Lowndes Yancey, during what may have been his first political speech, the men of the Revolution had "staked property, life and honor—all—that they might transmit to us, their posterity, freedom of conscience, freedom of opinion, and a good and wise government." The secessionist William Lowndes Yancey, some years later, made a similar point when he called upon his fellow Southerners to defend the rights of their region, expressing the hope that, in unity, they "may yet produce spirit enough to lead us forward, to call forth a Lexington, to fight a Bunker's Hill, to drive the foe from the city of our rights." In the violence of the Revolution, all that had been noble in men had met the challenge put to them. The event was a model for the people of Yancey's own time.[20]

But the testing character of the Revolution was never lost in the words of Southern orators. Far more than they emphasized the glories of the struggle, and however much they exalted the American spirit, they spoke most frequently of the war as a necessity which, having occurred, should never occur again. Hence, as they constructed their rhetorical history of the Revolution, there were certain features on which they tended to focus. As they talked about the causes of the war, for instance, they generally characterized it as a war of self-defense. James L. Petigru put the matter in fairly typical terms in 1834 when he suggested that because of Britain's violations of her own "constitution," Americans were left with "no alternative but revolution or treason," and that they thus, "with the intrepidity of men that could look danger in the face . . . proclaimed the independence of the United States."[21] In this,

Southern orators drew on the region's more general attitudes toward violence in making defense, founded on an aroused passion for self-respect, rather than an arrogant passion for independence, the background for Revolution.

Beyond that, however, by invoking the violence of Revolution, they particularly emphasized its element of disorder. One sees this, for example, in the frequent characterization of the Revolution as a war of brother against brother, but one sees it as well in the description Southerners often gave of the Constitution. The Revolution had been a period of antistructure, almost a rite of passage in which, to use South Carolina Senator James Hammond's words in his famous "mud-sill" speech, "We threw off a Government not adapted to our social system and made one for ourselves." But the Revolution had not put things in order by itself; it had merely destroyed an unsatisfactory form of government. Hence, according to the Alabama politician-rhetorician Henry Washington Hilliard, it had taken the Constitution to put an end to "wildness, madness, and selfishness" in American politics. The Constitution, in other words, had provided rules for political process which would put passion back under control, and in the absence of such rules, as at the time of the Revolution, disorder and violence had characterized the political scene.[22] In this, one may note, violent language was the direct descendant of those metaphors of disease and decay which had expressed Southern fears for the social organism in earlier times.

Such a view of the Revolution was also the basis on which Southern orators were able to come to terms with its rather uncomfortable ideology. It allowed them to dismiss Revolutionary rhetoric, although they would have put it differently, as a ritual necessity. Those who accepted social contract ideology—and, as Louis Hartz has suggested, most Southern leaders did, whether they said so or not—could see the Revolution as a temporary return to the state of nature, to a period before, or without society and government. Giving this context to the ideology of the Revolution meant that it had nothing to do with a future legacy for America but only with the need to declare independence at a particular point in history. Southern politicians were sure, then, that Revolutionary ideology was not to be taken seriously beyond its antistructural role. Its doctrine might have been necessary to cleanse the political sphere of its built-in impurities in 1776, but the ideology itself was, as John Randolph said of the principles of freedom as presented in the Declaration of Independence, "a falsehood, and a pernicious falsehood, even though I find them in the Declaration."[23]

Southerners' views of the antistructural character of the Revolution referred back to their most important beliefs about human nature and society. Humanly contrived rules controlled passion. Southern orators made that point in 1787 and 1788, when the states debated the Federal Constitution, and they would continue to make it until the Civil War by their use of violent images. Long before Calhoun had codified and attempted to rationalize Southern prejudices, politicians in the region had developed, with varying degrees of skill, a sociology of structure—which they identified with the South—and opposed that sociology to the tendency toward antistructure elsewhere. It was to evoke the evils of antistructure that political figures in the South commonly used violent imagery in their speeches.

Southern orators most liked to equate the politics of antistructure with those of the North, particularly as abolition or freesoil sentiment appeared to gain the upper hand with Northern political leaders. One may see this clearly in the way Yancey used violent language in his notorious speech before the 1860 Democratic Convention at Charleston. Invoking what might be called the "best people" theory of American government, Yancey lamented that Northern leaders had been caught up in the popular will against slavery, and that this popular will was like the force of a vast army. Northern politicians had "trembled before its march," making no effort to resist the attack. Indeed, in acknowledging themselves that slavery was wrong, Northern Democrats "gave up the real ground of battle," and before the combat had even been joined. They hardly measured up, one might add, to that model of Revolutionary fortitude for which Southerners proclaimed so much admiration.

Given his perspective, Yancey could easily contrast Northern and Southern positions, and, for this too, violent imagery was perfect. Uncontrolled violence was all on the side of the North. The doctrines of antislavery were "revolutionary and incendiary," founded only on "the passionate struggle of the masses for party or agrarian ascendancy." The result was most likely to be that "the wisdom, judgement and experience of the past be thrown down and trampled upon."[24]

Yancey captured much of what Southerners feared and disapproved in his remarks at Charleston, and he did so through the evocation of violence. Northern politics, he implied, was based on perpetual disorder, that is, on a conscious and constant disregard for proper structure in social relations. Thus, everything about the Northern position was suspect, because, like every violation of a proper order, the motives of those opposed to the South could not be good. Yancey was generous in attributing the views of Northern leaders to cowardice in the face of the popular will. Many orators felt it would be more accurate to describe Northern views as Thomas Clingman did, "as resting on the lust for power of your politicians, or on the rapacity of your people."[25] Had such words been spoken of a Southern leader, their aptness might have been tested on the field of honor.

The denigration of the popular will was, itself, a major theme in Southern oratory. It would be simple enough to ascribe such antidemocratic talk to the defense of slavery, but the equation of violence, antistructure, and democracy was made by Southern orators long before the need to defend slavery seemed pressing. Such Virginia leaders as James Madison, at the time of the debates on the Constitution in 1788, could attempt to make a case for its adoption by claiming that "on a candid examination of history, we shall find that turbulence, violence, and abuse of power, by the majority trampling on the rights of the minority, have produced factions and commotions, which, in republics, have more frequently than any other cause, produced despotism."[26] Replying to those who opposed the Federal scheme for fear of too much concentration of power, Madison nevertheless contributed to a formulation of an equation of democracy with violence that was to have great force in the South for years to come.

Later politicians would, in fact, make the connection increasingly direct. On the one hand they would see in the loss of structure, to use a common analogy, the makings of another Santo Domingo or Paris. Benjamin Watkins Leigh, a later Virginia conservative, went even further, grimly announcing that the very principles of democracy—white manhood suffrage, in this instance—

"were calculated in their nature to lead to rapine, anarchy and bloodshed, and in the end to military despotism." On the other hand, and more radically, some Southerners acknowledged the sense of Tocqueville's famous notion of the "tyranny of the majority" by equating majority rule with the rule of physical force. Fulminating against "King Numbers" in the Virginia Convention of 1830, John Randolph declared that there could only be one result from majoritarian government: "If we sanction this principle," he warned, "we shall prove that a state, not of nature, but of society, and of Constitutional Government, is a state of interminable war." His words would be echoed two decades later by Henry W. Hilliard, who would say in an address on the American government that "the Constitution—not the will of a majority—is the supreme law of the United States," concluding, "our system is one of consent, not of force." Government conducted by any but the strictest rules, with the most careful regulation, was in danger of becoming arbitrary, and hence a government of the strong over the weak. Since the Southern elite was outnumbered at home and in the sectional conflict, the evocation of such a fear obviously had some power. But one may also note the analogy that made the appeal work: just as passionate willfulness in the individual had to be restrained by careful behavior, so, too, did the naturally powerful will of the numerical majority—often called passionate or violent—have to be subordinated to the rules of Constitutional government.[27]

Violent imagery in Southern oratory was a way of fitting political situations into a cultural context and, because of this, Southern orators of all persuasions were remarkably consistent in their use of that imagery. So far as the rhetoric of political discussion was concerned, moreover, the gaps between public and private expression or between discourse in speech and in print were practically nonexistent. It is fitting to look at oratory, in particular, because of the primacy Southerners themselves gave it as a form of political expression, but other forms of expression also shared its characteristics. Even the most private correspondence had the formulaic properties of public speeches, and newspaper writing, less restrained because less direct, was certainly as full of stale metaphor as were the speeches of most Southern leaders. All made use of violent images and analogies and all paid the same attention to order as most of the oratory of the day.

The real power of the language of violence in oratory ultimately was shown by its capacity to characterize so many positions that Southerners took during the antebellum period. Nullifiers in the 1830s, for instance, could use such language to proclaim that they had been pushed reluctantly into taking their stand as easily as conservative antinullifiers could draw on the conventional imagery, as Hugh Swinton Legaré did, to accuse their opponents of proposing a "revolutionary measure—a remedy derived from a source above all law, and an authority which bows to no arbiter but the sword."[28] Violent rhetoric could evoke both resistance to oppression and a state of disorder, and seemed to cover so many matters in antebellum Southern political life.

Here, indeed, was the key to the use of violent language in Southern oratory. Such language, as we have seen, really referred to two things, both of which were important elements in elite Southern social ideals. On the one hand, political violence, like social violence, meant that there was disorder because proper relationships had broken down. On the other, violent action or the threat of it indicated that matters had become so desperate that violence was the only thing that would set things right. The notion of violence as a last resort was no less powerful in Southern political rhetoric than in other areas of Southern life. Essentially, the two notions were complementary. The threat of violence meant that relationships had become so unsatisfactory that they were worth destroying altogether—as had occurred, of course, in the American Revolution.

It was in terms of this dual meaning, in fact, that an interesting but subtle change in the violent rhetoric of Southern orators occurred in the nineteenth century. This may be seen by contrasting the words of Southern spokesmen during two of the tensest periods of sectional dispute during the nineteenth century, the debates over the admission of Missouri and Maine in 1819 and 1820 and the Congressional discussion of the organization of the Nebraska territory in 1854. In both cases Southern orators evoked the violence of America's birth to describe the crisis of the day and predicted a violent outcome in its wake. But they gradually shifted their focus away from disorder and toward self-defense in the years from 1820 to 1854.

As Southern Congressmen understood the situation in 1820,

Missouri had applied for admission as a slave state, and Eastern Congressmen would deny statehood by making it conditional on the extinction of slavery. This, to spokesmen for the South, had obvious parallels to 1776 and could only result in violence. Nathaniel Macon, of North Carolina, made a fairly typical approach to the situation when he described the consequences of admitting Missouri with conditions as no different from those of Great Britain's colonial tyranny. Forcing Missourians, at least, to extralegal means of securing their rights, the Congress would "order the father to march against the son, and brother against brother." Macon went on to declare: "It would be a terrible sight to behold these near relations plunging the bayonet into each other," and he reminded his hearers of how awful the sights of the Revolution had been.[29] Drawing on widely held attitudes toward the violence and danger of war, Macon described a scenario in which a nation, united and whole, would be plunged into a kind of interfamilial war. The imagery was apt. Macon clearly did not see a permanent sectional division in the country. His prediction was for the creation of such a division, and, thus, of an unnatural warfare over this single issue. Other Southern Senators shared Macon's point of view and even his words. There was balance in the country, a unity that could be maintained and which would only be disrupted by rash and untimely interference. The result would be, as Georgian Freeman Walker eloquently predicted, "a brother's sword crimsoned with a brother's blood,"[30] an evil of which no man could approve.

Southern congressional orators of the 1820s evoked violence mainly to express their fears for national unity. For those of the 1850s, sectional lines had become hard and fixed, and Revolutionary references thus took a different turn. Instead of predicting disruption and horrible warfare, they described a state of conflict in which the North had become the aggressor and the South was put in a posture of self-defense. Rhett, in 1850, had evoked the need of revolutionary response when he declared that, "to maintain the Constitution, we must dissolve the Union." Alexander Stephens, of Georgia, expressed his sense of the need even more clearly during the 1854 Nebraska debates in an attack on the free-soilers in Congress. Their doctrine, he declared, "is the doctrine of Lord North," and the implication was clear: the South would have to respond as the colonies had, three-quarters of a century before. Resistance to aggression, rather than the fear of disruption, became the dominant idea in violent imagery in the decade before the Civil War.[31]

References to the Revolution, and to the need for self-defense, were not, of course, new in 1854, nor was their application to the sectional dispute. It was simply that as sectional tensions heightened in the 1850s, the experience of the Revolution as a war of self-defense gave Southerners a notably good way of ascribing divisions in the nation to "acts of hostility" on the part of the North.[32] In doing so, like their colonial forebears,[33] these regional spokesmen were able to claim both their own desire to preserve good order and their sense of the necessity to destroy order temporarily to reestablish it more securely. Their rhetorical history of the Revolution, applied to so many situations, seemed especially appropriate for the events of the sectional debate over slavery, and provided the legitimation they needed for bold, even radical action.

Indeed, it was the debate over slavery that brought all of these issues to a head, and violent imagery was often used by those who wanted to preserve slavery in the South. The equation of Northern antislavery with violence had become pressing by the 1850s, and many Southerners were genuinely afraid that abolitionist and free-soil agitation could lead to slave violence in their own communities.[34] Their spokesmen encouraged that fear. Yancey told the Charleston convention,

> Ours is the property invaded; ours are the institutions which are at stake; ours is the peace that is to be destroyed; ours is the property that is to be destroyed; ours is the honor at stake—the honor of children, the honor of families, the lives, perhaps, of all— all of which rests upon what your course may ultimately make a great heaving volcano of passion and crime if you are able to consummate your designs. Bear with us then if we stand sternly upon what is yet a dormant volcano, and say we yield no position here until we are convinced we are wrong.[35]

In a manner consistent with proslavery predictions of impending race war, Yancey too asserted a violence just below the surface of Southern society. Any encouragement to the carefully-regulated slaves could trigger a chaos of violence and retribution.

The debate over slavery thus became peculiarly appropriate for violent description. Fearful of violent freedmen, and compounding metaphor with reality in their oratory, Southern politicians were no less distraught over their growing inequality in national politics, an inequality in what had for some years developed into a "fierce" rhetorical warfare between the North and the South. Every abolitionist success came to be understood as something which, to use the words of Mississippi's John Quitman, plainly showed "the deliberate intention of their instigators to wage a war of extermination against our most valued rights." In the debate over slavery, violent rhetoric reached its peak, for it was in that debate that the apparent need for self-defense and fears for the social order came unmistakeably together in the South.[36]

It would be an overstatement to blame Southern orators for the coming of the Civil War, although Tom Watson in his role of historian attempted to do just that. They exacerbated but did not create the kinds of tensions that ultimately led to secession and war. Nonetheless, one should not minimize their role in political events. In what everyone agreed was essentially an oral-aural community, their limited definitions of political developments must have carried a great deal of weight. More than that, their reliance on formula and convention, particularly the conventions of violence, must have had the effect of limiting the range of interpretations Southerners could give to these events as they occurred. They disposed Southerners to see war as a possibility—though not a necessity—when sectional tensions mounted.[37]

Southerners were not wholly irrational on the question of slavery, nor did they approach sectional issues with their minds completely set. They did, however, approach these extremely difficult questions with a sense that certain alternatives were possible courses of action, and that others were not. Acting with high emotions and strong fears during the crises of 1860–1861, Southerners had long been accustomed to talking about political difficulties in the language of violent revolution and self-defense, and such language undoubtedly affected their choices among the alternatives that presented themselves at that time. Their rhetorical tradition did not determine how people would act, but it undoubtedly influenced their perceptions of what sorts of actions were likely to be effective.[38]

Still, the violent imagery of Southern oratory had more than immediate relevance. The modes of using such imagery had, after all, changed little since the Revolution, and the range of specific situations to which that imagery was applied was extensive. Because of this, it seems likely that the appeal of violent rhetoric came more from its coherence with rather deep themes in Southern social ideals than from its relevance to particular, immediate situations. That is, violent rhetoric was not so much a function of circumstances as it was an attempt to place circumstances in a well-understood cognitive and affective context.

Indeed, if a study of violence in the form and substance of political rhetoric adds only a little to an understanding of what Southern political positions were during the antebellum period, it does show how deeply embedded those positions were in the culture. The rage for order and stability which violent imagery was used to connote went well beyond political affairs in Southern life, as did the sense that the meaning of order was the presence and careful observation of well-defined rules, for their own sake. Southerners, at least elite Southerners, had an ethic that was almost purely procedural, and it carried over into political as well as social life. However cynically the Southern orator appealed to constitutionalism and inveighed against "abstractions" or "higher law," his words could not have failed to strike a response among those who shared his ideals.

Similarly, the sense that violence was a "last resort" and that its threat meant precisely that such a measure of the last resort was called for was more than a political notion. It was a common way for Southerners to talk about situations of any kind, whether in social life, in raising their children, or, of course, in the duel. And the last resort, in all situations, usually meant the breakdown of an accepted pattern of relationships or, at least, someone's belief that the pattern was in danger.

One must, ultimately, turn the usual interpretation of Southern rhetoric around to see the penchant for violent words not so much as equivalent to a penchant for violence itself, but, rather, as a reflection of political proceduralism and an abiding fear for the fragility of any structure. The reason why such violent rhetoric worked, then, had little to do with the impetuosity of Southern politicians—some, like Louis Wigfall, fit the mold; others, Yancey, for instance, most definitely did not—but rather with their belief, which their constituents shared, that relationships could hold only so long as they were tightly regulated and that, once careful regulation ceased or was circumvented, the result would inevitably be chaos—and, of course, violence.

To threaten violence, or to acknowledge its necessity, was to make the rather large claim that things had fallen apart. It was also to point up the nature of what might be called the therapeutic role of violent action. Southerners were fearful of the unintended consequences of violence, as their attitudes toward every form of physical conflict from fighting to warfare make clear. Still, they were sure that violence would bring about change, whether it were for good or ill. Given both the fragility and the totality of the political organism, any sort of violence would inevitably and profoundly affect the whole system—just as applying the rod could reform the child or destroy any significant family ties. That one should turn to violence at all said much about the circumstances; expectations about the consequences of violence were proportionately radical.

Violent rhetoric thus put political situations in their place and encouraged certain kinds of expectations and responses in Southern political life. It was certainly not the only kind of rhetoric Southerners used, and one cannot get from it a summary of the region's politics. What one can get, though, is a clue to the close relationship between politics and culture as that relationship was expressed in one fairly important device of antebellum rhetoric.

9. Hunting, Violence, and Culture

SOUTHERN VIOLENCE was more than an outgrowth of certain predispositions in Southern life, but was, in addition, an expressive form of antebellum culture through which Southerners symbolically described, even acted out, many of their basic assumptions about the world. No form of violence brought out the truth of this proposition more clearly than hunting, when Southern gentlemen acted aggressively in the world of nature. Indeed, many Southerners believed that hunting and killing animals were the only ways in which one could understand nature and man's place in the world, a notion that informed one very popular genre of Southern writing, the hunting narrative. These narratives purported to be factual accounts of the exploits of Southern sportsmen, but, like so much popular writing, they were fairly standardized elaborations of the underlying ideology of the sport. And the underlying ideology of the hunt was an almost metaphysical encounter with the ideas and sentiments that pervaded all Southern ideas about the meaning of violence.

As was the case in regard to most things they did, Southerners talked about their hunting as though it were something unique to their region, claiming both a special appreciation for the hunt and a distinct adeptness in its pursuit. If other regions, the West, for instance, could boast of such remarkable species as the buffalo, none, so Southerners claimed, could equal their own South in either the diversity or the quantity of the sort of game that would engage the connoisseur of field sports. Those Southerners who, like George Anderson Mercer of Georgia, removed for a time to the North, soon felt a longing to return to a home where, as he said, "I could kill more birds there in one week, nay in one day, than I killed in New Haven during the year I spent there." The accuracy of his view may be doubted, but it is beyond question that Southern sportsmen tended to see hunting as a form of recreation with special ties to their region and to themselves.[1]

Moreover, if many Southerners, black and white, hunted out of necessity, Southern planters felt there were more important matters in hunting than gathering meat. In part, they valued hunting because they attached great value to all amusement, at least when pursued with proper moderation. As William Elliott of Beaufort, South Carolina, wrote, "*Amusement*, in some shape or other, is indispensable to [man]. And if this be so, it is a point of wisdom, and it is even promotive of virtue, to provide him such, as are innocent. Field sports are both innocent and manly." As Southerners practiced it, in the opinion of Elliott and many other writers on the subject, hunting not only provided great sport, but it also inculcated the high moral standards and ideas Southern gentlemen ascribed to their class.[2]

Engaging in field sports of various kinds contributed to the image of plantation splendor the Southern gentry hoped to project to themselves and to the outside world. Being well-equipped for the hunt was as necessary to a display of social refinement as were the other "amusements of cultured people," whether lavish parties, libraries of classics, or well-appointed tables. Many Southerners kept dogs of English or Irish blood for practicing the art of the chase—not only for fox and deer but also for exciting native quarry, including the wildcat—and planters often used the hunt to entertain visitors and share in the company of social peers.[3] Southern planters devoted as much attention as they could to insuring good sport, as is shown, for example, by Frederick G. Skinner's comment, in his memoirs, that everyday hunting in his area was always done at a distance from the home plantation in order "to reserve the home birds for expected guests." Hunts were frequently concluded by a gala evening and a substantial dinner, so that most hunts among the wealthy were part sport and part social affair.[4]

The camaraderie of the hunt was in itself valued by many Southern sportsmen, and for more reason than the fact that a day in the field was best concluded by a meeting over a "sparkling glass" to "fight the battle over" with one's companions.[5] Although there were some who enjoyed solitary hunting, most preferred to hunt with friends because the sport's social character increased its virtuous influences. John Stuart Skinner, Frederick's father, wrote in the introductory editorial for his popular *American Turf Register and Sporting Magazine,*

> The knowledge of mankind, so essential in every practical pursuit, nay the yet more essential knowledge of one's self, is not to be found alone in solitary labour nor in solitary meditation; neither is it in a state of isolation from society that the heart most quickly learns to answer to the calls of benevolence.—Sympathy springs from habits of association and a sense of mutual dependence on each other; and the true estimate of character, and friendly and generous dispositions, are under no circumstances more certainly acquired, nor more assuredly improved and quickened than by often meeting each other in the friendly contentions and rivalries that characterise field sports.[6]

For all the enjoyment hunting gave, it also developed character by giving the hunters a sense of what it meant to live in society.

As an element of the well-bred life, Southern hunting was viewed in much the same light as other endeavors. In particular, hunters liked to talk about their sport in such a way that the process—the chase itself—was emphasized over any possible ends. Such an emphasis was clearly behind their attitudes toward the spoils of the hunt. Nothing was more detrimental to good hunting, many declared, than to kill with any practical intent. Hunting solely or even primarily for food led inevitably to killing for quantity by any means available, and this was contrary to that "spice of chivalry" that every sportsman should have. Because of this, the term "pothunter" was the worst thing one Southern hunter could call another, since it implied not only that one's practices were unworthy of a gentleman, but also that one was more concerned with the killing than the chase. Not that all Southerners paid attention to the injunction against killing solely for the count. Some actually recorded their numerical successes with great pride. One Tennessee hunter, for instance, wrote to the editors of the *American Turf Register* to report that he had shot, in December, 1830, a total of 234 birds of various species.[7]

But most hunters would not have approved of the Tennessee marksman's boast. The same writer who decried the lack of chivalry among hunters warned that killing for quantity led hunters "to protract their hunt until many of the birds are spoiled by the heat and delay," and totally useless killing was condemned by most writers of the time. Still, the basic impracticality of the Tennes-seean's approach, though it could lead to the same results as pot-hunting, was accepted by many as the only valid attitude with which to approach the field. Even if books on hunting rarely lacked excellent recipes for the preparation of game, the meat was always to be considered as secondary in importance to the hunt itself. Few, perhaps, went so far as William Elliott in his claim that "the worst use you can make of your game, is to eat it yourselves," but most did feel that if one were too concerned with living off the spoils, it turned one's attention away from hunting and toward more ma-terial concerns. George Tucker drew on this belief when he tried to defend the importance of a classical education. "Classical learn-ing," he wrote, "is like many sorts of hunting, less valuable for the game than the exercise of pursuing it."[8]

Above all, Southern hunters valued the excitement of their sport, its thrills of danger and its intensity. William Elliott, writing about the popular foxhunt, described the ideal atmosphere for a chase once the dogs had found the trail of the prey.

> Gather, huntsmen! Now we shall see sport! The ground was fa-vorable for the sportsmen, for a road ran parallel with the direction of the cry, and thus the whole field got placed; and took a fair start with the dogs. "There they go! Look! for the hedge! Rouser leads,—he leaps the hedge!—ha! he has overrun the track! Black has caught it up!—it is all right! There they go!—look at them!— listen to them! Huntsmen, is it not charming? Does it make your pulse quicken? Is there not a thrill of pleasure shooting through your frame? Can you tell your name? Have you a wife? a child? *Have you a neck?*" If you can, at such a moment, answer such questions; you do not feel your position, and are but half a sports-man!![9]

Perhaps most hunters were able to remember their families and names, even when the chase got hot, but Elliott nevertheless evoked the kind of total involvement most sportsmen hoped to achieve when they took to the field.

Much of the excitement of a hunt derived from the fact that its outcome was never certain. A part of the uncertainty lay in the hunter himself. There was always a danger that upon sighting the prey the hunter would not only forget the existence of his neck, but would, in his anxiety, "forget to cock, or pull upon the guard of the trigger, or fire without effect."[10] Overcoming the weaknesses of one's own nature was a major task all hunters had to face, because it was a tendency of the human animal to lose composure. When the buck rushed by or the covey took wing, any hunter could become too eager and excited, and as a result, make a bad shot. And overcoming impetuosity was an important lesson the hunter learned from his sport. By the same token, many people recognized that too much composure could ruin whatever pleasure one might get from the sport. As one writer stated, the sportsman must curb his excitement to be a good shot with a steady aim, but no one could "commend or covet a degree of frigidity or nonchalance, and consequent certainty in shooting, which strips the sport of all its fascinations."[11] The problem was not so much to do away with anxiety and eagerness as it was to discipline one's excitement by concentrating on shooting the target.

The animals themselves added to the excitement of a hunt. The prey was supposed to provide a fair test of the hunter's skill, so that a fierce or cunning animal added to the problematic but fascinating character of the sport. To William Elliott, for example, the sport of going after devil fish grew out of the fact that "no precautions, can absolutely secure the sportsman against danger," in some cases mortal. Indeed, the excitement of the popular sport of wildcat hunting derived in part from the well-known ferocity of a species which, when overtaken, might well kill the hunters' dogs.[12]

Danger aside, however, the most skillful animal was thought to provide the best hunting. Foxhunts were seldom held, and even less approved, when the foxes could not run well, as in mating season, since the sport was more enjoyable when one pursued an animal at the peak of its ability to elude eager pursuers. This was one reason why Southern hunters repeatedly contrasted their reliance upon the wilderness for game with the preserve shooting found in the North and Europe—Elliott called it "popping over our own nurselings." Only the animal in nature had the freedom and wildness necessary to give the hunter both the pleasure and work of a proper chase, and without those elements there could be no real hunt.[13]

At the same time, Southerners felt that, however accomplished the prey, even the noblest animal, fallen, was "a legitimate prize to the prowess of man" by virtue of human superiority.[14] Men were superior to other creatures and could, if they so desired, kill any species in any quantity they desired. However much this superiority may have been a biological fact, it certainly could have ruined the excitement of a hunt. Most sportsmen recognized that there were proper and improper ways to go about their business.

No matter how much a man wanted to take the game, a sporting nature meant that the prey had to have a fair chance: unfair methods would, as one writer declared, make a true sportsman's blood "boil over with contemptuous indignation." And, indeed, the rules of the hunt were intended to make the contest fair by allowing the animal, in the words of an ardent foxhunter, "the advantage of a considerable 'law,' (he being one of the very few victims, to which the said monosyllable is ever beneficial)." One hoped for a good hunt pursuing a skillful quarry, but given the natural endowments of man, one also had to place limits on himself in the interest of a sporting contest. Such methods as night fire-hunting—in which the animal was temporarily blinded by a bright light and shot—or using a pointer to locate deer were definitely frowned upon by genuine sportsmen for whom chivalry, as they said, still had some meaning.[15]

But proper hunting was more than an expression of the Southern admiration for chivalry. A few writers, Thomas Bangs Thorpe, for example, considered the presence of limiting rules as evidence for the civilization of the hunt, and hunter-naturalist C. W. Webber believed that one could construct a sort of historical model relating advances in the code of the hunt to the progress of human society.[16] The main effect of rules, in any case, was to reinforce the hunter's focus on the process of the sport rather than on the achievement of results, regardless of method. Compatible with Southern proceduralism in much of life, hunting conventions preserved the sport's uncertainty by placing controls on the extent to which man could exercise his superior powers of reason so that the animal would have the opportunity to employ its wiles or ferocity to greatest advantage. The conventions lowered man, in other words, closer to the level of his prey. Such limitations were necessary if the hunt were to be exciting and in addition, if the hunter were to learn the important lesson of self-discipline from his sport.

Again, Southern sportsmen, like those anywhere, did not hunt merely to kill. The killing was interpreted more as a culmination of a much broader experience, a culmination which did not have to be inevitable. An old Virginia hunter put the case best, in the opinion of one writer: "An old sporting friend told us that he had no fancy for these perfect shots, who go through the operation with the coolness and composure of an automaton. He had seen many enjoy more pleasure in shooting and missing than these do shooting and killing. It was nothing with them but cold-blooded murder. But in hunting, as in politics, the mere pleasure of the chase will not satisfy—success to some extent must perch upon our banners to console for past defeats, and inspire hopes for future triumphs."[17] Never to have succeeded would have ruined the hunt, but inevitable success would have made the hunter something more like a killing machine than a man.

The uncertainty of the hunt, much as it was founded in rules for practical action intended to maintain self-discipline, also reflected a basic ambivalence in the Southern mind about nature as such—an ambivalence that appeared whenever Southerners talked about human nature, society, or the world in general. It took the form of the inevitable problem of achieving a proper balance between reason and passion. In the case of the hunt, the tension between these two sides of every man was most clearly shown in the attitudes Southerners expressed toward the character of the true man of nature, the hunter.

For many Southerners, the return to a natural humanity was what hunting was all about. The hunter felt he could be himself in the field, ignoring the constraints of society, since, as George Anderson Mercer said, in the "playground" of nature, "we can freely laugh and skip and dance, without fear of offending some would be critic, who deems a stern, stiff, silly dignity the only true index to a manly character."[18] It was along similar lines that Frederick G. Skinner wrote, after an extended outing, "Now when I look back on the ups and downs of a long career both at home and in foreign countries, I can candidly say that those seven months of isolation in the wilderness, deprived as I was of luxuries and with scarce enough of the necessities of civilization, are remembered as among the happiest of my life."[19]

It is not to be supposed, however, that everyone saw the man of nature as a childlike innocent. If some, like Mercer, could write of a freedom to laugh and play, many others would have agreed with the very different sentiment expressed by Thomas Bangs Thorpe, a Northerner who well understood the ways of the South, that the hunter was one who retained "enough of the old leaven of the wild man to love to destroy the birds of the air and the beasts of the field." The natural man who was the hunter was part of a web of interrelationships with everything in the world and, as the author C. W. Webber declared, "The law is, that animal life must be perpetuated through death and decay." The man of nature was, among other things, a killer, and the act of stalking and "destroying" the prey was an assertion of that natural quality, an act in which "the civilized man, the savage and the brute have been brought into extraordinary relations." In the hunt, in other words, the old problem of passion and reason—of natural ardor and social convention—received its clearest and most obvious exposition.[20]

The familiar drama of reason and passion entered into Southern thinking about hunting in a couple of ways. Of course, the dialogue between the two sides of human nature underlaid the concern for self-discipline in the field. But more profoundly, in their definition of the man of nature Southerners looked directly to the familiar dilemma of human nature for identifying what hunting did for the individual. The discipline of the field not only helped a man to contain his excitement and hence make a good shot, it also helped him to control his passions in a more profound way by placing limits on his desire to kill and destroy. Above all, the hunting narratives illustrate the depth of a paradox inherent in Southern conceptions of passion and reason because they show man as a creature who could, by virtue of his reason, engage in the most savage forms of hunting; whereas, by contrast, the hunter who most thoroughly entered into nature was the one who brought the highest level of civilized concern and a code of law into the pursuit of his game. Nothing mediated or resolved that paradox and, indeed, the ambiguity in the role of the hunter did nothing so much as to reveal the complexity of the antebellum conception of human nature.

But hunting, like other forms of violence, not only expressed the Southern sense of what self-discipline really meant. It also expressed that other paradoxical relationship Southerners so frequently saw in their discussions of violence, that between violence and order, in this case the order of nature. The hunter was, it seems, supposed to be something of a naturalist, and, in the opinion of several writers, the only sort of scientist who did adequate research. Southern natural history in general was methodologically based on observation rather than experimentation; and the hunter, whose powers of observation had been developed in actual contact with the creatures of nature, was clearly in a better position to understand living nature "than whole fleets of navigators and scientific pedants in silk stockings, could attain in half a century." It is small wonder that the peripatetic Southern immigrant John James Audubon, who combined natural science with prodigious hunting skill, was widely admired by Southern sportsmen.[21]

The hunt contributed more to an understanding of nature than the simple provision of a setting for focused observation of the species, for any genuine understanding of nature grew out of what the antebellum Southern scientist Stephen Elliott described as man's "mutual dependencies on every side with substances animate and inanimate." The hunter actually entered into that relationship of dependencies among the species when he practiced his sport correctly. Passive contemplation of nature was not only undesirable but, given human ties with all of nature, was not really possible. The understanding of nature was an *act* by which the successful naturalist became a part of the world in which he lived. It was, perhaps, this need that prompted Audubon to write to his sometime collaborator, the Reverend John Bachman of Charleston: "In my opinion there is more real merit in destroying one single nominal species, than in the publishing of six new good species, as the latter are always well able to speak for themselves *when found!*"[22]

The quality of man's relationship to his world was one of the major features of the hunt and was not a simple one. Man was thought to have dominion over the other creatures of the world and, in accord with prevailing ideology, the hunter was believed to be a necessary trailblazer for the settled husbandman and thus for civilization.[23] In this, the hunter was merely acting as the agent of inevitable human domination, making possible that conquest of the wilderness that was necessary to the spread of society.

Still, man's dominion over other creatures was not just a matter of superiority, for the relationship involved his view of the animals themselves. First, it was clear to many that human beings and other animals were not too far separate from each other but were part of a grand scheme of being. Webber described this scheme with particular vividness in his utterly remarkable review of Audubon and Bachman's *Viviparous Quadrupeds of North America.* Drawing first a major distinction between types of animals—birds and quadrupeds—Webber argued that birds "are a type of aspiration": "The bird has wings, and like the imagination or the soul, triumphs over time and space. It lives in the pure ether, all its modes and associations are those of the soul's life. Even its impulses are those of cold intellection." To the contrary, the animals, as Webber called mammals, appealed to the material, lower, and purely sensuous instincts, were cruel and vicious. Even in their modes of sustenance, the two types of creatures differed: "As with the higher intellect, alimentation is with them [birds] a means, not an end—life has higher blisses for them—they eat to live, while the animal lives to eat." While it would be tempting to draw a parallel between this view of the species and the studied impracticality of Southern hunting, Webber would not have agreed:

> Nevertheless, for all this, it must be confessed that as yet animals more closely approximate our sympathies—appeal through more numerous traits of consanguinity to our interest than birds. This, though honest and honorable, is somewhat humiliating to a transcendental pride. They who would sillily have the human all spiritualized, forget that such conditions belong to a remote development, or the other life; that linked as we are here with the material, it is as brave of us, and as necessary, that we should be true animals, as that we should be true angels. Our mingled being can as yet be neither one nor the other wholly, but must wisely compound between the extremes and be simply what we are—*men!*

Acknowledging man's passionate nature, Webber saw, as did many other Southerners, that much of the pleasure of the hunt grew out of the kinship that existed between the hunter and the hunted—the feeling that, though different, there was a basic similarity between the two types of creatures.[24]

Still, however much Southerners felt a closeness to the prey, the relationship was not one of equality. As the Spanish philosopher José Ortega y Gasset has said of hunting in general, "the question is always of one animal striving to hunt, while the other strives not to be hunted. Hunting is not reciprocal."[25] What did have to be present was an attitude of respect for the rights and abilities of the prey, and this view was generally acknowledged by Southern writers about hunting. It was this point that Audubon, for one, had in mind when he recorded in his journal, "Every time I read or hear of a stupid animal in a wild state, I cannot help but wishing that the stupid animal who speaks thus, was half as wise as the brute he despises, so that he might be able to thank his Maker for what knowledge he may possess."[26] The kinship between hunter and hunted was one of nature, enforced by convention, growing out of the common place both he and his prey occupied in a larger scheme.[27]

This sense of common existence with the animals led to the most significant and striking aspect of the hunt, its proclaimed inseparability from the love of nature. As in its ties to social class, hunting supported Southern claims to a distinctive identity inasmuch as Southerners' professed closeness to nature was yet another way in which they described their differences from people in the North. To many, this closeness was a product of the twin variables of climate and history and could be traced back to the earliest days of English settlement. In the case of the Southern settlers, according to William Lowndes Yancey, "Nature smiled upon them and invited them to repose upon a bosom that, warmed by a Southern sun, teemed with all the elements necessary to rational growth. With its umbrageous shades—its never ending verdure—its never tiring fertility—its crystal streams—it forms a strong contrast to New England. Slight efforts produced more than corresponding returns of all the necessaries of life. Nature was the friend of the Cavalier."[28] While, in Yancey's opinion, the product of nature's beneficence was a prosperity returned for slight effort, many other Southerners expressed their gratitude in terms of a deep and abiding love for the beauties and wilds of nature herself.

To an extent, hunting and the love of nature went together simply because to engage in the sport took one into the natural wilderness where, as young Mercer wrote, "No houses no works of men's hands, were there to mar the scene: it lay just as God had made it in its own beautiful freedom." This sense of freedom and unspoiled beauty was available to all hunters, and most seem to have taken great delight in it. Just as natural science could profit from the hunter's knowledge of nature's ways, so too could one develop a deeper affection for nature through venturing into the midst of an unspoiled wild. And the hunters frequently report having been moved, if not always, like one S. G. F., to the extent of quoting Byron, at least to a contemplation of the scenes upon which they entered.[29]

The depth of the association of hunting with a love of nature was shown most clearly in the way in which writers of hunting narratives juxtaposed scenes of pastoral peace with their outbursts of venatic fury. In fact, the two elements seem to have gone hand in hand in any fully experienced hunt, as one particularly vivid example in the reminiscences of Frederick G. Skinner shows:

> As soon as we caught the gleam of the distant water through the trees we dismounted and, masked by the procumbent trunk of an enormous tree, we crept to a spot which commanded the whole pool. We had the pleasure of seeing its black surface dotted over with wild-fowl mostly teal, with a few mallards at the far side, and all within easy range of our ten-bores. It was a most interesting sight to see these beautiful wild creatures gliding thither and thither and giving life and animation to this secluded pool in all freedom and confidence of unsuspected danger. We were in no hurry to convert this idyl of the wilderness into a scene of slaughter and terror, but the angel of mercy who hovered over us for a moment fled away on drooping wing before the fierce venatic instinct to kill. The Chief, pointing to the teal, which were all near together, gave a low whistle, when in obedience to a singular instinct, peculiar I believe to that family of ducks, they all huddle into a compact mass into which we poured our fire with murderous effect. As they took wing they received the contents of our second barrels, when three more victims were added to the number of the slain.[30]

Skinner's account was not unusual. The same S. G. F. who was moved to quote Byron concluded his poetic paean with the comment that "we met at the millpond into which we wished to drive the deer." Other Southern writers used the identical juxtaposition. Audubon, for example, once recalled an excursion to the "Great Pine Swamp," where, he noted, "My ears were greeted by the notes, always sweet and mellow, of the Wood Thrush and other songsters. Before I had gone many steps, the woods echoed to the report of my gun, and I picked from the leaves a lovely Sylvia, long sought for, but until then sought for in vain." Mercer, too, commonly connected pastoral scenes with accounts of shooting success.[31]

To understand the vivid juxtaposition of scenes of idyllic peace with those of "slaughter and terror," one must have some idea of major Southern conceptions of nature. In the opinion of many, nature was remarkably systematic. Although there was the view, widely shared, of such scientists as Dr. A. W. Ely that nature was too diverse for man to understand fully and that to grasp " 'in one organic whole the entire science of nature,' is a thing to man impossible," still most people, including Ely, would have concluded with the Alabama orator Henry Washington Hilliard, that "throughout the whole circle of created beings there is an endless diversity, and yet an unbroken order." Regardless of whether one could comprehend it, nature was ordered, regular, and, ultimately, an organic system of which man was himself a part.[32]

This conception of nature, connected as it frequently was with the defense of a conservative social order, and, more especially, with the justification of slavery, was a useful notion for many people in the South. For one thing, it allowed them to acknowledge a basic unity of mankind without denying the vaildity of social, temporal hierarchy. At the same time, because the conservative ideology of the South made many people look askance at all efforts for social change, such a conception of the world supported a belief that human beings had no business interfering with natural or social processes; or as Theodore Bozeman has put it, given such a view of the world, "reform could almost be equated with vivisection."[33] One Southerner summed up the matter in a critique of Jeffersonianism addressed to a friend. Citing the existence of "great minds" as evidence to disprove the doctrine of human equality, he went on to points of more general significance: "The universe & all creation contradict it God has made no two beings equal he has created no two things a like In his infinite wisdom he has decreed that those who see should lead the blind, that the wise should lead the ignorant that the head should direct the movements of the tow [*sic*] this is true of the great laws of nature & when one of these laws is over turned, chaos & confusion must follow."[34]

Given this view of nature, and its importance to Southern beliefs about social order, the symbolic role of the "slaughter and terror" becomes plain. Southerners believed strongly in the desirability of order, but they also believed that order was a fragile set of relationships, all too liable to disruption, especially in view of the nature of human beings. The hunter's acts of destruction paradoxically supported his belief in the permanence of nature since, events made plain, his actions did nothing to "over turn" any of the great laws upon which the world order was based.[35]

The Southern hunter loved nature for many things, but what he may have loved most about it was its order. The system of nature had a degree of stability which society could only approximate and which the hunter proved time and again he could not permanently disrupt. The hunt provided, to use Richard Slotkin's phrase, a "regeneration through violence," but it was not a regeneration of either self or society. Instead, for the Southern hunter there was something of an intellectual regeneration in the dramatized renewal of faith in the existence and permanence of a stable and orderly world.

Still, it is also important to bear in mind the more specific features of the Southern writers' pattern of association. Assuming that the writers were aware of a contradiction between peace and destruction—and Skinner's narrative indicates that he, at least, was—the metaphoric power of this pattern of association grew out of the actual meeting of the two elements in the hunters' narratives.[36] Killing was in some sense necessary for an appreciation of what nature meant to human beings. Precisely this need to kill was expressed by George Anderson Mercer when he shot his first woodcock: "He ran before me in a dense thicket, and, as I had never killed one, I shot him sitting. It was too thick to mark him, had he flown and I missed; so I was determined to make sure of him. I found but his head and wings."[37] Audubon, too, had a feeling like Mercer's when, spotting a kingfisher, he longed for a gun as he had never before seen one "fresh killed."[38]

The meaning of hunting and the deeper relationship of man and nature that was expressed in the narratives grew out of the tension between the elements of idyll and terror primarily in connection with the animals themselves, for the prey was present in both peace and destruction. The prey in the Southern hunt was both animal and more than animal insofar as the hunters were enabled, by their acts, to enter nature. To Audubon and Mercer, for example, one did not fully appreciate an animal unless he had killed a specimen, and one may note again Audubon's comment that he would prefer to destroy one single nominal species than to publish six new ones. One probable explanation for this attitude is that nature, for Southerners, was not just ordered, but vast, and if they were to lay claim to an appreciation of such an unfathomable system, they needed some sort of handle by which to grasp at least a portion.

The prey, because it was a part of both idyll and terror, met this need. As an animal, it could be killed, but the prey was more than animal since its destruction affirmed rather than destroyed the stable order of nature. The prey was, in other words, a metaphor for all of nature, and was brought by the hunt into a "collision" with man through which he was able to grasp, actively and intuitively, that sense of stability which contemplation could only approach. The process was not an unusual one, since much ritual and many popular beliefs depend upon a similar activity of using an accessible part to reach an inaccessible whole.[39] To the extent that patterned accounts of hunting summarized the main conventions of action and feeling in the experience itself, they show it to have been a kind of secular ritual for many sportsmen in the South. That it was, has much to do with its meaning for them.

When Southerners hunted animals, they were able to put a critical part of nature into a mode of expressive action. If one may interpret the prey as a synecdoche for all of nature, then the meaning of Skinner's reminiscences and similar narratives becomes clear. The fusion of concept and action brought about by the hunt was a way in which the Southerner could put into concrete modes of expression an otherwise inexpressible sense of what it meant to be a part of an orderly but awesome natural world, for in the hunt he acted in nature in a most profound way. Going a step further, it might be said that what the tension between peace and destruction accomplished intellectually, the synecdochic properties of the animals together with the expressive acts of hunting accomplished for the emotions. In both cases the hunter was enabled to get a deeper sense of his own character as a man of passion and reason while entering, as well, into a system of the most perfect order.

An analysis of hunting narratives should not obscure the simple fact that Southerners hunted for pleasure and that they wrote their narratives—like all sportsmen everywhere—mainly to relive the thrill of the chase and, of course, to brag about their accomplishments. Still, the role of the stories as entertainment did not preclude their authors' use of familiar themes and ideas in talking about the sport. In fact, Southern sportsmen-writers tended to talk about their kind of violence in a way that was quite consistent with the ways in which other members of the society talked about other kinds of violence, whether personal or political. The sporting accounts gave new elaborations to old themes, most significantly by extending them beyond the bounds of human life and into all of the natural world.

Moreover, the hunt, like the duel, emphasized the expressive character of violence in the Old South. It was not simply that when Southerners acted violently they did so in accordance with certain social values and beliefs. Instead, the violence itself could be an effective way to express certain assumptions about life and about the world. In the case of hunting—as the popularity of Audubon attests—it was a uniquely appropriate way of appreciating the orderly world of nature. When Southerners had a particularly difficult notion to express, violence was not an uncommon way of doing it.

10. *Violence in Southern Fiction*
Simms and the Southwestern Humorists

THE SYMBOLIC POWER of evoked violence was great in the Old South. It could define political situations; it was necessary for an understanding of nature and the world. Because of its power, violence was also a key element in antebellum Southern fiction. The use of violence was not, of course, unique to Southern writers during the first half of the nineteenth century. Most of the popular novelists of the day made violent conflict a part of their work. Nevertheless, those of the South did use violence in a way that was consistent with more widely held attitudes in the region, while portraying those attitudes in original and often surprising ways.

Southern writers were, above all, moral writers, concerned about their own culture and about the moral questions to which it gave rise. Not loath to experiment with literary form, and certainly concerned with questions of criticism and aesthetics, Southern writers nevertheless acknowledged a preference for literature that was morally as well as stylistically good—although with varying degrees of emphasis. Their readers, moreover, tended to place such concerns at the forefront of their own evaluations of most works. That a work express their sense of right social values, in one way or another, was a major concern for readers and writers alike in the Old South, and provides an important key to understanding relations between literature and culture during the period. This is not to say that fiction mirrored culture; it is to say that the two were intertwined.

Violence played an important part in connecting literature to culture. Southern writers used violence in ways that made their morals clear as they focused on problems of cause and effect and, more deeply, on the relationships of violence to human nature and society. Their fiction elaborated on the Southern conception of violence in often remarkable ways.

Of all writers of the Old South, William Gilmore Simms was the most "Southern." An ardent regional patriot, Simms's identity with his South grew as his career progressed. His defenses of the South and her institutions, including slavery, were important contributions to Southern polemic; his histories did much for the region's identity. Since the studies of Vernon Parrington, at least, Simms's role in the development of Southern Romanticism has been acknowledged, even if his marginal position in Southern society has been overemphasized.[1]

Simms was, to say the least, a prolific writer. One of the few professionals in the region, he was the author of some eighty-two volumes, not to mention essays and short stories. His novels of the American Revolution are generally accounted his best works, and, because they so clearly summarized Southern "cavalier" stereotypes, have received the greatest amount of scholarly attention.[2] But Simms wrote other kinds of works and these indicate no less clearly major elements in Southern culture. His "domestic" stories and "border romances," as well as his novel of the Revolution, are important for historical cultural analysis.

Taking Simms's work as a whole, it is possible to identify a single theme informing his use of violence. In his fiction, Simms represented life as a kind of test which everyone—every man, at least—had to undergo. The crux of the test was the traditional, familiar problem of balancing necessary passion with equally necessary restraint, and violence, in its occurrence or in the form it took, was a measure of how well one did in the test. In general, when one turned to violence, it meant failure, for it indicated an inability to cope properly with difficult situations. Even when violence itself was necessary, as in war or in the interest of law, it could go to excess, and this, too, was a sign of failure. Simms was, then, a novelist who dramatized the classical opposition between passion and restraint as Southerners had understood it throughout the period. His novels explored the meaning of that opposition and his treatment of violence showed the difficulties that opposion entailed in life.

The understanding of violence and its causes Simms showed in his works was subtle. If he saw himself as a moral writer, one who strove for a "consistency of moral drawing"[3] in his work, his moral vision was neither simple nor pedantic. In none of his stories, for instance, was violence rewarded for itself; its consequences were only rarely positive, whether the perpetrator was the hero or the villain. Good and bad alike suffered from the violence of a Simms novel. The reason for this was that, consistent with traditional morality, he saw the passion leading to violence as being itself incapable of completely positive or negative treatment. As he wrote in defense of his controversial story "The Loves of the Driver": "Active virtues can only live in the heart which is filled with active passions."[4] He might have added active evil, as well, for it was the conflict between the virtuous and sinful passions that formed the basis of all Simms's novels.

Simms used passion as a first cause in human affairs, a background upon which secondary, immediate motivations operated. Still, different situations created different needs and posed their own problems, and because of this, one may distinguish among the three groups into which Simms's works fall. In his domestic stories, Simms looked mainly at the passions which motivated the individual, and at their interplay with social reality. And, again, he recognized that passion could move men to good or to evil, depending upon the role it was given to play. Hence, the ambition of Edward Clifford, main character of Simms's psychological novel *Confession* (1841), led him to great attainment in his community. His wrongful exclusion from the household in which he was raised both encouraged his ambition and failed to dampen that sense of duty to others that led him to do noble deeds on their behalf. A passionate man, Edward Clifford was also a peculiarly virtuous man, and, Simms made plain, the one characteristic led to the other. Indeed, even Simms's most villainous figure, Martin Faber, was motivated to his first act of cruelty by a passionate defense of a friend against unjust punishment. Faber and Clifford were passionate characters from the beginning, and as Simms never failed to remind his readers, that passion gave them whatever virtue they had, even if it also led them to crime.[5]

Still, the protagonists in the domestic stories, whatever their virtues, were ultimately unsympathetic characters. Even their apologies for their crimes could never be taken as justifications for what they did. This was particularly so in the case of the thoroughgoing villain, Martin Faber. After bemoaning his failure to receive a sufficiently strict upbringing, this earliest of Simms's tragic figures was made to say, "You will argue from this against my notion of the destinies, since I admit, impliedly, that a different course of education, would have brought about different results. I think not. The case is still the same. I was fated to be so tutored."[6] Ascribing his tragedy to fate, Faber was engaging in "an ordinary habit of such persons," and the lesson the character claimed to have learned was not to be "charged upon the author." As Simms declared in one of his Revolutionary novels, "There is an argument . . . for every error, and poor Humanity will never want a lie to justify any of her failings to herself."[7]

Here, then, was a central point in Simms's domestic novels—the ability of men to rationalize and justify their own crimes to themselves. Again, Simms represented life as a test, and in domestic affairs a major reason some failed was because they could convince themselves, wrongly, that what they did represented no failure at all. Moral blindness was more than a feature of human nature; it was an achievement of all-too-human people.

The difficulty was compounded, moreover, by the uncontrollable character of the passions once given free rein. In *Confession*, this characteristic was crucial, as a seeming misconception on the part of Edward Clifford brought on a jealousy that fed on itself until, like a disease, it "was part of my very existence."[8] Even contrary evidence only confirmed Clifford's suspicions that his wife was having an affair with his best friend.

Jealousy and vengeance, unrequited love, all were pivotal to Simms's violent scenarios. As Simms used those evil passions, moreover, they informed not only protagonists' actions, but also their perceptions and interpretations of every event in their lives. Passion, always in the background, came to the fore as it gained control and became the primary motivation for every action, overriding and rendering irrelevant all other immediate motivations. Violence, ultimately, was a product of distorted morals only aided by circumstance.

Passion could get the upper hand in a Simms story because of the moral blindness of his characters. Such blindness, encouraged in part by the human ability to rationalize anything, was equally aided by characteristics of Southern society, at least as Simms represented that society in his fiction. Simms himself described his domestic works as having "a prevailing presence of vehement individuality of tone & temper" enhanced, as he saw it, by the frequent use of first-person narration to bring about "a certain intensifying egotism." Thus, in his domestic stories, Simms portrayed that tendency toward social exclusiveness and misanthropy which figured so prominently in many Southerners' discussions of social violence, displaying its consequences in a bold, exaggerated form.[9]

Simms constructed his domestic stories on the basis of that distance between self and others which Southerners talked about in so many areas of life, and it was a feeling about which he often raised grave doubts. In *Confession* he employed notions of distance to play off class, family, and friendship against each other in such a way that violence came to appear almost inevitable. The novel moved in two directions at once. On the one hand, it was a chronicle of the growing domination of jealousy ever Edward Clifford, a domination leading him ultimately to murder his wife and to instigate his best friend's suicide. At the same time, it was also a chronicle of the growing domination of jealousy over Edward Clifford changed from a man of strong friendships and a sense of social duty to one who saw only himself and his wife (and, ultimately, only himself) as important figures in the world. It was, in other words, a chronicle of "intensifying egotism"—an insiders' group with an ever diminishing membership ending, finally, at one.

Simms described this process with very little ambiguity, highlighting it by causing jealous passion to operate in a setting of marriage between cousins and suspicions against old friends. Marriage within his own family was Clifford's first step toward that inward turning that led to a loss of reality and a fantastic obsessive jealousy about his wife's liking for the friend. Certainly, moreover, marriage within his family, and to a woman with whom he had been raised in the same household, was the sort of inward turning that captured, dramatically, that sense of family-against-the-world which so many Southerners evoked in their letters to each other.[10] In this novel, however, Simms used it as a beginning for a continuing process of exclusion and misanthropy which led to a loss of sympathy for anyone, and, thus, to violence.

Most of Simms's domestic novels, like *Confession*, displayed an exaggerated but not unfamiliar way of looking at social relations. Misanthropy was a potential conclusion to Southern social philosophy, and such Simms characters as Edward Clifford or Martin Faber became thorough misanthropes, living on suspicion and fantasy rather than social understanding. As, for various reasons, they chose to isolate themselves from the larger society, their evil passions took over their minds and led them to tragic violence.

The central focus on morality-put-to-the-test which dominated Simms's domestic stories dominated his other forms of writing as well. In his very popular "border romances," for example, Simms posed the same sort of dilemma for his characters, that of maintaining moral virtue in the face of challenges posed by circumstances—here, the unsettled character of frontier life. His vision of the frontier was not a favorable one. The people, he once wrote, were "wild," and, under the circumstances, his stories could not avoid having "a gloomy and savage cast."[11] The test was, as a result, a difficult one.

Because of this, Simms saw the frontier as a perfect setting for a "romance." The romance was, for Simms, a special genre of writing, one different from the novel and, thus, one to which the rules of novel writing did not apply.[12] Truth had to be a part of a romance, to be sure, but it was to be truth of a particular sort. It had to be moral truth, accomplished, as he would say, by "consistency of moral drawing." Far less complex than Simms the domestic tragedian, Simms the border romancer, dealing with a "frontier and wild people," still gave a moral focus to his work, a focus developed through violence. But in the exaggerated frame of the frontier, violence took on a more elemental cast. There were few subtleties of good and evil on Simms' frontier.

The border romances drew to some extent on themes found in the domestic stories. This was certainly true of *Guy Rivers*, for example, a story in which a young gentleman, Ralph Colleton, went West after having been refused the hand of his cousin Edith. Ralph encountered Lucy Munro—whose own father was dead and who was currently under the guardianship of her somewhat shady uncle, a frontier innkeeper—and Guy Rivers, a notorious outlaw and suitor of Lucy. Rivers was the most fully drawn of Simms's frontier outlaws. Once known as Edward Creighton, Rivers had been an aspiring lawyer and politician in South Carolina, in the district, in fact, where Ralph's uncle exerted much influence. Desiring, as a young man, Edith's hand, Creighton, like Ralph, had gone West, but once there had changed his name and fallen into a life of crime under the tutelage of Lucy's guardian. Much of the plot revolved around Rivers's hatred for the other failed, but more proper rival, Ralph—a class hatred born out of his own failure as a suitor. Defeated in love, Rivers declared, "These defeats were wormwood to my soul; and if I am criminal, the parties concerned in them have been the cause of the crime."[13]

Thus, as in *Confession*, Simms constructed *Guy Rivers* as a tale of the noble passions blunted and thus perverted to evil ends. In a remarkable, long passage the outlaw gave an explanation of himself to Munro:

> Look, for instance, at the execution of a criminal. See the thousands that will assemble, day after day, after travelling miles for that single object, to gape and gaze upon the last agonizing pangs and paroxysms of a fellow-creature—not regarding for an instant the fatigue of their position, the press of the crowd, or the loss of a dinner—totally unsusceptable, it would seem, of the several influences of heat and cold, wind and rain, which at any other time would drive them to their beds or firesides. The same motive which provokes this desire in the spectator, is the parent, to a certain extent, of the very crime which has led to the exhibition. It is the morbid appetite, which sometimes grows to madness—the creature of unregulated passions, ill-judged direction, and sometimes, even of the laws and usages of society itself, which is so much interested in the promotion of characteristics the very reverse. It may be that I have more of this perilous stuff about me than the generality of mankind; but I am satisfied there are few of them, taught as I have been, and the prey of like influences, whose temper had been very different from mine . . . I was the victim of a tyranny, which, in the end, made me too a tyrant.[14]

The passage, which continues for several pages, expressed Simms's belief that passion could go for good or ill, just as it supported his view of the romance: jarringly out of place, the outlaw's apologia gave a decidedly moralistic undertone to the events of the tale.

Still, as Simms made plain, Rivers's self-defense, like Martin Faber's, was merely rationalization, and more insidious for that fact. Simms himself considered Guy Rivers "the monster of the book,"[15] and, for all that character's attempts to justify himself in terms of a past of social rejection, he was a thoroughgoing villain from his first appearance until his death at the end. With Rivers, that is,

Simms again pointed up the power of rationalization to excuse giving freedom to the worst, most fiendish passions.

But in *Guy Rivers*, as in all the border romances, the frontier itself did much to highlight Simms's characters. The frontier, according to Simms and others, was a force in itself on individual lives because of the nature of its settlement. Going to the frontier had been founded on a "spirit of adventure . . . not materially differing from that, which, at an earlier period of human history, though in a condition of society not dissimilar, begot the practices denominated, by a most licentious courtesy, those of chivalry." The problem here was, of course, "that the natural mixture was still incoherent—the parts had not grown together." The result was that "A mass so heterogeneous in its origin and tendency might not so readily amalgamate." And the ultimate end of that heterogeneity was violence: "wounds and bloodshed, and occasionally death."[16]

Simms appears at first to have shared in the more general American ambivalence about the frontier. Fearful of its regressive force on civilized people, he nevertheless recognized its role in building a distinctive American character, and it was in terms of this that he created the aptly named "Mark Forrester," a backwoodsman who saved Ralph Colleton's life and who, mistaken for the young gentleman, was murdered by Guy Rivers. Presented initially as a frontier type of high character but simple manners, Forrester proved, from the beginning, his ability to manage in the wilderness. He was the image of that Daniel Boone type which dominated American literature during the antebellum period. He dressed the part, and certainly talked it. Describing vigilantes to his shocked, civilized companion, Forrester declared, "What! you from Georgy, and never hear tell of the regilators." Misspellings were his stock in trade.[17]

Such a dialect could never fit a nobleman, especially not one with the finer feelings possessed by Forrester. He deeply loved Kate Allen; however, as a frontiersman, he was shy about telling her. Such feelings, the stuff of domestic romance, were not for the backwoodsman, and the Forrester who spoke in misspellings was no match for the romantic Forrester who took his farewell from Kate for what proved to be the last time. He asked of her a pledge; she asked what it might be, and he replied, "It shall come with no risk Kate, believe me, none. Heaven forbid that I should bring a solitary grief to your bosom; yet it may adventure in some respects both mind and person if you be not wary."[18] Noble sentiments required noble language, spelled correctly.

But still, Forrester was a creature of the frontier. He was himself involved in the vigilante movement he described to the horrified Colleton, and his own tragic death was due to his succumbing to the lawlessness of his society. This frontier failure was a pivotal episode in the book—a merciless massacre of the Georgia Regulars whose duty it was to keep squatters off "lands now known to be valuable." The frontier folk, not all of them outlaws, followed the detachment into a narrow gorge and buried its members beneath an avalanche of rocks and dirt. Forrester was among the killers, and though filled with remorse after the act, shared with his fellows a frontier short-sightedness which believed "ulterior consequences were as nothing in comparison with the excitement of the strife." Sacrificing long-term social good for short-term goals and for excitement was an act as characteristic of Forrester as of frontier people in general, and the consequences of such impetuosity could only be disastrous.[19]

Frontier people sometimes behaved nobly, but Simms ascribed no unqualified nobility to any frontier dweller. This one simple fact was clear enough in the character of Mark Forrester, but it underlay the whole of *Guy Rivers* and of the other border romances, as well. To the extent that active self-restraint was active virtue, and the key to Simms's moralism, the frontier represented a place where restraint was wholly absent and, thus, it was a place of violence.

In a strange and perverse way the frontier was also a place of exile, voluntary or otherwise, for those whose strong passions had been thwarted. Edward Clifford, of *Confession*, went to Texas after causing two deaths. Ralph Colleton and Guy Rivers both went to the frontier after their attempts to channel their passions in acceptable directions were thwarted by Ralph's uncle. A similar journey was chronicled in another border romance, *Richard Hurdis*, in which the title character went West having become convinced that his lover desired not him, but his brother, John. Leaving in a fit of pique, Hurdis acted in a way that exemplified that unbridled egotism Simms explored in his domestic stories. Indeed, Governor Hammond wrote to the author: "I do not like Richard, whom you have made as silly as he was surly. . . . I don't think even a novelist should allow any success to such perverse—coarse—sour tempered & jealous minded rascals as Richard Hurdis."[20] Only Harry Vernon, in *Border Beagles*, journeying West on a commission from a friend, showed much quality of character on the frontier.

Simms, like W. J. Cash in the twentieth century, saw the frontier as more than a place. As a novelist engaged in moral drawing, Simms found in the frontier an ideal evocation of that lack of restraint, permitting unvarnished egotism, which led to violence in human society. Simone Vauthier, in a superb essay on Simms, has suggested that the theme of escape and return was dominant in the border romances as characters sought to escape society only to return after an experience of frontier disorder. Although Vauthier interprets this theme in terms of the characters' recognition of their own failings, one may also see it as an escape prompted by selfish desires and a return inspired by a learned rejection of selfishness. This rejection was encouraged by the experience of a world based only on the gratification of immediate, egotistical passions. The "frontier," for Simms the border romancer, was just that, a place where one could see his darker passions in social form.[21]

If the frontier were a disorderly place, it was matched in violence by those periods of time in which disorder predominated, the times of war. Simms's eight novels of the American Revolution, together with *The Yemassee*, a tale of colonial Indian war, are his most noted works, and, perhaps because of their similarity to the works of Scott and Cooper, they have remained his most accessible writing. These works show an understanding of violence and warfare that not only elaborated on more generally held Southern attitudes, but also fit closely with Simms's own treatment of violence in his other novels.

Simms held no naive view of the nature of warfare. His Revolution, in particular, was no simple patriotic struggle motivated by ideals and marked by noble deeds. Like most Southerners, he conceived it as a war for independence, more a defense of homeland than an idealist revolution and, as Hugh Holman has suggested, issues tended to be "submerged in hatred, revenge, and cupidity."[22] Evil was found on both sides of the Revolutionary struggle—although only the Americans had any balancing virtues—because war, like the frontier, cancelled out all the usual restraints.

Whatever Simms's purposes in writing his Revolutionary novels, he saw America's War for Independence as a peculiarly fruitful field for the romancer. As he wrote in his preface to *The Forayers* (1855), the war allowed him "to illustrate the social condition of the country, under the influence of those strifes and trials which give vivacity to ordinary circumstances, and mark with deeper hues, and stronger colors, and sterner tones, the otherwise common progress of human hopes and fears, passions and necessities."[23] The American Revolution was a war in, as well as against, South Carolina society, and moral tensions no less than violent adventure were the subjects of Simms's works, moral tensions as they were heightened by war. The romances of the Revolution—and one may say *The Yemassee*, too—were not war stories, but stories of people in wartime, stories of morality and sentiment.

Simms's ideal warrior in his Revolutionary romances was, to use an overworked term, a man of "chivalry." But chivalry meant more than physical courage or even style as Simms used the term. It meant, as he enthused, "gallantry, stimulated by courage, warmed by enthusiasm, and refined by courtesy,"[24] and this in turn implied mainly that physical daring and enthusiasm in battle were well-tempered by restraint. His main character in *The Partisan* (1835)— perhaps, the best of the Revolutionary romances—was Major Robert Singleton, a figure in whom "true chivalry" found its purest expression. Singleton's understanding of himself as a warrior mirrored Simms's sense of war as a test, something to be undertaken out of duty and with an awareness of its potential for unleashing the most violent passions. For Singleton, as for any soldier, war meant struggle, chiefly the struggle of maintaining his own decency when violence was required. And he well understood the difficulty of the task. When a young lieutenant participated successfully in his first battle, Singleton was given to meditation:

> The boy had a new sentiment in his bosom, the contemplation of which made it eminently more familiar. He could destroy—and he could do so without his own rebuke. . . . He could now pluck with impunity—so he began to think—and his mind was on that narrow eminence which divides duty from an indulgence—which separates the close approach of a principle to an appetite—which changes the means into an end; and, identifying the excuse for violence, with an impelling motive to its commission, converts a most necessary agent of life into a powerful tyranny, which, in the end, runs riot, and only conquers to destroy.[25]

He then spoke his thoughts to the boy: "War is not a sport, but a duty, and we should not love it. It is a cruel necessity, and only to be resorted to as it protects from cruelty; and must be a tyranny, even though it shields us from a greater."[26] The real work of the soldier, then, was that of any man under provocation—to act firmly, but with restraint, and to give his passions only the freedom necessary for victory. The challenge was that one might feel pleasure from that necessary release of the passions. There were pleasures in war, but they were "dangerous pleasures," indeed.[27]

Singleton and his fellow partisans were singularly successful at confining passion to the battlefield. The only fiend among them had earlier been driven to insanity when the Tories murdered his wife. The British and Tories, on the other hand, had no success at all. "Sanguine" was the word Simms used most often to describe the enemy, and he never failed to show that bloodthirsty cruelty was their most salient characteristic. This was particularly true of the Tories. "If a rebel resisted, they slew him without quarter; if he submitted, they hung him without benefit of clergy." Indifferent to claims of humanity, the British and the loyalists were no more concerned with the laws of war. Their lust for fighting and for a "banquet of blood" overcame all their better feelings.[28]

Violence was at the center of Simms's Revolutionary novels. He portrayed war primarily in terms of its violence, of fighting and killing, and the trial war posed was that of maintaining one's humanity while acting with necessary violence. This was certainly true of *The Partisan*, in which the chivalrous Singleton contrasted sharply with the sanguine foes of independence. It was also true of the other books. The Tory villain of *Mellichampe* was motivated solely by a thirst for vengeance. The villain of *The Scout*, brother of the patriot hero, merely used Toryism as an excuse for an outlaw life, and Simms sharply contrasted outlaw violence with the self-discipline and restraint of even rough-hewn patriot forces.

Indeed, if there were a central episode in the works which summarized both the testing character of war and American virtue, it occurred in *Mellichampe* when a young, nonaristocratic patriot named Humphries captured a particularly troublesome spy, Blonay. With "malicious joy," he enclosed the spy in a hollow tree, where the unfortunate victim would die a slow, horrible death, buried alive. Such a death was not to occur, however. Tortured by guilt and remorse, and by nightmares, Humphries ultimately rushed back to release Blonay, giving him his freedom. Though it involved a minor character, the episode was important because it encapsulated a central point in all Simms's books on war, that of acting as violently as the battle required while refusing to let violence control one's will.[29]

Whether Simms wrote about war, or the frontier, or even domestic life, he used violence in a way that dramatized the traditional conflict between passion and reason. The situations he portrayed were all of the sort that made restraint difficult, and the real tension in most of his works came from his heroes' struggles to come to terms with themselves, keeping their excited passions under control. It is usual to consider Simms a Southern "Romantic," and, insofar as he emphasized the power and importance of the emotions, the consideration may be just. Yet it may be equally fair, and perhaps more accurate, to describe Simms as a Southern novelist of a more traditional and an older understanding of human nature and society, one which puts the greatest emphasis on the problems and possibilities of holding passion in check under trying circumstances. The difficulty of moderation was at the core of virtually all his works.

The South produced other writers than William Gilmore Simms. Some wrote novels which, focusing on war and adventure, were much like those of Simms in the understanding of violence and human nature they portrayed. Most of these writers were part-time authors who showed little of Simms's skill, but the well-known works of such men as Nathaniel Beverly Tucker, who published *The Partisan Leader* in 1836, or William Alexander Caruthers, whose *Knights of the Golden Horseshoe* (1845) virtually summarized the famous "cavalier" stereotype, also dramatized the testing character of violence as they exalted the man who could act competently and with restraint in trying circumstances. There were, however, other writers in the Old South whose works took a much different approach to Southern life from that of Simms and his fellow novelists. These were the "Southwestern humorists." Beginnings as composers of newpaper sketches of frontier life, many of the more prominent humorists published their better pieces in books and anthologies, reaching wide audiences. Their pictures of life in the Old Southwest became a major force in the development of long-enduring stereotypes of Southern poor whites and plain-folk, as fact and fancy merged in the minds of many readers.

It would, however, be a mistake to use the writings of the Southwestern humorists as data for the delineation of the "frontier mind" or of plain-folk culture. This is not to say that these writers did not draw extensively on the facts of rural and town life for their sketches; many of the practices they described were common occurrences in the lives of the people about whom they wrote. More significantly, many of the sketches drew heavily on oral tradition, on folktales and anecdotes current among whites, in the South, and some of the material was itself adopted into oral tradition, surviving into the twentieth century. There was, to be sure, a compatibility between the writings produced by the Southwestern humorists and the people they wrote about, but this is not to say that Southwestern humor was a reflection of frontier life. The authors put tradition into literary form, for one thing; but, more than that, they never lost sight of the potential for entertainment, especially for humor, in their accounts of frontier folk.[30] While they did not falsify life in plain-folk society, they did dress it up a bit, highlighting and exaggerating those features that made it differ from elite community ideals. The society they portrayed was recognizably that of the Southern frontier, but its ways were described in a manner that emphasized how different the folk were from those who wrote about them.

The Southwestern humorists accomplished this feat by, structurally, dissociating their readers from the events they described. Indeed, as Mody C. Boatright pointed out, "they were not writing about events, but about concepts." The key to the humor was what Walter Blair called the "box-like" structure which framed most of the stories the humorists wrote. The stories themselves were often told in dialect, but the narratives were almost invariably introduced and concluded by the more correctly written words of, presumably, the author himself—a gentleman-outsider, not a frontiersman. The overall effect of this box-like structure was three-fold. For one thing, it served to establish the incongruity between the narrator and his subjects, between propriety and frontier life. Secondly, it encouraged identification *not* with the subjects, but with the observer, the often condescending outsider looking in. The reader was to watch, not participate in frontier life. Third, and related to the other two, this structure emphasized the bounded character of the story's events. The narrator's world, however extensive his contacts with frontier folk, never lost its integrity. His subjects lived in a separate world, one which was amusing, but also safely at a distance from his own. The stories were, then, far less a reflection of life on the Southern frontier than they were evocations of a frontier setting in order to talk about significant "concepts" in antebellum Southern culture in an interesting but controlled way.[31]

Augustus Baldwin Longstreet's *Georgia Scenes* has rightly been considered the groundwork for all Southwestern humor. Published in 1835, it had but a few predecessors and many followers.[32] Not as earthy as some writers, Longstreet still portrayed a Georgia frontier that differed little from such later settings as Johnson Jones Hooper's Alabama or, to take the boldest of them all, George Washington Harris's Tennessee. Longstreet's use of violence, moreover, may be taken as a virtual model for all the Southwestern humorists who would follow him.

The one notion that predominated in Longstreet's treatment of the violence among frontier folk was his subjects' lack of understanding of or appreciation for the intense symbolic importance of physical violence. He made this notion clear in his classic story of "The Fight," an account of a rough and tumble battle between two friends. The fight was almost archetypal—although it lacked a gouging—complete with lost ears and noses and concluding with the victor grinding dirt and sand into his opponent's eyes. The causes of the fight were unimportant. The people of the area had longed for a match between Bob and Billy, the two combatants, and had sought to provoke it in every way possible, but without success. When it finally occurred, it was the result of a quarrel between the champions' wives and was encouraged by a little dirt-eater named Ransy Sniffle primarily to gratify his own curiosity.

Once the fight had been agreed to, it began at once and was the object of intense public interest. The townsfolk picked sides and cheered the partisans on with bloodthirsty frenzy. After the fight and after the two had recovered from their wounds, the business was forgotten. Billy, the loser, decided he must have been in the wrong in the dispute, since he had been licked in a "fair fight," and the two resumed their friendship. The fight had settled all.[33]

The attitudes toward violence portrayed here, like those on

Simms's frontier, were quite different from those of the Southern elite. If, ostensibly, family feeling was at issue in the quarrel between the two wives, the immediate cause of tht fight was trivial—tempers had flared over who should be served first at the local store. Beyond that, Longstreet's violent world had its own properties. One was the kind of impermanence that could allow the healed warriors to make up and be friends again. Violence, here, was not the culmination of passion gone out of control, an irrevocable act that meant the triumph of passion and the loss of the will, but was a natural part of a society in which self-control and restraint were not prevalent.

This sense of the nonclimactic character of violence was emphasized by the community's encouragement of the fighters. Gathering around, making predictions, and yelling such things as "That'll do for his face; now feel his short ribs, Billy!" the lookers-on showed their indifference not only to the pain of the combatants but to any potential consequences the fight might have had, as well. Simms and others interpreted violence as a threat to the community, as the signal of a rending of the social fabric. The short-sighted people of Longstreet's frontier assigned no such importance to violence. It was a matter of short-term amusement, and they were largely indifferent to either causes or social consequences.[34]

Such indifference was a dominant element in Longstreet's treatment of frontier violence, not only in "The Fight," but in other sketches, too. For example, in "The Gander Pulling," a day of sporting ended in a free-for-all, "after which all parted good friends." Similarly, in his account of "The Turf," the day of the races was marked by "two little boys engaged in a fight, and not less than fifty grown men gathered around them to witness the conflict, with as great an uproar as if a town were on fire." Thoughts were not on developing discipline in "the moral garden" of childhood, but only on the good fun (and fights among "grown persons") the conflict produced.[35]

Short-sightedness and a lack of concern for social order were characteristics of Longstreet's frontier as much as they were of Simms's, and they were summarized by the character of a "fair fight." Here was violence for its own sake, with all attention directed toward immediate victory and away from long-term effects.

Thus, one may say, the importance of maiming as a part of that violence: within the short-run context of a fight, to maim one's opponent would have been a certain way to win, but there was no sign that, in the heat of battle either combatant worried much about a life without a nose or an ear—or eyes. Maiming was a sign of the frontiersman's moral myopia.

Other Southwestern humorists treated violence and fighting in much the same way Longstreet did. The fight stories William T. Porter published in his anthology of Southwestern humor, *Big Bear of Arkansas* (1846), all emphasized the insensitivity of backwoods characters to the importance of violence. A fight need have no cause beyond a desire to show off, and once begun, a fight had to be bloody, complete with gouging and biting. Thus, one "Uncle Johnny" characterized election day in Mississippi as a time for "the peculiar pleasure of witnessing the beginning—ay, the 'opening of the ball' of the 'Fall Fighting Campaign.'" Hamilton Jones further emphasized the indifference of frontier folk to violence in his classic story of "Cousin Sally Dilliard," a popular tale in which an old man, asked to give testimony in an assault-and-battery case, talked about everything but the fight. What the lawyer described by saying, "a more diabolical breach of the peace, has seldom happened in a civilized country" had made no impression on the old man, nor on any other witness called before the court.[36]

The dynamics of fighting were also set forth by Harden Taliaferro—"Skitt"—in his *Fisher's River* in a way that complemented Longstreet's accounts. Even more than Longstreet, however, Taliaferro described the frontier as a tense society, one in which social relations were marked by a hostility maintained for its own sake and one in which violence was indulged with little regard for its consequences. People loved a good, long fight, and fighters became wholly unconcerned for themselves or their opponents in the midst of a contest: "no cool man," according to Taliaferro's account of a fight, "would have taken the knocks, kicks, bites, gougings, battings, etc., that were given and received by those two duelists for a trifle."[37]

Like Longstreet, Taliaferro described a social context in which fighting was so important that preparedness was a great concern. Just as Longstreet's narrator in "Georgia Theatrics" came upon a young man rehearsing a gouging match, complete with screams, so

Taliaferro described a backwoods life in which "bullies would keep their thumb-nails oiled and trimmed as sharp as hawk's claws. Ask them why, they would reply, 'To feel fur a feller's eye-strings, and make him tell the news.' "[38] Frontier folks not only lived with violence, according to these writers, they encouraged it and were disappointed in its absence.

Now, Southwestern humorists often used fight stories in their writings, but it was not simple violence that they were most concerned to describe, since stories focusing solely on violence occupied a relatively minor place in Southwestern humor, whether in books or newspapers.[39] Violence was a part of a larger pattern of frontier life as the humorists described it, and it was as a place without community, a place of social disorder, that the humorists' frontier was most distinguished. Thus, for example, all of Longstreet's characters, even his gentleman on the frontier Ned Brace, were marked by a desire to put self above society regardless of the social costs of doing so, and this generally involved the creation and manipulation of disorder for selfish ends. Ned Brace, for one, was quite willing to prevent a fire company from doing its job in order to satisfy his love of "fun." Or, in Longstreet's classic story of frontier economics, "The Horse-Swap," cheating for profit and for fun provided the major motivating force for his characters. Longstreet's frontier was a place of disordered relations, given the Southern understanding of order, and the disorder was itself indulged, even enjoyed, by the people he described. Violence, with no thought of its deeper significance, was one element of that disorder.

Writers who followed Longstreet also followed his characterization of the frontier as a milieu of purposeful disorder. Some, like Harden Taliaferro, used violence to exemplify that disorder by emphasizing a readiness to fight whether the situation called for it or not. John S. Robb, for another, put violence in the context of a disorder wrought by the absence of law, and, in an especially chilling story, created a frontier where the ability to shoot was sufficient claim to anything.[40] But even nonviolent stories could have a violent undertone, particularly when the humor grew out of a hero's ability to create disorder while dodging its violent consequences. Johnson Jones Hooper's Simon Suggs was one who thrived on the disorderly condition of frontier and town life. His "life story" opened with an account of the young Simon's avoiding a whipping for gambling while at the same time cheating his pious father out of a horse, and the episode was a virtual paradigm for a life spent skirting violence and convention for profit.[41]

The tradition received its artistic, if not chronological culmination, however, in the character of one Sut Lovingood, created by George Washington Harris. Sut's world was one of almost total anarchy, and his view of social relations showed a complete disregard for the stability and form which elite Southerners prized so highly. It was not that Sut was especially cruel or violent. Indeed, he was not, and violence was rarely a part of a Lovingood story, at least not violence growing out of conflict. What one did see in Sut, however, was an almost militant dislike for social order, and especially for those institutions which contributed most to stability on the frontier. Sut's sharpest barbs were inevitably aimed at such upholders of order as preachers, "ole field schoolmasters," and officers of the law.[42] Indeed, he fairly spat contempt on the sheriffs, declaring, "Sheriffs am awful 'spectable people; everybody looks up to 'em. I never exactly seed the 'spectable part myself. I'se too feared of 'em, I reckon, to examine for it too much. One thing I knows: no country atwixt here and Tophet kin ever elect me to sell out widders' plunder or poor men's corn, and the thoughts of it gives me a good feeling; it sorta flashes through my heart when I thinks of it." As for the sheriff of his own county, "Ole John Dolton were a 'spectable sheriff, monstrously so, and had the best scent for poor, fugitive devils—and women—I ever seed; he were surefire."[43] Harris, the Democrat, was not entirely off the mark in capturing something of plain-folk class resentments. Undoubtedly, too, he effectively satirized the pretensions of some frontier folk to civility in a way that readers of all classes felt they could appreciate. The humor in Harris' satire should not, however, lead to the conclusion that his readers were somehow expected to share Sut's point of view.

The satire of institutions in the Sut Lovingood stories may have been pointed, but one cannot get away from the character in whose words the satire was put. To be sure, Sut was not a cruel figure, but he was remarkably indifferent to human nature and social needs. Painfully blunt in his dealings with strangers—a wrongly proffered question could lead him to exclaim, "You go to *hell*, mistofer. You bothers me"[44]—Sut was no less insensitive to the efforts of others to create a satisfying life on the frontier nor, indeed, to any discomfort others suffered. He caused a share of it himself. Equally important was Sut's failure to take himself at all seriously. He was, he said frequently, "a natural-born durned fool," and he was not about to make any efforts to change. Sut disapproved of social institutions and he also found irrelevant the cultivation of those skills which many of his readers would have felt made society work.

Maybe Sut's adventures did point up pretensions. And it may have been that some readers found in Sut's point of view a healthy honesty and a vicarious release from the constricting attachment to form that marked Southern social ideals. But, ultimately, Sut himself was not a sympathetic character. Whatever the humor in Sut's attacks on formal society, his disregard for others and his unwillingness to respect efforts toward "improvement" marked him off as one dedicated to producing disorder in society. Indeed, even his relations with his own family were distinguished by a callous indifference, especially toward his father, that most of his readers would not have found acceptable. Readers may have found Harris's stories funny, but they would have had to distance themselves from Sut in order to laugh.

The same was true of most of the characters of Southwestern humor. Not only did most of the authors manage structurally to distance their readers from the characters of the narratives, but the figures they portrayed, for all their abilities to profit at the expense of social convention, were never able to triumph fully over those conventions. Their poverty was chronic, and temporary successes tended to be accompanied by sudden losses as profit, like Simon Suggs's ill-gotten gains, "melted away and was gone forever."[45] At the same time, the connections between the humorists' works and life on the frontier were complex. In portraying a plain-folk readiness to fight founded on mistrust of others, these writers certainly drew on the facts of frontier society. The same may be said of their portrayal of violence as essentially lacking the symbolic significance it had in more elite circles. But the creative disorder of a Sut or a Simon Suggs was not prized by the people of the Southern frontier, nor were they the simple dupes of such types that writers portrayed. Plain-folk were, after all, known to lynch outlaws and gamblers. The people of the frontier valued order, and their violence was often intended to maintain it. In their image of frontier disorder, then, the Southwestern humorists may have come closer to capturing plain-folk fears than frontier values. What the writers did show, more certainly, was a graphic image of the significance of their own beliefs.

It was in terms of this that one can see the function of violence in the works of the Southwestern humorists. These writers were constructing a fantasy world out of the frontier, and, in this context, were displaying the image of man in a world ruled by passion. Like Simms, the humorists claimed that the world they described had disappeared. Longstreet closed his fight story with the assurance that "thanks to the Christian religion, to schools, colleges, and benevolent associations, such scenes of barbarism and cruelty as that which I have been just describing are now of rare occurrence." The Southwestern humorists' frontier was a setting in which they and their readers could, in a sense, play with passion, exploring its meaning and social implications, and constructing a fantasy-world in which it predominated. They were not of the frontier, and frontier reality was, itself, a thing of the past, so that the dangers of such a world need not trouble them in their exploration of it. They could, in the context of humor, look at the dreadful and the forbidden, but they could do so safely at a distance.[46]

Because of distance and context, violence could be funny; but the humorists had a concept of violence which differed little from that of serious-minded Southern writers. It was, to them, a natural concomitant of an absence of social restraint and of a self-centeredness that triumphed over social demands—a potential selfishness that all men shared and had to guard against. Conceptually, it was a very short step from the misanthropy and cruelty portrayed by Simms to the world view of Hooper's Simon Suggs, whose "whole ethical system lies snugly in his favourite aphorism—'IT IS GOOD TO BE SHIFTY IN A NEW COUNTRY.' "[47] The worlds portrayed by both Simms and the humorists were contradictions of that social organicism, preserved by formalized self-interest, which was the elite Southern ideal. And violence was inseparable from such a situation.

Conclusion
Edgar Allan Poe and the Southern World View

PROBLEMS of passion and restraint occupied a central place in antebellum Southern thinking about human relationships. Given their tie to human violence, these themes also took on pressing practical importance for Southerners both within and outside their society. As a result, the evocation of violence in everything from political rhetoric to literature had the power to call forth very deep assumptions about human nature and the world. We have, up to this point, examined what Southerners thought about passion and the ways in which, by stressing self-discipline and restraint, they sought to control and guide passion in order to avoid crisis, disruption, and violence. But, as we have seen, Southerners were never completely secure about anyone's ability to keep passion in check. The one Southern figure who detailed this problem of security with the greatest power, though his focus, on the surface, differed markedly from that implied by traditional views, was Edgar Allan Poe. His conception of passion was not, to be sure, unlike that of Simms, but Poe virtually abandoned altogether the claim that restraint could hold passion in check. As a result, Poe, more than any other writer, explored the meaning of predominating passion, forcing his readers to experience its overwhelming power and grotesqueness. Indeed, however untraditional his treatment of passion may have been, Poe presented more fully than any other writer the deepest of Southern fears.

Poe's place in Southern literary tradition, to the extent that one may speak of such a tradition in the nineteenth century, has never been clear and has occasioned much debate. Parrington emphasized Poe's alienation from the Virginia background, but saw, nevertheless, that his Southern upbringing had much to do with the author's life and career. He finally concluded that Poe "got from Virginia what was bad rather than good." Other critics and historians have assigned more importance to Poe's Southern background, but have felt that whatever "Southern" there was in Poe's work was a good deal more "elusive" than matters of locale or plot. Whether it were, as Ellen Glasgow once wrote, a question of style or, as Robert Jacobs suggested, Poe's understanding of terror, the Southernness of Poe has been appreciated if not entirely understood.[1]

One reason Poe's place in Southern literary tradition has been obscured is that, unlike most antebellum writers, Poe rarely chose Southern settings for his works. When he did, as in "The Gold Bug," he seemed wholly unconcerned to make anything of it. Poe was more comfortable with remote or unspecifiable settings in his tales, so that the circumstances were removed as much as possible from convenient reference. Thus, for example, when Poe wrote "Politian" to dramatize a classic Southern legend, the Kentucky tragedy, he set the action in Rome, apparently in the sixteenth century. And even though it has become fashionable to read his novel, *The Narrative of Arthur Gordon Pym* (1838), as the product of a Virginian's fear of slave insurrection—and of memories of Nat Turner—Poe still set his tale of black violence in what was decidedly a fantasy world in the Antarctic.[2]

If anything, the very vagueness of Poe's settings increased the power of his tales by decreasing the possibility for detachment. The terror and violence could not be ascribed to such unusual social conditions as those of wartime or the frontier. His characters were men and women, unplaced in time or space, and whatever violence they did to each other grew wholly out of their natures, unaided by social peculiarities. Poe's tales were unframed and, as a result, dealt more in apparent universals than did the works of any other Southern author. Still, if Poe did deal in "universals," his key concepts and sentiments cohered with Southern social and moral concerns. In Poe, that is, the classical concern for passion and reason which survived in the South was taken over and its universal status reasserted, made to speak to essential questions of human nature and conduct rather than to the identifiable realities of Southern life. It is not so much that Poe was a "Southern writer" as that, playing out the causes and consequences of violence and passion through the experience of terror, Poe created a world in which one may see the darkest streaks of the antebellum Southern world view in their most general form.

Violence was an important element in many of Poe's stories. Like Simms and most Southern writers, Poe portrayed violence as a certain sign of passion's victory over self-restraint; however, Poe was far less concerned with any material causes of that triumph. There was nothing in Poe, for example, to correspond to Guy Rivers's apologia nor to the mixed virtue and misanthropy of an Edward Clifford or a Martin Faber. Poe's was less an exploration of character than of passion itself, in terms of its power over the individual. Thus, his use of violence was both simpler and deeper than that of Simms and other Southern writers.[3]

It is possible to isolate several themes which Poe dramatized through violence, but the dominant one in the tales was what he termed "monomania." His central character in the early "Berenice" represented monomania in its most exaggerated form, but differed little from the more fully drawn monomaniacs of later tales. Egaeus had a problem with the attentive properties of his mind, leading him so to focus on the frivolous as to lose all consciousness of time or place, or even of himself. Living in a world of imagination, "the realities of the world affected me as visions, and as visions only, while the wild ideas of the land of dreams became, in turn—not the materials of my everyday existence—but in very deed that existence utterly and solely in itself."[4] It was in this context of monomania as a delusive fantasy that Poe set his violence.

Berenice, Egaeus's cousin, was on her deathbed, victim to a lingering illness. True to his monomania, Egaeus was obsessed with her *physical* demise, to the exclusion of everything else. As he glanced at her face, she smiled weakly, and he saw her teeth: "In the multiplied objects of the external world I had no thoughts but for the teeth. For these I longed with a phrenzied desire. . . . I felt that their possession could alone ever restore me to peace, in giving me back to reason." And he got the teeth. Berenice had been buried alive, but Egaeus, wholly unconscious of his act, had dug her up and pulled out all the teeth. He was awakened the next morning by a servant: "He pointed to my garments:—they were muddy and clotted with gore. I spoke not, and he took me gently by the hand:—it was indented with the impress of human nails." The teeth and some dental instruments were next to him on the table.[5]

Poe's dramatization of monomania and violence in "Berenice" was less skillful than in his later works, but it was not atypical. The violent act was without rational motive and was entirely the product of a fantastic, distorted vision held by the actor, a vision informed only by monomania. Moreover, the power of monomania was irresistible. Whereas Simms had treated such a notion as a failure of the will, Poe expressed no doubts about the power of the irrational and wrote many stories—not just "Berenice," but such other tales as "The Tell-Tale Heart" or "The Black Cat"—to make his point. For Poe, an obsession could be blinding in its intensity: Berenice's assaulter was not even aware of his act. Where Simms, the moralist, would have urged self-discipline as a protection against being overcome by passion, Poe dramatized the irrelevance of self-discipline in the face of monomania.

Poe's view of monomania was the Southern concept of passion in a particularly intense form, for it involved the triumph of the inner self, subject to delusion, over every other consideration. Indeed, if it be the case, as Edward H. Davidson has suggested, that horror was Poe's insight into Romantic self-consciousness, no insight could have been more compatible with Southern beliefs than one which viewed heightened subjectivity as tending toward moral blindness and violence. Simms and even the Southwestern humorists put a similar view in more moderate form. Thus, one can see the accuracy of Daniel Hoffman's likening of the horror in Poe's tales to the treatment of beauty in his poems. In both cases, passion was grown so obsessive as to overcome all restraint and control. Poe's insight was not at all eccentric, but was, rather, an exploration of Romantic self-consciousness from a perspective more compatible with classical than Romantic viewpoints, retaining strong fears of passion and its power. Poe saw in that self-consciousness not so much the hope of human fulfillment as, instead, the danger of horror. Romantic and classical views were brought head-on in the world of Poe's tales. [6]

Because of this, Poe, even more than Simms or the Southwestern humorists—whose grotesque world was, after all, passing fast—captured that pessimism which pervaded thought and action in the Old South. He did so in "Berenice," for example, when he characterized monomania as a "disease" which could only be explained by reference to heredity. Poe may have made much of the relationship of man to his environment,[7] but he was no environmentalist. The obsessions that led to violence—Berenice's teeth or the old man's eye in "The Tell-Tale Heart"—were hardly common spurs to violence. Poe's point was, however, the irrelevance of cause. The seeds of evil and destruction were already present in any character, could begin to grow at any moment, and once started would exert complete control. The moral fears of many Southerners were brilliantly dramatized in many of Poe's characters, including Egaeus.

"Berenice" was one of Poe's earliest stories. Its exaggerations were in some ways greater than those in later works, for it was written as a virtual parody of the kind of work that sold magazines. Whether it and stories like it were "in bad taste" was, to the young Poe, "little to the purpose. To be appreciated you must be *read*, and these things are invariably sought after with avidity."[8] But, parody or not, the story expressed an understanding of human passion that Poe would sustain in much of his subsequent work. In the independent and horrible power he ascribed to passion, Poe achieved one of his most significant effects.

In humanity, however, there was more than passion trying to get control. Like many Southerners, Poe accepted a rather dark view of human nature, a view he sometimes called "perverseness." According to the murderer in "The Black Cat," the spirit of perverseness was the ultimate conclusion of a process of moral degeneration, and he added, "Of this spirit philosophy takes no account. Yet I am not more sure that my soul lives, than I am that perverseness is one of the primary impulses of the human heart—one of the indivisible primary faculties, or sentiments, which give direction to the character of Man." Like passion, moreover, perverseness needed no external motivation. It was, in the words of the narrator of "The Imp of the Perverse," a "mobile without a motive," and it meant only that "we act, for the reason that we should *not*. . . . the assurance of the wrong or error of any action is often the unconquerable *force* which impels us, and alone impels us to its prosecution." Perverseness, was, then, simply the will to do wrong for its own sake and, like passion, was internally derived, without reference to the external world.[9]

David Brion Davis has suggested that "Man, according to Poe, had an instinct to submit to the compulsions of society, but he also had a counterimpulse to do wrong for wrong's sake."[10] Yet, as Poe handled the two impulses, they were hardly equal, nor were they ever expressed in quite the same way. Perverseness, which Poe's characters called a primary impulse, was also the active one, able to take control of the individual and, certainly, to triumph over other instincts. Like passion, too, the effect of controlling perverseness was a snowballing one, leading to greater and greater wrong. The narrator of "The Black Cat" began his own cruelties to his cat quite trivially, with minor torments. Once he had begun to act, however, he found himself completely unable to stop harming the animal, even maiming it, until ultimately, purely out of perverseness, he hung it. The more he knew he was acting evilly, according to Poe, the more he felt that such action had to continue, and that it must take increasingly awful forms. Later, a monomaniac because of his crime, the narrator would murder his wife. Knowledge and morality were wholly unconnected in Poe's tales of the perverse, just as knowledge was rendered irrelevant in a setting where passion had become the guiding force.

Poe's understanding of the depths of human perversity was expressed even more powerfully, if symbolically, in his treatment of death. The corpse, especially the quickness and ugliness of its decay, was a motif appearing in many of Poe's stories, and it was his most vivid statement of his conception of human nature. By his descriptions of death, and the ugliness of decay, Poe presented his vision of humanity's essence. It was a motif he would use to striking effect in the repulsive "Facts in the Case of M. Valdemar," a story of suspended animation through mesmerism, the hypnotizing of a man on the point of death. Valdemar had been kept in that state for nearly seven months when it was decided to awaken him. The effort was made, and "his whole frame at once—within the space of a single minute, or even less, shrunk—crumbled—absolutely *rotted* away beneath my hands. Upon the bed, before that whole company there lay a nearly liquid mass of loathsome—of detestable putridity." But the important thing in this story was the surprise of the mesmerist; the rapid decay striking him as something for which "it is quite impossible that any human could have been prepared."[11] If this was what man ultimately came to, in nature, the living man with his rational or moral delusions could never fail to be surprised by the ugly reality of that end. Here, above all, one may contrast Poe's view of man with the positive, even comfortable assessment of humanity implied in the Romantic treatment of death that marked much of American literature during the antebellum period. Poe's accounts could not have been in greater opposition to the beautiful, fulfilling deaths of America's Romantic tradition.[12]

Perverseness was a complement to passion, as Poe used both notions. Human nature provided explanation enough for the evil in the world, because within man was the seed of a horrible corruption, including a will to turn his efforts toward harming others. Even reason provided no check against such a desire, since the most careful plans and strongest arguments could be made to support the most heinous actions—the murder and burial of "The Tell-Tale Heart" or the entombment of a living man in "The Cask of Amontillado." Once the mind was set on doing evil, all that was human could be bent toward the task. The thrust of Poe's use of the perverse, then, was to show that evil needed no motivation beyond itself in order to occur. The violence in Poe's fiction was a display of what human nature could lead men to do in society, but to understand violence one need look nowhere but the human heart.

Poe was a Southern writer who was willing to carry the region's pessimism much further than most people were prepared to do. Southerners in general tended to claim that a clinging to standards was protection against passion and wildness, whether they were talking about behavior in everyday life, about political affairs, or in their literature. Where standards were enforced, violence could be minimized as passion was controlled. Civilization depended upon the effort. Poe portrayed this effort as, essentially, hopeless. Civilization could bring, at best, feelings of guilt, a nagging moral sense which, to be sure, could not be completely destroyed. In such tales as "The Tell-Tale Heart" or "The Imp of the Perverse," this moral conflict led to both crime and confession. Still, the crime occurred and, ultimately, was less a matter of rational choice than of the irresistible power of passion and perversity. Both of these properties of human nature, in Poe's view, rendered the advice of standard morality irrelevant to the problems of life and society.

Poe's presentation of human nature as powerfully passionate and perverse was but a slight exaggeration of Southern ideas examined throughout this study. The veneer of manners and sociability Southerners cultivated was feared to be dangerously thin protection from the inner man whose passions and cruelties were likely to break out at any moment. At the same time, Poe's assertion of the inability of mere reason to hold passion and perverseness in check starkly illuminated the kinds of fears for the fragility of social order that so many Southerners seemed to see. Poe made his readers experience inevitable and horrible violence in his tales and, hence, made public what many Southerners thought but could not admit so boldly—that there was something essential in man's nature that made him unable to find protection from the dangers of life, especially from those that lay within himself. There was, in other words, no security in a human world.

Just as George Fitzhugh has been said to have presented the "logical outcome" to Southern philosophy in his proslavery arguments,[13] Poe expressed the logical outcome of many Southerners' world view in his tales. This is not to say that most Southerners would have found his picture of the world attractive or even agreeable. It is to say that as Southerners found themselves in an increasingly optimistic and individualistic nation—a nation that could produce, for instance, a Whitman—they held to views which asserted traditional forms of pessimism and fear. Poe himself expressed such views, though he took them to striking extremes. In doing so, whether many Southerners would have said so or not, he dramatized the Southern world view in its most powerful and essential elements.

Given this world view, it would have been hard to argue against violence with antebellum Southerners, not because they thought it was good, but because, with their sense of impotence in the face of a perverse humanity, they were resigned to its necessity. Tradition and experience conspired to dispose Southerners to pessimism, founded on strong doubts about human nature. While those doubts held, violence would seem to Southerners to be a natural part of life.

Notes

INTRODUCTION

1. W. J. Cash, *The Mind of the South*, p. 43. The most useful criticism of Cash's book is C. Vann Woodard, "W. J. Cash Reconsidered," *New York Review of Books*, (December 4, 1969), pp. 28–34. Buckingham's comments appeared in J. S. Buckingham, Esq., *The Slave States of America*, 1: 557. The best general study of the South's reputation for violence, and this reputation's relation to fact is John Hope Franklin, *The Militant South, 1800–1861*, especially chapter 1.

2. For a contrast between Southern and non-Southern violence, with a defense of the former, see the letter of "O'Trigger" to the *Charleston Mercury*, August 13, 1856. The "baby ethics" of the North are noted in C. W. Webber, "The Viviparous Quadrupeds of North America," a review of Audubon's book, in the *Southern Quarterly Review* 12 (1847): 277.

3. The quotation is from S. C. Carpenter, *Report of the Trial of Richard Dennis, the Younger, for the Murder of James Shaw, on the 20th of August, 1804*, p. 10. For significant comments denying Southern violence, or imputing worse to the North, see Matthew Estes, *A Defense of Negro Slavery, as It Exists in the United States*, p. 153: or, A Lady of Georgia, "Southern Slavery and Its Assailants," *De Bow's Review* 16 (1854): 48–49. Apparently the view was widely shared. John Hope Franklin reports that Southern travelers to the North often expressed a dread of Northern crime, in his *A Southern Odyssey: Travelers in the Antebellum North*, p. 179. It is probably worth noting my own impression that one can learn more about Northern than Southern crime in Southern newspapers.

4. See Augustus Baldwin Longstreet, *A Voice from the South: Comprising Letters from Georgia to Massachusetts, and to the Southern States*, p. 50. De Bow's effort is in his *Statistical View of the United States*, p. 167.

This is not intended to be a quantitative study of Southern violence, and I have not pursued the kinds of sources which would be necessary for such a study. Still, a few points ought to be made. Murder figures given in the mortality statistics of the 1850 and 1860 censuses confirm the South's right to a violent reputation, at least in comparison to the North. Identifying Southern states as those which would join the Confederacy, plus Kentucky, and excluding Texas and California because of abnormally high murder rates, one finds that the South's 1850 murder rate of 2.28 per 100,000 population was over seven times that of the North's 0.31. Region itself, moreover, accounted for a difference in murder rates that was statistically significant ($F = 19.01$, $p = .001$). The figures are from J. D. De Bow, *Mortality Statistics of the Seventh Census of the United States, 1850*, passim.

The situation for 1860 was more complex, due largely to the addition of new states in the West, but also to a dramatic rise in murder rates in the North. Nevertheless, in 1860 for those states which had been states in 1850, the difference between North and South remained statistically significant ($F = 7.014$, $p = .05$). Among all states in 1860, however, the most telling variable was difference in the length of time a state had been in the Union ($F = 10.069$, $p = .01$), so that frontier conditions undoubtedly had much to do with violence. The figures here are from *Statistics of the United States, (Including Mortality, Property, &c.,) in 1860*.

One could conclude a number of things from this, but, most importantly, region did affect variations in murder rates in the United States in 1850 and 1860, and the South tended to be more violent than the North—confirming, I think, popular opinion. Any stronger conclusions would depend on more extensive testing of more thorough data. One might point out, finally, however, and by way of putting the whole matter in perspective, that murder *and* homicide rates from the antebellum period were far lower than those of our own time. The national murder and homicide rate in 1860 was 3.45 per 100,000 population; that of the United States in 1975, as reported in the FBI's *Uniform Crime Reports for the United States, 1975*, was 9.6 (p. 50).

5. The existence of slavery was used to account for the violence of Southern life, first, and classically, by Thomas Jefferson in his *Notes on the State of Virginia*, ed. William Peden, pp. 162–163. See also Francis Pendleton Gaines, *The Southern Plantation: A Study in the Development and Accuracy of a Tradition*, p. 159.

6. See Everett Dick, *The Dixie Frontier: A Social History of the*

Southern Frontier from the First Transmontane Beginnings to the Civil War, pp. 140–141; Arthur K. Moore, *The Frontier Mind*, pp. 110–112.

7. On the fear of black violence in white society, see, of course, Winthrop D. Jordan, *White Over Black: American Attitudes Toward the Negro, 1550–1812*, chapters 3, 10. On violence in the slave community, see Eugene D. Genovese, *Roll, Jordan, Roll: The World the Slaves Made*, pp. 625–630.

8. Southern moralism has also been noted in William L. Barney, *The Road to Secession: A New Perspective on the Old South*, p. 73. Cash, in spite of his emphasis on hedonism, also notes both moralism and pessimism among antebellum Southerners: *Mind of the South*, p. 54.

9. For a brief but fascinating discussion of violence in the history of Western thought, see George Boas, "Warfare in the Cosmos," in *Violence and Aggression in the History of Ideas*, ed. Philip P. Wiener and John Fisher, pp. 3–14. On the importance of cultural norms to a society's potential for violence, see Rex Nettleford, "Aggression, Violence and Force: Containment and Eruption in the Jamaican History of Protest," ibid., pp. 133–157. The notion that a callousness toward violence itself has long been a part of the American ethos is advanced in various ways by Robert Brent Toplin in *Unchallenged Violence: An American Ordeal*, pp. 153, 157, 182. The phrase "violent tenor of life" is, of course, J. Huizinga's, from *The Waning of the Middle Ages: A Study of the Forms of Life, Thought, and Art in France and the Netherlands in the XIVth and the XVth Centuries*, chapter 1. I am not the only one to notice the relevance of Huizinga's remarkable book to the understanding of the Old South. See also Genovese, *Roll, Jordan, Roll*, p. 687 n. 66.

10. See note 5, above. See also Franklin, *The Militant South*; Herbert Aptheker, *American Negro Slave Revolts*; Richard Maxwell Brown, *Strain of Violence: Historical Studies of American Violence and Vigilantism*, especially chapter 7; Steven A. Channing, *Crisis of Fear: Secession in South Carolina*.

11. Cash, *Mind of the South*, part I. For a similar view, see James C. Bonner, "The Historical Basis of Southern Military Tradition," *Georgia Review* 9 (1955): 74–85. For a somewhat different opinion, see W. Eugene Hollon, *Frontier Violence: Another Look*.

12. The best recent discussions of the notion of passion in Western political and economic thought are these: J. G. A. Pocock, *The Machiavellian Moment: Florentine Political Thought and the At-*

lantic Republican Tradition, chapters 14–15; Albert O. Hirschman, *The Passions and the Interests: Political Arguments for Capitalism before Its Triumph*, especially part I. See also Arthur O. Lovejoy, *Reflections on Human Nature*, pp. 38–39.

13. This discussion owes much to Hirschman, *Passions and Interests*.

14. Ibid., part III. See also Howard Mumford Jones, *Revolution and Romanticism*, chapter 4.

15. George Fitzhugh, *Cannibals All! or Slaves Without Masters*, ed. C. Vann Woodard, p. 27.

16. One should note, in connection with this discussion, the material presented in Richard Sennett, *The Fall of Public Man*, pp. 107–109.

17. Everard Green Baker, Diary, June 30, 1861, typed copy of original on file in the Southern Historical Collection, University of North Carolina, Chapel Hill.

18. Jack P. Greene, *Landon Carter: An Inquiry into the Personal Values and Social Imperatives of the Eighteenth-Century Virginia Gentry*, pp. 13–15.

19. James K. Stringfield, "Pride," March 14, 1856, ms. school essay in the William Williams Stringfield Collection, University Archives, Western Carolina University, Cullowhee, N.C.

20. For a good if critical account of late eighteenth-century Virginia Anglicanism, see *Life of the Rev. Devereaux Jarratt*, e.g., p. 34.

21. See Donald G. Mathews, *Religion in the Old South*, pp. 62, 64–65.

22. Dickson D. Bruce, Jr., *And They All Sang Hallelujah: Plain-Folk Camp-Meeting Religion, 1800–1845*, pp. 98–103.

23. For a detailed account of Southern deathbed scenes, see Dickson D. Bruce, Jr., "Death as Testimony in the Old South," *Southern Humanities Review* 12 (1978): 123–132.

24. [John Taylor], *An Enquiry into the Principles and Tendency of Certain Public Measures*, p. 30.

25. See on this Jesse T. Carpenter, *The South as a Conscious Minority, 1789–1861: A Study in Political Thought*.

26. Much of my information on Northern thought derives from Rush Welter, *The Mind of America, 1820–1860*, chapters 1, 6.

1. THE SOUTHERN DUEL

1. Thomas Lanier Clingman, *Selections from the Speeches and Writings of Hon. Thomas L. Clingman of North Carolina: With Additions and Explanatory Notes*, pp. 175–176, 182, 195.

2. *Charleston Courier*, January 16, 1845.

3. "Speech of Mr. Yancey of Alabama, on the Annexation of Texas,

delivered in the House of Representatives of the U.S. on the 7th of January, as reported for the National-Intelligencer," typed copy in W. L. Yancey papers, Alabama Department of Archives and History, Montgomery.

4. *Mobile Register and Journal*, January 17, 1845; *New Orleans Bee*, January 17, 1845.

5. John M. Huger, comp., "Memoranda of the Late Affair of Honor between Hon. T. L. Clingman, of North Carolina, and Hon. William L. Yancey, of Alabama," p. 3. Huger's "Memoranda," containing all the correspondence between the two principals, is the basis for the account that follows.

6. John Hope Franklin, *The Militant South, 1800–1861*, p. 35.

7. *Charleston Courier*, January 16, 1845.

8. Huger, "Memoranda," pp. 5–6, 8.

9. Ibid., p. 8.

10. *Jonesborough Whig*, January 29, 1845. Actually, the fight occurred in South Carolina, where Yancey had accidentally and under great provocation killed his wife's uncle, Robert Earle. For an account, see John Witherspoon DuBose, *The Life and Times of William Lowndes Yancey: A History of Political Parties in the United States, from 1834 to 1864: Especially as to the Origin of the Confederate States*, 1: 74–75. For Yancey's side of the story, see Letter from William Lowndes Yancey to Benjamin C. Yancey, September 8, 1838, Yancey papers.

11. *Houston Telegraph and Texas Register*, February 5, 1845.

12. "Communication from the Hon. W. L. Yancey to the Editors of the 'Alabama Baptist,'" February 10, 1845, typed copy in Yancey papers.

13. Ibid.

14. Franklin, *Militant South*, p. 55.

15. Wilmuth S. Rutledge, "Dueling in Antebellum Mississippi," *Journal of Mississippi History* 26 (1964): 182. Don Carlos Seitz, *Famous American Duels: With Some Account of the Causes That Led Up to Them and the Men Engaged*, p. 30. Guion Griffis Johnson, *Ante-bellum North Carolina: A Social History*, p. 44.

16. Johnson, *North Carolina*, p. 44; Rutledge, "Dueling," p. 190.

17. Francis Gildart Ruffin, Diary, June 13, 1838, Virginia Historical Society, Richmond.

18. Henry S. Foote, *Casket of Reminiscences*, pp. 185–186. One might also note that when one North Carolina politician was involved in an affair that was successfully adjusted before it could reach the field, his reputation so suffered that his failure to fight was considered a major factor in his failure to win reelection. See Norman

D. Brown, *Edward Stanly: Whiggery's Tarheel "Conqueror"*, p. 91.

19. George Anderson Mercer, Diary, October 18, 1859, typed copy, Southern Historical Collection, University of North Carolina, Chapel Hill.

20. J. D. B. De Bow, "Louisiana," *De Bow's Review* 1 (1846): 428.

21. William Hooper Haigh, Diary, May 17, 1844, typed copy, Southern Historical Collection, University of North Carolina, Chapel Hill. John Lyde Wilson, *The Code of Honor; or, Rules for the Government of Principals and Seconds in Duelling*, p. 9.

22. John Berkley Grimball, Diary, June 12, 1858, typed copy, Southern Historical Collection, University of North Carolina, Chapel Hill.

23. "Difficulty between Messrs. Clingman & Stanley," [*sic*] March, 1850, Clingman-Puryear papers, Southern Historical Collection, University of North Carolina, Chapel Hill. *Charleston Mercury*, September 24, 30, 1856.

24. "The Bladensburg Dueling Ground," *Harper's* 16 (1858): 472.

25. Reverend John D. Blair, "A Sermon on the Impetuosity and Bad Effects of Passion," p. 6. Honestus, "On Fashionable Manners," *American Gleaner* 1 (1807): 6. Robert C. McLean, *George Tucker: Moral Philosopher and Man of Letters*, pp. 215–216. Wilson, *Code*, p. 7.

26. Marquis James, *The Life of Andrew Jackson, Complete in One Volume*, p. 46.

27. Wilson, *Code*, p. 12.

28. Ibid., pp. 10–13, passim. See also Thomas Hart Benton, *Thirty Years' View; or, A History of the Working of the American Government for Thirty Years, from 1820 to 1850*, 2: 148.

29. *Charleston Courier*, January 13, 1845.

30. T. P. Chisman, note appended to a letter from Roger Pryor to John Potter, April 13, 1860, Williiam Porcher Miles papers, Southern Historical Collection.

31. "The Dugger-Dromgoole Duel," unidentified newspaper clipping [1899], Edward Dromgoole papers, Southern Historical Collection. All information on the duel, unless otherwise noted, comes from this account originally published by the seconds.

32. Hiram Haines to Edward Dromgoole, January 8, 1838; R. R. Brown to George C. Dromgoole, November 2, 1837, Edward Dromgoole papers. The date of the latter is incorrect because the duel was fought on November 6. In any case, Dromgoole suffered no major political harm.

33. "Duelling in America," *Living Age* 15 (1847): 468.

34. *Columbus Enquirer*, January 29, 1845.

35. In Robert Manson Myers, ed., *The Children of Pride: A True Story of Georgia and the Civil War*, p. 457. My own very rough count shows that by far the majority of duels ended short of mortal injury.

36. *Cheraw Gazette*, August 9, 1837; *Raleigh Semi-weekly Register*, October 6, 1858; Wilson, *Code*, pp. 27–28.

37. *Charleston Mercury*, August 28, 1856.

38. "The Cheves-Trapier Duel" typescript in the South Carolina Historical Society, Charleston; Francis Gildart Ruffin, Diary, June 13, 1838; *Charleston Southern Patriot*, October 15, 1836.

39. This was one virtue of dueling noted by the Virginia philosopher George Tucker in his *Essays on Various Subjects of Taste, Morals, and National Policy. By a Citizen of Virginia*, pp. 255–256.

40. Harnett T. Kane, *Gentlemen, Swords and Pistols*, pp. ix–x.

41. Ibid., p. ix. Richard Buel, Jr., *Securing the Revolution: Ideology in American Politics, 1789–1815*, pp. 80–81. See also Guy A. Cardwell, "The Duel in the Old South: Crux of a Concept," *South Atlantic Quarterly* 66 (1967): especially 68.

42. Wilson, *Code*, p. 19.

43. John Randolph, *Letters of John Randolph, to a Young Relative; Embracing a Series of Years, from Early Youth, to Mature Manhood*, p. 25.

44. David Hackett Fischer, *The Revolution in American Conservatism: The Federalist Party in the Era of Jeffersonian Democracy*, pp. 33, 49. Contrast the discussion in chapter 8, below.

45. Robert Hendrickson, *Hamilton*, 2: 635.

46. See on this James T. Moore, "The Death of the Duel: The *Code Duello* in Readjuster Virginia, 1879–1883," *Virginia Magazine of History and Biography* 83 (1975): 259–266.

2. PREPARATION FOR VIOLENCE

1. Michael Paul Rogin, *Fathers and Children: Andrew Jackson and the Subjugation of the American Indian*, p. 43; and compare chapter 5, below.

2. Peter Laslett, *Family Life and Illicit Love in Earlier Generations: Essays in Historical Sociology*, p. 13.

3. William S. Pettigrew to James C. Johnston, August 4, 1846, in the Pettigrew family papers, Southern Historical Collection, University of North Carolina, Chapel Hill. Unless otherwise noted, all citations to Pettigrew family papers are from this collection.

4. For biographical information, see Bennett H. Wall, "The Founda-

tion of the Pettigrew Plantations," in *Plantation, Town, and Country: Essays on the Local History of American Slave Society*, ed. Elinor Miller and Eugene D. Genovese, pp. 163–185. See also Sarah McCulloh Lemmon, "Introduction: The Pettigrew Family," in *The Pettigrew Papers, 1685–1818*, pp. xi–xx.

5. Ebenezer Pettigrew to Charles L. Pettigrew, date torn [1831].
6. Charles Pettigrew, *Last Advice of the Rev. Charles Pettigrew to His Sons, 1797*, p. 3.
7. Ibid., p. 5.
8. Ibid., pp. 4, 5, 6, 9.
9. Ibid., p. 5.
10. Rev. Charles Pettigrew to Rev. Joseph Caldwell, November 10, 1797; Rev. Charles Pettigrew to John Pettigrew, October 8, 1797; John Pettigrew to Rev. Charles Pettigrew, April 12, 1796; Ebenezer Pettigrew to John Loudon, September 29, 1798; Lemmon, *Pettigrew Papers*, p. 333.
11. George Fitzhugh, "The English Reviews," *De Bow's Review* 28 (1860): 401.
12. Ebenezer Pettigrew to Charles L. Pettigrew, [1831].
13. In Lemmon, *Pettigrew Papers*, p. 361. Bennett H. Wall describes this letter as containing "the first strain of mystic melancholia" that was to characterize Ebenezer Pettigrew's later correspondence, in "Ebenezer Pettigrew, an Economic Study of an Antebellum Planter" (Ph.D. dissertation, University of North Carolina, 1946), pp. 20–21. Ebenezer Pettigrew to James C. Johnston, April 15, 1842.
14. Charles L. Pettigrew to James Johnston Pettigrew, March 31, 1845.
15. William Gilmore Simms, quoted in Clement Eaton, *The Growth of Southern Civilization, 1790–1860*, p. 297; Robert Manson Myers, ed., *A Georgian at Princeton*, p. 100.
16. Vindex Veritatis, "Importance of Home Education," *Southern Ladies' Book* 2 (1840): 2.
17. Wall, "Ebenezer Pettigrew," p. 27; William S. Pettigrew, "A Dream," August 14, 1848; "A Dream²," August 24, 1848; "A Dream⁴," September 28, 1848, mss.
18. Myers, ed., *Georgian at Princeton*, p. 195; Ninian Edmonston to Polly Ann Edmonston, December 19, 1831, in the Ninian Edmonston Collection, University Archives, Western Carolina University, Cullowhee, N.C.; Charles Minor, Diary, 1837, ms. copy by Virginia Carr Minor, 1906, of a copy by John B. Minor, 1902, Virginia Historical Society, Richmond.
19. Philippe Ariès, *Centuries of Childhood: A Social History of Family Life*, trans. Robert Baldick. These developments have been

traced in English society in Lawrence Stone, *The Family, Sex and Marriage in England, 1500–1800*, p. 221.

20. William Hooper Haigh, Journal of William Hooper Haigh, Esqr^e, Raleigh, N. Carolina, September 11, 1844, typed copy in the Southern Historical Collection. Stone, *The Family*, pp. 268–269. On the pursuit of sentiment in nineteenth-century America, see Ann Douglas, *The Feminization of American Culture*, especially chapter 2.

21. Ebenezer Pettigrew to Ann B. Pettigrew, March 15, 1816.

22. Ebenezer Pettigrew to William S. Pettigrew, February 18, 1836.

23. On the relationship between language use and child-rearing practices, see Basil Bernstein, "Aspects of Language and Learning in the Genesis of the Social Process," in *Language in Culture and Society: A Reader in Linguistics and Anthropology*, ed. Dell Hymes, pp. 251–263. Bernstein distinguishes between "restricted" and "elaborated" coding in language, the former emphasizing fixed forms in language use, the latter involving more individual choice and creativity in the formulation of utterances, and he relates these two types of coding to family orientation. The former tends to correlate with what he has called the "positional" family, one in which roles and patterns of authority are clearly defined, while elaborated coding tends to accompany the "personal" family in which every individual is encouraged to have a sense of his own personality. Dell Hymes, in his discussion of Bernstein's work, makes the distinction between "now-coding," by which he refers to ad hoc elaborations of thoughts and feelings, and "then-coding," which relies on "preformulated expressions." Although Hymes questions whether then-coding and positional control are necessarily connected, such a connection does seem to have been present in the Pettigrew family. See Dell Hymes, *Foundations in Sociolinguistics: An Ethnographic Approach*, pp. 39n., 115. Restricted speech may be said to have been characteristic in Southern education generally, if the oft-noted inability of even educated Southerners to rise above conversational banality is any indication. See on this H. Peter Pudner, "People not Pedagogy: Education in Old Virginia," *Georgia Review* 25 (1971): 274, 280. William Lowndes Yancey to Dr. W. O. Baldwin, November 24, 1843, William Lowndes Yancey papers, Alabama Department of Archives and History, Montgomery.

24. Ebenezer Pettigrew to James Johnston Pettigrew, September 2, 1839. The classic work on this question is, of course, Ruth Benedict, "Continuities and Discontinuities in Cultural Conditioning,"

in *Childhood in Contemporary Cultures*, ed. Margaret Mead and Martha Wolfenstein, pp. 21–30.

25. William S. Pettigrew to James Johnston Pettigrew, September 26, 1843; William Bingham to Ebenezer Pettigrew, July 1, 1839; December 1, 1841. On this point, see Betram Wyatt-Brown, "The Ideal Typology and Ante-Bellum Southern History: A Testing of a New Approach," *Societas* 5 (1975): 26.

26. John Randolph, *Letters of John Randolph to a Young Relative; Embracing a Series of Years, from Early Youth, to Mature Manhood*, pp. 25–26.

27. Ann B. Pettigrew to William S. Pettigrew, March 1, 1830; W. J. Bingham to Ebenezer Pettigrew, April 4, 1840.

28. Richard Sennett, *The Fall of Public Man*, pp. 179–181.

29. Susanna Clay to her son, C. C. Clay, October 30, 1860, Clement Claiborne Clay papers, Manuscript Department, William R. Perkins Library, Duke University, Durham, N.C.

30. Philip Greven, *The Protestant Temperament: Patterns of Child-Rearing, Religious Experience, and Self in Early America*, pp. 265–266, 275, 206.

31. Ibid., p. 202.

32. Everard Green Baker, Diary, June 30, 1861; Launcelot Minor Blackford, Diary, June 12, 1849; typed copies of each in the Southern Historical Collection.

33. Mrs. Eliza Clitherall, Autobiography and Diary, 1751–1860, in 17 vols.; 7:16 (ca. 1829), typed copy in the Southern Historical Collection; E.B.C., "The Mothers and Children of the Present Day," *Southern Literary Messenger* 22 (1856): 392, 393. According to Robert Sunley, corporal punishment was generally out of favor in American child-rearing during the years before the Civil War. See his "Early Nineteenth-Century American Literature on Child Rearing," in *Childhood*, ed. Mead and Wolfenstein, pp. 152–153.

34. C. C., "Corporal Punishment: Its Use in the Discipline of Children," *Southern Literary Messenger* 7 (1841): 575.

35. Charles Minor, Autobiography (ms. 1835), Virginia Historical Society.

36. W. J. Bingham to Ebenezer Pettigrew, April 4, 1840.

37. Blackford, Diary, February 15, 1849.

38. Ibid., April 16, 1852.

39. William S. Pettigrew to James Johnston Pettigrew, September 2, 1846; William Williams Stringfield, unpublished memoirs (1899–1914), in the William Williams Stringfield Collection, University Archives, Western Carolina University, Cullowhee, N.C. Violence

seems to have been fairly common in college literary and debating societies. See for example Charles W. Watts, "Student Days at Old LaGrange, 1844–45," *Alabama Review* 24 (1971): 68.

40. See Watts, "Student Days," p. 74, see also E. Merton Coulter, *College Life in the Old South*, p. 95; Edmund Hubard to Robert Hubard, n.d., "On the manners and ways of the Students" in the Hubard family papers, Southern Historical Collection.

41. R. M. Cahusac to William Porcher, February 17, 1822, miscellaneous manuscripts, South Carolina Historical Society, Charleston; Myers, ed., *Georgian at Princeton*, pp. 3–4; William Bolling, Diary, November 14, 1840, Virginia Historical Society.

42. William John Grayson, "The Autobiography of William John Grayson," ed. Samuel Gaillard Stoney, *South Carolina Historical Magazine* 49 (1948): 91.

43. For a useful survey of the literature on defensive masculinity, see Robert L. Munroe and Ruth H. Munroe, *Cross-Cultural Human Development*, p. 123.

44. See for example Alvy L. King, *Louis T. Wigfall: Southern Fire-Eater*, p. 21. Wigfall was one of those who never seemed to grow up, but at least he worried about it.

45. Ebenezer Pettigrew to James C. Johnston, July 30, 1839; Norman D. Brown, *Edward Stanly: Whiggery's Tarheel "Conqueror,"* p. 86. I am grateful to Professor Brown for pointing this episode out to me.

46. Bernstein, "Aspects of Language," p. 260.

47. See chapter 5, below.

48. The frustration-aggression hypothesis is cogently presented in Ted Robert Gurr, *Why Men Rebel*, pp. 36–37.

3. FEELING AND FORM

1. C. Vann Woodward, *American Counterpoint: Slavery and Racism in the North-South Dialogue*, p. 30. Meta M. Grimball to Elizabeth Grimball, October 31, 1860, in the Grimball papers, Southern Historical Collection, University of North Carolina, Chapel Hill. For a good treatment of Southern notions of community and their relationships to social and political values, see Robert M. Weir, "The South Carolinian as Extremist," *South Atlantic Quarterly* 74 (1975): 86–103.

2. An Edistonian, "The Successful Planter, or Memoirs of My Uncle Ben," *Southern Agriculturalist* 4 (1831): 570. Letter to Mrs. Thom-

as E. Buchanan from her sister, May 22, 1833, in Thomas E. Buchanan papers, Manuscript Department, William R. Perkins Library, Duke University, Durham, N.C. John Berkley Grimball, Diary, June 26, 1835, typed copy of originals in the Southern Historical Collection.

3. D. R. Hundley, esq., *Social Relations in Our Southern States*, p. 71. J. B. Grimball, Diary, October 15–16, 1832.

4. J. Huizinga, *The Waning of the Middle Ages: A Study of the Forms of Life, Thought and Art in France and the Netherlands in the XIVth and the XVth Centuries*, p. 40. For a treatment of Southern play and its relationships to social values, see Dickson D. Bruce, Jr., "Play, Work, and Ethics in the Old South," *Southern Folklore Quarterly*, in press.

5. Francis Gildart Ruffin, Diary, Septtmber 4, 1835, Virginia Historical Society, Richmond.

6. Hans Toch, *Violent Men: An Inquiry into the Psychology of Violence*, pp. vi, 183.

7. Hundley, *Social Relations*, p. 242. To the extent that statistics can tell one anything at all in this matter, it is worth noting that most murder victims in the South were white males, ages twenty to fifty. In 1849–50, such victims accounted for about three-quarters of those whites killed in the South, although the statistics are not entirely clear. This suggests, though it does not prove, that most murders probably grew out of conflicts rather than, say, being incident upon muggings or robberies. Indeed, it is definitely to the point that, excepting Kentucky, no white women was reported murdered in any Southern state in 1849–50. The same cannot be said of the North. This, of course, is not to mention slave murders. See J. D. B. De Bow, *Mortality Statistics of the Seventh Census of the United States, 1850*, passim.

8. [Augustus Baldwin Longstreet], *A Voice from the South: Comprising Letters from Georgia to Massachusetts, and to the Southern States*, p. 50. See on this H. C. Brearly, "The Pattern of Violence," in *Culture in the South*, ed. William T. Couch, p. 687.

9. *An Authenticated Report of the Trial of Myers and Others, for the Murder of Dudley Marvin Hoyt*, drawn up by the editor of the Richmond Southern Standard, p. 4. William Bolling, Diary, February 1, 1838, typed copy in Virginia Historical Society. Jacob Schirmer, Records, April 26, 1844, South Carolina Historical Society, Charleston.

10. Edward Ryland Randolph to John Witherspoon Dubose, March 21, 1903, in John Witherspoon DuBose papers, Alabama Depart-

ment of Archives and History, Montgomery. Andrew Pickens Butler, *Speech of Hon. A. P. Butler, of South Carolina, on the Difficulty of Messrs. Brooks and Sumner, and the Causes Thereof. Delivered in the Senate of the United States, June 12–13, 1856*, p. 15.

11. *Report of the Trials of Capt. Thomas Wells, before the County Court of Nottoway; Sitting as an Examining Court, at the August Term, 1816—Charged with Feloniously and Maliciously Shooting, With Intent to Kill Peter Randolph, Esq. Judge of the 5th Circuit; and Col. Wm. C. Greenhill*, by a Member of the Bar, p. 24. On young Jones, see *The Children of Pride: A True Story of Georgia and the Civil War*, ed. Robert Manson Myers, p. 42. On this point in general, see Jack K. Williams, "Crime and Punishment in Alabama, 1819–1840," *Alabama Review* 6 (1953): 25; and idem, *Vogues in Villainy: Crime and Retribution in Antebellum South Carolina*, p. 9.

12. Sheldon Hackney, "Southern Violence," *American Historical Review* 74 (1969): 917.

13. William John Grayson, "The Autobiography of William John Grayson," ed. Samuel Gaillard Stoney, *South Carolina Historical Magazine* 49 (1948): 28. Edwin J. Scott, *Random Recollections of a Long Life, 1806–1876*, p. 57.

14. Copy of a letter written by William Lowndes Yancey to Benjamin C. Yancey, September 8, 1838, in William Lowndes Yancey papers, Alabama Department of Archives and History, Montgomery.

15. See also Williams, "Crime," p. 24.

16. Miles Taylor, *Speech of Hon. Miles Taylor, of Louisiana, On the Assault by Mr. Brooks on Mr. Sumner. Delivered in the House of Representatives, July 12, 1856*, pp. 3–4.

17. S. C. Carpenter, *Report of the Trial of Richard Dennis, the Younger, for the Murder of James Shaw, on the 20th of August, 1804*, p. 75.

18. Everard Green Baker, Diary, May 29, 1860, typed copy in Southern Historical Collection.

19. Schirmer, Records, May 7, 1842. Petition of Ferdinand S. Heiskill, Augusta County, January 17, 1849, in Virginia Legislative Petitions, Virginia State Library, Richmond.

20. Petitions of Citizens of Bath County, February 3, 1840, and Citizens of Accomac County, March 3, 1840, in Virginia Legislative Petitions.

21. George Fitzhugh, "Love of Danger and of War," *De Bow's Review* 28 (1860): 297.

22. Butler, *Speech on Brooks and Sumner*, p. 16.
23. W. J. Cash, *The Mind of the South*, p. 86.
24. See for example the various comments of Mary Boykin Chesnut in *A Diary from Dixie*, ed. Ben Ames Williams.
25. The best discussion of this is in Eugene D. Genovese, *The World the Slaveholders Made: Two Essays in Interpretation*, pp. 120, 137–143.
26. Hundley, *Social Relations*, pp. 71, 170. For a good discussion of Hundley, see Tommie W. Rogers, "D. R. Hundley: A Multi-Class Thesis of Social Stratification in the Antebellum South," *Mississippi Quarterly* 24 (1970): 137–138.
27. Hundley, *Social Relations*, pp. 224–225.
28. Ibid., p. 239.
29. Ibid., p. 243.
30. "Domestic Improvements," *Southern Literary Journal* n.s. 3 (1838): 3.
31. *A Report (in Part) of the Trial of Thomas Gayner, for the Alleged Murder of His Wife*, p. 19.
32. *Report of the Trials of . . . Wells*, p. 60.
33. "Relation of Education to the Prevention of Crime," *De Bow's Review* 18 (n.s. 1) (1855): 419.
34. Elwood Fisher, "The North and the South," *De Bow's Review* 7 (1849): 306–307.
35. "Public Amusements and Social Enjoyments," *De Bow's Review* 29 (1860): 330–334.
36. The classic discussion of Southern attitudes toward the law is Charles S. Sydnor, "The Southerner and the Laws," in *The Pursuit of Southern History: Presidential Addresses of the Southern Historical Association, 1935–1963*, ed. George Brown Tindall, pp. 62–76. The matter is also taken up in Cash, *Mind of the South*, p. 34.
37. William L. Yancey, Speech to the Gentlemen of the Erosophic and Philomathic Societies, n.d., ms. in Yancey papers.
38. Rev. Dr. Hamilton, "On the Majesty of Law," *New Orleans Miscellany* 1 (1847): 17.
39. "The Utility, Studies, and Duties of the Profession of Law," *De Bow's Review* 2 (1846): 142.
40. *Trial of William Dandridge Epes, for the Murder of Francis Adolphus Muir, Dinwiddie County, Virginia*, p. 61.
41. J. A. G. Davis, *A Treatise on Criminal Law, with an Exposition of the Office and Authority of Justices of the Peace in Virginia; Including Forms of Practice*, p. 17. For sentiment opposed to capi-

tal punishment, see "The Criminal Law," *Southern Quarterly Review* 3 (1843): 391, 394; J. B. White, "Capital Punishment," *Southern Literary Journal* 1 (1836): 302–310.

42. "Utility . . . of Law," p. 151; John Belton O'Neall, *Biographical Sketches of the Bench and Bar of South Carolina*, 2: 248–249; Grayson, "Autobiography," p. 223.

43. See for example Bolling, Diary, April 10, 1838. Richard Maxwell Brown, *Strain of Violence: Historical Studies of American Violence and Vigilantism*, p. 21.

44. P. P., "Uses and Abuses of Lynch Law," *American Whig Review*, n.s.5 (1850), pp. 459–60; *Hints on Three Defects in the Criminal Laws of Virginia. Addressed to the Legislature*, p. 2.

45. Brown, *Strain of Violence*, pp. 104–105. See for example Secretary's Book, Pineville Association, 1823–1840, South Carolina Historical Society.

46. The claim was probably accurate. See the list of vigilante organizations in Brown, *Strain of Violence*, Appendix 3, pp. 305–319.

47. "Utility . . . of Law," p. 147.

48. Hamilton, "On the Majesty of Law," p. 19.

49. Davis, *Treatise*, p. 70.

50. Carpenter, *Report of the Trial of Richard Dennis*, pp. 48–49.

51. Going armed caused many problems. See for example C. J. Elford to Hon. B. F. Perry, February 18, 1833, in B. F. Perry letters, Alabama Department of Archives and History; see also *Report of the Trials of . . . Wells*, p. 12.

52. Davis, *Treatise*, p. 23.

53. *Authenticated Report . . . of Myers*, p. 32.

54. James S. Hamm to Edward F. Birkhead, March 7, 1844, in Edward F. Birkhead letters and papers, Duke University.

55. Carpenter, *Report of the Trial of Richard Dennis*, p. 164.

56. Ibid., pp. 132, 149.

4. VIOLENCE IN PLAIN-FOLK SOCIETY

1. Everett Dick, *The Dixie Frontier: A Social History of the Southern Frontier from the First Transmontane Beginnings to the Civil War*, pp. 148–149.

2. See chapter 10, below.

3. Jane Caroline North, Journal of an Excursion to the Virginia Springs, July 31–October 12, 1851, entry for August 4, 1851, 3 ms.

vols. in the Pettigrew family papers, Southern Historical Collection, University of North Carolina, Chapel Hill. This diary provides an excellent and entertaining view of Southern social life. Charles Minor, Diary, 1837, ms. copy by Virginia Carr Minor, 1906, of a copy by John B. Minor, 1902, Virginia Historical Society, Richmond. Jacob Young, *Autobiography of a Pioneer: or, The Nativity, Experience, Travels, and Ministerial Labors of Rev. Jacob Young, with Incidents, Observations, and Reflections*, p. 113; see also James B. Finley, *Autobiography of Rev. James B. Finley; or Pioneer Life in the West*, ed. W. P. Strickland, p. 330.

4. Philip Paxton [Samuel A. Hammett], *A Stray Yankee in Texas*, p. x; see also Mody C. Boatright, *Folk Laughter on the American Frontier*. For an example of such a hoax, see the *Arkansas Gazette*, August 11, 1830; March 2, 23, 1831.

5. I am taking the term "plain folk" from Frank Lawrence Owsley, *Plain Folk of the Old South*. Some may object to an apparent melding of plain-folk and poor whites, but the data do not indicate any significant differences in attitudes toward violence. I have adopted the term "plain-folk," hyphen included, to avoid awkward construction. On plain-folk participation in lynchings, see P. P., "Uses and Abuses of Lynch Law," *American Whig Review* n.s. 5 (1850), p. 460. That there was some rioting in Southern cities, although less than in the North, is mentioned in Leonard P. Curry, "Urbanization and Urbanism in the Old South: A Comparative View," *Journal of Southern History* 40 (1974): 58.

6. Finley, *Autobiography*, p. 154.

7. Reuben Davis, *Recollections of Mississippi and Mississippians*, p. 19.

8. Jeremiah Bell Jeter, *The Recollections of a Long Life*, p. 15.

9. Dickson D. Bruce, Jr., *And They All Sang Hallelujah: Plain-Folk Camp-Meeting Religion, 1800–1845*, pp. 99–106.

10. W. H. Sparks, *The Memories of Fifty Years*, p. 69.

11. Ibid., p. 24.

12. David Theo. Hines, *The Life, Adventures and Opinions of David Theo. Hines, of South Carolina*, pp. 101–102.

13. On "fighting words," see H. C. Brearly, "The Pattern of Violence," in *Culture in the South*, ed. William Terry Couch, p. 687.

14. For differential rates of mobility, see Fabian Linden, "Economic Democracy in the Slave South: An Appraisal of Some Recent Views," *Journal of Negro History* 31 (1946): 140–189.

15. Mody C. Boatright, "The Myth of Frontier Individualism," in *Turner and the Sociology of the Frontier*, ed. Richard Hofstadter and Seymour Martin Lipset, pp. 43–64.

16. Richard A. Bartlett, *The New Country: A Social History of the American Frontier, 1776–1890,* p. 362.

17. See for example Daniel Drake, M.D., *Pioneer Life in Kentucky, 1785–1800,* ed. Emmet Field Horine, M.D., pp. 94–98.

18. Bartlett, *New Country,* p. 362. See also Michael Paul Rogin, *Fathers and Children: Andrew Jackson and the Subjugation of the American Indian,* p. 28.

19. Bartlett, *New Country,* p. 362; David Crockett, *A Narrative of the Life of David Crockett of the State of Tennessee,* pp. 30–31, 43.

20. Jeter, *Recollections,* p. 5.

21. *Sketches and Recollections of Lynchburg, by the Oldest Inhabitant,* p. 28.

22. Mary J. Welsh, "Recollections of Pioneer Life in Mississippi," *Publications,* Mississippi Historical Society, 4 (1901): 349.

23. Finley, *Autobiography,* p. 164. For a similar report from a very different sort of man, see George H. Devol, *Forty Years a Gambler on the Mississippi,* p. 9.

24. Drake, *Pioneer Life,* p. 154.

25. Rogin, *Fathers and Children,* p. 44; William Physick Zuber, *My Eighty Years in Texas,* ed. Janis Boyle Mayfield, p. 24. For a statement of concern, see the *Houston Morning Star,* June 18, 1842.

26. Jeter, *Recollections,* pp. 11–12.

27. Davis, *Recollections,* p 19.

28. Jeter, *Recollections,* p. 18.

29. See for example Drake, *Pioneer Life,* pp. 55–56, 187; Amos Kendall, *Autobiography of Amos Kendall,* ed. William Stickney, p. 124; Sparks, *Memories,* p. 24.

30. In *Richardson's Virginia and North Carolina Almanac, for the Year of our Lord 1855.* Cottom's Edition. p. [15].

31. Francis James Child, *The English and Scottish Popular Ballads.* On the origins of ballads, see M. J. C. Hodgart, *The Ballads,* pp. 66–75.

32. *The Forget Me Not Songster, Containing a Choice Collection of Old Ballad Songs, as Sung by Our Grandmothers* contains "Barbara Allan'" ("Bonny Barbara Allen," Child, No. 84), and "Lord Thomas and Fair Eleanor" ("Lord Thomas and Fair Annet," Child, No. 73). *The United States Songster* also contains "Barbara Allen." On the social context of ballad singing, see John Harrington Cox, *Folk-Songs of the South,* p. xxv.

33. Hodgart, *Ballads,* p. 134; Alan Lomax, *The Folk Songs of North America in the English Language,* p. 261.

34. The specific ballads referred to are "Lord Bateman" ("Young Beichan," Child, No. 53), in Cox, *Folk-Songs,* p. 36; "The Brown

Girl" ("Lord Thomas and Fair Annet," Child, No. 73), ibid., p. 45; "Johnnie Randal" ("Lord Randal," Child, No. 12), ibid., p. 25.

35. "House Carpenter" ("James Harris [The Daemon Lover]," Child, No. 243), ibid., p. 139. It is instructive, on this point, to compare "Willie o Winsbury" as collected in West Virginia by Josiah Combs with the versions recorded by Child. In the apparently older versions in Child, a young girl whose father is away is made pregnant, and the father, on returning, threatens to hang the young man. However, when he sees the youth, the father is so struck by his beauty that he offers his daughter's hand and a handsome dowry. In the West Virginia version, no such revelation takes place. The father's threat is simply answered by the daughter with a threat of her own: "You'll get no more good of me." See Child, *English and Scottish Popular Ballads*, 2: 398–399; Josiah H. Combs, *Folk-Songs of the Southern United States*, ed. D. K. Wilgus, pp. 123–124.

36. Dick, *Dixie Frontier*, p. 141.

37. An Engineer, "Notes on Texas," *Southern Literary Journal* n.s. 3 (1838): 134; the article was meant to counter such a reputation. Mark E. Nackman, "Anglo-American Migrants to the West: Men of Broken Fortunes? The Case of Texas, 1821–46," *Western Historical Quarterly* 5 (1974): 453. For interesting evidence of the spread of Texas' reputation, see John Q. Anderson, ed., *Tales of Frontier Texas, 1830–1860*, p. v.

38. *Houston Telegraph and Texas Register*, June 24, 1840.

39. Francis Richard Lubbock, *Six Decades in Texas, or, Memoirs of Francis Richard Lubbock; a Personal Experience in Business, War, and Politics*, ed. C. W. Raines, p. 55.

40. Gustav Dresel, *Houston Journal: Adventures in North America and Texas, 1837–1841*, ed. and trans. Max Freund, pp. 36–37; William Kennedy, Esq., *Texas: The Rise, Progress, and Prospects of the Republic of Texas*, 2: 390–391. B. H. Carroll, Jr., *Standard History of Houston, Texas: From a Study of the Original Sources*, pp. 86–87; see also Lubbock, *Six Decades*, p. 55.

41. Lubbock, *Six Decades*, p. 57. Note again the implication that fighting is a concomitant of openness.

42. *Houston Telegraph and Texas Register*, November 18, 1837.

43. Ibid., January 20, 1838.

44. Lubbock, *Six Decades*, p. 57.

45. *Houston Telegraph and Texas Register*, June 24, 1837.

46. See Robert R. Dykstra, *The Cattle Towns*, chapter 3, passim. The

stereotyped form of more contemporary fights need not include an exchange of words. See James P. Leary, "Fists and Foul Mouths: Fights and Fight Stories in Contemporary Rural American Bars," *Journal of American Folklore* 89 (1976): 31.

47. *Houston Telegraph and Texas Register*, June 14, 1843; *Houston Morning Star*, May 19, 1842.

48. *Houston Telegraph and Texas Register*, June 24, 1840; *Houston Morning Star*, May 5, 1842; Dresel, *Houston Journal*, p. 38.

49. Dresel, *Houston Journal*, p. 36; Lubbock, *Six Decades*, pp. 54–55; *Texas in 1840, or the Emigrant's Guide to the New Republic; Being the Result of Observation, Enquiry and Travel in that Beautiful Country. By an Emigrant, Late of the United States*, p. 229.

50. Paxton, *Stray Yankee*, pp. 341–346, xiv; see also William Ransom Hogan, "Rampant Individualism in the Republic of Texas," *Southwestern Historical Quarterly* 44 (1941): 459–461.

51. *Houston Telegraph and Texas Register*, June 24, 1840; Report of the Grand Jurors, Spring Term, 1839, in the Minutes, 11th Judicial District Court, Harris County, District Clerk's Office, vol. B., p. 172.

52. Edward Stiff, *A New History of Texas*, p. 70; *Houston Telegraph and Texas Register*, July 8, 1840; see Minutes, 11th Judicial District Court, 1838–41, passim.

53. Lubbock, *Six Decades*, pp. 56–57; *Houston Telegraph and Texas Register*, January 20, March 31, 1838.

54. For a related view, see Dykstra, *Cattle Towns*, pp. 142–148; see also W. Eugene Hollon, *Frontier Violence: Another Look*, p. 211. For a fascinating study which highlights both the similarities and differences between the nineteenth and twentieth centuries, see Henry P. Lundsgaarde, *Murder in Space City: A Cultural Analysis of Houston Homicide Patterns*.

55. P. P., "Uses and Abuses," 5: 462; Richard Maxwell Brown, *Strain of Violence: Historical Studies of American Violence and Vigilantism*, pp. 116–117.

56. *Natchitoches Herald*, rpt. in the *Asheville (N.C.) Highland Messenger*, November 12, 1841.

57. Richard Maxwell Brown, "The History of Vigilantism in America," in *Vigilante Politics*, ed. H. Jon Rosenbaum and Peter C. Sederberg, pp. 98–99; *Houston Morning Star*, October 4, 1842.

58. Brown, "History of Vigilantism," p. 89; Rosenbaum and Sederberg, *Vigilante Politics*, p. 269; *Houston Morning Star*, September 25, 1841.

59. James E. Cutler, *Lynch-Law: An Investigation into the History of Lynching in the United States*, pp. 100–111; James G. Leyburn, *Frontier Folkways*, p. 216.

60. H. S. Fulkerson, *Random Recollections of Early Days in Mississippi*, p. 95.

61. James W. Bragg, "Captain Slick, Arbiter of Early Alabama Morals," *Alabama Review* 11 (1958): 130–131.

62. See on this Edward Stettner, "Vigilantism and Political Theory," in *Viligante Politics*, ed. Rosenbaum and Sederberg, pp. 67–70.

63. Davis, *Recollections*, p. 19.

64. Bruce, Jr., *And They All Sang Hallelujah*, p. 118.

65. Walter Blair and Franklin J. Meine, eds., *Half Horse Half Alligator: The Growth of the Mike Fink Legend*, pp. 216–217; see also Finley, *Autobiography*, pp. 327–329.

66. Peter Cartwright, *Autobiography of Peter Cartwright*, pp. 160–161, 177. Robert Paine, D.D., *Life and Times of William McKendree, Bishop of the Methodist Episcopal Church*, p. 80.

67. Finley, *Autobiography*, p 155; Young, *Autobiography*, p. 336.

68. Young, *Autobiography*, pp. 295–296.

5. SLAVERY AND VIOLENCE: THE MASTERS' VIEW

1. John A. Calhoun, E. E. DuBose, and Virgil Bubo, Committee of the Barbour County (Ala.) Agricultural Society, "Report on the Management of Slaves," *American Farmer* 4th ser. 2 (1846): 76. See also in a different context, J. A. G. Davis, *A Treatise on Criminal Law, with an Exposition of the Office and Authority of Justices of the Peace in Virginia; Including Forms of Practice*, p. 21.

2. Thomas Jefferson, *Notes on the State of Virginia*, ed. William Peden, p. 162. Charles Pettigrew, *Last Advice of the Rev. Charles Pettigrew to His Sons, 1797*, p. 10.

3. "The People," *Southern Quarterly Review* 25 (n.s. 9) (1854): 52.

4. [John L. Carey], *Some Thoughts Concerning Domestic Slavery, in a Letter to ——— ———, Esq. of Baltimore*, pp. 20–21.

5. Bertram W. Doyle, *The Etiquette of Race Relations in the South: A Study in Social Control*, p. 31. See also N. Herbemont, "On the Moral Discipline and Treatment of Slaves," *Southern Agriculturalist* 9 (1836): 71; "The People," p. 49.

6. "Management of Slaves, &c.," *Farmers' Register* 5 (1837): 32.

7. John S. Skinner, "Mortality among Slaves in Mississippi," *American Farmer* 3d ser. 2 (1840): 170.

8. Ibid.; "Management," p. 32.

9. Calhoun et al., "Report," pp. 78–79.

10. Harris Smith Evans, "Rules for the Government of the Negroes, Plantation, &c. at Float Swamp, Wilcox County, South Alabama," *Southern Agriculturalist* 5 (1832): 233; see also Calhoun et al., "Report," p. 79.

11. [Hill Carter], "On the Management of Negroes," *Farmers' Register* 1 (1834): 564; see also An Overseer, "On the Conduct and Management of Overseers, Drivers, and Slaves," *Farmers' Register* 4 (1836): 115.

12. H. H., "A Louisiana Plantation," *American Farmer* 4th ser. 12 (1856): 132; see also H., "Remarks on Overseers, and the Proper Treatment of Slaves," *Farmer's Register* 5 (1837): 302; Carter, "On the Management," p. 564.

13. R. S. Blackburn, "Management of Negroes," *American Farmer* 4th ser. 7 (1852): 397.

14. Pee Dee, "The Management of Negroes," *Southern Agriculturalist* 11 (1838): 513.

15. See especially Eugene D. Genovese, *Roll, Jordan, Roll: The World the Slaves Made*. Thomas R. R. Cobb, *An Historical Sketch of Slavery, from the Earliest Periods*, p. clx.

16. William Bolling, Diary, October 29–November 2, 1838; December 3, 1838; typed copy in the Virginia Historical Society, Richmond. See on this Genovese, *Roll, Jordan*, p. 14; Pee Dee, "Management," p. 513; A Southern Lady, "British Philanthropy and American Slavery," *De Bow's Review* 14 (1853): 271.

17. William Gilmore Simms, *The Letters of William Gilmore Simms*, collected and ed. by Mary C. Simms Oliphant, Alfred Taylor Odell, and T. C. Duncan Eaves, 3: 174. Michael Wallace, "Paternalism and Violence," in *Violence and Aggression in the History of Ideas*, ed. Phillip P. Wiener and John Fisher, pp. 203–204, 211.

18. The history of proslavery thought has been traced by William Sumner Jenkins in *Pro-Slavery Thought in the Old South*. For the historical background to these problems, see Winthrop D. Jordan, *White over Black: American Attitudes toward the Negro, 1550–1812*.

19. Edmund Ruffin, *African Colonization Unveiled*, p. 26, pamphlet in Edmund Ruffin papers, Virginia Historical Society. See on this George M. Frederickson, *The Black Image in the White Mind: The Debate on Afro-American Character and Destiny, 1817–1914*, pp. 45–46. See also John C. Greene, "The American Debate on the

Negro's Place in Nature, 1780–1815," *Journal of the History of Ideas* 15 (1954): 384–396.

20. [S. A.] Cartwright, "Dr. Cartwright on the Caucasians and the Africans," *De Bow's Review* 25 (1858): 47–48.

21. H., "Remarks," p. 302.

22. Carey, *Some Thoughts*, p. 29; W. J. Cash, *The Mind of the South*, p. 83.

23. H. H., "Louisiana Plantation," p. 132; An Edistonian, "The Successful Planter, or Memoirs of My Uncle Ben," *Southern Agriculturalist* 5 (1832): 26.

24. Overseer, "On the Conduct," p. 115; William Galt, "Farm Diary, Stud Book, &c. of William Galt of 'Point of Fork' Fluvanna Co., Va.," Virginia Historical Society; Agricola, "Management of Negroes," *De Bow's Review* 19 (1855): 362.

25. Overseer, "On the Conduct," p. 115.

26. Cartwright, "Dr. Cartwright," p. 54.

27. Chancellor [Robert] Harper, "Slavery in the Light of Social Ethics," in *Cotton Is King, and Pro-Slavery Arguments*, ed. E. N. Elliott, p. 576; Matthew Estes, *A Defense of Negro Slavery, as It Exists in the United States*, pp. 135–137.

28. Thomas Cooper, "Slavery," *Southern Literary Journal* 1 (1835): 193; [Zaphaniah Kingsley], *A Treatise on the Patriarchal, or Co-Operative System of Society as It Exists in Some Governments, and Colonies in America, and in the United States, under the Name of Slavery, with Its Necessity and Advantages*, pp. [3], 8 I am grateful to Mr. Philip Lapsansky of the Library Company of Philadelphia for pointing out Kingsley's work to me.

29. [James Warley Miles], *The Relation between the Races at the South*, p. 4n.

30. J. F. H. Claiborne, *Life and Correspondence of John A. Quitman, Major-General, U.S.A., and Governor of the State of Mississippi*, 1: 84.

31. Frederickson, *Black Image*, p. 53.

32. A Small Farmer, "Management of Negroes," *De Bow's Review* 11 (1851): 371; Robert E. Lee to William Henry Fitzhugh Lee, May 30, 1858, in the George Bolling Lee papers, Virginia Historical Society.

33. Peter G. Camden, *A Common-Sense, Matter-of-Fact Examination and Discussion of Negro Slavery in the United States of America, in Connection with the Questions of Emancipation and Abolition*, quotation printed on the back; Mary Boykin Chesnut, *A Diary from Dixie*, ed. Ben Ames Williams, especially p. 147.

34. See Kenneth M. Stampp, *The Peculiar Institution: Slavery in the Antebellum South*, pp. 220–221. On due process, note the entries in Jacob Schirmer, Records from October 1826 to December 1846, relating to slave trials in Charleston (for example, June 30, 1838), South Carolina Historical Society, Charleston. A good summary of the issue is Daniel J. Flanigan, "Criminal Procedure in Slave Trials in the Antebellum South," *Journal of Southern History* 40 (1974): 537–564. Michael S. Hindus, in his excellent study of South Carolina's criminal prosecutions of blacks, shows a system which was anything but fair. He also shows, however, the extent to which many prominent men were deeply concerned about the situation. See his "Black Justice under White Law: Criminal Prosecutions of Blacks in Antebellum South Carolina," *Journal of American History* 53 (1976): 575–599.

35. Estes, *Defense of Negro Slavery*, p 108.

36. S. A. Cartwright, "Slavery in the Light of Ethnology," in *Cotton is King*, ed. Elliott, p. 701.

37. See Ruffin, *African Colonization*, p. 3; W. S. Brown, *A Plan of National Colonization Adequate to the Removal of Free Blacks*, p. 491; C. S. Morgan, letter, in "Slavery and Slave Statistics of the South, &c.," *De Bow's Review* 14 (1853): 593.

38. See on this Leslie Howard Owens, *This Species of Property: Slave Life and Culture in the Old South*, pp. 104–105.

39. Ruffin, *African Colonization*, p. 24.

40. Overseer, "On the Conduct," p. 116; Cobb, *Historical Sketch*, p. cxi. Reverend Charles Pettigrew to Ebenezer Pettigrew, May 10, 1802, in the Pettigrew family papers, Southern Historical Collection, University of North Carolina, Chapel Hill. See also "Observations, &c.—Olives, Grapes, Wool and Silk," *American Farmer* 4 (1822): 274; Chesnut, *Diary*, p. 139; Cooper, "Slavery," p. 193; Harper, "Slavery," pp. 607–608; A Lady of Georgia, "Southern Slavery and Its Assailants," *De Bow's Review* 16 (1854): 49.

41. Cartwright, "Dr. Cartwright," p. 52.

42. Edwin A. Miles, "The Mississippi Slave Insurrection Scare of 1835," *Journal of Negro History* 42 (1957): 48–60, is the best account. Miles reports that the scare was probably a hoax (p. 56). For an interestingly biased contemporary account, see P. P., "Uses and Abuses of Lynch Law," *American Whig Review* n.s. 6 (1850): 494–501.

43. Letter to Mrs. Thomas E. Buchanan from her mother, July 6, 1847, in Thomas E. Buchanan papers, Manuscript Department, William R. Perkins Library, Duke University, Durham, N.C.; see

also William L. Barney, *The Secessionist Impulse: Alabama and Mississippi in 1860,* p. 168.

44. William Drayton, *The South Vindicated from the Treason and Fanaticism of the Northern Abolitionists,* p. 72.

45. William Bolling, Diary, February 19, 1839; the best survey is Clement Eaton, "Mob Violence in the Old South," *Mississippi Valley Historical Review* 29 (1942): 351–370.

46. Stephen B. Oates, *The Fires of Jubilee: Nat Turner's Fierce Rebellion,* pp. 99–100, 103; Miles, "Mississippi Scare," pp. 50–55.

47. Mary E. McPhail to Miss Mary V. Carrington, September 30, 1831, in the Carrington family papers, Virginia Historical Society; John A. Chandler, *The Speech of John A. Chandler (of Norfolk County), in the House of Delegates of Virginia, on the Policy of the State with Respect to Her Slave Population,* p. 7; Females of Augusta County, Legislative Petition, January 19, 1832, Virginia Legislative Petitions, Virginia State Library, Richmond. On challenges to the system, see Barney, *Secessionist Impulse;* Steven A. Channing, *Crisis of Fear: Secession in South Carolina.*

48. Cobb, *Historical Sketch,* p. cxxxiv; John Fletcher, of Louisiana, *Studies on Slavery, in Easy Lessons,* p. 151; Nott, cited in Brown, *A Plan,* p. [3]; Robert Toombs, *A Lecture Delivered in the Tremont Temple, Boston, Massachusetts, on the 24th of January, 1856,* p. 12.

49. Jefferson, *Notes,* pp. 162–163.

50. Drayton, *South Vindicated,* p. 227.

51. [Augustus Baldwin Longstreet], *A Voice from the South: Comprising Letters from Georgia to Massachusetts, and to the Southern States,* p. 19.

52. Carey, *Some Thoughts,* p. 43.

53. See David Donald, "The Proslavery Argument Reconsidered," *Journal of Southern History* 37 (1971): 5–6; see also Bert E. Bradley and Jerry L. Tarver, "John C. Calhoun's Rhetorical Method in Defense of Slavery," in *Oratory in the Old South, 1828–1860,* ed. Waldo W. Braden, pp. 169–189. Bradley and Tarver see the expository style of Calhoun's defense as a weakness insofar as the persuasion of outsiders is concerned. The point is, of course, that it was that very "weakness" that gave the argument strength in the South since it was a matching of "facts" to assumptions. See especially pp. 180–182.

54. Drayton, *South Vindicated,* p. 72; Claiborne, *Life of Quitman,* 1: 79, 81; Cooper, "Slavery," p. 190. David Donald says that one purpose of proslavery writing was to celebrate a "bygone age which

Southern life had had" ("Proslavery Argument," p. 12), but I disagree.

55. Toombs, *Lecture*, p. 15.
56. Donald, "Proslavery Argument," pp. 8–9; Eugene D. Genovese, *The World the Slaveholders Made: Two Essays in Interpretation*, p. 146.

6. SLAVERY AND VIOLENCE: THE SLAVES' VIEW

1. The best account of the characteristics of ex-slave materials is John W. Blassingame, "Using the Testimony of Ex-Slaves: Approaches and Problems," *Journal of Southern History* 41 (1975): 473–492. Ira Berlin has rightly questioned studies of the antebellum South that somehow see the years 1830–1860 as stable and points to the existence of great changes in Southern society, especially in regard to Southern blacks. Still, in terms of traditional ideas and values held in both black and white society, one may point to certain persistent features that did remain relatively constant throughout the period—although their manifestations may have changed over time. See Berlin's *Slaves without Masters: The Free Negro in the Antebellum South*, pp. xv–xvi.
2. Carter G. Woodson, ed., *The Mind of the Negro as Reflected in Letters Written During the Crisis, 1800–1860*, p. 264. George P. Rawick, general editor, *The American Slave: A Composite Autobiography*, 19 vols. *Texas Narratives*, 4, part 2, p. 82. Rawick's collection includes interviews collected by the Work Projects Administration during the 1930s, volumes 2–17, and two volumes of narratives published originally by Fisk University, *The Unwritten History of Slavery* and *God Struck Me Dead*, vols. 18 and 19. Future citations will be abbreviated in the following form, using the note above, as Rawick, ed., *Tex. Narr.*, 4 (2), 82. I have reluctantly retained the often strange and probably inaccurate versions of black speech developed by the WPA. interviewers.
3. Rawick, ed., *Ark. Narr.*, 11 (7), 100.
4. Rawick, ed., *Fla. Narr.*, 17, 146–147.
5. Benjamin Drew, *The Refugee: A North-Side View of Slavery*, p. 129.
6. John Thompson, *The Life of John Thompson, a Fugitive Slave; Containing His History of 25 Years in Bondage, and His Providential Escape, Written By Himself*, p. 20.
7. Louis Hughes, *Thirty Years a Slave. From Bondage to Freedom.*

The Institution of Slavery as Seen on the Plantation and in the Home of the Planter, p. 73.

8. See on this Ronald G. Walters, "The Erotic South: Civilization and Sexuality in American Abolitionism," *American Quarterly* 25 (1973): 177–201. Eugene D. Genovese, *Roll, Jordan Roll: The World the Slaves Made*, p. 371. For some representative stories, see Rawick, ed., *S.C. Narr.*, 2 (2), 304; *Ga. Narr.*, 12 (2), 118; *N.C. Narr.*, 15 (2), 208; Drew, *The Refuge*, p. 159; Thompson, *Life*, pp. 31–32.

9. Rawick, ed., *S.C. Narr.*, 2 (2), 81.

10. Hughes, *Thirty Years a Slave*, p. 20.

11. Rawick, ed., *Ark. Narr.*, 11 (7), 203.

12. J. Ralph Jones, "Portraits of Georgia Slaves," *Georgia Review* 21 (1967): 269–270.

13. J. W. Loguen, *The Rev. J. W. Loguen as a Slave and as a Freeman: A Narrative of Real Life*, p. 239.

14. Rawick, ed., *Tex. Narr.*, 4 (2), 256.

15. This was also noted by Genovese, in *Roll, Jordan*, p. 124. See as well *The Negro in Virginia*, comp. by workers of the Writers' Program of the Work Projects Administration in the State of Virginia, p. 156. The Virginians, however, fail to discuss the possible significance of the remark.

16. Rawick, ed., *S.C. Narr.*, 2 (1), 162.

17. Genovese, *Roll, Jordan*, p. 91. Peter Wood has suggested that Genovese's conclusions about slavery, advancing as they do a reciprocal relationship between slaves and masters, represent a case of turning U. B. Phillips "upside down." See his "Phillips Upside Down: Dialectic or Equivocation?" *Journal of Interdisciplinary History* 6 (1975): 289–297, especially p. 297. My own view, by contrast, may be said to do the same thing for Stanley Elkins— to turn him "upside down"—by suggesting that, indeed, slavery was supposed to be a total institution, but that the slaves themselves were aware of it and sought adjustments to the institution on the basis of that understanding (*Slavery: A Problem in American Institutional Life*, especially chapter 3). This, I take it, is also the point of Kenneth M. Stampps's superb essay, "Rebels and Sambos: The Search for the Negro's Personality in Slavery," *Journal of Southern History* 37 (1971): 397–392, also p. 384.

18. For an argument that cognitive nonuniformity is a functional prerequisite of society, see Anthony F. C. Wallace, *Culture and Personality*, pp. 34–36. My understanding of this point has profited greatly from discussions with James Flink.

19. Rawick, ed., *Okla. Narr.*, 7, 78. See on this issue Dickson D. Bruce, Jr., "Religion, Society and Culture in the Old South: A Comparative View," *American Quarterly* 26 (1974): 411–412. The story itself is almost certainly a folktale. Another version is found in Lawrence W. Levine, *Black Culture and Black Consciousness: Afro-American Folk Thought from Slavery to Freedom*, p. 98.

20. Kenneth M. Stampp, *The Peculiar Institution: Slavery in the Antebellum South*, p. 174.

21. See for example "The Hog Thief," *Southern Workman* 26 (April 1897): 79.

22. *Southern Workman* 25 (September 1896): 185. This story was sometimes told in such a way that John himself was the butt of the joke.

23. Portia Smiley, "Folklore from Virginia, South Carolina, Georgia, Alabama and Florida," *Journal of American Folklore* 32 (1919): 370; "Morality and Religion in Slavery Days," *Southern Workman* 26 (October 1897): 210.

24. See Dickson D. Bruce, Jr., "The 'John and Old Master' Stories and the World of Slavery: A Study in Folktales and History," *Phylon* 35 (1974): 423, 427–428.

25. Drew, *The Refugee*, p. 144; Rawick, ed., *Ga. Narr.*, 12 (1), 164.

26. John Blassingame, *The Slave Community: Plantation Life in the Antebellum South*, p. 204; Stampp, "Rebels and Sambos," p. 388. On the interviews, see Blassingame, "Using the Testimony of Ex-Slaves," pp. 481–489. Allen is quoted in Jones, "Portraits," p. 273, and his case is discussed specifically in Blassingame, "Using the Testimony of Ex-Slaves," p. 485. Even the Reverend Allen was not always so outspoken.

27. *Negro in Virginia*, p. 158.

28. Herbert Gutman, *The Black Family in Slavery and Freedom, 1750–1925*, p. 32; on slave religion—with specific focus on its comparison to that of whites and on the influence of the plantation setting—see Bruce, Jr., "Religion, Society and Culture."

29. Rawick, ed., *S.C. Narr.*, 2 (1), 67; *Unwritten History*, 18, 305.

30. Henry Bibb, *Narrative of the Life and Adventures of Henry Bibb, an American Slave, Written by Himself*, p. 13. J. F. White said he was "brought up, or rather whipped up, in Kentucky," in Drew, *The Refugee*, p. 238.

31. *Aunt Sally; or, The Cross the Way to Freedom. A Narrative of the Slave-Life and Purchase of the Mother of Rev. Isaac Williams, of Detroit, Michigan*, p. 27; Rawick, *Ga. Narr.*, 12 (2), 128. Blassingame ("Using the Testimony of Ex-Slaves," p. 478) considers

Aunt Sally to be of questionable reliability; however, the main themes in the descriptions of slave life are quite compatible with those in other autobiographies and in the various collections of interviews.

32. Thompson, *Life*, p. 20.
33. Clifton H. Johnson, ed., *God Struck Me Dead: Religious Conversion Experiences and Autobiographies of Ex-Slaves*, p. 78; Rawick, ed., *Unwritten History*, 18, 306–307; *Mo. Narr.*, 11, 86.
34. Moses Roper, *A Narrative of the Adventures and Escape of Moses Roper, from American Slavery*, p. 66.
35. Genovese, *Roll, Jordan*, p. 636; see, e.g., Rawick, ed., *Tex. Narr.*, 4 (1) 241; *Okla. Narr.*, 7, 142; *Ga. Narr.*, 12 (2), 108. See also Loguen, *Rev. J. W. Loguen*, p. 239; Frederick Douglass, *Life and Times of Frederick Douglass*, p. 70. There is a data problem in regard to the question of violence in the slave community. Fugitives and ex-slaves simply did not talk about it much, other than to indicate, very clearly, that such violence occurred. Court records are only slight help since most cases of assault between slaves only reached the courts if they were between plantations and one of the owners wanted to bring action against the other for damages to his valuable property. See the records collected in Helen Tunnicliff Catterall, ed., *Judicial Cases Concerning American Slavery and the Negro*. A good, recent local study is Royce Gordon Shingleton, "The Trial and Punishment of Slaves in Baldwin County, Georgia, 1812–1826," *Southern Humanities Review* 8 (1974): 67–73.
36. Solomon Northrup, *Twelve Years a Slave*, ed. Sue Eakin and Joseph Logsdon, p. 136; Rawick, ed., *Tex. Narr.*, 4 (1), 192.
37. Rawick, ed., *Ga. Narr.*, 12 (2), 120; *N.C. Narr.*, 15 (2), 424; H. C. Bruce, *The New Man: Twenty-Nine Years a Slave. Twenty-Nine Years a Free Man*, p. 41; Jones, "Portraits," p. 191. On the slaves' desire for an orderly community, see Genovese, *Roll, Jordan*, p. 91.
38. Charles S. Johnson, *Shadow of the Plantation*.
39. Ibid., p. 191; John Dollard, *Caste and Class in a Southern Town*, p. 271; Allison Davis and John Dollard, *Children of Bondage: The Personality Development of Negro Youth in the Urban South*, pp. 270–271. See also on this William Lynwood Montell, *The Saga of Coe Ridge: A Study in Oral History*, Chapter 4. The violence Montell describes, from 1888, followed the pattern set forth here, but was directed against whites.
40. Dollard, *Caste and Class*, pp. 267–268.
41. Bruce, Jr., "John and Old Master," p. 426. On religion, see Zora

Neale Hurston, *Mules and Men*, p. 19. Hurston, who tended to romanticize and overdraw elements of Afro-American culture—especially those that went against the grain of what she believed to be white American ideals—raised conflict to a central theme of black social life. See particularly her "Characteristics of Negro Expression," in *Negro Anthology Made by Nancy Cunard, 1931–1933*, p. 44. On blues, see Howard W. Odum and Guy B. Johnson, *Negro Workaday Songs*, p. 135.

42. Bruce, *New Man*, p. 34; Rawick, ed., *Ala. Narr.*, 6, 85.

43. Bruce, *New Man*, p. 48; Douglass, *Life and Times*, p. 145; Drew, *The Refugee*, p. 46; Rawick, ed., *Okla. Narr.*, 7, 141.

44. Bruce, *New Man*, p. 40; Loguen, *Rev J. W. Loguen*, p. 20; Rawick, ed., *Ark. Narr.*, 8 (1), 78.

45. George P. Rawick, *From Sundown to Sunup: The Making of the Black Community (Vol. 1 in The American Slave: A Composite Autobiography)* p. 55; George Fredrickson and Christopher Lasch, "Resistance to Slavery," *Civil War History* 13 (1967): 318. My view of resistance is in disagreement with Leslie Howard Owens, *This Species of Property: Slave Life and Culture in the Old South*, pp. 103–105, which describe forms of resistance as threats to the total system.

46. John B. Cade, "Out of the Mouths of Ex-Slaves," *Journal of Negro History* 20 (1935): 308.

47. On those who refused, see Genovese, *Roll, Jordan*, p. 619; Blassingame, *Slave Community*, pp. 133–134.

48. For accounts of brawls, see Rawick, ed., *Ala. Narr.*, 6, 417; Austin Steward, *Twenty-Two Years a Slave, and Forty Years a Freeman: Embracing a Correspondence of Several Years, While President of Wilberforce Colony, London, Canada, West*, pp. 33–38. Steward is quoted in Rawick, ed., *N.C. Narr.*, 15 (2), 321.

49. Jones, "Portraits," p. 273.

50. Drew, *The Refugee*, p. 28; Johnson, *God Struck Me Dead*, p. 103.

51. Loguen, *Rev. J. W. Loguen*, p. 242; Drew, *The Refugee*, p. 129. See also Cade, "Out of the Mouths of Ex-Slaves," p. 315; Douglass, *Life and Times*, p. 142; Drew, *The Refugee*, p. 177.

52. Thompson, *Life*, p. 46. Similar stories appear in Douglass, *Life and Times*, p. 52, and Bruce, *New Man*, p. 69. Stories of suicide are in, for example, Rawick, ed., *S.C. Narr.*, 2 (2), 81; Northrup, *Twelve Years a Slave*, p. 187.

53. Bruce, *New Man*, 32; Douglass, *Life and Times*, p. 169.

54. *The Life and Writings of Frederick Douglass*, ed. Philip S. Foner, 1: 157.

55. Douglass, *Life and Times*, pp. 78, 84–85, 87.

56. Woodson, *Mind of the Negro*, p. 204.
57. *The Confessions of Nat Turner, Leader of the Late Insurrection in Southampton, Va.*, p. 3. Turner's *Confessions* have encouraged much debate as to their validity. Stephen B. Oates finds the document reliable, and describes it as Turner's "last opportunity to strike back at the slave world he hated, to flay it with verbal brilliance and religious prophecy." See Oates, *The Fires of Jubilee: Nat Turner's Fierce Rebellion*, pp. 121, 123. Others have attacked the authenticity of the confessions Thomas Gray published. See especially Seymour L. Gross and Eileen Bender, "History, Politics and Literature: The Myth of Nat Turner," *American Quarterly* 23 (1971): 487–518. For the background of William Wells Brown, see William Edward Farrison, *William Wells Brown: Author and Reformer*, pp. 18, 22.
58. Oates, *Fires of Jubilee*, p. 41. On this point, see also Marion D. deB. Kilson, "Towards Freedom: An Analysis of Slave Revolts in the United States," *Phylon* 25 (1964): 183–184.
59. Douglass, *Life and Times*, p. 145; *Life and Writings of Douglass*, 1: 301; Oates, *Fires of Jubilee*, p. 42; Turner's *Confessions*, p. 3.
60. John Lofton, *Insurrection in South Carolina: The Turbulent World of Denmark Vesey*, p. 131.
61. In Herbert Aptheker, ed., *Documentary History of the Negro People in the United States*, p. 56; *An Account of the Late Intended Insurrection Among the Blacks of This City*, published by the Authority of the Corporation of Charleston, p. 35.
62. Benjamin Quarles, *Black Abolitionists*, p. 10. The best account of Douglass's move toward favoring violence is Leslie Friedman Goldstein, "Violence as an Instrument for Social Change: The Views of Frederick Douglass (1817–1895)," *Journal of Negro History* 41 (1976): 61–72. Quarles, in *Black Abolitionists*, notes that Douglass would come to feel "a state of war existed in the South" (p. 228).
63. *Minutes of the National Convention of Colored Citizens: Held at Buffalo, on the 15th, 16th, 17th, 18th and 19th of August, 1843, For the Purpose of Considering Their Moral and Political Condition as American Citizens*; rpt. in *Minutes and Proceedings of the National Negro Conventions, 1830–1864*, ed. Howard Holman Bell, p. 13; Farrison, *William Wells Brown*, p. 77; *Life and Writings of Douglass*, 1: 164.
64. *Life and Writings of Douglass*, 2: 128.
65. Ibid., pp. 206, 460, 487.
66. Woodson, *Mind of the Negro*, p. 267.
67. Rawick, ed., *Okla. Narr.*, 7, 209.

7. MILITARISM AND VIOLENCE

1. The best summaries of the image of the martial spirit are Robert
   D. Meade, "The Military Spirit of the South," *Current History* 30
   (1929): 55–60; and James C. Bonner, "The Historical Basis of
   Southern Military Tradition," *Georgia Review* 9 (1955): 74–85.

2. "Military Education," *Magnolia; or Southern Monthly* 4 (1842):
   256; D. R. Hundley, esq., *Social Relations in Our Southern States*,
   p. 56.

3. George Fitzhugh, "Frederick the Great, by Thomas Carlyle," *De
   Bow's Review* 29 (1860): 155–156.

4. John Hope Franklin, *The Militant South, 1800–1861*, pp. 191–192.
   On the ring tournaments, including survivals into the twentieth
   century, see Majorie Craig, "Survivals of the Chivalric Tournament
   in Southern Life and Literature" (M.A. thesis, University of North
   Carolina, 1935); see also Esther Josephine and Ruth W. Crooks,
   The Ring Tournament in the United States. For a good description of "dashing" uniforms see Mary Boykin Chesnut, *A Diary
   from Dixie*, ed. Ben Ames Williams, p. 35.

5. James Lawson Kemper, "The Mexican War Diary of James Lawson Kemper," ed. Robert R. Jones, *Virginia Magazine of History
   and Biography* 74 (1966): 428; J. F. H. Claiborne, *Life and Correspondence of John A. Quitman, Major-General, U.S.A., and
   Governor of the State of Mississippi*, 2: 56.

6. Franklin, *Militant South*, p. 4; Peter Karsten, "The American
   Democratic Citizen Soldier: Triumph or Disaster," *Military Affairs*
   30 (1966): 36. For two instances, see Andrew Pickens Butler,
   *Speech of Hon. A. P. Butler, of South Carolina, on the Difficulty
   of Messrs. Brooks and Sumner, and the Causes Thereof*, p. 8;
   Meta Morris Grimball, Journal, January 12, 1861, typed copy of
   original on file in the Southern Historical Collection, University of
   North Carolina, Chapel Hill.

7. "The State of Georgia," *De Bow's Review* 10 (1851): 245; "Mili-
   tary Defenses of Virginia," ibid. 19 (1855): 446–447; Nathaniel
   Francis Cabell to H. S. Randall, January 6, 1860, typed copy in the
   Virginia Historical Society, Richmond.

8. "The Army in Mexico," *De Bow's Review* 6 (1848): 369; Lee A.
   Wallace, Jr., "The First Regiment of Virginia Volunteers, 1846–
   1848," *Virginia Magazine of History and Biography* 77 (1969):
   52. For an excellent treatment of the question of whether there
   was a martial spirit, see Robert E. May, "Recent Trends in the
   Historiography of Southern Militarism," *The Historian*, in press.

Professor May was kind enough to furnish me with a typescript of his essay.

9. In Robert Manson Myers, ed., *A Georgian at Princeton*, pp. 222, 226.

10. Hundley, *Social Relations*, p. 175.

11. "Halleck's Military Art and Science," *Southern Quarterly Review* 10 (1846): 419.

12. "Our Army in Mexico," *De Bow's Review* 2 (1846): 430.

13. Claiborne, *Life of Quitman*, 2: 297; J. D. B. De Bow, "The Late Cuba Expedition," *De Bow's Review* 9 (1850): 165 et passim.

14. Marcus Cunliffe, *Soldiers and Civilians: The Martial Spirit in America, 1775–1865*, pp. 342, 358, 381.

15. George Fitzhugh, "Love of Danger and of War," *De Bow's Review* 28 (1860): 302; Col. Gardner, "The Army of the United States," ibid. 15 (1853): 449; Claiborne, *Life of Quitman*, 2: 297.

16. "State of Georgia," p. 245; see Augustus Baldwin Longstreet, *Georgia Scenes: Characters, Incidents, &c., in the First Half Century of the Republic*, pp. 131–137.

17. "A Virginia Militia Training of the Last Generation," *Harper's* 45 (1872): 245, 243.

18. Moreau B. C. Chambers, "The Militia Crisis," *Virginia Cavalcade* 16, no. 4 (Spring 1967): 10; "State of Georgia," p. 246.

19. The figures are in "United States Militia," *De Bow's Review* 13 (1852): 621. John Gideon Harris, Diary, March 2, 1859, typed copy in the Southern Historical Collection; John Coles Rutherfoord, Diary, May 15, 1847, Virginia Historical Society.

20. John H. Napier III, "Martial Montgomery: Antebellum Military Activity," *Alabama Historical Quarterly* 29 (1967): 116; William Hooper Haigh, Journal, January 3, 1844, typed copy in Southern Historical Collection.

21. Richard W. Barsness, "John C. Calhoun and the Military Establishment, 1817–1825," *Wisconsin Magazine of History* 50 (1966): 43–53; Cunliffe, *Soldiers and Civilians*, p. 197; "Interesting Correspondence," *Crisis* 1 (1840): 113. One may note Ritchie's use of capital letters.

22. Lee A. Wallace, Jr., "The Alexandria Militia," *Virginia Cavalcade* 16, no. 3 (Winter 1967): 13–15.

23. B. J. Barbour, "Address Delivered before the Literary Societies of the Virginia Military Institute, July 4, 1854," *Southern Literary Messenger* 20 (1854): 513.

24. "Halleck's Military Art," pp. 424, 428–429.

25. "Battle of Buena Vista," *Southern Quarterly Review* 19 (1851): 155; "Our Army in Mexico," p. 428.

26. "South Carolina Military Academies," *Southern Quarterly Review* 26 (1854): 201; see also "Southern School Books," *De Bow's Review* 13 (1852): 266.
27. Barbour, "Address," p. 513.
28. Daniel R. Whitaker, "Letter from Daniel Whitaker," *New Orleans Miscellany* 1 (1847): 54.
29. Peter W. Hairston, ed., "J. E. B. Stuart's Letters to His Hairston Kin, 1850–1855," *North Carolina Historical Review* 51 (1974): 274.
30. "Military Schools of South Carolina," *Southern Quarterly Review* 18 (1850): 529; Franklin, *Militant South*, pp. 15, 17. For a contrary view, see Cunliffe, *Soldiers and Civilians*, pp. 352–353; May, "Recent Trends," pp. 13–14.
31. Paul F. Lambert, "The Movement for the Acquisition of All Mexico," *Journal of the West* 11 (1972): 320, 323–324; Ernest M. Lander, Jr., "The Reluctant Imperialist: South Carolina, the Rio Grande, and the Mexican War," *Southwestern Historical Quarterly* 78 (1975): 254–270; Frederick Merk, *Manifest Destiny and Mission in American History: A Reinterpretation*, pp. 157–169.
32. Robert E. May, *The Southern Dream of a Caribbean Empire, 1854–1861*, p. 194. On the character and motivations of the filibusters themselves, see Joe A. Stout, Jr., "Idealism or Manifest Destiny? Filibustering in Northwestern Mexico, 1850–1865," *Journal of the West* 11 (1972): 348, 360.
33. Henry W. Hilliard, *Speeches and Addresses*, pp. 91, 156.
34. De Bow, "Late Cuba Expedition," p. 173; "The Invasion of Cuba," *Southern Quarterly Review* 21 (1852): 11, 4.
35. Claiborne, *Life of Quitman*, 1: 311.
36. Ibid., 2: 113; De Bow, "Late Cuba Expedition," p. 158.
37. George Fitzhugh, "Acquisition of Mexico—Filibustering," *De Bow's Review* 25 (1858): 617; George Frederick Holmes, "Relations of the Old and the New Worlds," ibid. 20 (1856): 529.
38. S. C. Carpenter, *Report of the Trial of Richard Dennis, the Younger, for the Murder of James Shaw, on the 20th of August, 1804*, p. 115.
39. "Our Army in Mexico," p. 426.
40. "Halleck's Military Art," p. 422.
41. Ibid., p. 423.
42. De Bow, "Late Cuba Expedition," p. 165.
43. Fitzhugh, "Love of Danger," p. 303; "War and Its Incidents," *Southern Quarterly Review* 13 (1848): 2; "The Northern Pacific: California, Oregon and the Oregon Question," ibid. 8 (1845): 241; "Halleck's Military Art," p. 432.

8. VIOLENCE AND SOUTHERN ORATORY

1. The term "fire-eater" was, in fact, originally applied to Southern duelists. See H. Hardy Perritt, "The Fire Eaters," in *Oratory in the Old South, 1828–1860*, ed. Waldo W. Braden, p. 234 n. 2.

2. William L. Barney emphasizes the entertainment value of Southern oratory, and its value for diverting the Southern people from their real interests in *The Secessionist Impulse: Alabama and Mississippi in 1860*, p. 38—although, it must be added, he does not minimize the power of oratory in the secessionist movement. The classic statement of oratory as romanticism is W. J. Cash, *The Mind of the South*, pp. 51–52.

3. See on this Dell Hymes, "Linguistic Aspects of Comparative Political Research," in *The Methodology of Comparative Research*, ed. Robert T. Holt and John E. Turner, p. 309. See also Roger D. Abrahams, "Introductory Remarks to a Rhetorical Theory of Folklore," *Journal of American Folklore* 81 (1968): 148, and Doris A. Graber, *Verbal Behavior and Politics*, p. 48. An excellent discussion of the relationship between rhetoric and morality, and thus of rhetoric to culture, is Parke G. Burgess, "The Rhetoric of Moral Conflict: Two Critical Dimensions," *Quarterly Journal of Speech* 56 (1970): 120–130.

4. James Johnston Pettigrew to Ebenezer Pettigrew, May 7, 1848, in the Pettigrew family papers, Southern Historical Collection, University of North Carolina, Chapel Hill. Edward K. Graham suggested that before 1820, Northern and Southern oratory were indistinguishable and that after that date the distinction was as much one of content as of style, in "The History of Southern Oratory during the Federal Period, 1788–1861," in *History of Southern Oratory*, ed. Thomas E. Watson, p. 35. The "myth of a southern orator" is thoroughly deflated in Braden, ed., *Oratory in the Old South*, especially pp. 17–18. I agree with his contention that individual styles were too varied for one to speak of a genre of Southern oratory, but this does not mean that antebellum standards, or conventions, of rhetorical criticism were not both fairly consistent and widespread.

5. John Witherspoon DuBose, *The Life and Times of William Lowndes Yancey: A History of Political Parties in the United States, from 1834 to 1864; Especially as the Origin of the Confederate States*, 2: 79, 186.

6. William L. Yancey, Speech to the Gentlemen of the Erosophic and Philomathic Societies, n.d., ms. in William Lowndes Yancey pa-

pers, Alabama Department of Archives and History, Montgomery.

7. Perritt, "Fire-Eaters," p. 255. It may have been, as Perritt suggests, that many were disappointed in Yancey's manner, but it could only have added to his rhetorical effectiveness.

8. *Vicksburg Sentinel,* June 24, 1844, in *The Papers of Jefferson Davis,* ed. Haskell M. Monroe, Jr., and James T. McIntosh, 2: 166.

9. Charles Colcock Jones, Jr., to his parents in *A Georgian at Princeton,* ed. Robert Manson Myers, p. 83.

10. The connection between violence and oratory is made in John Hope Franklin, *The Militant South, 1800–1860,* p. 132; Letter from Burwell Boykin to C. C. Clay, in Clement Claiborne Clay papers, Manuscript Department, William R. Perkins Library, Duke University, Durham, N.C.; Watson, ed., *History of Oratory,* p. 87.

11. Prentiss, in Dallas C. Dickey, *Seargent S. Prentiss: Whig Orator of the Old South,* p. 344; see also pp. 348, 351. For a fairly typical statement of the importance of fusing reason and passion, see Dunbar Rowland, "Political and Parliamentary Orators and Oratory of Mississippi," *Publications,* Mississippi Historical Society 4 (1901): 370.

12. Hugh R. Pleasants, "Sketches of the Virginia Convention of 1829–30," *Southern Literary Messenger* 17 (1851): 297. William Gilmore Simms, *The Letters of William Gilmore Simms,* collected and ed., Mary C. Simms Oliphant, Alfred Taylor Odell, and T. C. Duncan Eaves, 4: 52.

13. See Graham, "History of Southern Oratory," p. 37; Perritt, "Fire-Eaters," p. 250.

14. See on this Joseph J. Hemmer, Jr., "The Charleston Platform Debate in Rhetorical-Historical Perspective," *Quarterly Journal of Speech* 56 (1970): 414. Robert G. Gunderson has remarked that the metaphors of Southern oratory were stale even to nineteenth-century tastes in "The Southern Whigs," in *Oratory in the Old South,* ed. Braden, p. 139.

15. John Quincy Adams, *Lectures on Rhetoric and Oratory, Delivered to the Classes of Senior and Junior Sophisters in Harvard University,* 1: 402.

16. Robert M. Weir, "The South Carolinian as Extremist," *South Atlantic Quarterly* 74 (1975): 90.

17. Laura A. White, *Robert Barnwell Rhett: Father of Secession,* p. 28.

18. Ibid., p. 98.

19. For one study of the rise of military imagery in oratory and its connection to party politics, see Perry M. Goldman, "Political Rhetoric in the Age of Jackson," *Tennessee Historical Quarterly*

29 (1970): 360–371. Goldman accounts for martial imagery in terms of both the rise of partisanship as a way of political life and its suitability to a society which had been through at least one serious war and any number of skirmishes. Both facts undoubtedly increased its appeal, but, as I shall argue, this combining of metaphor and reality was most effective because of deeper concerns about order growing out of Southern conceptions of human nature and society.

20. William Lowndes Yancey, "Extracts from the Address delivered at Lodi, Abbeville District, on the 4th inst. by W. L. Yancey," *Greenville Mountaineer*, July 12, 1834, typed copy in Yancey papers. Robert Gunderson writes that Benjamin Watkins Leigh, using similar words, brought a North Carolina crowd to tears and says that this was not an unusual occurrence, in "Southern Whigs," p. 139. DuBose, *Life and Times*, p. 361.

21. In James Petigru Carson, ed., *The Life, Letters and Speeches of James Louis Petigru, the Union Man of South Carolina*, p. 143.

22. "Speech of Hon. J. H. Hammond, of South Carolina," *Charleston Mercury*, March 8, 1858. Henry W. Hilliard, *Speeches and Addresses*, p. 365. The term "antistructure" is used in the sense developed by Victor W. Turner in, for example, *Dramas, Fields, and Metaphors: Symbolic Action in Human Society*, p. 202.

23. Louis Hartz, *The Liberal Tradition in America: An Interpretation of American Political Thought Since the Revolution*, p. 161. On the conflicting ideals of American "freedom" see Major L. Wilson, *Space, Time, and Freedom: The Quest for Nationality and the Irrepressible Conflict, 1815–1861*. David Brion Davis, looking at the issue from the antislavery point of view, has written of "the perishability of Revolutionary time" in *The Problem of Slavery in the Age of Revolution, 1770–1823*, pp. 306–308. For Southerners, "perishability" was its greatest virtue. A good general discussion of this issue is Philip F. Detweiler, "The Changing Reputation of the Declaration of Independence," *William and Mary Quarterly* 3rd ser. 19 (1962): 557–574. Most early Americans, and particularly the Federalists, would not have found the Southern view strange. The quotation from Randolph is in William Sumner Jenkins, *Pro-Slavery Thought in the Old South*, p. 60.

24. "Speech of the Hon. William L. Yancey, of Alabama, Delivered in the National Democratic Convention, Charleston, April 28, 1860. With the Protest of the Alabama Delegation," pp. 7, 11.

25. Thomas Lanier Clingman, "Speech: Defense of the South against

the Aggressive Movement of the North; Delivered in the House of Representatives, January 22, 1850," p. 4.

26. *Debates and other Proceedings of the Convention of Virginia, Convened at Richmond, on Monday the 2d day of June, 1788, for the purpose of deliberating on the Constitution recommended by the Grand Federal Convention*, p. 71.

27. *Proceedings and Debates of the Virginia State Convention of 1829–30. To Which Are Subjoined, the New Constitution of Virginia, and the Votes of the People*, pp. 53, 317; Hillard, *Speeches*, p. 365.

28. Minority Report of the Committee on the South Carolina Documents, published in the *Western Carolinian*, Salisbury, Rowan County, N.C., January 14, 1833, typed copy in John Lancaster Bailey papers, Southern Historical Collection. Hugh Swinton Legaré, *Writings of Hugh Swinton Legaré*, ed. his sister, 1: 274.

29. *Annals of the Congress*, Senate, 16 Cong., 1 Sess., p. 224.

30. Ibid., p. 175.

31. In White, *Robert Barnwell Rhett*, p. 107; *Congressional Globe*, 33 Cong., 1 Sess., appendix, p. 195.

32. See e.g. Hilliard, *Speeches*, p. 312. An earlier version of this idea as it was expressed by a North Carolinian in the Continental Congress appears in John Richard Alden, *The First South*, pp. 61–62.

33. See e.g. Rev. David Griffith, "Passive Obedience Considered, in a Sermon Preached at Williamsburg, December 13, 1775," p. 22. This was a popular motif in Revolutionary propaganda; see Bernard Bailyn, *Ideological Origins of the American Revolution*, pp. 132–140.

34. See Barney, *Secessionist Impulse*, pp. 180–181; Steven A. Channing, *Crisis of Fear: Secession in South Carolina*, p. 24.

35. Yancey, "Speech . . . in the National Democratic Convention," p. 4.

36. J. F. H. Claiborne, *Life and Correspondence of John A. Quitman, Major-General, U.S.A., and Governor of the State of Mississippi*, 2: 23n. See on this David Potter, *The Impending Crisis, 1848–1861*, completed and ed. Don E. Fehrenbacher, pp. 469, 484.

37. Watson, *History of Oratory*, p. 88. Perritt ("Fire-Eaters," p. 249) suggests that the fire-eaters provided "ready-made arguments for people to use when the conditions made the arguments palatable," and thus advanced the cause of secession by giving "continuity and credibility to conditions which the South was reluctant to accept." Given the widespread use of similiar arguments and images over a long period of time and dealing with a great variety of

conditions, I would suggest that the continuity was already there and that in drawing upon it the fire-eaters lent credibility to their own interpretation of events.

38. On this I am in agreement with Potter, *Impending Crisis*, pp. 501, 516, 532.

9. HUNTING, VIOLENCE, AND CULTURE

1. Clarence Gohdes, ed., *Hunting in the Old South: Original Narratives of the Hunters*, pp. xi–xii; George Anderson Mercer, Scrapbook, Southern Historical Collection, University of North Carolina, Chapel Hill.

2. The Hon. Wm. Elliott, of Beaufort, S.C., *Carolina Sports by Land and Water; Including Incidents of Devil-Fishing, &c.*, p. 162. See also D. R. Hundley, esq., *Social Relations in Our Southern States*, pp. 28–29, 35.

3. John Witherspoon DuBose, "Recollections of the Plantation," ms. (1916), Dubose papers, Alabama Department of Archives and History, Montgomery; idem, *The Life and Times of William Lowndes Yancey*, 1: 80. See also Rollin G. Osterweis, *Romanticism and Nationalism in the Old South*, p. 84.

4. Frederick Gustavus Skinner, "Reminiscences of an Old Sportsman," in *A Sporting Family of the Old South*, ed. Harry Worcester Smith, p. 64; Alatamaha, "Deer Hunting on the Seaboard of Georgia," *American Turf Register and Sporting Magazine* 3 (1831): 29–30.

5. Elliott, *Carolina Sports*, p. 83.

6. J. S. Skinner, "Introduction," *American Turf Register and Sporting Magazine* 1 (1829): 2.

7. Topthorn, "Foxhunting, Its Pleasures and Its Uses, with Anecdotes of Men, Horses, and Hounds," *American Turf Register and Sporting Magazine* 4 (1832): 80; A., "Woodcock," ibid. 1 (1830): 303; A Hunter, "Shooting in Tennessee," ibid. 2 (181): 391.

8. A., "Woodcock," p. 303; Elliott, *Carolina Sports*, p. 107; George Tucker, *Essays on Various Subjects of Taste, Morals, and National Policy. By a Citizen of Virginia*, p. 102.

9. Elliott, *Carolina Sports*, p. 88.

10. Alatamaha, "Deer Hunting," p. 29.

11. "Field Sports in Virginia," *American Turf Register and Sporting Magazine* 9 (1838): 510.

12. Elliott, *Carolina Sports*, p. 52; C. W. Webber, "The Viviparous

Quadrupeds of North America," *Southern Quarterly Review* 12 (1847): 296.

13. "The Chase," *Spirit of the Times*, May 12, 1832; Elliott, *Carolina Sports*, p. 108; John James Audubon, *Audubon and His Journals*, ed. Maria R. Audubon, 1: 116.

14. Thomas Bangs Thorpe, "The American Deer: Its Habits and Associations," *Harper's* 17 (1858): 618.

15. "North American Foxes," *Southern Quarterly Review* 13 (1848): 413; Pholo-therus, "Foxhunting in Washington [D.C.]," *American Turf Register and Sporting Magazine* 6 (1835): 292.

16. Thomas Bangs Thorpe, "Woodcock Fire-Hunting," in *Hunting*, ed. Gohdes, p. 114; Webber, "Viviparous Quadrupeds," p. 282.

17. "Field Sports," p. 510.

18. Mercer, Diary, May 23, 1855.

19. Frederick Skinner, "Reminiscences," pp. 240–241.

20. Thorpe, "Woodcock Fire-Hunting," p. 114; Webber, "Viviparous Quadrupeds," pp. 276, 284.

21. Theodore Dwight Bozeman, "Joseph LeConte: Organic Science and a 'Sociology for the South,'" *Journal of Southern History* 39 (1973): 576; Webber, "Viviparous Quadrupeds," p. 285.

22. Stephen Elliott, "Views of Nature," *The Southern Review* 2 (1828): 413; John James Audubon, *The Letters of John James Audubon, 1826–1840*, ed. Howard Corning, 2: 192.

23. Elliott, *Carolina Sports*, p. 166; see also Richard Slotkin, *Regeneration through Violence: The Mythology of the American Frontier, 1600–1860*, p. 274.

24. Webber, "Viviparous Quadrupeds," pp. 273–275, passim.

25. José Ortega y Gasset, *Meditations on Hunting*, trans. Howard B. Wescott, p. 55.

26. Audubon, *Journals*, 1: 374.

27. Expressions of such feelings appeared frequently. See for example John Bachman, "The Insect World: Morals of Entomology, etc.," *De Bow's Review* 25 (1858): 434; "Deer Hunting," *Spirit of the Times*, March 24, 1832; A., "Woodcock," p. 304. William Elliott even had a feeling of sadness upon the death of a devil fish because of "something almost *human* in the attitude and the expression of his agony," *Carolina Sports*, p. 41.

28. William L. Yancey, Speech to the Gentlemen of the Erosophic and Philomathic Societies, n.d., ms. in Yancey papers, Alabama Department of Archives and History.

29. Mercer, Scrapbook, May 9, 1855; S. G. F., "Deer-Hunting at Berkely Springs, Va.," *Spirit of the Times*, September 15, 1832.

30. Frederick Skinner, "Reminiscences," p. 124.
31. S. G. F., "Deer-Hunting;" John James Audubon, *Journals*, 2: 316.
32. A. W. Ely, "Phenomena of Nature," *De Bow's Review* 12 (1852): 378; Henry Washington Hilliard, *Speeches and Addresses*, p. 478. On this general point, see Bozeman, "Joseph LeConte." See also Daniel J. Boorstin, *The Lost World of Thomas Jefferson*, p. 49.
33. Bozeman, "Joseph LeConte," p. 581.
34. James C. Johnston to William S. Pettigrew, June 28, 1848, Pettigrew family papers, Southern Historical Collection.
35. Victor W. Turner, "Liminal to Liminoid, in Play, Flow, and Ritual: An Essay in Comparative Symbology," in *The Anthropological Study of Human Play*, ed. Edward Norbeck, Rice University Studies 60, no. 3 (Summer 1974), pp. 85–86. Max Gluckman, *Order and Rebellion in Tribal Africa*, pp. 129–130.
36. Philip Wheelwright, *Metaphor and Reality*, p. 46.
37. Mercer, Scrapbook, December 26, 1855.
38. Audubon, *Journals*, 1: 261.
39. S. J. Tambiah, "The Magical Power of Words," *Man* 3 (1968): 194.

10. VIOLENCE IN SOUTHERN FICTION

1. See on this John W. Higham, "The Changing Loyalties of William Gilmore Simms," *Journal of Southern History* 9 (1943): 210–223. Vernon Louis Parrington, *Main Currents in American Thought*, 2: 119.
2. Donald Davidson, Introduction to *The Letters of William Gilmore Simms*, collected and ed. Mary C. Simms Oliphant, Alfred Taylor Odell, and T. C. Duncan Eaves, 1: li; see for example William R. Taylor, *Cavalier and Yankee: The Old South and American National Character*.
3. Simms, *Letters*, 1: 155.
4. William Gilmore Simms, "A Letter to the Editor by the Author of 'The Loves of the Driver,'" *Magnolia* 3 (1841): 378; see also David Brion Davis, *Homicide in American Fiction, 1798–1860: A Study in Social Values*, pp. 142–143.
5. William Gilmore Simms, *Confession; or, The Blind Heart. A Domestic Story;* idem, *Martin Faber, The Story of a Criminal*.
6. Simms, *Martin Faber*, p. 13.
7. Simms, *Letters*, 2: 224; idem, *Katharine Walton; or, The Rebel of Dorchester*, p. 224.

8. Simms, *Confession*, p. 180.

9. Simms, *Letters*, 2: 224; Davis, *Homicide*, p. 190.

10. Along these lines, see Simms, *Letters*, 2: 493, for the author's strongly negative view of marriages between cousins.

11. Simms, *Letters*, 1: 55; Simms, *Richard Hurdis: A Tale of Alabama*, p. 10.

12. Simms, *Letters*, 1: 153.

13. William Gilmore Simms, *Guy Rivers: A Tale of Georgia*, p. 284.

14. Ibid., p. 280.

15. Simms, *Letters*, 2: 225; see also J. V. Ridgely, *William Gilmore Simms*, p. 48.

16. Simms, *Guy Rivers*, p. 229.

17. Ibid., p. 70. See on this Slotkin, *Regeneration through Violence*, especially chapters 12–13.

18. Simms, *Guy Rivers*, p. 229.

19. Ibid., pp. 169, 172.

20. Simms, *Letters*, 2: 548 n. 166; see also Simone Vauthier, "Of Time and the South: The Fiction of William Gilmore Simms," *Southern Literary Journal* 5 (1972): 21.

21. Vauthier, "Of Time and the South," pp. 20–21, 24–25.

22. C. Hugh Holman, *The Roots of Southern Writing: Essays on the Literature of the American South*, p. 40.

23. William Gilmore Simms, *The Forayers; or, the Raid of the Dog-Days*, p. 5.

24. William Gilmore Simms, *The Partisan: A Tale of the Revolution*, 1: 10, 2: 10.

25. Ibid., 2: 145–146.

26. Ibid., 2: 147–148.

27. Ibid., 2: 148.

28. Ibid., 1: 14–15; 2: 134–135, 219.

29. William Gilmore Simms, *Mellichampe: A Legend of the Santee*, pp. 401–408.

30. For folklore in one Southwestern humorist's works, see Ormonde Plater, "Before Sut: Folklore in the Early Works of George Washington Harris," *Southern Folklore Quarterly* 34 (1970): 104–115. For an example of a Southwestern humorist's work that entered into oral tradition, see B. A. Botkin, ed., *A Treasury of Southern Folklore: Stories, Ballads, Traditions, and Folkways of the People of the South*, p. 112. On the complex relationship of tradition to the genre, see Joseph J. Arpad, "The Fight Story: Quotation and Originality in Native American Humor," *Journal of the Folklore Institute* 10 (1973): 153.

31. Mody C. Boatright, *Folk Laughter on the American Frontier*, p. 26; Walter Blair, *Native American Humor (1800–1900)*, p. 91; Shields McIlwaine, *The Southern Poor-White from Lubberland to Tobacco Road*, p. 55.

32. John D. Wade, *Augustus Baldwin Longstreet: A Study of the Development of Culture in the South*, pp. 164–167.

33. Augustus Baldwin Longstreet, *Georgia Scenes: Characters, Incidents, &c., in the First Half Century of the Republic*, pp. 42–53.

34. Ibid., p. 51.

35. Ibid., pp. 105, 145.

36. William T. Porter, ed., *The Big Bear of Arkansas, and Other Sketches, Illustrative of the Characters and Incidents of the South and South-West*, pp. 167, 178.

37. Harden E. Taliaferro, *Fisher's River (North Carolina) Scenes and Characters. By "Skitt," "Who Was Raised Thar,"* p. 203.

38. Ibid., p. 198.

39. See Nancy B. Sederberg, "Antebellum Southern Humor in the *Camden Journal:* 1826–1840," *Mississippi Quarterly* 27 (1974): 41–74; James L. W. West III, "Early Backwoods Humor in the Greenville *Mountaineer,* 1826–1840," ibid. 25 (1971): 69–82.

40. Harden E. Taliaferro, "Fun in North Carolina," *Southern Literary Messenger* 31 (1860): 106; John Robb, *Streaks of Squatter Life, and Far-West Scenes*, p. 132.

41. Johnson Jones Hooper, *Adventures of Captain Simon Suggs, Late of the Tallapoosa Volunteers*, pp. 15–25.

42. George Washington Harris, *Sut Lovingood*, ed. Brom Weber, pp. 48–49.

43. Ibid., pp. 121–122.

44. Ibid., pp. 124.

45. Hooper, *Adventures*, p. 113.

46. Longstreet, *Georgia Scenes*, p. 52. See on this Arlin Turner, "Realism and Fantasy in Southern Humor," *Georgia Review* 12 (1958): 455.

47. Hooper, *Adventures*, p. 8.

CONCLUSION

1. Vernon Louis Parrington, *Main Currents in American Thought*, 2: 55. Jay B. Hubbell, "Poe and the Southern Literary Tradition," *Texas Studies in Literature and Language* 2 (1960): 153–154; Glasgow is quoted on p. 154. Jacobs, in *Southern Literary Study: Prob-*

lems and Possibilities, ed. Louis D. Rubin, Jr., and C. Hugh Holman, p. 110. See also Thomas Hubert, "The Southern Element in Poe's Fiction," *Georgia Review* 28 (1974): 200–212.

2. Hubbell, "Poe," p. 153. For such a reading of *Pym*, see Sidney Kaplan, introduction to the Hill and Wang edition, 1960, pp. xxiii–xxv; see also Leslie Fiedler, *Love and Death in the American Novel*, pp. 379–380.

3. Edgar Allan Poe, *The Complete Works of Edgar Allan Poe*, ed. James A. Harrison, 10: 54. For Poe's favorable opinion of Simms's *Martin Faber*, see ibid., 10: 50. On the contrast between Simms and Poe see also David Brion Davis, *Homicide in American Fiction, 1798–1860: A Study in Social Values*, pp. 108–109.

4. Edgar Allan Poe, *Complete Stories and Poems of Edgar Allan Poe*, pp. 71–72.

5. Ibid., pp. 175–176.

6. Edward H. Davidson, *Poe: A Critical Study*, p. 125; Daniel Hoffman, *Poe Poe Poe Poe Poe Poe Poe*, p. 113.

7. Leo Spitzer, "A Reinterpretation of 'The Fall of the House of Usher,'" *Comparative Literature* 4 (1952): 360.

8. Edgar Allan Poe, *The Letters of Edgar Allan Poe*, ed. John Ward Ostrom, 1: 58.

9. Poe, *Complete Stories*, pp. 65, 272.

10. Davis, *Homicide*, p. 123.

11. Poe, *Complete Stories*, pp. 282–283.

12. See on this Fiedler, *Love and Death*. See also Ann Douglas, "Heaven Our Home: Consolation Literature in the Northern United States, 1830–1880," in *Death in America*, ed. David E. Stannard, pp. 49–68.

13. Eugene D. Genovese, *The World the Slaveholders Made: Two Essays in Interpretation*, part II, passim.

Bibliography

MANUSCRIPT SOURCES

Asterisk indicates typed copy.

Chapel Hill. Southern Historical Collection, University of North Carolina.
    John Lancaster Bailey papers.
    Everard Green Baker diaries and plantation notes.*
    Launcelot Minor Blackford diary.*
    Clingman-Puryear papers.
    Mrs. Eliza Clitherall autobiography and diary.*
    Edward Dromgoole papers.
    Grimball papers.
    John Berkley Grimball diaries.*
    Meta Morris Grimball journal.*
    William Hooper Haigh journal.*
    John Gideon Harris diary.*
    Hubard family papers.
    George A. Mercer diary.*
    William Porcher Miles papers.
    Pettigrew family papers.
Charleston, South Carolina Historical Society.
    R. M. Cahusac to William Porcher, Pineville, February 17, 1822.
    The Cheves-Trapier Duel.*
    Jacob Schirmer, records from October 1826 to December 1846.
    Secretary's Book, Pineville Association, 1823–1840.
Cullowhee, N. C. University Archives, Western Carolina University.
    Ninian Edmonston collection.
    William Williams Stringfield collection.
Durham, N. C. William R. Perkins Library, Duke University.
    Edward F. Birkhead letters and papers.
    Thomas E. Buchanan papers.
    Clement Claiborne Clay papers.
Harris County, Texas, District Clerk's Office.
    Minutes, 11th Judicial District Court, 1838–1844.

Montgomery. Alabama Department of Archives and History.
  John Witherspoon Dubose papers.
  Benjamin Franklin Perry letters.
  William Lowndes Yancey papers.
Richmond, Virginia Historical Society.
  William Bolling diary, 1836–1839.*
  William Bolling diary, 1840–1842.
  Nathaniel Francis Cabell to H. S. Randall, January 6, 1860.*
  Carrington family papers.
  William Galt farm diary.
  George Bolling Lee papers.
  Charles Minor diary (ms. copy).
  Edmund Ruffin papers.
  Francis Gildart Ruffin diary.
  John Coles Rutherfoord diary.
Richmond, Virginia State Library.
  Virginia Legislative Petitions.

NEWSPAPERS

Annals of the Congress.
Arkansas Gazette.
Asheville (N.C.) *Highland Messenger.*
Charleston Courier.
Charleston Mercury.
Charleston Southern Patriot.
Cheraw (S.C.) *Gazette.*
Columbus (Ga.) *Enquirer.*
Congressional Globe.
Houston Morning Star.
Houston Telegraph and Texas Register.
Jonesborough (Tenn.) *Whig and Independent Journal.*
Mobile Register and Journal.
New Orleans Bee.
Raleigh Semi-Weekly Register.

BOOKS AND ARTICLES

A. "Woodcock." *American Turf Register and Sporting Magazine* 1
  (1830): 302–304.
Abrahams, Roger D. "Introductory Remarks to a Rhetorical Theory of

Folklore." *Journal of American Folklore* 81 (1968): 143–158.

An Account of the Late Intended Insurrection among the Blacks of This City. Published by the authority of the Corporation of Charleston, 1822. Rpt. Westport, Conn.: Negro Universities Press, 1970.

Adams, John Quincy. *Lectures on Rhetoric and Oratory, Delivered to the Classes of Senior and Junior Sophisters in Harvard University*. 2 vols. Cambridge, Mass.: Hilliard and Metcalf, 1810.

Agricola. "Management of Negroes." *De Bow's Review* 19 (1855): 358–363.

Alatamaha. "Deer Hunting on the Seaboard of Georgia." *American Turf Register and Sporting Magazine* 3 (1831): 28–30.

Alden, John Richard. *The First South*. Baton Rouge: Louisiana State University Press, 1961.

Anderson, John Q., ed. *Tales of Frontier Texas, 1830–1860*. Dallas: Southern Methodist University Press, 1966.

Aptheker, Herbert. *American Negro Slave Revolts*. 1943. Rpt. New York: International Publishers, 1963.

————, ed. *Documentary History of the Negro People in the United States*. 2 vols. 2nd paperback ed, New York: Citadel Press, 1963.

Ariès, Philippe. *Centuries of Childhood: A Social History of Family Life*. Translated by Robert Baldick. New York: Vintage Books, 1962.

"The Army in Mexico." *De Bow's Review* 6 (1848): 369.

Arpad, Joseph J. "The Fight Story: Quotation and Originality in Native American Humor." *Journal of the Folklore Institute* 10 (1973): 141–172.

Audubon, John James. *Audubon and His Journals*. Edited by Maria R. Audubon. 2 vols. 1897. Rpt. New York: Dover, 1960.

————. *The Letters of John James Audubon, 1826–1840*. Edited by Howard Corning. 2 vols. Boston: The Club of Odd Volumes, 1930.

Aunt Sally; or, The Cross the Way to Freedom. A Narrative of the Slave-life and Purchase of the Mother of Rev. Isaac Williams, of Detroit, Michigan. 1858. Rpt. Miami: Mnemosyne, 1969.

An Authenticated Report of the Trial of Myers and Others, for the Murder of Dudley Marvin Hoyt. Drawn up by the editor of the Richmond Southern Standard. New York: Richards and Co., 1846.

Bachman, John. "The Insect World: Morals of Entomology, etc." *De Bow's Review* 25 (1858): 430–435.

Bailyn, Bernard. *Ideological Origins of the American Revolution*. Cambridge, Mass.: Harvard University Press, 1967.

Barbour, B. J. "Address Delivered before the Literary Societies of the

Virginia Military Institute, July 4, 1854." *Southern Literary Messenger* 20 (1854): 513–528.

Barney, William L. *The Road to Secession: A New Perspective on the Old South.* New York: Praeger, 1972.

———. *The Secessionist Impulse: Alabama and Mississippi in 1860.* Princeton: Princeton University Press, 1974.

Barsness, Richard W. "John C. Calhoun and the Military Establishment, 1817–1825." *Wisconsin Magazine of History* 50 (1966): 43–53.

Bartlett, Richard A. *The New Country: A Social History of the American Frontier, 1776–1890.* New York: Oxford University Press, 1974.

"Battle of Buena Vista." *Southern Quarterly Review* 19 (1851): 146–189.

Benedict, Ruth. "Continuities and Discontinuities in Cultural Conditioning," In *Childhood in Contemporary Cultures*, edited by Margaret Mead and Martha Wolfenstein, pp. 21–30. Chicago: University of Chicago Press, 1954.

Benton, Thomas Hart. *Thirty Years' View; or, A History of the Working of the American Government for Thirty Years, From 1820 to 1850.* 2 vols. New York: D. Appleton and Co., 1856.

Berlin, Ira. *Slaves without Masters: The Free Negro in the Antebellum South.* 1974. Rpt. New York: Vintage, 1976.

Bernstein, Basil. "Aspects of Language and Learning in the Genesis of the Social Process." In *Language in Culture and Society: A Reader in Linguistics and Anthropology*, edited by Dell Hymes, pp. 251–263. New York: Harper, 1964.

Bibb, Henry. *Narrative of the Life and Adventures of Henry Bibb, an American Slave, Written by Himself.* 3d ed., 1850. Rpt. Miami: Mnemosyne, 1969.

Blackburn, R. S. "Management of Negroes." *American Farmer* 4th ser. 7 (1852): 397.

"The Bladensburg Dueling Ground." *Harper's* 16 (1858): 471–481.

Blair, Rev. John D. "A Sermon on the Impetuosity and Bad Effects of Passion." Richmond: Lynch and Southgate, 1809.

Blair, Walter. *Native American Humor (1800–1900).* New York: American Book Co., 1937.

———, and Meine, Franklin J., eds. *Half Horse Half Alligator: The Growth of the Mike Fink Legend.* Chicago: University of Chicago Press, 1956.

Blassingame, John W. *The Slave Community: Plantation Life in the Antebellum South.* New York: Oxford University Press, 1972.

———. "Using the Testimony of Ex-Slaves: Approaches and Problems." *Journal of Southern History* 41 (1975): 473–492.

Boas, George. "Warfare in the Cosmos." In *Violence and Aggression in the History of Ideas,* edited by Philip P. Wiener and John Fisher, pp. 3–14. New Brunswick: Rutgers University Press, 1974.

Boatright, Mody C. *Folk Laughter on the American Frontier.* Gloucester, Mass.: Peter Smith, 1971.

———. "The Myth of Frontier Individualism." In *Turner and the Sociology of the Frontier,* edited by Richard Hofstadter and Seymour Martin Lipset, pp. 43–64. New York: Basic Books, 1968.

Bonner, James C. "The Historical Basis of Southern Military Tradition." *Georgia Review* 9 (1955): 74–85.

Boorstin, Daniel J. *The Lost World of Thomas Jefferson.* 1948. Rpt. Boston: Beacon Press, 1960.

Botkin, B. A., ed. *A Treasury of Southern Folklore: Stories, Ballads, Traditions, and Folkways of the People of The South.* New York: Crown Publishers, 1949.

Bozeman, Theodore Dwight. "Joseph LeConte: Organic Science and a 'Sociology for the South.' " *Journal of Southern History* 39 (1973): 565–582.

Braden, Waldo W., ed. *Oratory in the Old South, 1828–1860.* Baton Rouge: Louisiana State University Press, 1970.

Bradley, Bert E. and Tarver, Jerry L. "John C. Calhoun's Rhetorical Method in Defense of Slavery." In *Oratory in the Old South, 1828–1860,* edited by Waldo W. Braden, pp. 169–189. Baton Rouge: Louisiana State University Press, 1970.

Bragg, James W. "Captain Slick, Arbiter of Early Alabama Morals." *Alabama Review* 11 (1958): 125–134.

Brearly, H. C. "The Pattern of Violence." In *Culture in the South,* edited by William Terry Couch, pp. 678–692. 1934. Rpt. Westport, Conn.: Negro Universities Press, 1970.

Brown, Norman D. *Edward Stanly: Whiggery's Tarheel "Conqueror."* University: University of Alabama Press, 1974.

Brown, Richard Maxwell. "The History of Vigilantism in America." In *Vigilante Politics,* edited by H. Jon Rosenbaum and Peter C. Sederberg, pp. 79–109. Philadelphia: University of Pennsylvania Press, 1976.

———. *Strain of Violence: Historical Studies of American Violence and Vigilantism.* New York: Oxford University Press, 1975.

Brown, W. S., M.D. "Strictures on Abolitionism." In *Bible Defense of Slavery, by Josiah Priest, to which is added A Plan of National Colonization Adequate to the Removal of Free Blacks,* by W. S. Brown, M.D., pp. 437–569, [1–8]. Glasgow, Ky.: Rev. W. S. Brown, M.D., 1853.

Bruce, Dickson D., Jr. *And They All Sang Hallelujah: Plain-Folk*

Camp-Meeting Religion, 1800–1845. Knoxville: University of Tennessee Press, 1974.

————. "Death as Testimony in the Old South." *Southern Humanities Review* 12 (1978): 123–132.

————. "Hunting: Dimensions of Antebellum Southern Culture." *Mississippi Quarterly* 30 (1977): 259–281.

————. "The 'John and Old Master' Stories and the World of Slavery: A Study in Folktales and History." *Phylon* 35 (1974): 418–429.

————. "Religion, Society and Culture in the Old South: A Comparative View." *American Quarterly* 26 (1974): 399–416.

Bruce, H. C. *The New Man: Twenty-Nine Years a Slave. Twenty-Nine Years a Free Man.* 1895. Rpt. Miami: Mnemosyne, 1969.

Buckingham, J. S., Esq. *The Slave States of America.* 2 vols. 1842. Rpt. New York: Negro Universities Press, 1968.

Buel, Richard, Jr. *Securing the Revolution: Ideology in American Politics, 1789–1815.* Ithaca: Cornell University Press, 1972.

Burgess, Parke G. "The Rhetoric of Moral Conflict: Two Critical Dimensions." *Quarterly Journal of Speech* 56 (1970): 120–130.

Butler, Andrew Pickens. *Speech of Hon. A. P. Butler, of South Carolina, on the Difficulty of Messrs. Brooks and Sumner, and the Causes Thereof. Delivered in the Senate of the United States, June 12–13, 1856.* Washington, D.C.: The Congressional Globe Office, 1856.

C. C. "Corporal Punishment: Its Use in the Discipline of Children." *Southern Literary Messenger* 7 (1841): 575–576.

Cade, John B. "Out of the Mouths of Ex-Slaves." *Journal of Negro History* 20 (1935): 294–337.

Calhoun, John A.; DuBose, E. E.; and Bubo, Virgil. Committee of the Barbour County (Ala.) Agricultural Society. "Report on the Management of Slaves." *American Farmer* 4th ser. 2 (1846): 77–79.

Camden, Peter G. *A Common-Sense, Matter-of-Fact Examination and Discussion of Negro Slavery in the United States of America, in Connection with the Questions of Emancipation and Abolition.* St. Louis, 1855.

Cardwell, Guy A. "The Duel in the Old South: Crux of a Concept." *South Atlantic Quarterly* 66 (1967): 50–69.

[Carey, John L.] *Some Thoughts Concerning Domestic Slavery, in a Letter to ———— ————, Esq. of Baltimore.* Baltimore: Joseph N. Lewis, 1838.

Carpenter, Jesse T. *The South as a Concious Minority, 1789–1861: A Study in Political Thought.* New York: New York University Press, 1930.

Carpenter, S. C. *Report of the Trial of Richard Dennis, the Younger, for the Murder of James Shaw, On the 20th of August, 1804.* Charleston: G. M. Bounetheu, 1805.

Carroll, B. H., Jr., *Standard History of Houston, Texas: From a Study of the Original Sources.* Knoxville: H. W. Crew, 1912.

Carson, James Petigru, ed. *The Life, Letters and Speeches of James Louis Petigru, the Union Man of South Carolina.* Washington, D.C.: W. H. Lowdermilk, 1920.

[Carter, Hill.] "On the Management of Negroes." *Farmers' Register* 1 (1834): 564–565.

Cartwright, Peter. *Autobiography of Peter Cartwright.* Centennial Edition. Nashville: Abingdon Press, 1956.

Cartwright, [S. A.] "Dr. Cartwright on the Caucasians and the African." *De Bow's Review* 25 (1858): 45–56.

———. "Slavery in the Light of Ethnology." In *Cotton Is King, and Pro-Slavery Arguments,* ed. E. N. Elliott, pp. 690–728. 1860. Rpt. New York: Negro Universities Press, 1969.

Cash, W. J. *The Mind of the South.* New York: Knopf, 1941.

Catterall, Helen Tunnicliff, ed. *Judicial Cases Concerning American Slavery and the Negro.* 5 vols. 1926. Rpt. New York: Octagon Books, 1968.

Chambers, Moreau B. C. "The Militia Crisis." *Virginia Cavalcade* 16, no. 4 (Spring 1967): 10–14.

Chandler, John A. *The Speech of John A. Chandler (of Norfolk County), in the House of Delegates of Virginia, on the Policy of the State with Respect to Her Slave Population.* Richmond: Thomas W. White, 1832.

Channing, Steven A. *Crisis of Fear: Secession in South Carolina.* New York: Simon and Schuster, 1970.

"The Chase." *Spirit of the Times,* May 12, 1832.

Chesnut, Mary Boykin. *A Diary from Dixie.* Edited by Ben Ames Williams. Boston: Houghton Mifflin, 1949.

Child, Francis James. *The English and Scottish Popular Ballads.* 5 vols. Boston: Houghton Mifflin, 1882–1898.

Claiborne, J. F. H. *Life and Correspondence of John A. Quitman, Major-General, U.S.A., and Governor of the State of Mississippi.* 2 vols. New York: Harper, 1860.

Clingman, Thomas Lanier. *Selections from the Speeches and Writings of Hon. Thomas L. Clingman of North Carolina; with Additions and Explanatory Notes.* Raleigh: John Nichols, 1877.

———. "Speech: Defense of the South against the Aggressive Movement of the North; Delivered in the House of Representatives, January 22, 1850." [Washington, D.C.]: Gideon, [1850?].

Cobb, Thomas R. R. *An Historical Sketch of Slavery, from the Earliest*

Periods. Philadelphia: T. & J. W. Johnson; Savannah: W. Thorne Williams, 1858.

Combs, Josiah H. *Folk-Songs of the Southern United States.* Edited by D. K. Wilgus. Austin: University of Texas Press, 1967.

The Confessions of Nat Turner, Leader of the Late Insurrection in Southampton, Va. 1861. Rpt. Miami: Mnemosyne, 1969.

Cooper, Thomas. "Slavery." *Southern Literary Journal* 1 (1835): 188–193.

Coulter, E. Merton. *College Life in the Old South.* Athens: University of Georgia Press, 1928.

Cox, John Harrington. *Folk-Songs of the South.* 1925. Rpt. New York: Dover, 1967.

Craig, Marjorie. "Survivals of the Chivalric Tournament in Southern Life and Literature." M.A. thesis, University of North Carolina, 1935.

"The Criminal Law." *Southern Quarterly Review* 3 (1843): 388–406.

Crockett, David. *A Narrative of the Life of David Crockett of the State of Tennessee.* A facsimile ed. with annotations by James A. Shackford and Stanley J. Folmsbee. Knoxville: University of Tennessee Press, 1973.

Crooks, Esther Josephine and Ruth W. *The Ring Tournament in the United States.* Richmond: Garrett and Massie, 1936.

Cunliffe, Marcus. *Soldiers and Civilians: The Martial Spirit in America, 1775–1865.* Boston: Little, Brown, 1968.

Curry, Leonard P. "Urbanization and Urbanism in the Old South: A Comparative View." *Journal of Southern History* 40 (1974): 43–60.

Cutler, James E. *Lynch-Law: An Investigation into the History of Lynching in the United States.* 1905. Rpt. New York: Negro Universities Press, 1969.

Davidson, Edward H. *Poe: A Critical Study.* Cambridge, Mass.: Harvard University Press, 1957.

Davis, Allison, and Dollard, John. *Children of Bondage: The Personality Development of Negro Youth in the Urban South.* 1940. Rpt. New York: Harper and Row, 1964.

Davis, David Brion. *Homicide in American Fiction, 1798–1860: A Study in Social Values.* Ithaca: Cornell University Press, 1957.

———. *The Problem of Slavery in the Age of Revolution, 1770–1823.* Ithaca: Cornell University Press, 1975.

Davis, J. A. G. *A Treatise on Criminal Law, with an Exposition of the Office and Authority of Justices of the Peace in Virginia; Including Forms of Practice.* Philadelphia: C. Sherman & Co., 1838.

Davis, Jefferson. *The Papers of Jefferson Davis.* Edited by Haskell M.

Monroe, Jr., and James T. McIntosh. 2 vols. Baton Rouge: Louisiana State University Press, 1971.

Davis, Reuben. *Recollections of Mississippi and Mississippians*. Boston: Houghton Mifflin, 1889.

Debates and Other Proceedings of the Convention of Virginia, Convened at Richmond, on Monday the 2d day of June, 1788, for the purpose of deliberating on the Constitution recommended by the Grand Federal Convention. 2nd ed. Richmond: Ritchie and Worsley and Augustine Davis, 1805.

De Bow, J. D. B. "The Late Cuba Expedition." *De Bow's Review* 9 (1850): 164–177.

———. "Louisiana." *De Bow's Review* 1 (1846): 85–433.

———. *Mortality Statistics of the Seventh Census of the United States, 1850*. Washington, D.C.: House of Representatives, Ex. Doc. No. 98, 1855.

———. *Statistical View of the United States*. Washington, D.C.: Beverly Tucker, Senate Printer, 1854.

"Deer Hunting." *Spirit of the Times*, March 24, 1832.

Detweiler, Philip F. "The Changing Reputation of the Declaration of Independence." *William and Mary Quarterly* 3rd ser. 19 (1962): 557–574.

Devol, George H. *Forty Years a Gambler on the Mississippi*. 1887. Rpt. Austin: Steck-Vaughn, 1967.

Dick, Everett. *The Dixie Frontier: A Social History of the Southern Frontier from the First Transmontane Beginnings to the Civil War*. New York: Capricorn Books, 1964.

Dickey, Dallas C. *Seargent S. Prentiss: Whig Orator of the Old South*. Baton Rouge: Louisiana State University Press, 1946.

Dollard, John. *Caste and Class in a Southern Town*. 3rd ed. Garden City: Doubleday Anchor, 1957.

"Domestic Improvements." *Southern Literary Journal* n.s. 3 (1838): 1–6.

Donald, David. "The Proslavery Argument Reconsidered." *Journal of Southern History* 37 (1971): 3–18.

Douglas, Ann. *The Feminization of American Culture*. New York: Knopf, 1977.

———. "Heaven Our Home: Consolation Literature in the Northern United States, 1830–1880." In *Death in America*, edited by David E. Stannard, pp. 49–68. Philadelphia: University of Pennsylvania Press, 1975.

Douglass, Frederick. *Life and Times of Frederick Douglass*. 1892. Rpt. New York: Collier, 1962.

Doyle, Bertram W. *The Etiquette of Race Relations in the South: A*

Study in Social Control. 1937. Rpt. Port Washington, N.Y.: Kennikat Press, 1968.

Drake, Daniel, M.D. *Pioneer Life in Kentucky, 1785–1800.* Edited by Emmet Field Horine, M.D. New York: Henry Schuman, 1948.

Drayton, William. *The South Vindicated from the Treason and Fanaticism of the Northern Abolitionists.* 1836. Rpt. New York: Negro Universities Press, 1969.

Dresel, Gustav. *Houston Journal: Adventures in North America and Texas, 1837–1841.* Edited and translated by Max Freund. Austin: University of Texas Press, 1954.

Drew, Benjamin. *The Refugee: A North-Side View of Slavery.* 1856. Rpt. Reading, Mass.: Addison-Wesley, 1969.

Du Bose, John Witherspoon. *The Life and Times of William Lowndes Yancey: A History of Political Parties in the United States, from 1834 to 1864: Especially as to the Origin of the Confederate States.* 2 vols. 1892. Rpt. New York: Peter Smith, 1942.

"Duelling in America." *Living Age* 15 (1847): 467–471.

Dykstra, Robert R. *The Cattle Towns.* New York: Knopf, 1968.

E. B. C. "The Mothers and Children of the Present Day." *Southern Literary Messenger* 22 (1856): 391–393.

Eaton, Clement. *The Growth of Southern Civilization, 1790–1860.* New York: Harper, 1961.

——. "Mob Violence in the Old South." *Mississippi Valley Historical Review* 29 (1942): 351–370.

An Edistonian. "The Successful Planter, or Memoirs of My Uncle Ben." *Southern Agriculturalist* 4 (1831): 569–572, 638–640; 5 (1832): 24–28, 82–85, 132–136, 300–304.

Elkins, Stanley M. *Slavery: A Problem in American Institutional Life.* Chicago: University of Chicago Press, 1959.

[Elliot, Stephen.] "Views of Nature." *The Southern Review* 2 (1828): 408–431.

Elliot, The Hon. Wm., of Beaufort, S.C. *Carolina Sports by Land and Water; Including Incidents of Devil-Fishing, &c.* Charleston: Burges and James, 1846.

Ely, A. W., M.D. "Phenomena of Nature." *De Bow's Review* 12 (1852): 370–380.

An Engineer. "Notes on Texas." *Southern Literary Journal* n.s. 3 (1838): 131–138.

Estes, Matthew. *A Defense of Negro Slavery, as It Exists in the United States.* Montgomery: Press of the "Alabama Journal," 1846.

Evans, Harris Smith. "Rules for the Government of the Negroes, Plantation, &c. at Float Swamp, Wilcox County, South Alabama." *Southern Agriculturalist* 5 (1832): 231–234.

Farrison, William Edward. *William Wells Brown: Author and Reformer*. Chicago: University of Chicago Press, 1969.

Fiedler, Leslie A. *Love and Death in the American Novel*. New York: Criterion, 1960.

"Field Sports in Virginia." *American Turf Register and Sporting Magazine* 9 (1838): 508–511.

Finley, James B. *Autobiography of Rev. James B. Finley; or, Pioneer Life in the West*. Edited by W. P. Strickland. Cincinnati: The Methodist Book Concern, 1853.

Fischer, David Hackett. *The Revolution in American Conservatism: The Federalist Party in the Era of Jeffersonian Democracy*. New York: Harper, 1965.

Fisher, Elwood. "The North and the South." *De Bow's Review* 7 (1849): 304–316.

Fitzhugh, George. "Acquisition of Mexico—Filibustering." *De Bow's Review* 25 (1858): 613–626.

———. *Cannibals All! or Slaves without Masters*. Edited by C. Vann Woodward. Cambridge, Mass.: Belknap Press of Harvard University Press, 1960.

———. "The English Reviews." *De Bow's Review* 28 (1860): 392–405.

———. "Frederick the Great, by Thomas Carlyle." *De Bow's Review* 29 (1860): 151–167.

———. "Love of Danger and of War." *De Bow's Review* 28 (1860): 294–305.

Flanigan, Daniel J. "Criminal Procedure in Slave Trials in the Antebellum South." *Journal of Southern History* 40 (1974): 537–564.

Fletcher, John, of Louisiana. *Studies On Slavery, in Easy Lessons. Compiled into Eight Studies, and Subdivided into Short Lessons for the Convenience of Readers*. Natchez: Jackson Warner, 1852.

Foner, Philip S. *The Life and Writings of Frederick Douglass*. 5 vols. New York: International Publishers, 1950–1975.

Foote, Henry S. *Casket of Reminiscences*. 1874. Rpt. New York: Negro Universities Press, 1968.

The Forget Me Not Songster, Containing a Choice Collection of Old Ballad Songs, as Sung by Our Grandmothers. New York: Nafis & Cornish, n.d.

Franklin, John Hope. *The Militant South, 1800–1861*. Cambridge, Mass.: Belknap Press of Harvard University Press, 1956.

———. *A Southern Odyssey: Travelers in the Antebellum North*. Baton Rouge: Louisiana State University Press, 1976.

Fredrickson, George M. *The Black Image in the White Mind: The Debate on Afro-American Character and Destiny, 1817–1914*. New York: Harper, 1971.

Fredrickson, George M., and Lasch, Christopher. "Resistance to Slavery." *Civil War History* 13 (1967): 315–329.
Fulkerson, H. S. *Random Recollections of Early Days in Mississippi.* 1885. Rpt. Baton Rouge: Otto Claitor, 1937.
Gaines, Francis Pendleton. *The Southern Plantation: A Study in the Development and Accuracy of a Tradition.* 1924. Rpt. Gloucester, Mass.: Peter Smith, 1962.
Gardner, Col. "The Army of the United States." *De Bow's Review* 15 (1853): 448–459.
Genovese, Eugene D. *Roll, Jordan, Roll: The World the Slaves Made.* New York: Pantheon, 1974.
———. *The World the Slaveholders Made: Two Essays in Interpretation.* New York: Pantheon, 1969.
Gluckman, Max. *Order and Rebellion in Tribal Africa.* London: Cohen and West, 1963.
Gohdes, Clarence, ed. *Hunting in the Old South: Original Narratives of the Hunters.* Baton Rouge: Louisiana State University Press, 1967.
Goldman, Perry M. "Political Rhetoric in the Age of Jackson." *Tennessee Historical Quarterly* 29 (1970): 360–371.
Goldstein, Leslie Friedman. "Violence as an Instrument for Social Change: The Views of Frederick Douglass (1817–1895)." *Journal of Negro History* 41 (1976): 61–72.
Graber, Doris A. *Verbal Behavior and Politics.* Urbana: University of Illinois Press, 1976.
Graham, Edward K. "The History of Southern Oratory during the Federal Period, 1788–1861." In *History of Southern Oratory,* edited by Thomas E. Watson (*The South in the Building of the Nation,* vol. 9), pp. 30–52. Richmond: Southern Historical Publication Society, 1909.
Grayson, William John. "The Autobiography of William John Grayson." Edited by Samuel Gaillard Stoney. *South Carolina Historical Magazine* 48–51 (1947–1950).
Greene, Jack P. *Landon Carter: An Inquiry into the Personal Values and Social Imperatives of the Eighteenth-Century Virginia Gentry.* Charlottesville: University Press of Virginia, 1967.
Greene, John C. "The American Debate on the Negro's Place in Nature, 1780–1815." *Journal of the History of Ideas* 15 (1954): 384–396.
Greven, Philip. *The Protestant Temperament: Patterns of Child-Rearing, Religious Experience, and Self in Early America.* New York: Knopf, 1977.
Griffith, Rev. David. "Passive Obedience Considered, in a Sermon

Preached at Williamsburg, December 13, 1775." Williamsburg: Alexander Purdie, 1776.

Gross, Seymour L., and Bender, Eileen. "History, Politics and Literature: The Myth of Nat Turner." *American Quarterly* 23 (1971): 487–518.

Gunderson, Robert G. "The Southern Whigs." In *Oratory in the Old South, 1828–1860*, edited by Waldo W. Braden, pp. 104–141. Baton Rouge: Louisiana State University Press, 1970.

Gurr, Ted Robert. *Why Men Rebel*. Princeton: Princeton University Press, 1970.

Gutman, Herbert G. *The Black Family in Slavery and Freedom, 1750–1925*. New York: Pantheon, 1976.

H. "Remarks on Overseers, and the Proper Treatment of Slaves." *Farmers' Register* 5 (1837): 301–302.

H. H. "A Louisiana Plantation." *American Farmer* 4th ser. 12 (1856): 131–132.

Hackney, Sheldon. "Southern Violence." *American Historical Review* 74 (1969): 906–925.

Hairston, Peter W., ed. "J. E. B. Stuart's Letters to His Hairston Kin, 1850–1855." *North Carolina Historical Review* 51 (1974): 261–333.

"Halleck's Military Art and Science." *Southern Quarterly Review* 10 (1846): 418–440.

Hamilton, Rev. Dr. "On the Majesty of Law." *New Orleans Miscellany* 1 (1847): 12–20.

Harper, Chancellor [Robert.] "Slavery in the Light of Social Ethics." In *Cotton Is King, and Pro-Slavery Arguments*, edited by E. N. Elliott, pp. 547–626. 1860. Rpt. New York: Negro Universities Press, 1969.

Harris, George Washington. *Sut Lovingood*. Edited by Brom Weber. New York: Grove Press, 1954.

Hartz, Louis. *The Liberal Tradition in America: An Interpretation of American Political Thought Since the Revolution*. New York: Harcourt, 1955.

Hemmer, Joseph J., Jr. "The Charleston Platform Debate in Rhetorical-Historical Perspective." *Quarterly Journal of Speech* 56 (1970): 406–416.

Hendrickson, Robert. *Hamilton*. 2 vols. New York: Mason/Charter, 1976.

Herbemont, N. "On the Moral Discipline and Treatment of Slaves." *Southern Agriculturalist* 9 (1836): 70–75.

Higham, John W. "The Changing Loyalties of William Gilmore Simms." *Journal of Southern History* 9 (1943): 210–223.

Hilliard, Henry W. *Speeches and Addresses*. New York: Harper, 1855.
Hindus, Michael S. "Black Justice under White Law: Criminal Prosecutions of Blacks in Antebellum South Carolina." *Journal of American History* 53 (1976): 575–599.
Hines, David Theo. *The Life, Adventures and Opinions of David Theo. Hines, of South Carolina*. New York: Bradley and Clark, 1840.
Hints on Three Defects in the Criminal Laws of Virginia. Addressed to the Legislature. N.p., 1845.
Hirschman, Albert O. *The Passions and the Interests: Political Arguments for Capitalism before Its Triumph*. Princeton: Princeton University Press, 1977.
Hodgart, M. J. C. *The Ballads*. New York: Norton, 1962.
Hoffman, Daniel. *Poe Poe Poe Poe Poe Poe Poe*. Garden City: Doubleday, 1972.
Hogan, William Ransom. "Rampant Individualism in the Republic of Texas." *Southwestern Historical Quarterly* 44 (1941): 454–480.
Hollon, W. Eugene. *Frontier Violence: Another Look*. New York: Oxford University Press, 1974.
Holman, C. Hugh. *The Roots of Southern Writing: Essays on the Literature of the American South*. Athens: University of Georgia Press, 1972.
Holmes, George Frederick. "Relations of the Old and the New Worlds." *De Bow's Review* 20 (1856): 521–540.
Honestus. "On Fashionable Manners." *The American Gleaner* 1 (1807): 5–7.
Hooper, Johnson Jones. *Adventures of Captain Simon Suggs, Late of the Tallapoosa Volunteers*. 1845. Rpt. Chapel Hill: University of North Carolina Press, 1969.
Hubbell, Jay B. "Poe and the Southern Literary Tradition." *Texas Studies in Literature and Language* 2 (1960): 151–171.
Hubert, Thomas. "The Southern Element in Poe's Fiction," *Georgia Review* 28 (1974): 200–212.
Huger, John M. "Memoranda of the Late Affair of Honor between Hon. T. L. Clingman, of North Carolina, and Hon. William L. Yancey, of Alabama." [Washington, D.C.]: For private circulation by W. L. Yancey, February 13, 1845.
Hughes, Louis. *Thirty Years a Slave. From Bondage to Freedom. The Institution of Slavery as Seen on the Plantation and in the Home of the Planter*. 1897. Rpt. New York: Negro Universities Press, 1969.
Huizinga, J. *The Waning of the Middle Ages: A Study of the Forms of Life, Thought, and Art in France and the Netherlands in the

XIVth and the XVth Centuries. Garden City: Doubleday Anchor, 1954.

Hundley, D. R., esq. *Social Relations in Our Southern States.* New York: Henry B. Price, 1860.

A Hunter. "Shooting in Tennessee." *American Turf Register and Sporting Magazine* 2 (1831): 391.

Hurston, Zora Neale. "Characteristics of Negro Expression." In *Negro Anthology Made by Nancy Cunard, 1931–1933,* pp. 39–46. 1934. Rpt. New York: Negro Universities Press, 1969.

————. *Mules and Men.* 1935. Rpt. New York: Harper, 1970.

Hymes, Dell. *Foundations in Sociolinguistics: An Ethnographic Approach.* Philadelphia: University of Pennsylvania Press, 1974.

————. "Linguistic Aspects of Comparative Political Research." In *The Methodology of Comparative Research,* edited by Robert T. Holt and John E. Turner, pp. 295–341. New York: Free Press, 1970.

"Interesting Correspondence." *Crisis* 1 (1840): 113–115.

"The Invasion of Cuba." *Southern Quarterly Review* 21 (1852): 1–47.

James, Marquis. *The Life of Andrew Jackson, Complete in One Volume.* Indianapolis: Bobbs-Merrill, 1938.

Jefferson, Thomas. *Notes on the State of Virginia.* Edited by William Peden. Chapel Hill: University of North Carolina Press, 1955.

Jenkins, William Sumner. *Pro-Slavery Thought in the Old South.* 1935. Rpt. Gloucester, Mass.: Peter Smith, 1960.

Jeter, Jeremiah Bell. *The Recollections of a Long Life.* Richmond: Religious Herald Co., 1891.

Johnson, Charles S. *Shadow of the Plantation.* Chicago: University of Chicago Press, 1934.

Johnson, Clifton H., ed. *God Struck Me Dead: Religious Conversion Experiences and Autobiographies of Ex-Slaves.* Philadelphia: Pilgrim Press, 1969.

Johnson, Guion Griffis. *Ante-bellum North Carolina: A Social History.* Chapel Hill: University of North Carolina Press, 1937.

Jones, Howard Mumford. *Revolution and Romanticism.* Cambridge, Mass.: Belknap Press of Harvard University Press, 1974.

Jones, J. Ralph. "Portraits of Georgia Slaves." *Georgia Review* 21 (1967): 126–131, 268–273, 407–411, 521–525; 22 (1968): 125–127, 254–257.

Jordan, Winthrop D. *White over Black: American Attitudes toward the Negro, 1550–1812.* Chapel Hill: University of North Carolina Press, 1968.

Kane, Harnett T. *Gentlemen, Swords and Pistols.* New York: William Morrow, 1951.

Karsten, Peter. "The American Democratic Citizen Soldier: Triumph or Disaster." *Military Affairs* 30 (1966): 34–40.

Kemper, James Lawson. "The Mexican War Diary of James Lawson Kemper." Edited by Robert R. Jones, *Virginia Magazine of History and Biography* 74 (1966): 387–428.

Kendall, Amos. *Autobiography of Amos Kendall.* Edited by William Stickney. 1872. Rpt. New York: Peter Smith, 1949.

Kennedy, William, Esq. *Texas: The Rise, Progress, and Prospects of the Republic of Texas.* 2 vols. London: R. Hastings, 1841.

Kilson, Marion D. de B. "Towards Freedom: An Analysis of Slave Revolts in the United States." *Phylon* 25 (1964): 175–187.

King, Alvy L. *Louis T. Wigfall: Southern Fire-Eater.* Baton Rouge: Louisiana State University Press, 1970.

[Kingsley, Zaphaniah.] *A Treatise on the Patriarchal, or Co-operative System of Society as It Exists in Some Governments, and Colonies in America, and in the United States, under the Name of Slavery, with Its Necessity and Advantages.* By an Inhabitant of Florida. 2nd ed. [Tallahassee], 1829.

A Lady of Georgia. "Southern Slavery and Its Assailants." *De Bow's Review* 16 (1854): 46–62.

Lambert, Paul F. "The Movement for the Acquisition of All Mexico." *Journal of the West* 11 (1972): 317–327.

Lander, Ernest M., J. "The Reluctant Imperialist: South Carolina, the Rio Grande, and the Mexican War." *Southwestern Historical Quarterly* 78 (1975): 254–270.

Laslett, Peter. *Family Life and Illicit Love in Earlier Generations: Essays in Historical Sociology.* Cambridge: Cambridge University Press, 1977.

Leary, James P. "Fists and Foul Mouths: Fights and Fight Stories in Contemporary Rural American Bars." *Journal of American Folklore* 89 (1976): 27–39.

Legaré, Hugh Swinton. *Writings of Hugh Swinton Legaré.* Edited by his sister. 2 vols. 1846. Rpt. New York: DaCapo, 1970.

Lemmon, Sarah McCulloh, ed. *The Pettigrew Papers, 1685–1818.* Raleigh: State Department of Archives and History, 1971.

Levine, Lawrence W. *Black Culture and Black Consciousness: Afro-American Folk Thought from Slavery to Freedom.* New York: Oxford University Press, 1977.

Leyburn, James G. *Frontier Folkways.* New Haven: Yale University Press, 1935.

Life of the Rev. Devereaux Jarratt. Richmond: Office of the Southern Churchman, [1840].

Linden, Fabian. "Economic Democracy in the Slave South: An Appraisal of Some Recent Views." *Journal of Negro History* 31 (1946): 140–189.

Lofton, John. *Insurrection in South Carolina: The Turbulent World of Denmark Vesey.* Yellow Springs, Ohio: Antioch Press, 1964.

Loguen, J. W. *The Rev. J. W. Loguen as a Slave and as a Freeman. A Narrative of Real Life.* 1859. Rpt. New York: Negro Universities Press, 1968.

Lomax, Alan. *The Folk Songs of North America in the English Language.* Garden City: Doubleday, 1960.

Longstreet, Augustus Baldwin. *Georgia Scenes: Characters, Incidents, &c., in the First Half Century of the Republic.* 1835. Rpt. Gloucester, Mass.: Peter Smith, 1970.

———. *A Voice from the South: Comprising Letters from Georgia to Massachusetts, and to the Southern States.* Baltimore: Western Continent Press, 1847.

Lovejoy, Arthur O. *Reflections on Human Nature.* Baltimore: Johns Hopkins Press, 1961.

Lubbock, Francis Richard. *Six Decades in Texas, or, Memoirs of Francis Richard Lubbock; a Personal Experience in Business, War, and Politics.* Edited by C. W. Raines. Austin: Ben C. Jones, 1900.

Lundsgaarde, Henry P. *Murder in Space City: A Cultural Analysis of Houston Homicide Patterns.* New York: Oxford University Press, 1977.

McIlwaine, Shields. *The Southern Poor-White from Lubberland to Tobacco Road.* Norman: University of Oklahoma Press, 1939.

McLean, Robert C. *George Tucker: Moral Philosopher and Man of Letters.* Chapel Hill: University of North Carolina Press, 1961.

"Management of Slaves, &c." *Farmers' Register* 5 (1837): 32–33.

Mathews, Donald G. *Religion in the Old South.* Chicago: University of Chicago Press, 1977.

May, Robert E. "Recent Trends in the Historiography of Southern Militarism." *The Historian*, in press.

———. *The Southern Dream of a Caribbean Empire, 1854–1861.* Baton Rouge: Louisiana State University Press, 1973.

Meade, Robert D. "The Military Spirit of the South." *Current History* 30 (1929): 55–60.

Merk, Frederick. *Manifest Destiny and Mission in American History: A Reinterpretation.* New York: Knopf, 1963.

Miles, Edwin A. "The Mississippi Slave Insurrection Scare of 1835." *Journal of Negro History* 42 (1957): 48–60.

[Miles, James Warley.] *The Relation between the Races at the South.* Charleston: Steam-Power Presses of Evans & Cogswell, 1861.

"Military Defences of Virginia." *De Bow's Review* 19 (1855): 445–450.

"Military Education." *Magnolia; or Southern Monthly* 4 (1842): 256.

"Military Schools of South Carolina." *Southern Quarterly Review* 18 (1850): 527–534.

Minutes of the National Convention of Colored Citizens: Held at Buffalo, on the 15th, 16th, 17th, 18th and 19th of August, 1843, For the Purpose of Considering Their Moral and Political Condition as American Citizens. 1843. Rpt. in *Minutes and Proceedings of the National Negro Conventions, 1830–1864*, edited by Howard Holman Bell. New York: Arno Press and the New York Times, 1969.

Montell, William Lynwood. *The Saga of Coe Ridge: A Study in Oral History.* Knoxville: University of Tennessee Press, 1970.

Moore, Arthur K. *The Frontier Mind.* 1957. Rpt. New York: McGraw-Hill, 1963.

Moore, James T. "The Death of the Duel: The *Code Duello* in Readjuster Virginia, 1879–1883." *Virginia Magazine of History and Biography* 83 (1975): 259–276.

"Morality and Religion in Slavery Days." *Southern Workman* 26 (October 1897): 210.

Morgan, C. S. Letter in "Slavery and Slave Statistics of the South, &c." *DeBow's Review* 14 (1853): 593–595.

Munroe, Robert L. and Ruth H. *Cross-Cultural Human Development.* Monterey, Cal.: Brooks/Cole, 1975.

Myers, Robert Manson, ed. *The Children of Pride: A True Story of Georgia and the Civil War.* New Haven and London: Yale University Press, 1972.

Myers, Robert Manson, ed. *A Georgian at Princeton.* New York: Harcourt, 1976.

Nackman, Mark E. "Anglo-American Migrants to the West: Men of Broken Fortunes? The Case of Texas, 1821–46." *Western Historical Quarterly* 5 (1974): 441–455.

Napier, John H., III. "Martial Montgomery: Antebellum Military Activity." *Alabama Historical Quarterly* 29 (1967): 107–131.

The Negro in Virginia. Compiled by workers of the Writers' Program of the Work Projects Administration in the State of Virginia. 1940. Rpt. New York: Arno Press and the New York Times, 1969.

Nettleford, Rex. "Aggression, Violence and Force: Containment and Eruption in the Jamaican History of Protest." In *Violence and Aggression in the History of Ideas*, edited by Philip P. Wiener and John Fisher, pp. 133–157. New Brunswick: Rutgers University Press, 1974.

"North American Foxes." *Southern Quarterly Review* 13 (1848): 403–427.

"The Northern Pacific: California, Oregon and the Oregon Question." *Southern Quarterly Review* 8 (1845): 191–243.

Northrup, Solomon. *Twelve Years a Slave*. Edited by Sue Eakin and Joseph Logsdon. Baton Rouge: Louisiana State University Press, 1968.

Oates, Stephen B. *The Fires of Jubilee: Nat Turner's Fierce Rebellion*. New York: Harper, 1975.

"Observations, &c.–Olives, Grapes, Wool and Silk." *American Farmer* 4 (1822): 274–276.

Odum, Howard W., and Johnson, Guy B. *Negro Workaday Songs*. Chapel Hill: University of North Carolina Press, 1926.

O'Neall, John Belton. *Biographical Sketches of the Bench and Bar of South Carolina*. 2 vols. Charleston: S. G. Courtenay, 1859.

Ortega y Gasset, José. *Meditations on Hunting*. Translated by Howard B. Wescott. New York: Charles Scribner, 1972.

Osterweis, Rollin G. *Romanticism and Nationalism in the Old South*. 1949. Rpt. Baton Rouge: Louisiana State University Press, 1971.

"Our Army in Mexico." *De Bow's Review* 2 (1846): 426–430.

An Overseer. "On the Conduct and Management of Overseers, Drivers, and Slaves." *Farmers' Register* 4 (1836): 114–116.

Owens, Leslie Howard. *This Species of Property: Slave Life and Culture in the Old South*. New York: Oxford University Press, 1976.

Owsley, Frank Lawrence. *Plain Folk of the Old South*. 1949. Rpt. Chicago: Quadrangle, 1965.

P. P. "Uses and Abuses of Lynch Law." *American Whig Review* n.s. 5 (1850): 459–476; n.s. 6 (1850): 494–501; n.s. 7 (1851): 213–220.

Paine, Robert, D.D. *Life and Times of William McKendree, Bishop of the Methodist Episcopal Church*. Nashville: Publishing House of the Methodist Episcopal Church, South, 1880.

Parrington, Vernon Louis. *Main Currents in American Thought*. 2 vols. 1927. Rpt. New York: Harcourt, 1954.

Paxton, Philip [Samuel A. Hammett]. *A Stray Yankee in Texas*. New York: Redfield, 1853.

Pee Dee. "The Management of Negroes." *Southern Agriculturalist* 11 (1838): 512–514.

"The People." *Southern Quarterly Review* 25 (n.s. 9) (1854): 32–57.

Perritt, H. Hardy. "The Fire-Eaters." In *Oratory in the Old South, 1828–1860*, edited by Waldo W. Braden, pp. 234–257. Baton Rouge: Louisiana State University Press, 1970.

Pettigrew, Charles. *Last Advice of the Reverend Charles Pettigrew to His Sons, 1797*. N.p., n.d.

Pholo-therus. "Foxhunting in Washington." *American Turf Register and Sporting Magazine* 6 (1835): 292–295.

Plater, Ormonde. "Before Sut: Folklore in the Early Works of George Washington Harris." *Southern Folklore Quarterly* 34 (1970): 104–115.

Pleasants, Hugh R. "Sketches of the Virginia Convention of 1829–30." *Southern Literary Messenger* 17 (1851): 147–154, 297–304.

Pocock, J. G. A. *The Machiavellian Moment: Florentine Political Thought and the Atlantic Republican Tradition*. Princeton: Princeton University Press, 1975.

Poe, Edgar Allan. *Complete Stories and Poems of Edgar Allan Poe*. Garden City: Doubleday, 1966.

———. *The Complete Works of Edgar Allan Poe*. Edited by James A. Harrison. 17 vols. New York: Thomas Y. Crowell, 1902.

———. *The Letters of Edgar Allan Poe*. Edited by John Ward Ostrom. 2 vols. New York: Gordian Press, 1966.

Porter, William T., ed. *The Big Bear of Arkansas, and Other Sketches, Illustrative of the Characters and Incidents of the South and South-West*. Philadelphia: T. B. Peterson and Bros., 1846.

Potter, David. *The Impending Crisis, 1848–1861*. Completed and edited by Don E. Fehrenbacher. New York: Harper 1976.

Proceedings and Debates of the Virginia State Convention of 1829–30. To Which Are Subjoined, the New Constitution of Virginia, and the Votes of the People. Richmond: Ritchie and Cook, 1830.

"Public Amusements and Social Enjoyments." *De Bow's Review* 29 (1860): 330–334.

Pudner, H. Peter. "People Not Pedagogy: Education in Old Virginia." *George Review* 25 (1971): 263–285.

Quarles, Benjamin. *Black Abolitionists*. New York: Oxford University Press, 1969.

Randolph, John. *Letters of John Randolph, to a Young Relative; Embracing a Series of Years, from Early Youth, to Mature Manhood*. Philadelphia: Carey, Lea and Blanchard, 1834.

Rawick, George P. *From Sundown to Sunup: The Making of the Black Community*. Westport, Conn.: Greenwood Press, 1972.

———, general ed. *The American Slave: A Composite Autobiography*. 19 vols. Westport, Conn.: Greenwood Press, 1972.

"Relation of Education to the Prevention of Crime." *De Bow's Review* 18 (n.s. 1) (1855): 409–421.

A Report (in Part) of the Trial of Thomas Gayner, for the Alleged Murder of His Wife. Charleston: W. P. Young, 1810.

Report of the Trials of Capt. Thomas Wells, before the County Court of Nottoway; Sitting as an Examining Court, at the August Term,

1816—Charged with Feloniously and Maliciously Shooting, with Intent to Kill Peter Randolph, Esq. Judge of the 5th Circuit; and Col. Wm. C. Greenhill. By a Member of the Bar. Petersburg: Marvel W. Dunnavant, 1816.

Richardson's Virginia and North Carolina Almanac, for the Year of Our Lord 1855. Cottom's Edition. Richmond: J. W. Randolph, 1855.

Ridgely, J. V. *William Gilmore Simms.* New York: Twayne Publishers, 1962.

Robb, John. *Streaks of Squatter Life, and Far-West Scenes.* 1847. Rpt. Gainesville, Fla.: Scholars' Facsimiles and Reprints, 1962.

Rogers, Tommie W. "D. R. Hundley: A Multi-Class Thesis of Social Stratification in the Antebellum South." *Mississippi Quarterly* 24 (1970): 135–154.

Rogin, Michael Paul. *Fathers and Children: Andrew Jackson and the Subjugation of the American Indian.* New York: Knopf, 1975.

Roper, Moses. *A Narrative of the Adventures and Escape of Moses Roper, from American Slavery.* 2nd ed., 1838. Rpt. New York: Negro Universities Press, 1970.

Rosenbaum, H. John, and Sederberg, Peter C., eds. *Vigilante Politics.* Philadelphia: University of Pennsylvania Press, 1976.

Rowland, Dunbar. "Political and Parliamentary Orators and Oratory of Mississippi." *Publications*, Mississippi Historical Society 4 (1901): 357–400.

Rubin, Louis D., Jr., and Holman, C. Hugh. *Southern Literary Studies: Problems and Possibilities.* Chapel Hill: University of North Carolina Press, 1975.

Rutledge, Wilmuth S. "Dueling in Antebellum Mississippi." *Journal of Mississippi History* 26 (1964): 181–191.

S. G. F. "Deer-Hunting at Berkeley Springs, Va." *Spirit of the Times*, September 5, 1832.

Scott, Edwin J. *Random Recollections of a Long Life, 1806–1876.* 1884. Rpt. Columbia: R. L. Bryan, 1969.

Sederberg, Nancy B. "Antebellum Southern Humor in the *Camden Journal* 1826–1840." *Mississippi Quarterly* 27 (1974): 41–74.

Seitz, Don Carlos. *Famous American Duels: With Some Account of the Causes That Led Up to Them and the Men Engaged.* New York: Thomas Y. Crowell, 1929.

Sennett, Richard. *The Fall of Public Man.* New York: Knopf, 1977.

Shingleton, Royce Gordon. "The Trial and Punishment of Slaves in Baldwin County, Georgia, 1812–1826." *Southern Humanities Review* 8 (1974): 67–73.

Simms, William Gilmore. *Confession; or, The Blind Heart. A Domestic*

Story. "New and Revised Edition," 1885. Rpt. New York: AMS Press, 1970.

————. *The Forayers; or, The Raid of the Dog-Days.* "New and Revised Edition," 1885. Rpt. New York: AMS Press, 1970.

————. *Guy Rivers: A Tale of Georgia.* "New and Revised Edition." Chicago: Donohue, Henneberry, 1890.

————. *Katharine Walton; or, The Rebel of Dorchester.* "New and Revised Edition." Chicago: Donohue, Henneberry, 1890.

————. "A Letter to the Editor by the Author of 'The Loves of the Driver.'" *Magnolia* 3 (1841): 376–380.

————. *The Letters of William Gilmore Simms.* Collected and edited by Mary C. Simms Oliphant, Alfred Taylor Odell, and T. C. Duncan Eaves. 5 vols. Columbia: University of South Carolina Press, 1952–1956.

————. *Martin Faber; The Story of a Criminal.* New York: Harper, 1833.

————. *Mellichampe: A Legend of the Santee.* "New and Revised Edition." Chicago: Donohue, Henneberry, 1890.

————. *The Partisan: A Tale of the Revolution.* 2 vols. 1835. Rpt. Ridgewood, N.J.: Gregg Press, 1968.

————. *Richard Hurdis: A Tale of Alabama.* "New and Revised Edition." New York: W. J. Widdleton, 1878.

Sketches and Recollections of Lynchburg, by the Oldest Inhabitant. Richmond: C. H. Wynne, 1858.

Skinner, Frederick Gustavus. "Reminiscences of an Old Sportsman." In *A Sporting Family of the Old South,* by Harry Worcester Smith, pp. 61–402. Albany: J. B. Lyon, 1936.

Skinner, J. S. "Introduction." *American Turf Register and Sporting Magazine* 1 (1829): 1–3.

Skinner, John "Mortality among Slaves in Mississippi." *American Farmer* 3rd ser. 2 (1840): 170.

Slotkin, Richard. *Regeneration through Violence: The Mythology of the American Frontier, 1600–1860.* Middletown, Conn.: Wesleyan University Press, 1973.

A Small Farmer. "Management of Negroes." *De Bow's Review* 11 (1851): 369–372.

Smiley, Portia. "Folklore from Virginia, South Carolina, Georgia, Alabama and Florida." *Journal of American Folklore* 32 (1919): 357–383.

"South Carolina Military Academies." *Southern Quarterly Review* 26 (n.s. 10) (1854): 191–204.

A Southern Lady. "British Philanthropy and American Slavery." *De Bow's Review* 14 (1853): 258–280.

"Southern School Books." *De Bow's Review* 13 (1852): 258–266.

Sparks, W. H. *The Memories of Fifty Years.* 3rd ed. Philadelphia: Claxton, Remsen and Haffelfinger, 1872.

Spitzer, Leo. "A Reinterpretation of 'The Fall of the House of Usher.'" *Comparative Literature* 4 (1952): 351–363.

Stampp, Kenneth M. *The Peculiar Institution: Slavery in the Antebellum South.* New York: Vintage, 1956.

———. "Rebels and Sambos: The Search for the Negro's Personality in Slavery." *Journal of Southern History* 37 (1971): 367–392.

"The State of Georgia." *De Bow's Review* 10 (1851): 243–252.

Statistics of the United States (Including Mortality, Property, &c.,) in 1860. Washington, D.C.: Government Printing Office, 1866.

Stettner, Edward. "Vigilantism and Political Theory." In *Vigilante Politics,* edited by H. Jon Rosenbaum and Peter C. Sederberg, pp. 64–75. Philadelphia: University of Pennsylvania Press, 1976.

Steward, Austin. *Twenty-two Years a Slave, and Forty Years a Freeman; Embracing a Correspondence of Several Years, While President of Wilberforce Colony, London, Canada West.* 1856. Rpt. New York: Negro Universities Press, 1968.

Stiff, Edward. *A New History of Texas.* Cincinnati: George Conclin, 1847.

Stone, Lawrence. *The Family, Sex and Marriage in England, 1500–1800.* New York: Harper, 1977.

Stout, Joe A., Jr. "Idealism or Manifest Destiny? Filibustering in Northwestern Mexico, 1850–1865." *Journal of the West* 11 (1972): 348–360.

Sunley, Robert. "Early Nineteenth-Century American Literature on Child Rearing." In *Childhood in Contemporary Cultures,* edited by Margaret Mead and Martha Wolfenstein, pp. 150–167. Chicago: University of Chicago Press, 1954.

Sydnor, Charles S. "The Southerner and the Laws." In *The Pursuit of Southern History: Presidential Address of the Southern Historical Association, 1935–1963,* edited by George Brown Tindall, pp. 62–76. Baton Rouge: Louisiana State University Press, 1964.

Taliaferro, Harden E. *Fisher's River (North Carolina) Scenes and Characters. By "Skitt," "Who Was Raised Thar."* New York: Harper, 1859.

———. "Fun in North Carolina." *Southern Literary Messenger* 31 (1860): 105–110.

Tambiah, S. J. "The Magical Power of Words." *Man* 3 (1968): 175–206.

[Taylor, John.] *An Enquiry into the Principles and Tendency of Certain Public Measures.* Philadelphia: Thomas Dobson, 1794.

Taylor, Miles. *Speech of Hon. Miles Taylor, of Louisiana, on the Assault by Mr. Brooks on Mr. Sumner. Delivered in the House of Representatives, July 12, 1856.* Washington, D.C.: Congressional Globe Office, 1856.

Taylor, William R. *Cavalier and Yankee: The Old South and American National Character.* 1961. Rpt. Garden City: Doubleday Anchor, 1963.

Texas in 1840, or the Emigrant's Guide to the New Republic; Being the Result of Observation, Enquiry and Travel in that Beautiful Country. By an Emigrant, Late of the United States. New York: William W. Allen, 1840.

Thompson, John. *The Life of John Thompson, a Fugitive Slave; Containing His History of 25 Years in Bondage, and His Providential Escape, Written by Himself.* 1856. Rpt. New York: Negro Universities Press, 1968.

Thorpe, Thomas Bangs. "The American Deer: Its Habits and Associations." *Harper's* 17 (1858): 606–621.

————. "Woodcock Fire-Hunting." In *Hunting in the Old South: Original Narratives of the Hunters,* edited by Clarence Gohdes. Baton Rouge: Louisiana State University Press, 1967.

Toch, Hans. *Violent Men: An Inquiry into the Psychology of Violence.* Chicago: Aldine, 1969.

Toombs, Robert. *A Lecture Delivered in the Tremont Temple, Boston, Massachusetts, on the 24th of January, 1856.* N.p., 1856.

Toplin, Robert Brent. *Unchallenged Violence: An American Ordeal.* Westport, Conn.: Greenwood Press, 1975.

Topthorn. "Foxhunting, Its Pleasures and Its Uses, with Anecdotes of Men, Horses, and Hounds." *American Turf Register and Sporting Magazine* 4 (1832): 77–80.

Trial of William Dandridge Epes, for the Murder of Francis Adolphus Muir, Dinwiddie County, Virginia. Petersburg, Va.: J. M. H. Brunet, Reporter, 1849.

Tucker, George. *Essays on Various Subjects of Taste, Morals, and National Policy. By a Citizen of Virginia.* Georgetown, D.C.: Joseph Mulligan, 1822.

Turner, Arlin. "Realism and Fantasy in Southern Humor." *Georgia Review* 12 (1958): 451–457.

Turner, Victor W. *Dramas, Fields, and Metaphors: Symbolic Action in Human Society.* Ithaca: Cornell University Press, 1974.

————. "Liminal to Liminoid, in Play, Flow, and Ritual: An Essay in Comparative Symbology." In *The Anthropological Study of Human Play,* edited by Edward Norbeck. Rice University Studies 60, no. 3 (Summer 1974): 53–92.

Uniform Crime Reports for the United States, 1975. Washington, D.C.: Government Printing Office, n.d.

The United States Songster. Cincinnati: U. P. James, 1836.

"The Utility, Studies, and Duties of the Profession of Law." *De Bow's Review* 2 (1846): 142–152.

Vauthier, Simone. "Of Time and the South: The Fiction of William Gilmore Simms." *Southern Literary Journal* 5 (1972): 3–45.

Vindex Veritatis. "Importance of Home Education." *Southern Ladies' Book* 2 (1840): 1–7.

"A Virginia Militia Training of the Last Generation." *Harper's* 45 (1872): 243–245.

Wade, John D. *Augustus Baldwin Longstreet: A Study of the Development of Culture in the South.* New York: Macmillan, 1924.

Wall, Bennett H. "Ebenezer Pettigrew, an Economic Study of an Antebellum Planter." Ph.D. dissertation, University of North Carolina, 1946.

———. "The Foundation of the Pettigrew Plantations." In *Plantation, Town, and County: Essays on the Local History of American Slave Society,* edited by Elinor Miller and Eugene D. Genovese, pp. 163–185. Urbana: University of Illinois Press 1974.

Wallace, Anthony F. C. *Culture and Personality.* 2nd ed. New York: Random House, 1970.

Wallace, Lee A., Jr. "The Alexandria Militia." *Virginia Cavalcade* 16, no. 3 (Winter 1967): 12–21.

———. "The First Regiment of Virginia Volunteers, 1846–1848." *Virginia Magazine of History and Biography* 77 (1969): 46–77.

Wallace, Michael. "Paternalism and Violence." In *Violence and Aggression in the History of Ideas,* edited by Philip P. Wiener and John Fisher, pp. 203–220. New Brunswick: Rutgers University Press, 1974.

Walters, Ronald G. "The Erotic South: Civilization and Sexuality in American Abolitionism." *American Quarterly* 25 (1973): 177–201.

"War and Its Incidents." *Southern Quarterly Review* 13 (1848): 1–54.

Watson, Thomas E., ed. *History of Southern Oratory.* The South in the Building of a Nation, vol. 9. Richmond: Southern Historical Publication Society, 1909.

Watts, Charles W. "Student Days at Old LaGrange, 1844–45." *Alabama Review* 24 (1971): 63–76.

Webber, C. W. "The Viviparous Quadrupeds of North America." *Southern Quarterly Review* 12 (1847): 273–306.

Weir, Robert M. "The South Carolinian as Extremist." *South Atlantic Quarterly* 74 (1975): 86–103.

Welsh, Mary J. "Recollections of Pioneer Life in Mississippi." *Publications*, Mississippi Historical Society 4 (1901): 343–356.

Welter, Rush. *The Mind of America, 1820–1860.* New York: Columbia University Press, 1975.

West, James L. W., III. "Early Backwoods Humor in the Greenville *Mountaineer*, 1826–1840." *Mississippi Quarterly* 25 (1971): 69–82.

Wheelwright, Philip. *Metaphor and Reality.* Bloomington: Indiana University Press, 1968.

Whitaker, Daniel R. "Letter from Daniel Whitaker." *New Orleans Miscellany* 1 (1847): 52–54.

White, J. B. "Capital Punishment." *Southern Literary Journal* 1 (1836): 302–310.

White, Laura A. *Robert Barnwell Rhett: Father of Secession.* 1931. Rpt. Golucester, Mass.: Peter Smith, 1965.

Williams, Jack Kenny. "Crime and Punishment in Alabama, 1819–1840." *Alabama Review* 6 (1953): 14–30.

———. *Vogues in Villainy: Crime and Retribution in Antebellum South Carolina.* Columbia: University of South Carolina Press, 1959.

Wilson, John Lyde. *The Code of Honor; or, Rules for the Government of Principals and Seconds in Duelling.* 1838. Rpt. Charleston: J. Phinney, 1858.

Wilson, Major L. *Space, Time, and Freedom: The Quest for Nationality and the Irrepressible Conflict, 1815–1861.* Westport, Conn.: Greenwood Press, 1974.

Wood, Peter H. "Phillips Upside Down: Dialectic or Equivocation?" *Journal of Interdisciplinary History* 6 (1975): 289–297.

Woodson, Carter G., ed. *The Mind of the Negro as Reflected in Letters Written During the Crisis, 1800–1860.* Washington: Association for the Study of Negro Life and History, 1926.

Woodward, C. Vann. *American Counterpoint: Slavery and Racism in the North-South Dialogue.* Boston: Little, Brown, 1971.

———. "W. J. Cash Reconsidered." *New York Review of Books*, December 4, 1969, pp. 28–34.

Wyatt-Brown, Bertram. "The Ideal Typology and Ante-Bellum Southern History: A Testing of a New Approach." *Societas* 5 (1975): 1–29.

Yancey, William Lowndes. "Speech of the Hon. William L. Yancey, of Alabama, Delivered in the National Democratic Convention, Charleston, April 28, 1860 .With the Protest of the Alabama Delegation." Charleston: Walker, Evans, 1860.

Young, Jacob. *Autobiography of a Pioneer: or, The Nativity, Experi-*

ence, Travels, and Ministerial Labors of Rev. Jacob Young, with Incidents, Observations, and Reflections. Cincinnati: L. Swormstedt and A. Poe, 1858.

Zuber, William Physick. *My Eighty Years in Texas.* Edited by Janis Boyle Mayfield. Austin: University of Texas Press, 1971.

Index

Abolitionism: blacks in, 155, 158–160; and sectional rhetoric, 187–188; on slaveholder violence, 140; and slave insurrections, 129–130
Adams, John Quincy, 183
Africa: as source for slave culture, 6, 146; white ideas of, 132
Alabama, 111
Alabama Baptist, 26
Allen, W. B., 141, 145, 153
"All Mexico," 172
American Farmer, 119
American Revolution, rhetorical image of, 184–186; and constitutionalism, 185–186; and disorder, 186–187, 276 n. 23; and sectionalism, 190–192
American Turf Register and Sporting Magazine, 198
Arminianism, 12. *See also* Religion
Asbury, Francis, 113
Audubon, John James, 204, 205, 206, 207, 209, 210; *Viviparous Quadrupeds of North America* (Audubon and Bachman), 205
Auld, Thomas, 156

Bachman, John, 204; *Viviparous Quadrupeds of North America* (Audubon and Bachman), 205
Badgett, Joseph, 152

Baker, Everard Green, 10–11, 60, 74
Balladry, 99–102, 258 n. 35
Baltimore, 24
Baptist church, 13
Barbour, B. J., 170
Bartlett, Richard, 94, 95
"Berenice" (Poe), 235–236
Bernstein, Basil, 249 n. 23
Bibb, Henry, 147
Big Bear of Arkansas (Porter), 228
Bingham, William James, 55, 56, 61, 95
Blackburn, R. S., 119
"Black Cat, The" (Poe), 236, 237, 238
Black drivers, 119, 123
Blackford, Launcelot Minor, 62
Blair, Rev. John, 31
Blair, Walter, 225
Blount, Mary, 46
Boatright, Mody C., 225
Bolling, William, 120, 130
Boone, Daniel, 219
Border Beagles (Simms), 221
Boulware, Samuel, 147
Boykin, Burwell, 181
Bozeman, Theodore Dwight, 208
Brooks, Preston, 71, 74, 76
Brown, John, 159
Brown, Norman D., 245–246 n. 18

Brown, William Wells, 156, 157, 158
Brownlow, William G., 25
Bruce, Henry Clay, 152
Buckingham, J. S., 3
Buel, Richard, 40
Burr, Aaron, 42
Butler, Andrew Pickens, 76
Butler, Pierce, 68
Butler, Solbert, 142
Byron, [George Gordon] Lord, 207

Cabell, Nathaniel Francis, 163
Calhoun, John C., 168, 187
California, 4, 5
Calvinism, 12. *See also* Religion
Camden, Peter, *Common-Sense, Matter-of-Fact Examination and Discussion of Negro Slavery, A*, 126–127
Camp-meetings, 112–113
Carey, John L., 123, 133
Carter, Landon, 11
Cartwright, Peter, 112
Cartwright, Samuel, 122, 124, 127, 129
Caruthers, William Alexander, *Knights of the Golden Horseshoe*, 224
Cash, W. J., 3, 7, 76, 123, 221
"Cask of Amontillado, The" (Poe), 239
Cavalier image, 161, 166, 213
Chandler, John A., 131
Charleston, 78, 187, 192
Charleston Courier, 22
Charleston Gospel Messenger and Protestant Episcopal Register, 14
Charleston Mercury, 30, 183–184
Charlottesville, Virginia, 90

Chesnut, Mary Boykin, 127, 131
Cheves, Joseph, 37–38
Child, Francis James, 99, 100
Child-rearing: frontier, 94–97; role of pessimism in, 44, 57; slave, 147, 149; and social class, 44, 76–78; and violence, 18, 44, 64–66. *See also* Discipline; Family; Language-use; Passion; Pessimism
Chivalry: and hunting, 198, 201; and martial spirit, 161, 162, 164–165, 171, 177; in Simms, 222
Christian Register (Kentucky), 14
Civil War: and martial spirit, 163; and rhetoric, 193–194, 277–278 n. 37; and views on war, 176–177
Claiborne, J. F. H., 133, 166, 174, 175
Clay, Clement Claiborne, 57, 181
Clay, Henry, 21
Clay, Susanna, 57
Clemens, Sherrard, 37
Clingman, Thomas Lanier: disputes Stanly, 30; duels Yancey, 21–26, 27–38 passim; sectionalism of, 188
Cobb, Thomas R. R., 120, 132
Code of Honor (Wilson), 29, 32–33
College rioting, 62–64
Columbia College (South Carolina), 62
Columbian Orator, 156
Columbus (Georgia) *Enquirer*, 36
Common-Sense, Matter-of-Fact Examination and Discussion of Negro Slavery, A (Camden), 126–127

Confession (Simms), 214, 215, 216–217, 218
Confessions of Nat Turner, 270 n. 57
Conflict model: in master-slave relationship, 145, 160; in slave community, 150–151, 268–269 n. 41
Conquest, theories of, 174–175
Constitutionalism: in argument, 182; and Revolutionary imagery, 185–186, 189
Coope., James Fenimore, 221
Cooper, Thomas, 125
Corporal punishment: in child-rearing, 60–61, 95–96, 250 n. 33; and house slaves, 65–66; and racial ideas, 124–125; in slavery, 115, 123, 124–125, 135; slaves' views of, 140–142
Craft, William, 138
Crime of passion, in planter society, 71, 86
Crockett, David, 95
Cuba, military expeditions to, 164, 172, 173
Cunliffe, Marcus, 165

Davidson, Edward H., 236
Davis, David Brion, 237, 276 n. 23
Davis, J. A. G.: death of, 63; on law, 81, 84, 85
Davis, Jefferson, 180–181
Davis, Reuben, 91, 97–98, 112
Death, concepts of: evangelical, 14; in Poe, 238–239
Debating, 181–182
De Bow, J. D. B., 4, 165, 173, 176
De Bow's Review, 27, 79, 122, 162, 165
Declaration of Independence, 187, 276 n. 23

Deference, slave, 145
Democracy, Southern ideas on, 187, 188–189
Democratic party, 21–22, 187
Dennis, Richard, 84–85, 86–87, 175
Deportment. *See* Discipline
Discipline, 74; in child-rearing, 48, 50; and dueling, 35, 38–39; in hunting, 199–204; in military education, 170–171; in oratory, 182; and pessimism, 17; plantation, 123, 124, 128, 148; Poe's views on, 236–237, 239–240; and self-will, 56–57; Simms's views on, 220; and social class, 76, 79; and social life, 17, 68–69; and violence, 65, 76, 79, 80. *See also* Proceduralism
Douglass, Frederick, 155, 157, 160; on abolitionist methods, 158–159; on desires for freedom, 155–156; on racism, 159; on resistance, 154–155; sources of his opposition to slavery, 156
Drake, Daniel, 96
Drayton, William, 130, 132, 133
Dresel, Gustav, 104
Drinking, as cause of violence, 74–75, 106
Dromgoole, George C., 34–35
DuBose, John Witherspoon, 180
Dueling: "bloodless" duels, 36, 37; and debating, 181, 182, 274 n. 1; discipline in, 35, 38–39; fighting contrasted with, 73–74; laws on, 27–28; and passion, 31–32, 35, 38–39; and pessimism, 28–29, 35; and political office, 33, 42, 245–246 n. 18; proceduralism in, 39; and religion, 28; and sectionalism, 42; and

social class, 40; Southern opposition to, 27; Southern reputation for, 4–5, 26–27, 39–41
Dugger, Daniel, 34–35

Earle, Robert, 73
Edmonston, Ninian, 52
Education, military, 169–171
Egotism: in Poe's works, 235–236; in Simms's works, 216. *See also* Individualism; Monomania
Elements of Military Art and Science (Halleck), 169
Elkins, Stanley, 266 n. 17
Elliott, Stephen, 204
Elliott, William, 197, 199, 200
Ellison, Ralph, *Invisible Man*, 149
Ely, A. W., 208
Emancipation: and slave insurrection, Virginia, 131
Estes, Matthew, 124–125, 127
Etiquette. *See* Discipline; Proceduralism
Evangelicalism, 13. *See also* Religion
Exordiums, 183
Expansionism, 172–175
Ex-slave sources, 137, 265 n. 1, 267–268 n. 31

"Facts in the Case of M. Valdemar" (Poe), 238
Family: black, 150; distinctiveness of Southern planter, 45, 52–53, 57; frontier, 94–95; importance of affection in, 51–54, 95, 150; as metaphor for slavery, 58, 66, 120–121, 123; presence of house slaves in, 58–60, 65–66; as refuge from society, 49, 50–51, 79, 216. *See also* Child-rearing; Passion; Pessimism; Social Class
Federalists, 40, 41

Fighting: among children, 62, 96–97; contrast with dueling, 73–74; plantation, 148–151
"Fighting words," 71, 93. *See also* Language-use
Filibusters, 172–173, 173–174
Fink, Mike, 112
Finley, James, 91, 96, 113
Fisher's River (Taliaferro), 228–229
Fitzhugh, George, 3, 240; on child-rearing, 49; on conquest, 175; on martial spirit, 162, 165; on politics, 10; on sex roles, 75; on war, 177
Fletcher, John, 132
Folklore: Afro-American, 144–145, 146, 150–151; plain-folk, 99–102; in Southwestern humor, 225
Foote, Henry S., 28
Forayers, The (Simms), 222
Formality. *See* Discipline; Proceduralism
Foster, Charlotte, 140
Franklin, John Hope, 23–24, 163
Fredrickson, George M., 126
Free blacks, white attitudes toward, 125, 127–128, 129–130
Frontier: in Longstreet, 226–228; reputation of, for violence, 5, 89–91; in Simms, 217, 219, 220–221; social conditions of, 93–94; social life of, 92; as source for Southern violence, 7
Fulkerson, H. S., 111
Furman, Richard, 86

Game (hunting), 198–199, 200–201, 204–206, 209–210
Garnet, Henry Highland, 158, 159
Garrison, William Lloyd, 159

Genovese, Eugene D., 149, 266 n. 17

Georgia, militia in, 167

Georgia Scenes (Longstreet), 167, 226–228, 229

Glasgow, Ellen, 234

"Gold Bug, The" (Poe), 234

Graber, Doris, 179

Grant, Austin, 138

Grayson, William, 63

Greven, Philip, 58–59

Grimball, John Berkley, 68, 69

Gutman, Herbert, 146

Guy Rivers (Simms), 217–220

Hackney, Sheldon, 72

Haigh, William Hooper, 29, 53, 168

Haines, Hiram, 34–35

Hall, Lucendy, 153

Halleck, Henry Wager, *Elements of Military Art and Science*, 169

Hamilton, Alexander, 42

Hammond, James, 186, 220

Harper, Robert (Chancellor), 124

Harper's Magazine, 30

Harris, George Washington, 226, 230, 231

Harris, John Gideon, 167

Harris, Shang, 149

Hartz, Louis, 186

Hawkins, Tom, 147

Henry, Patrick, 183

Hierarchy, 17, 40–41, 208. *See also* Social class

Hilliard, Henry Washington, 173, 186, 189, 208

Hines, David Theo., 92

Hoffman, Daniel, 236

Holman, Hugh, 221

Holmes, George Frederick, 175

Honor, 29–30, 48

Hooper, Johnson Jones, 226, 229–230, 232

Houston: as frontier community, 105; law in, 108; reputation of, for violence, 103–104; violence in, 104, 106–107

Houston Morning Star, 106, 110, 111

Houston Telegraph and Texas Register, 25–26, 103, 106, 108

Huger, John M., 24, 33

Hughes, Louis, 140, 141

Huizinga, J., 69

Hundley, Daniel R., 70, 97, 162, 164; *Social Relations in Our Southern States*, 76–78

Hunting: discipline in, 199–204; narratives of, 196, 210–211; and order, 208–209; passion in, 202; proceduralism in, 201; and social class, 197–198; and social life, 197–198; Southern reputation for, 196

Hurston, Zora Neale, 268–269 n. 41

Hymes, Dell H., 249 n. 23

"Imp of the Perverse, The" (Poe), 237, 239

Individualism, 44, 48, 99; as self-will, 56–57; in social life, 68–69; in Southwestern humor, 231–232. *See also* Discipline; Egotism

Invisible Man (Ellison), 149

Jackson, Andrew, 97, 98

Jacobs, Robert, 234

James, Marquis, 32

Jefferson, Thomas, 115, 132

Jeter, Jeremiah, 91, 95, 97, 98

"John and Old Master" stories, 144–145, 146, 151

Johnson, Charles S., 150
Johnston, James C., 46
Jones, Charles Colcock, 51, 52
Jones, Mrs. Charles Colcock
   (Mary), 51, 53
Jones, Charles Colcock, Jr., 72,
   164
Jones, Charles Lee, 24, 33
Jones, David, 104, 108
Jones, Hamilton, 228
Jonesborough Whig, 25

Kemper, James Lawson, 163
Kennedy, John Pendleton, 120
Kennedy, William, 104
Kentucky Tragedy, 234
Kilgore, Sam, 142
Kingsley, Zaphaniah, 125
Knights of the Golden Horseshoe
   (Caruthers), 224

Language-use: codes for, 249 n.
   23; in dueling, 32, 35; in oratory, 182–183; and passion, 53–
   54, 182–183; plain-folk attitudes
   toward, 92–93, 98–99; planter
   attitudes toward, 53–54, 65, 249
   n. 23; and violence, 65, 70–71,
   72, 93, 98–99. *See also* Discipline; Social class
*Last Advice of the Rev. Charles
   Pettigrew to His Sons, 1797*,
   47–49
Law: attitudes toward, 80–82;
   and dueling, 27–28; in Houston,
   108; and passion, 81, 84–87; and
   self-defense, 83–84; and slaves,
   127, 263 n. 34, 268 n. 35
Legaré, Hugh Swinton, 190
Leigh, Benjamin Watkins, 188
Leyburn, James, 111
Liberator, The, 138
Little, John, 145

Loguen, J. W., 141, 152, 154, 159–
   160
Lomax, Alan, 100
Longstreet, Augustus Baldwin:
   on abolition, 132; on frontier,
   232; *Georgia Scenes*, 167, 226–
   228, 229; Simms contrasted
   with, 227–228; on violence, 4,
   70–71
Louisiana, 28
"Loves of the Driver, The"
   (Simms), 214
Lubbock, Francis R., 103, 104,
   105
Lynching, 82–83, 110–111

McCord, D. J., 73
McCray, Stephen, 160
McKendree, William, 113
Macon, Nathaniel, 92, 191
Madison, James, 188
Magrath, A. G., 30, 31
Magrath, Edward, 30
Maine, 190
Manifest Destiny, 172
Manners. *See* Discipline
Martial spirit, 5, 161–162, 163–
   165, 171, 172, 177
Martin Faber (Simms), 214–215,
   216–217, 218
Massachusetts, 163
Mellichampe (Simms), 223–224
Mercer, George Anderson, 28,
   196, 202, 206, 207, 209
Methodist Episcopal church, 13,
   113
Mexico: conquest of, 172, 173,
   174; war with, 163, 164, 165,
   173
Miles, William Porcher, 182
Militia, 166–169
Minor, Charles, 52, 61, 90
Mississippi: laws in, on dueling,

27–28; slave insurrection scare in, 129, 131; slavery in, 116–117
Missouri, 190–191
Mobile Register and Journal, 23
Monomania (Poe), 235–236
Montgomery (Alabama) True Blues, 168
Moralism, 6, 114, 213–214
Murrel, John A., 92, 129, 131

Narrative of Arthur Gordon Pym, The (Poe), 234
National Negro Convention (1843), 158
Natural science, 204
Nature: and civilization, 201–203; human place in, 204; and order, 204, 208–209; and passion, 11–12, 38, 202–203, 205
Nebraska, 190, 191–192
Negro in Virginia, The, 146
New Mexico, 4
New Orleans, 37, 52
New Orleans Bee, 21
Nichols, Christopher, 152
North, Caroline, 90
North Carolina: laws in, on dueling, 27, 28; Pettigrew family in, 46; University of, 46, 48
Northrup, Solomon, 149
Nott, Josiah, 132
Nullification, 190

Oates, Stephen, 157
Oratory: and Civil War, 193; and culture, 179; discipline in, 182; and passion, 180–183; Southern attitudes toward, 178, 179–180, 181, 274 n. 4; violent imagery in, 184–185, 275–276 n. 19
Organicism, 14–15, 208–209, 232
Ortega y Gasset, José, 205
Overseers, 116, 119

Parrington, Vernon L., 213, 233
Partisan, The (Simms), 222–223
Partisan Leader, The (Tucker), 224
Passion: and civilization, 11–12, 38–39, 203, 239; concept of, 8–12; and corporal punishment, 60–61, 117–118; and democracy, 189; discipline and, 38–40, 74; in dueling, 30–32, 35–36, 38–40, 73; in family relations, 53, 57; and language-use, 53–54, 182–183; in oratory, 180–183; Poe's use of, 233–235, 237–240; and political disorder, 186; and racial ideas, 134–135; religious views on, 13; Simms's use of, 213–215, 222–223; and slavery, 115–119, 138; and social class, 40–41, 76; in social life, 70; Southwestern humorists' use of, 232; and violence, 39, 44, 73–75, 80, 85–86; and war, 175. *See also* Discipline; Law; Pessimism.
Paternalism, 119–121
Peers, as "bad company," in child-rearing, 48–49, 55–56
Pennsylvania, 46
Perverseness (Poe), 237–239. *See also* Passion; Pessimism
Pessimism: in balladry, 101; in child-rearing, 18, 44, 47–48, 57, 66; and dueling, 28–29, 35; in family relations, 55–58, 60; and organicism, 14–15; and passion, 11–12, 17, 72–73; plain-folk, 92, 98–99; in Poe, 239; in religion, 12–14, 92; and sectionalism, 16–17, 193; in slave culture, 146; and slavery, 16, 134; in social life, 15, 67, 70; as theme in Southern culture, 12–17, 19, 240; and violence, 18, 39, 66,

87–88, 98–99, 240; and war,
175–176, 177

Petigru, James L., 185

Pettigrew, Charles (Rev.): background of, 46; family as refuge,
53; *Last Advice of the Rev.
Charles Pettigrew to His Sons,
1797*, 47–49; on slavery, 115,
128

Pettigrew, Charles (son of Ebenezer), 50, 53

Pettigrew, Ebenezer, 46–61 passim, 94, 95, 128; on affection,
51, 53–54; on age relations,
55–56; pessimism of, 50; on
violence, 64, 65

Pettigrew, James, 46

Pettigrew, James Johnston, 50–51,
61; and age relations, 55, 56–57;
and fight at school, 62, 64–65;
on Southern eloquence, 179–180

Pettigrew, John, 46, 49

Pettigrew, William S., 52, 54, 55,
64

Pettigrew family, background
of, 46

Phillips, Ulrich B., 226 n. 17

Plain-folk, 91, 256 n. 5. *See also*
Frontier

Plantation: essays on management
of, 119–120; order on, 116–119;
as violent and nonviolent, in
ex-slave testimony, 142

Pleasants, Hugh R., 182

Poe, Edgar Allan: on horror, 237;
passion used by, 233–235, 237–
240; pessimism in, 239; Simms
compared with, 233, 235, 236;
and slavery, 234; and Southern
culture, 240; in Southern literary tradition, 233–234. Works:
"Berenice," 235–236; "The
Black Cat," 236, 237, 238; "The

Cask of Amontillado," 239;
"Facts in the Case of M. Valdemar," 238; "The Gold Bug,"
234; "The Imp of the Per-
verse," 237, 239; *The Narrative
of Arthur Gordon Pym*, 234;
"Politian," 234; "The Tell-Tale
Heart," 236, 237, 239

Poinsett, Joel R., 168–169

"Politian" (Poe), 234

Polk, James K., 21, 22, 173

Porter, William T., *Big Bear of
Arkansas*, 228

Potter, John, 33–34

Prentiss, Seargent S., 180, 181

Proceduralism: in child-rearing,
65; and constitutional arguments, 182; in dueling, 39; in
hunting, 201; and language-use,
65; and law, 80–82; and passion,
17, 70; and pessimism, 194;
plain-folk attitudes toward,
92–93; in plantation management, slaveholders' view, 116–
117, 127; in plantation management, slaves' view, 138–139; in
political ideas, 187–189, 194;
in social life, 17, 69, 72, 80; and
violence, 65, 72, 107. *See also*
Discipline

Proslavery argument, 133, 135–
136, 264–265 nn. 53–54

Prosser, Gabriel, 158

Protestant Episcopal church, 12,
13

Protestantism, 12. *See also* Religion

Pryor, Roger, 33–34

Punishment (legal), 81–82. *See
also* Corporal punishment

Quarles, Benjamin, 158

Quick, John C. C., 108

Quitman, John L., 126, 132, 163, 166, 173, 193

Race and racism: Douglass on, 159; and opposition to expansionism, 172; and slavery, 121–123, 125–127, 128, 130, 132, 134–136
Randolph, John, 40–41, 56, 187, 189
Randolph, Peter, 71
Rawick, George, 152
Regulators, 110
Religion: and dueling, 28; frontier, and violence, 112–113; and pessimism, 12–14, 92; slave, 146; and slave rebellion, 156, 157–158
Rhett, Robert Barnwell, 183, 191
Richard Hurdis (Simms), 220–221
Richmond, 71
Ring tournament, 5
Ritchie, Thomas, 169
Robb, John S., 229
Robinson, J. W., 108
Roles, social. *See* Discipline; Proceduralism
Romanticism: and passion, 9–10; and Poe, 236, 238–239; and Simms, 224; Southern, 213
Roper, Moses, 149
Rosenbaum, H. Jon, 110
Rousseau, Jean Jacques, 9
Ruffin, Edmund, 122, 128
Ruffin, Francis, 28, 38, 70

"Sambo," 125, 132, 133, 266 n. 17. *See also* Race and racism, and slavery
Satisfaction (dueling), 38
Schirmer, Jacob, 71, 75
Scotland, 46
Scott, Sir Walter, 161, 221

Scout, The (Simms), 223
Seconds (dueling), 32–35
Sectionalism, 3–4, 16–17, 70–71, 131, 187–188, 192, 206
Sederberg, Peter C., 110
Self-defense, legal, 84
Sennett, Richard, 57
Sentimentalism, 53
Sex, in plantation violence, 140
Sex roles, 44–45, 63–64, 75
Shaw, James, 84, 87, 175
Shelby County (Texas), Regulators, 110
Simms, William Gilmore: on American Revolution, 221–223; background of, 213; border romances by, 217; domestic novels by, 214–217; on family, 51, 65; frontier used by, 217, 219, 220–221, 232; Longstreet, compared with, 227–228; on moral blindness, 215–216, 218–219; on oratory, 182; and passion, 214–215; Poe, compared with, 233, 235, 236; Revolutionary novels by, 221; and romance, 217; and Romanticism, 224; on slavery, 120; on violence, 65, 215; on war, 222. Works: *Border Beagles*, 221; *Confession*, 214, 215, 216–217, 218; *The Forayers*, 222; *Guy Rivers*, 217–220; "The Loves of the Driver," 214; *Martin Faber*, 214–215, 216–217, 218; *Mellichampe*, 223–224; *The Partisan*, 222–223; *Richard Hurdis*, 220–221; *The Scout*, 223; *The Yemassee*, 221, 222
Skinner, Frederick G., 197, 202, 207, 209, 210
Skinner, John Stuart, 116, 117, 197–198

Slaveholder: self-image of, 117–119; slaves' ideas of, 142–146

Slavery: blacks' and whites' views of, compared, 138–139, 143, 148; influence of, on black culture, 5, 146; master-slave relationship in, 116, 120, 129–130, 142–146; and passion, 115–116, 118–119, 134; and pessimism, 16–17, 134–136; and planter family relations, 58–60, 65–66; and racial ideas, 122–123, 127, 135–136; and sectionalism, 16, 192–193; and social class, 119; and Southern propensity for violence, 5, 7, 115; and Southern reputation for violence, 5, 7, 114, 116

Slaves: African sources for culture of, 6, 146; attitudes of, toward resisters, 152; childhood among, 147–148; families, 150; ideas of, about slaveholders, 142–146; and insurrections, 128–131, 155; presence of, in white households, 58–60, 65–66; and religion, 146; and resistance, 126–128, 151–155; social relations among, 150; sources for opposition by, to slavery, 155–158, 159; violence among, 5, 123, 149–151. *See also* Abolitionism; Corporal punishment

Slicks (vigilantes), 111

Slotkin, Richard, 209

Smith, Adam, 9

Social class: and child-rearing, 44, 76–78; and discipline, 76, 79; and dueling, 40–41; and passion, 40–41, 76; and slavery, 119; and violence, 78–79, 89, 124–125. *See also* Hierarchy

Social life, 17, 67–69

Social Relations in Our Southern States (Hundley), 76–78

South Carolina, 46

Southern Quarterly Review, 115–116, 169, 170, 173

Southwestern humor: background of, 224–225; and frontier's reputation for violence, 90; on frontier violence, 229; individualism in, 229–232; relation of, to plain-folk life, 225, 231–232; structure of, 225–226

Spain, 173

Sparks, W. H., 92

Stampp, Kenneth M., 143

Standing armies, 166, 168–169, 172

Stanly, Edward, 30, 64

Stephens, Alexander, 191

Stewart, Sam T., 153

Stone, Lawrence, 53

Stringfield, William Williams, 62

Stuart, J. E. B., 170–171

Sumner, Charles, 71, 74, 76

Taber, William R., 30

Taliaferro, Harden E., *Fisher's River*, 228–229

Taylor, John, of Caroline, 14

Taylor, Miles, 74

"Tell-Tale Heart, The" (Poe), 236, 237, 239

Tennessee, 27, 46

Texas, 4, 21–22, 103

Thompson, John, 140, 148, 154

Thorpe, Thomas Bangs, 201, 203

Titles, military, 162, 167–168

Toch, Hans, 70

Tocqueville, Alexis de, 189

Toombs, Robert, 133, 134

Trapier, William, 37–38

Tucker, George, 3, 31, 199
Tucker, Nathaniel Beverly, *The Partisan Leader*, 224
Tucker, Thomas Goode, 35
Turner, Nat, 130, 131, 156, 157, 158, 160, 234; *The Confessions of Nat Turner*, 270 n. 57

Vauthier, Simone, 221
Vesey, Denmark, 130, 157, 158
Vicksburg, Mississippi, 111
Vigilantism, 91, 109–112
Violence: in abolitionism, 158–159; causes of, 70–74, 93, 106–107, 111–112, 252 n. 7; explanations for, 7; expressive character of, in South, 211; in master-slave relationship, 137–139, 142–146, 160; and order, 80, 194–195, 204; and passion, 74, 80, 85–86; and pessimism, 17–18, 39, 44, 67, 87; plain-folk and planter attitudes toward, contrasted, 91, 97–98, 105, 109; and rhetoric, 194–195; and sex roles, 63, 75; and slavery, 5, 7, 114–116; among slaves, 5, 123, 149–151; and social class, 76–80, 85, 89, 124, 134–135; Southern reputation for, 3–6, 241 n. 4. *See also* Corporal punishment; Dueling; Fighting
Virginia: Convention of 1829–1830 in, 189; emancipation movement in, 131; Federal Convention of 1788 in, 188; and Mexican War, 164; Military Institute, 170; militia in, 167, 169; temperance sentiment in, 75; University of, 63; and War of 1812, 163
Viviparous Quadrupeds of North America (Audubon and Bachman), 205

Walker, Freeman, 191
Walker, William, 173
Wallace, Michael, 120
War: Simms on, 222; Southern views on, 174–177
War Hawks, 163
War of 1812, 163
Warren, John, 140
Washington, D.C., 24, 27
Watson, Thomas E., 181, 193
Weapons, carrying of, 71–72, 105
Webber, C. W., 201, 203, 205
Wesmoland, Maggie, 139
West Point (United States Military Academy), 170
Whig party, 21–22, 30, 173
Whipping, slave accounts of, 141–143. *See also* Corporal punishment
Whitman, Walt, 240
Wigfall, Louis T., 173, 194
Williams, Sally, 147, 267–268 n. 31
Wilson, John Lyde, 29, 31, 32, 33, 40; *Code of Honor*, 29, 32–33
Winston, John A., 86
Wise, Henry, 64
Wise, O. Jennings, 37
Women, idealization of, 76. *See also* Sex roles
Wood, Peter, 266 n. 17
Woodward, C. Vann, 68
Wright, Anna, 149

Yancey, William Lowndes, 180, 194; and duel with Clingman, 21–26, 27–38 passim; and fight with Robert Earle, 25, 73; on filibusters, 173; on language-use, 54; on law, 81; on nature, 206; on oratory, 180; Revolutionary imagery used by, 185; speech by, in 1860 Democratic convention, 187–188, 192; violence of his son, 71

Yemassee, The (Simms), 221, 222
Young, Jacob, 90, 113

Zuber, William Physick, 97

CPSIA information can be obtained at www.ICGtesting.com
Printed in the USA
LVOW061211311012

305186LV00002B/20/P